Mastering React Test-Driven Development

Build rock-solid, well-tested web apps with React, Redux and GraphQL

Daniel Irvine

BIRMINGHAM - MUMBAI

Mastering React Test-Driven Development

Commissioning Editor: Amarabha Banerjee
Acquisition Editor: Trusha Shriyan
Content Development Editor: Keagan Carneiro
Technical Editor: Sachin Sunilkumar
Copy Editor: Safis Editing
Project Coordinator: Kinjal Bari
Proofreader: Safis Editing
Indexer: Rekha Nair
Graphics: Alishon Mendonsa
Production Coordinator: Jayalaxmi Raja

First published: May 2019

Production reference: 1020519

Published by Packt Publishing Ltd.
Livery Place
35 Livery Street
Birmingham
B3 2PB, UK.

ISBN 978-1-78913-341-7

www.packtpub.com

To Nige, my first mentor, who taught me the importance of slowing down.

– Daniel Irvine

`mapt.io`

Mapt is an online digital library that gives you full access to over 5,000 books and videos, as well as industry leading tools to help you plan your personal development and advance your career. For more information, please visit our website.

Why subscribe?

- Spend less time learning and more time coding with practical eBooks and Videos from over 4,000 industry professionals

- Improve your learning with Skill Plans built especially for you

- Get a free eBook or video every month

- Mapt is fully searchable

- Copy and paste, print, and bookmark content

Packt.com

Did you know that Packt offers eBook versions of every book published, with PDF and ePub files available? You can upgrade to the eBook version at `www.packt.com` and as a print book customer, you are entitled to a discount on the eBook copy. Get in touch with us at `customercare@packtpub.com` for more details.

At `www.packt.com`, you can also read a collection of free technical articles, sign up for a range of free newsletters, and receive exclusive discounts and offers on Packt books and eBooks.

Contributors

About the author

Daniel Irvine is a software consultant based in London. He is a member of the European software craft community and works with a variety of languages including C#, Clojure, JavaScript, and Ruby. He's a mentor and coach for junior developers and runs TDD and XP workshops and courses. When he's not working, he spends time cooking and practicing yoga. He co-founded and runs the Queer Code London meetup.

This book would not be what it is without the input of my technical reviewer, Raimo Radczewski, who is also the author of the expect-redux package that is used in this book. I met Raimo a few years ago through the European software craft community. We bonded at a SoCraTes conference and found that we shared many of the same driving forces. Through many conversations, I learned to respect his thoughtfulness, kindness, and, of course, his deep knowledge of JavaScript and the React ecosystem. So, when I first took on this project, I immediately asked Raimo to come on board. Thankfully, he said yes. In the following eight months, he had a difficult job of reading though many drafts of—shall we say—variable quality. Those who have worked with me know that I can be lazy, careless, brazen, and inconsistent. Well, Raimo has seen it all and more, so firstly, I must thank him for continuing with the project in spite of the early drafts. I must also thank him for teaching me about many of JavaScript's nuances, of which I simply wasn't aware. He also guided me back toward idiomatic React code, because until I wrote this book I had really been writing JavaScript "out in the wilderness," with my own style. He brought me back in from the cold. He suggested some simplifications to my implementations; for example, the undo/redo reducer in Section 3, which would have been a great deal more complicated without his critical eye. I blamed my terrible code on burn-out, but actually, Raimo is a fantastic programmer and I look forward to the next occasion that we get to work together.

My editor, Keagan Carneiro, has been constantly positive and supportive, not once ever judging me for missing my self-imposed deadlines, which toward the end I missed consistently. We got through it in the end. Of all the wonderful things he did for me, perhaps the most powerful was the push to embrace hooks. When I first informed him in November 2018 that the React team had announced this weird thing called hooks that looked horrendous and that I couldn't ever imagine taking off, but that we might have to consider doing a chapter on, he turned around and suggested that I rewrite the entire text entirely to use hooks. Bearing in mind we were halfway through at this point, it was a pretty big ask. Of course, I knew he was right and I trusted his assessment, so I had to go through the five stages of grief of denial, anger, bargaining, depression, and acceptance in super-quick time, before getting on with it. (I believe Raimo is still hovering somewhere around the bargaining stage.) In the end, we were only delayed by a month, so I have to thank Keagan for ensuring that the book wasn't out of date before it was even published.

Sachin Sunilkumar, my technical editor, was wonderfully patient with me as I was reworking code snippets right until the last moment. He went on a journey of discovery with me as we built and tested against alpha releases of React. That was fun and stressful in equal amounts!

There are a number of other friends who stepped in at the last moment to review content when I was rushing with the final draft. Their assistance was invaluable. The text is much better for their efforts. Charlotte Payne, Dan Pelensky, Isidro López, Makis Otman, Sam Szreter, Zach Shaw: thank you. I hope you enjoy seeing your suggested improvements in print.

To the development team at Idean—in particular, Brendan Murphy, Lucy Monie Hall, and Zach Shaw—thank you for listening to me bang on about "my book" at least once a week.

I cannot finish without thanking my partner, Phillipe, who has suffered as I embarked on this project, my first book. Staying on track while still having a day job was a mammoth effort for me. It really took it out of me. Phillipe put up with me as I was tired, distracted, creatively drained, emotionally distraught, unavailable, and—toward the end—burned out, monosyllabic, and not much fun. He supported me through the project from start to finish. Thank you.

About the reviewer

Raimo Radczewski is an IT consultant from Berlin, Germany. His journey through the world of software engineering has taught him not just quite a few languages and paradigms, but also how to build and lead engineering teams. He's an advocate for test-driven development and maintains testing tools for the React ecosystem. He organizes SoCraTes Day Berlin and the Global Day Of Coderetreat, two grassroots communities for IT workers who are curious about software crafting and eXtreme Programming. His current focus is founding a tech cooperative to support clients in building a professional and mindful engineering culture. He tweets under @rradczewski.

Thank you, Daniel, for giving me the opportunity to help create this most excellent introduction to TDD in React. It will surely land on the bookshelves of many of my clients. Thank you, Andreas and Jan, for being the first people to show me Test-Driven-Development and for introducing me to the communities that I continue to learn so much from.

Packt is searching for authors like you

If you're interested in becoming an author for Packt, please visit authors.packtpub.com and apply today. We have worked with thousands of developers and tech professionals, just like you, to help them share their insight with the global tech community. You can make a general application, apply for a specific hot topic that we are recruiting an author for, or submit your own idea.

Table of Contents

Section 3: Interactivity

Preface

This is a book about dogma. *My* dogma. It is a set of principles, practices, and rituals that I have found to be extremely beneficial when building React applications. I try to apply these ideas in my daily work, and I believe in them so much that I take every opportunity to teach others about them. That's why I've written this book: to show you the ideas that have helped me be successful in my own career.

As with any dogma, you are free to make your own mind up about it. There are people who will dislike everything about this book. There are those who will love everything about this book. Yet more people will absorb some things and forget others. All of these are fine. The only thing I ask is that you maintain an open mind while you follow along, and prepare to have your own dogmas challenged.

Test-driven development (TDD) did not originate in the JavaScript community. However, it is perfectly possible to test-drive JavaScript code. And although TDD is not common in the React community, there's no reason why it shouldn't be. In fact, React as a UI platform is a much better fit for TDD than older UI platforms, due to its elegant model of functional components and state.

So what is TDD, and why should you use it? Test-driven development is a process for writing software that involves writing tests, or specifications, before writing any code. Its practitioners follow it because they believe that it helps them build and design higher-quality software with longer life spans, at a lower cost. They believe it offers a mechanism for communicating about design and specification that *also* doubles up as a rock-solid regression suite. There isn't much empirical data available that *proves* any of that to be true, so the best you can do is try it out yourself and make your own mind up.

Perhaps most importantly for me, I find that TDD removes the *fear* of making changes to my software, and that this makes my working days much less stressful than they used to be. I don't worry about introducing bugs or regressions into my work, because the tests protect me from that.

TDD is often taught with 'toy' examples: todo lists, temperature converters, Tic Tac Toe, and so on. This book teaches two real-world applications. Often, the tests get hairy. We will hit many challenging scenarios and come up with solutions for all of them. There are over 450 tests contained within this book, and every one will teach you something.

So, before we begin, a few words of advice.

This is a book about **first principles**. I believe that learning TDD is about understanding the process in exceptional detail. For that reason, we do *not* use Enzyme or react-testing-library. Instead, we build our own test helpers. Doing so is not very complicated. The benefit of doing so is a deeper understanding and awareness of what those testing libraries are doing for you. I am not suggesting that you shouldn't use these tools in your daily work—I use them myself—but I am suggesting that going without them is a worthwhile adventure.

This book uses **React hooks**. These are a new feature in version 16.8, and we also make use of the **act** function, which became usable in version 16.9. There are no class components in this book. I believe that we should embrace hooks because functional components using hooks are simpler than class components. I embraced hooks during the process of writing this book, which originally started out as a book with class components. Halfway through, we decided to scrap classes entirely and instead, focus on the future.

On that topic, the JavaScript and React landscape changes at such a pace that I can't claim that this book will remain 'current' for very long. That is another reason why I use a first-principles approach. My hope is that when things *do* change, you'll still be able to use this book and apply what you've learned to those new scenarios.

There are a variety of themes that run throughout the book. The theme of first principles is one I've already mentioned. Another is **systematic refactoring**, which can come across as rather laborious, but is a cornerstone of TDD and other good design practices. I have provided many examples of that within these pages, but for brevity, I sometimes jump straight to a 'post-refactored' solution. For example, I often choose to extract methods *before* they are written, whereas in the real world, I would usually write methods inline and only extract when the containing method (or test) becomes too long.

Yet another theme is that of **cheating**, which you won't find mentioned in many TDD books. It's an acknowledgment that TDD is really a scaffold around which you can build your own rules. Once you've learned and practiced the strict version of TDD for a while, you can learn what **cheats** you can use to cut corners. What tests won't provide much value in the long run? How can you speed up repetitive tests? So, a **cheat** is almost like saying you cut a corner in a way that wouldn't be obvious to an observer if they came to look at your code tomorrow. Maybe, for example, you implement three tests at once, rather than one at a time.

Finally, do not for a second think that I wrote this book in a linear sequence from start to finish, or that I knew exactly what order to write the tests. It took a great deal of spiking, trial and error, and making horrendous mistakes before I ended up with the text you have before you. Needless to say, I am now an expert with `git rebase`.

Who this book is for

If you're a React programmer, this book is for you. I aim to show you how TDD can improve your work.

If you're already knowledgeable with TDD, I hope there's still a lot you can learn from comparing your own process with mine.

If you don't know already know React, you will benefit from spending some time running through the *Getting Started* guide on the React website. That being said, TDD is a wonderful platform for explaining new technologies, and it's entirely plausible that you'll be able to pick up React simply by following this book.

This book covers in-depth usage of React hooks, which are very new at the time of writing. If you're a React developer and hoping to learn how to use React without classes, then you will indeed learn that by reading this book.

What this book covers

Chapter 1, *First Steps with Test-Driven Development*, introduces Jest and the test-driven development cycle. We use them to build a rendering of customer information on a page.

Chapter 2, *Test-driving Data Input with React*, covers using React component state to manage the display and saving of forms.

Chapter 3, *Exploring Test Doubles*, introduces various types of test double that are necessary for testing collaborating objects. The collaborator we use in this chapter is the browser fetch API to send and receive data from our application backend.

Chapter 4, *Creating a User Interface*, ties everything with a root component that threads together a user journey.

Chapter 5, *Humanizing Forms*, continues with form building by looking at dealing with client- and server-side validation errors, and adding an indicator to show that data is being submitted.

Chapter 6, *Filtering and Searching Data*, shows building a search component with some complex interaction requirements, in addition to complex fetch request requirements.

Chapter 7, *Test-driving React Router*, introduces the React Router library to simplify navigation with our user journeys.

Chapter 8, *Test-driving Redux*, introduces Redux into our application in an effort to simplify our components and evolve our application architecture into something that will support larger use cases.

Chapter 9, *Test-driving GraphQL*, introduces the GraphQL library to communicate with a GraphQL endpoint that's provided by our application backend.

Chapter 10, *Building a Logo Interpreter*, introduces a fun application that we begin to explore by building out features across both React components and Redux middleware: undo/redo, persisting state across browser sessions with `LocalStorage` API, and programmatically managing field focus.

Chapter 11, *Adding Animation*, covers adding animations to our application using the browser `requestAnimationFrame` API, all with a test-driven approach.

Chapter 12, *Working with WebSockets*, adds support for WebSocket communication with our application backend.

Chapter 13, *Writing Your First Acceptance Test*, introduces CucumberJS and Puppeteer, which we use to build acceptance tests for existing functionality.

Chapter 14, *Adding Features Guided by Acceptance Tests*, integrates acceptance testing into our development process by first building acceptance tests, before dropping down to unit tests.

Chapter 15, *Understanding TDD in the Wider Testing Landscape*, finishes the book by looking at how what we've learned fits in with other test and quality practices, and provides some suggestions about where to go from here.

To get the most out of this book

There are two ways to read this book.

The first is to use it as a reference when you are faced with specific testing challenges. Use the index to find what you're after and move to that page.

The second, and the one I'd recommend starting with, is to follow the walk-throughs step by step, building your own code base as you go along. In this section, I'll detail how to do that.

You will need to be at least a little proficient with Git: a basic understanding of the `branch`, `checkout`, `clone`, `commit`, `diff`, and `merge` commands should be sufficient.

Keeping up with the book's Git history

This section details all you need to know to work effectively with Git while you're following along with the walk-throughs.

 This book is up-to-date with the latest version of React (16.9.0-alpha.0). Packt will update the code repository for future release cycle of React 16.9. Please note this version is not yet production ready. A production release of 16.9 is due for release soon.

Getting started before Chapter 1

The book has an accompanying GitHub repository that contains all of the walk-throughs already implemented in a series of commits. You should clone this to your local development machine as you'll be working within it.

1. If you have a GitHub account, I suggest you fork the repo so that you can push your work to keep a copy safe. Use the **Fork** button in the top-right hand corner of the GitHub page to do this.

   The repository is located at `https://github.com/PacktPublishing/Mastering-React-Test-Driven-Development`.

2. Once forked, you can then clone this locally by going to a terminal window and typing the following command, replacing **<username>** with your GitHub username:

   ```
   git clone git@github.com:<username>/Mastering-React-Test-Driven-
   Development.git
   ```

3. You may wish to rename the directory to something shorter. On my machine, I've used the name `react-tdd`.
4. Change into this directory using the `cd` command.
5. Issue the command `git checkout tags/starting-point`.
6. Finally, issue the command `git checkout -b starting-point-mine` to create your own branch from this point.

You're now ready to begin Chapter 1. If the last two commands didn't make any sense, don't panic: I'll explain about tags and branches now.

Working with section tags

There are two separate code bases in this book, and they have their own branches: `appointments` and `spec-logo`. `Chapter 1` to `Chapter 9` cover `appointments`; `Chapter 10` to `Chapter 14` cover `spec-logo`. (`Chapter 15` doesn't have any code.)

If you were to check out these branches, you'd get the final, completed versions of the code. This is an interesting sneak peak but it's not how you'll get started.

Instead, many sections have a designated tag, so you can skip to the tag and examine the code at that point. If you see a callout like this:

The Git tag for this section is `animation`.

...then you can skip to this tag by issuing the following command:

```
git checkout tags/animation
```

Once you've output that command, you will be in the *detached head* state. If you want to begin making changes at that point, you should create a new branch from the tag and work on that. I'd suggest suffixing the name with `-mine` so that your branches are clearly distinguishable from tags:

```
git checkout -b animation-mine
```

You can then commit to this branch. If you have been following along judiciously within your own branch, then you do *not* need to check out each tag, since you'll already have all of the same code.

However, sometimes you will see a callout like the one that follows, and that means you *will* need to check out the new tag:

The Git tag for this section is `load-available-time-slots`. It contains solutions to the exercises from the previous chapter, so if you haven't completed the *Exercises* section yourself, then you should move to this tag now so that you're up to date.

For more detailed instructions, see the *To get the most out of this book* section in the `Preface`.

This type of callout means that the code base now contains additional changes since the last edits covered in the book. It often happens at the start of each chapter when the preceding chapter had exercises, but it also happens when the code base skips ahead with changes that are uninteresting or not related to the content of the book.

When you see this callout, you have two options:

- You can choose to check out the new tag and start a new branch, starting afresh. In this case, the instructions are the same as before, except now you'd need a different branch name from your existing branch:

```
git checkout tags/load-available-time-slots
git checkout -b load-available-time-slots-mine
```

- You can choose to continue working on the branch you have. This could be because you've been creative and made changes that aren't covered in the book (which I fully support). In this case, `git diff` and `git merge` are your friends. You will want to review the changes in the latest tag, and then git merge them in. You may need to handle conflicts:

```
# to view the differences in the new tag
git diff tags/load-available-time-slots

# to auto-merge those differences into your branch
git merge tags/load-available-time-slots
```

The second option is not entirely risk free, mainly due to the *Exercises* section at the end of each chapter.

Solving the exercises

Almost every chapter has an *Exercises* section at the end. These exercises are designed to give you ideas for how you continue practicing what you've learned. They have already been solved in the GitHub repository so you can see how I've solved them. The next chapter always starts from the point where I've solved the exercises.

Should you choose to solve the exercises—which I encourage you to do—then the likelihood is that you'll have solved them in a different way than I would have. Unfortunately, this might leave you in merge hell when you begin the next chapter.

If you find yourself in this situation, I suggest you first study the differences between your approach and mine. Think about how they differ and the relative merits of each. (Do not think that mine will be any better than yours.)

Then, ensuring you've committed and successfully stored your code, move to a new tag and a new branch, starting again.

In other words, be pragmatic and don't spend an inordinate amount of time fighting the system. It's better to keep moving and not get stuck or frustrated.

Pro tip: always keep your exercise solutions in a separate commit. When you move on to the next chapter, branch from your pre-*Exercises* commit and merge in the official exercise solutions instead.

Debugging when things go wrong

Should you get stuck, or your tests fail in a way that you weren't expecting, feel free to launch the application and see what the console is telling you. Add in `console.log` statements to help you debug.

The best defense against getting stuck is committing early and often. Any time you have a working feature, commit it!

Download the example code files

In addition to the GitHub repository, if you prefer you can download the example code files for this book from your account at `www.packt.com`. If you purchased this book elsewhere, you can visit `www.packt.com/support` and register to have the files emailed directly to you.

You can download the code files by following these steps:

1. Log in or register at `www.packt.com`.
2. Select the **SUPPORT** tab.
3. Click on **Code Downloads & Errata**.
4. Enter the name of the book in the **Search** box and follow the onscreen instructions.

Once the file is downloaded, please make sure that you unzip or extract the folder using the latest version of:

- WinRAR/7-Zip for Windows
- Zipeg/iZip/UnRarX for Mac
- 7-Zip/PeaZip for Linux

We also have other code bundles from our rich catalog of books and videos available at `https://github.com/PacktPublishing/`. Check them out!

Conventions used

There are a number of text conventions used throughout this book.

`CodeInText`: Indicates code words in text, React component names, test names, directory names, filenames, file extensions, pathnames, dummy URLs, user input, and Twitter handles. Here is an example: "In `test/domManipulators.js`, add the following new property to the return object of `createContainer`."

Any command-line input or output is written as follows:

```
$ mkdir css
$ cd css
```

Bold: Indicates a new term, an important word, or words that you see onscreen. For example, words in menus or dialog boxes appear in the text like this. Here is an example: "The final test for the **Undo** button is to check that it dispatches an UNDO action when it is clicked."

Warnings or important notes appear like this.

Tips and tricks appear like this.

Understanding code snippets

A block of code is set as follows:

```
const handleBlur = ({ target }) => {
  const result = required(target.value);
  setValidationErrors({
    ...validationErrors,
    firstName: result
  });
};
```

There are two important things to know about the code snippets that appear in this book.

The first is that some code samples show modifications to existing sections of code. When this happens, the changed lines appear in **bold**, and the other lines are simply there to provide context:

```
const handleBlur = ({ target }) => {
  const validators = {
    firstName: required
  };
  const result = validators[target.name](target.value);
  setValidationErrors({
    ...validationErrors,
    [target.name]: result
  });
};
```

The second is that, often, some code samples will skip lines in order to keep the context clear. When this occurs, you'll see this marked by a line with three dots:

```
if (!anyErrors(validationResult)) {
  ...
} else {
  setValidationErrors(validationResult);
}
```

Sometimes this happens for function parameters too:

```
if (!anyErrors(validationResult)) {
  setSubmitting(true);
  const result = await window.fetch(...);
  setSubmitting(false);
  ...
}
```

JavaScript syntax

As much as possible, the book aims to be consistent with its approach to syntax. There are some choices that may be contentious but I hope that they won't put you off reading. For example, I use semi-colons throughout. If you'd prefer to not use semi-colons, please feel free to ignore them in your own code.

Prettier

I have used Prettier to format code samples, and its configuration is set within `package.json` in each of the `appointments` and `spec-logo` projects. Here it is:

```
"prettier": {
  "singleQuote": true,
  "printWidth": 67,
  "jsxBracketSameLine": true
}
```

Feel free to change this to your own configuration and reformat files as you see fit. The line width of 67 characters is particularly short but ensures that, for the most part, code snippets do not suffer from line breaks.

The one place this is not true is with test descriptions:

```
it('passes from and to times through to appointments when retrieving
appointments', async () => {
```

In these cases, although the text is printed over two lines, you should enter it on one line only. If you are copy and pasting code samples from the electronic version of this book, you'll need to remove the extra line breaks that are inserted by your editor.

Arrow functions

The book almost exclusively uses arrow functions for defining functions. The only exceptions are when we write generator functions, which must use the standard function's syntax. If you're not familiar with arrow functions, they look like this, which defines a single-argument function named `inc`:

```
const inc = arg => arg + 1;
```

They can appear on one line or broken into two:

```
const inc = arg =>
  arg + 1;
```

Functions that have more than one argument have the arguments wrapped in brackets:

```
const add = (a, b) => a+ b;
```

If a function has multiple statements, then the body is wrapped in curly braces and the return keyword is used to denote when the function returns:

```
const dailyTimeSlots = (salonOpensAt, salonClosesAt) => {
  const totalSlots = (salonClosesAt - salonOpensAt) * 2;
  const startTime = new Date().setHours(salonOpensAt, 0, 0, 0);
  const increment = 30 * 60 * 1000;
  return timeIncrements(totalSlots, startTime, increment);
};
```

If the function returns an object, then that object must be wrapped in brackets so that the runtime doesn't think it's executing a block:

```
setAppointment(appointment => ({
  ...appointment,
  [name]: value
}));
```

Object and array destructuring

This book makes liberal use of destructuring techniques in an effort to keep the code base as concise as possible. As an example, object destructuring generally happens for function parameters:

```
const handleSelectBoxChange = ({ target: { value, name } }) => {
  ...
};
```

This is equivalent to saying this:

```
const handleSelectBoxChange = ({ target: { value, name } }) => {
  const target = event.target;
  const value = target.value;
  const name = target.name;
  ...
};
```

Return values can also be destructured in the same way. More frequently, you'll see return values destructured. This happens with the useState hook:

```
const [customer, setCustomer] = useState({});
```

This is equivalent to:

```
const customerState = useState({});
const customer = customerState[0];
const setCustomer = customerState[1];
```

Directory structure

Finally, both code bases suffer from a distinct lack of civilized directory structure. I hope this isn't an issue for you; I just didn't want to spend time discussing building directories and moving files when it isn't the focus of the book.

Get in touch

Feedback from our readers is always welcome.

General feedback: If you have questions about any aspect of this book, mention the book title in the subject of your message and email us at `customercare@packtpub.com`.

Errata: Although we have taken every care to ensure the accuracy of our content, mistakes do happen. If you have found a mistake in this book, we would be grateful if you would report this to us. Please visit `www.packt.com/submit-errata`, selecting your book, clicking on the Errata Submission Form link, and entering the details.

Piracy: If you come across any illegal copies of our works in any form on the Internet, we would be grateful if you would provide us with the location address or website name. Please contact us at `copyright@packt.com` with a link to the material.

If you are interested in becoming an author: If there is a topic that you have expertise in and you are interested in either writing or contributing to a book, please visit `authors.packtpub.com`.

Reviews

Please leave a review. Once you have read and used this book, why not leave a review on the site that you purchased it from? Potential readers can then see and use your unbiased opinion to make purchase decisions, we at Packt can understand what you think about our products, and our authors can see your feedback on their book. Thank you!

For more information about Packt, please visit `packt.com`.

Section 1: First Principles of TDD

This section is an exploration of the principles of test-driven development. You'll test drive the rendering of data and the loading of data from our server, and in the process, you'll build your own test helpers that help to simplify and accelerate your testing. By the end of the section, you'll have a working application.

This section includes the following chapters:

- Chapter 1, *First Steps with Test-Driven Development*
- Chapter 2, *Test-driving Data Input with React*
- Chapter 3, *Exploring Test Doubles*
- Chapter 4, *Creating a User Interface*

First Steps with Test-Driven Development

1

This book follows a simple format: it's a walk-through of building React applications using a test-driven approach. We'll touch on many different parts of the React experience, including building forms, composing interfaces, and animating elements. We'll also integrate React Router, Redux, and GraphQL, all guided by tests. The focus isn't on how these features of React work, but rather on how to test them and make sure you're using them with confidence.

Modern JavaScript programmers rely heavily on packages that other people have developed. This allows us to concentrate on innovating, not reinventing, the wheel. The downside, however, is that we don't always have a full understanding of the technologies we're dealing with. We simply don't need to learn them.

Among other things, **Test-Driven Development** (TDD) is an effective technique for learning new frameworks and libraries. That makes it very well suited for a book on React and its ecosystem. This book will allow you to explore React in a way that you may not have experienced before.

If you're new to TDD, some of the steps outlined may leave you scratching your head. You may find yourself wondering why we're going to such Herculean efforts to build an application. There is tremendous value to be gained in specifying our software in this way. By being crystal clear about our requirements, we gain the ability to adapt our code without fear of change. We gain automated regression testing by default. Our tests comment our code, and those comments are verifiable when we run them. We gain a method of communicating our decision-making process with our colleagues. And you'll soon start to recognize the higher level of trust and confidence you have in the code you're working on. If you're anything like me, you'll get hooked on that feeling and find it hard to work without it.

Sections 1 and *2* of this book involve building an appointments system for a hair salon—nothing too revolutionary, but as sample applications go, it offers plenty of scope. We'll get started with that in this chapter. *Sections 3* and *4* use an entirely different application: a Logo interpreter. Building that offers a fun way to explore more of the React landscape.

This chapter, and in fact this whole book, takes a *first principles* approach to React. We start with minuscule steps to slowly uncover the TDD story. We'll prefer rolling our own code to using libraries and packages. We will start from an empty directory and begin building out our application, test by test. Along the way, we'll discover a lot of the fundamental ideas behind test-driven development and React.

The following topics will be covered in this chapter:

- Creating a new React project from scratch
- Displaying data with your first test
- Refactoring your work
- Writing great tests
- Rendering lists and detail views

Technical requirements

Later in this chapter, you'll be required to install **Node Package Manager** (**npm**) together with a whole host of packages. You'll want to ensure you have a machine capable of running the Node.js environment.

You'll also need access to the command line.

In addition, you should choose a good editor or **Integrated Development Environment (IDE)** to work with your code.

Creating a new React project from scratch

There's a standard template for creating React apps: the `create-react-app` application template. This includes some standard dependencies and boilerplate code that all React applications need. However, it also contains some extra items such as `favicon.ico`, a sample logo, and CSS files. While these are undoubtedly useful, having them here at the very start of a project is at odds with one of the test-driven developer's core principles: **You Ain't Gonna Need It** (**YAGNI**).

This principle says that you should hold off adding anything to your project until you're really sure that it's necessary. Perhaps that's when your team adds a user story for it into the iteration, or maybe it's when a customer asks for it. Until then, YAGNI.

It's a theme that runs throughout this book and we'll start right now by choosing to avoid `create-react-app`. You can always start every JavaScript project from scratch, and there's a certain joy to be found in going over the basics each time.

Installing NPM

We'll be making extensive use of the `npm` command-line tool and the Node.js execution environment. Each time you run your tests, which will be very frequently, you'll be required to run an `npm` command.

Toward the end of the chapter, we'll also use `npm` to package our application.

You can find out if you already have it installed on your machine by opening a Terminal window (or Command Prompt if you're on Windows) and typing the following:

```
npm -v
```

If the command isn't found, head on over to the Node.js website for details on how to install. The URL is included at the end of this chapter.

The `npm` program knows how to update itself, so if it's installed, I recommend you ensure you're on the latest version. You can do this on the command line by typing this:

```
npm install npm@latest -g
```

I'm using version 6.9.0 to write this book. If you have any issues with the code samples contained here, differing NPM versions could be one of the causes, so please bear that in mind as you continue.

Yet another resource negotiator (YARN) is an alternative to NPM, and I won't hold it against you if you choose to use it. There are only a handful of `npm` commands in this book—I assume that if you're sticking with YARN, then you'll already know how to convert `npm` commands to `yarn` commands.

Creating a new Jest project

The Git tag for this section is `starting-point`. It doesn't contain any code; just a `README.md` file. If you want to follow along using the book's Git repository then you should ensure you've branched from this tag. Detailed instructions from doing that are in the *Getting started before Chapter 1* section of the `Preface`.

Now that NPM is installed, we can create our project:

1. If you're following along with the book's Git repository, open a Terminal window and navigate to the repository directory that you cloned in the *Getting started before Chapter 1* section of the `Preface`. Otherwise, simply navigate to your local projects directory.

2. Create a new directory using `mkdir appointments` and then change to it using `cd appointments`.

3. Enter the `npm init` command, which begins the process of initializing a new NPM project and generating a `package.json` file for you.

4. The first questions ask you to provide a package name, version, description, and an entrypoint. Since we're building an appointments system, you can call it `appointments`. Accept the default version (by just hitting *Enter*), and enter a description of `Appointments system`. You can accept the default entrypoint too.

5. Next, you'll be asked for a `test` command, for which you should type in `jest`. This will enable you to run tests by using the `npm test` shortcut command.

Don't worry if you miss this; you can set it afterward by adding `"test":` `"jest"` to the `scripts` section of the generated `package.json`.

6. You'll be asked to specify a repository, which you could just set as `example.com` for now. If you don't fill these fields in, `npm` will print warnings every time you run a command.

7. You can accept the defaults for everything else.

You may wonder why we filled out the repository field. TDD loves fast feedback cycles. Prioritize cleaning your screen and command outputs of as much noise as possible. Any time you see something that is destroying clarity, either fix it right then and there, or put it as an action at the top of your to-do list.

In this particular case, you could also add `"private": true` to your `package.json`, instead of setting the repository field.

8. Hit *Enter* on the remaining questions to finish the initialization process.
9. Install Jest using `npm install --save-dev jest`.

You will see the bottom line of your Terminal fill up with a fast-changing stream of package information as NPM installs dependent packages (a paltry 553 packages at the time of writing). You may see some warnings depending on the platform you are installing on, but these can be ignored. Once complete, you should see this:

```
npm notice created a lockfile as package-lock.json. You should commit this
file.

+ jest@24.7.1
+ added 553 packages from 373 contributors and audited 849842 packages in
16.304s
+ found 0 vulnerabilities
```

Commit early and often

The second sentence of that command output (*You should commit this file*) is a good cue for us to commit for the first time.

TDD provides natural breakpoints for you to commit code. If you're starting out with TDD, I'd recommend committing to source control after every single test. That might seem like overkill for your projects at work, but as you're learning, it can be a very effective tool.

If you've ever watched *The Weakest Link*, you'll know that contestants can choose to bank their winnings at any time, which decreases their risk of losing money but reduces their earning potential. With `git`, you can use `git add` to effectively *bank* your code. This saves a snapshot of your code but does not commit it. If you make a mess in the next test, you can revert to the last banked state. I tend to do this after every test. And, unlike in *The Weakest Link*, there's no downside to banking!

Committing early and often simplifies commit messages. If you have just one test in a commit, then you can use the test description as your commit message. No thinking is required.

If you're using `git`, use the following commands to `commit` what you've done so far:

```
git init
echo "node_modules" > .gitignore
git add .
git commit -m "Blank project with Jest dependency"
```

Bringing in React and Babel

Let's install React. That's actually two packages:

```
npm install --save react react-dom
```

React makes heavy use of **JavaScript XML (JSX)**, which we need Babel to transpile for us. Babel also transpiles our modern ES6 and ES7 constructs for us.

 The following information is accurate for Babel 7. If you're using a later version, you may need to adjust the installation instructions accordingly.

Thankfully, Jest already includes Babel, so we just need to install presets and plugins:

```
npm install --save-dev @babel/preset-env @babel/preset-react
npm install --save-dev @babel/plugin-transform-runtime
npm install --save @babel/runtime
```

A Babel preset is a set of plugins. Each plugin enables a specific feature of the ECMAScript standards, or a preprocessor such as JSX.

The `env` preset brings in essentially everything possible. It should really be configured with target execution environments. See the *Further reading* section at the end of this chapter for more information.

We need to enable the packages we've just installed. Create a new file, `.babelrc`, and add the following:

```
{
  "presets": ["@babel/env", "@babel/react"],
  "plugins": ["@babel/transform-runtime"]
}
```

With that, you're all set to write some tests. You may wish to check in at this point.

Displaying data with your first test

 The Git tag for this section is `appointment-first-name`.

In this section, we'll discover the TDD cycle for the first time.

We'll start our application by building out an appointment view. We won't get very far; the tests we'll create in this chapter will simply display the customer who made the appointment. As we do so, we'll discuss the TDD process in detail.

We'll build a React functional component called `Appointment`. It is used for displaying the details of a single appointment in our system. The component will be passed in a data structure that represents `Appointment`, which we can imagine looks a little something like this:

```
{
   customer: { firstName: 'Ashley', lastName: 'Jones', phoneNumber: '(123)
555-0123' },
   stylist: 'Jay Speares',
   startsAt: '2019-02-02 09:30',
   service: 'Cut',
   notes: ''
}
```

We won't manage to get all of that information displayed by the time we complete the chapter; in fact, we'll only display the customer's `firstName`, and we'll make use of the `startsAt` timestamp to order a list of today's appointments.

But before we get on to that, let's explore Jest a little.

Writing a failing test

What exactly *is* a test? We'll discover that by writing one. In your project directory, type the following commands:

```
mkdir test
touch test/Appointment.test.js
```

Open the `test/Appointment.test.js` file in your favorite editor or IDE and enter the following:

```
describe('Appointment', () => {
});
```

The `describe` function defines a *test suite*, which is simply a set of tests with a given name. The first argument is the name (or `description`) of the unit you are testing. It could be a React component, a function, or a module. The second argument is a function inside of which you define your tests.

 All of the Jest functions are already required and available in the global namespace when you run the `npm test` command. You don't need to import anything.

For React components, it's good practice to give your describe blocks the same name as the component itself.

You should run this code right now in the Jest test runner. It will give us valuable information about what to do next. You might think that running tests now is pointless, since we haven't even written a test yet, but with TDD, it's normal to run your test runner at every opportunity.

On the command line, run the `npm test` command:

```
> appointments@1.0.0 test /home/daniel/work/react-tdd/ch1
> jest

FAIL test/Appointment.test.js
● Test suite failed to run

Your test suite must contain at least one test.

  at node_modules/jest/node_modules/jest-cli/build/TestScheduler.js:225:24

Test Suites: 1 failed, 1 total
Tests: 0 total
Snapshots: 0 total
Time: 0.917s
Ran all test suites.
npm ERR! Test failed. See above for more details.
```

You can see Jest helpfully tells us `Your test suite must contain at least one test`. Test-driven developers rely heavily on listening to the test runner and what it tells us. It usually tells them exactly what to do next. In this case, it's telling us to create a test. So, let's do that.

Where should you place your tests?

If you do try out the `create-react-app` template, you'll notice that it contains a single unit test file, `App.test.js`, which exists in the same directory as the source file, `App.js`.

I don't recommend mixing production code with test code. For a start, it isn't the conventional unit-testing approach, which uses two separate directories for production code and test code. More importantly, however, it's likely that you won't have a one-to-one mapping between production and test files.

Writing your first expectation

Change your `describe` call to this:

```
describe('Appointment', () => {
  it('renders the customer first name', () => {
  });
});
```

The `it` function defines a single test. The first argument is the description of the test and always starts with a present-tense verb, so that it reads in plain English. The `it` in the function name refers to the noun you used to name your test suite (in this case, `Appointment`). In fact, if you run tests now, with `npm test`, remember, it should make sense:

```
PASS test/Appointment.test.js
  Appointment
    ✓ renders the customer first name (1ms)
```

You can read the `describe` and `it` descriptions together as one sentence: *Appointment renders the customer first name*. You should aim for all of your tests to be readable in this way.

As we add more tests, Jest will show us a little checklist of passing tests.

 You may have used the `test` function for Jest, which is equivalent to `it`. Since we're doing behavior driven development style of TDD, you should stick with `it`.

Empty tests, such as the one we just wrote, always pass. Let's change that now. Let's add an *expectation* to our test. Change `test` to read as follows:

```
it('renders the customer first name', () => {
  expect(document.body.textContent).toMatch('Ashley');
});
```

This `expect` call is an example of a fluent API. Like the test description, it reads like plain English. You can read it like this: I expect `document.body.textContent toMatch` the string `Ashley`.

Although it might look complicated, it's quite a simple idea: each expectation has an expected value that is compared against a received value. In this example, the expected value is `Ashley` and the received value is whatever is stored in `document.body.textContent`.

The `toMatch` function is called a `matcher` and there are a whole lot of different matchers that work in different ways. In this case, the expectation passes if `document.body.textContent` has the word `Ashley` anywhere within it.

Each individual test can have as many expectations in it as you like, and we'll see examples of multiple expectations in a test later in this chapter.

Before we run this test, spend a minute thinking about the code. You might have guessed that the test will fail. The question is, how will it fail?

Let's run `test` now, with `npm test`, and find out:

```
FAIL test/Appointment.test.js
  Appointment
    X renders the customer first name (10ms)

  ● Appointment › renders the customer first name

    expect(received).toMatch(expected)

    Expected value to match:
      "Ashley"
```

```
Received:
  " "

1 | describe('Appointment', () => {
2 |   it('renders the customer first name', () => {
> 3 |     expect(document.body.textContent).toMatch('Ashley');
  |                                        ^
4 |   });
5 | });
6 |

at Object.toMatch (test/Appointment.test.js:3:39)
```

There are four parts to the test output that are relevant to us:

- The name of the failing test
- The expected answer
- The actual answer
- The location in the source where the error occurred

All of these help us to pinpoint where our tests failed: `document.body.textContent` is empty. This isn't surprising really, since we've not done anything to set the body text.

But, hold on a second. Where did `document.body` come from? No one defined that yet. Shouldn't we expect the test to fail with an error saying that the *document is undefined*?

Jest magically includes a DOM implementation for us, which is why we have access to `document` and `document.body`. It uses `jsdom`, a headless implementation of the DOM. We can do test browser interactions on the command line, which is much simpler than involving a browser in our work.

In Jest lingo, this is called the **Jest environment** and it defaults to `jsdom`. If you want to verify that this is happening, add the following config to your `package.json` file:

```
"jest": {
  "testEnvironment": "node"
}
```

Re-run tests and observe the different output to convince yourself that JSDOM is no longer present.

Be sure to remove this extra configuration before you continue, as we'll be relying on the JSDOM environment from now on.

Rendering React from a test

In order to make this test pass, we'll have to write some code above the expectation that will call into our production code.

Since we're testing what happens when a React component is rendered, we'll need to call the `ReactDOM.render` function. This function takes a `component` (which in our case will be called `Appointment`), performs the React `render` magic, and replaces an existing DOM node with the newly rendered node tree. The DOM node it replaces is known as the React `container`.

Here's the method signature:

```
ReactDOM.render(component, container)
```

In order to call this in our test, we'll need to define both `component` and `container`. Let's piece the test together before we write it out in full. It will have this shape:

```
it('renders the customer first name', () => {
  const component = ???
  const container = ???
  ReactDOM.render(component, container);
  expect(document.body.textContent).toMatch('Ashley');
});
```

Since we're rendering `Appointment`, we know what we need to put for `component`. It's a JSX fragment that takes our `customer` as a prop:

```
const customer = { firstName: 'Ashley' };
const component = <Appointment customer={customer} />;
```

 Back when we were considering our design, we came up with a whole object format for our appointments. You might think the definition of a customer here is very sparse, as it only contains a first name. But we don't need anything else for a test about customer names.

What about `container`? We can use the DOM to create a `container` element:

```
const container = document.createElement('div');
document.body.appendChild(container);
```

Now let's take a look at that test in full. Change your test in `test/Appointments.test.js` to match the following:

```
it('renders the customer first name', () => {
  const customer = { firstName: 'Ashley' };
```

```
const component = <Appointment customer={customer} />;
const container = document.createElement('div');
document.body.appendChild(container);

ReactDOM.render(component, container);

expect(document.body.textContent).toMatch('Ashley');
});
```

As we're using both `ReactDOM` and JSX, we'll need to include the two standard `React` `import` at the top of our test file for this to work, as follows:

```
import React from 'react';
import ReactDOM from 'react-dom';
```

Go ahead and run the test. Within the output, you'll see the following:

```
ReferenceError: Appointment is not defined
```

This is subtly different from the test failure we saw previously. This is a run-time exception, not an expectation failure. Thankfully, though, the exception is telling us exactly what we need to do, just as a test expectation would. We need to define `Appointment`.

Make it pass

We're now ready to make failing test pass:

1. Add `import` to `test/Appointment.test.js`, below the two React imports:

    ```
    import { Appointment } from '../src/Appointment';
    ```

2. Run tests with `npm test`. You'll get a different error this time:

    ```
    Cannot find module '../src/Appointment' from 'Appointment.test.js'
    ```

    Although `Appointment` was defined as an export, it wasn't defined as a *default* export. That means we have to import it using the curly brace from of import (`import { ... }`). I tend to avoid using default exports; doing so keeps the name of my component and its usage in sync: if I change the name of a component, then every place where it's imported will break unless I change those too. This isn't the case with default exports. Once your names are out of sync, it can be hard to track where components are used.

3. Let's create that module. Type the following at your command line:

```
mkdir src
touch src/Appointment.js
```

4. In your editor, add the following content to `src/Appointment.js`:

```
export const Appointment = () => {};
```

Why have I created a shell of an `Appointment` without actually creating an implementation? This might seem pointless, but another core principle of the test-driven developer is *always do the simplest thing to pass the test*. We could rephrase this as *always do the simplest thing to fix the error you're working on*.

Remember when I mentioned that we listen carefully to what the test runner tells us? In this case, the test runner said `Cannot find module Appointment`, so what was needed was to create that module:

1. Run `npm test`. You'll get a lot of React output as a large stack trace. If you scroll up to the top, you'll see this:

```
Error: Uncaught [Invariant Violation: Appointment(...): Nothing was
returned from render. This usually means a return statement is
missing. Or, to render nothing, return null.]
```

2. To fix that, we need to do what it's telling us: we need to return something "from render". So, let's return something. Change the file to read as follows:

```
import React from 'react';

export const Appointment = () => <div></div>;
```

3. Now, if you run the test, you should get a test failure:

```
FAIL test/Appointment.test.js
  Appointment
    ✕ renders the customer first name (23ms)

  ● Appointment › renders the customer first name

    expect(received).toMatch(expected)

    Expected value to match:
      "Ashley"
    Received:
      ""
```

4. To fix the test, change the `Appointment` definition to look like this:

```
export const Appointment = () => (
  <div>Ashley</div>
);
```

But, wait a second. This test isn't using our `appointment` variable that we defined in our test. We just hard-coded a value of `Ashley` in there!

Remember our principle: always implement the simplest thing that will possibly work. That includes hard-coding, when it's possible. In order to get to the real implementation, we need to add more tests. This process is called **triangulation**. The more specific our tests get, the more general our production code needs to get.

 This is one reason why pair programming using TDD can be so fun. Pairs can play *ping pong*. Sometimes, your pair will write a test that you can solve trivially, perhaps by hard-coding, and then you force them to do the hard work of both tests by triangulating. They need to remove the hard-coding and add the generalization.

Let's triangulate:

1. Make a copy of your first test, pasting it just under the first test, and change the test description and the name of `Ashley` to `Jordan`, as follows:

```
it('renders another customer first name', () => {
  const customer = { firstName: 'Jordan' };
  const component = <Appointment customer={customer} />;
  const container = document.createElement('div');
  document.body.appendChild(container);

  ReactDOM.render(component, container);

  expect(document.body.textContent).toMatch('Jordan');
});
```

2. Run tests with `npm test`. We expect this test to fail, and it does. Take a careful look at this output:

```
FAIL test/Appointment.test.js
  Appointment
  ✓ renders the customer name (19ms)
  ✗ renders another customer name (20ms)

  ● Appointment › renders another customer name
```

```
expect(received).toMatch(expected)

Expected value to match:
  "Jordan"
Received:
  "AshleyAshley"
```

Yes, it did fail—but with the text `AshleyAshley`!

This kind of repeated text is an indicator that our tests are not running independently of one another. There is some shared state that isn't being cleared. We need to change course and uncover what's going on.

Unit tests should be independent of one another. The simplest way to achieve this is to not have any shared state between tests. Each test should only use variables that it has created itself.

Backtracking on ourselves

There's only one piece of shared state that our tests use and that's `document`. It must not be getting cleared each time the tests are run, and so we see the output of each test inside the document.

Even if we fixed our production code to remove the hard-coding, it still wouldn't pass; instead, we'd see the text `AshleyJordan`.

One solution is to clear the document DOM tree before each test run. But there's a simpler solution: we can rework our tests to not append our `container` element to the DOM at all, and instead work directly with the `container` element. In other words, we can change our expectation to check not `document.body.textContent` but `container.textContent`.

There may come a time that we actually need to attach our nodes to the DOM, and at that point, we'll need to fix this problem properly. But for now, *you ain't gonna need it*. So, let's solve this by avoiding the DOM tree altogether. It's the simplest way forward.

Unfortunately, there's a problem. We're in the middle of a *red* test. We should never refactor, rework, or otherwise change course while we're red.

What we'll have to do is *ignore*, or *pend*, this test we're working on. We do that by changing the word `it` to `it.skip`. Do that now for the second test:

```
it.skip('renders another customer first name', () => {
```

Run tests. You'll see Jest ignores the second test, and the first one still passes:

```
PASS test/Appointment.test.js
  Appointment
    ✓ renders the customer first name (19ms)
    ○ skipped 1 test

Test Suites: 1 passed, 1 total
Tests: 1 skipped, 1 passed, 2 total
```

For this refactor, we need to make two changes:

- Change the expectation to match on `container.textContent`.
- Remove the line that calls `appendChild` on the document body.

We can also take this opportunity to inline the `component` variable. Change the test to read as follows:

```
it('renders the customer first name', () => {
  const customer = { firstName: 'Ashley' };
  const container = document.createElement('div');
  ReactDOM.render(<Appointment customer={customer} />, container);
  expect(container.textContent).toMatch('Ashley');
});
```

Run your tests: the result should be the same as earlier, with one passing test and one skipped.

It's time to bring that second test back in, by removing the `.skip` from the function name, and this time, let's update the test code to make the same changes we made in the first, as follows:

```
it('renders another customer first name', () => {
  const customer = { firstName: 'Jordan' };
  const container = document.createElement('div');
  ReactDOM.render(<Appointment customer={customer} />, container);
  expect(container.textContent).toMatch('Jordan');
});
```

Running tests now should give us the error that we were originally expecting:

```
FAIL test/Appointment.test.js
  Appointment
    ✓ renders the customer first name (18ms)
    ✗ renders another customer first name (8ms)

  ● Appointment › renders another customer first name

    expect(received).toMatch(expected)

    Expected value to match:
      "Jordan"
    Received:
      "Ashley"
```

To fix this, we need to introduce the variable and use it within our JSX, which supports embedding JavaScript expressions within elements. We can also use destructuring assignment to avoid creating unnecessary variables.

Change the definition of `Appointment` to look as follows:

```
export const Appointment = ({ customer }) => (
  <div>{customer.firstName}</div>
);
```

Note that I haven't *fully* destructured this. I could have written this function like this:

```
export const Appointment = ({ customer: { firstName } }) => (
  <div>{firstName}</div>
);
```

The first version is no longer than the second; however, if you're counting tokens, it has one less set of curly braces. The most concise solution always wins!

Run tests; we expect this test to now pass, as follows:

```
PASS test/Appointment.test.js
  Appointment
    ✓ renders the customer first name (21ms)
    ✓ renders another customer first name (2ms)
```

Great work! We're done with our passing test.

Refactoring your work

The next step of the TDD cycle is to refactor your work. This step is often the hardest, because our natural impulse can be to get straight into the next feature. *Chasing green*, as I like to call it: building more and more functionality is much more exciting. Refactoring, however, is much more zen.

The rule "more haste; less speed" applies to coding, just as in many other areas of life. If you skip the refactoring phase, your code quality will deteriorate. If you develop a habit of skipping refactoring, your code base will soon become difficult to work with.

It takes a lot of personal discipline to consistently refactor, but you will reap the rewards of a code base that remains maintainable as it ages.

Right now, we have some repeated code between our two tests. Let's fix that.

 Test code needs as much care and attention as production code. The number one principle you'll be relying on when refactoring your tests is **Don't Repeat Yourself (DRY)**. *Drying up tests* is a phrase all TDDers repeat often.

Promoting variables

Both of our tests use the same two variables: `container` and `customer`. We can pull up these declarations to the outer describe scope, but leave the definitions within the tests. Since we'll be splitting declaration and definition, that also means we'll need to use `let` instead of `const`:

Just above the first test, write the following two lines:

```
let container;
let customer;
```

Then, remove the word `const` from both of the tests, and re-run your tests, which should still be passing.

Using a beforeEach block

Both of our tests start with some setup or arrangement. When that setup is common to all tests, we can promote them into a beforeEach block instead. Code in this block is executed before each test.

Above your first test, write the following code, and delete the corresponding call to createElement from each of your two tests:

```
beforeEach(() => {
  container = document.createElement('div');
});
```

Since we defined container in the scope of the describe block, the value set here in the beforeEach block will be available to our test once it executes.

Be careful when you use variables defined within the describe scope. These variables are not cleared between each test execution, so you are running the risk of non-independent tests. Therefore, any variable you declare in the describe scope should be assigned to a new value in a corresponding beforeEach block, or in the first part of each test, just as we've done here.

Extracting methods

The call to ReactDOM.render is the same in both methods. Since it's the same in both methods, it makes sense to pull it out.

However, rather than pull it out as-is, we can create a new function that takes the Appointment component as its parameter. This way, we can clearly see how our test data objects are woven through the object under test. If we hid that within an extracted method, the test would be less clear.

The parts of a test that you want to see are the parts that differ between tests. Usually, some data remains the same (container in this example) and some differs (customer in this example). Do your best to hide away whatever is the same and proudly display what differs.

Above the first test, write the following definition:

```
const render = component => ReactDOM.render(component, container);
```

Now, replace the call to `ReactDOM.render` in each test with this line:

```
render(<Appointment customer={customer} />);
```

Re-run your tests now—they should still be passing.

Writing great tests

The first test now looks like this:

```
it('renders the customer first name', () => {
  customer = { firstName: 'Ashley' };
  render(<Appointment customer={customer} />);
  expect(container.textContent).toMatch('Ashley');
});
```

This is concise and clearly readable.

A *good* test has three distinct sections:

- *Arrange*: Sets up test dependencies
- *Act*: Executes production code under test
- *Assert*: Checks expectations are met

A *great* test is not just good but is also the following:

- Short
- Descriptive
- Independent of other tests
- Has no side-effects

Red, green, refactor

We've covered a lot of ground, and we have gone into excruciating detail for a very simple test. All of the ground work is now done for us to speed up.

Let's look at the red, green, refactor cycle:

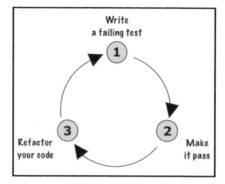

The steps of the TDD cycle are as follows:

1. **Write a failing test**: Write a short test that describes some functionality you want. Execute your test and watch it fail. If it doesn't fail, then it's not a good test; go back and try again.
2. **Make it pass**: Make the test green. Do the simplest thing that will work. Feel free to make a mess; you can clean it up later.
3. **Refactor your code**: Stop, slow down, and resist the urge to move on to the next feature. Work hard to make your code—both production and test code—as clean as it can be.

Streamlining your testing process

Think about the effort you've put into this book so far. What actions have you been doing the most? Most likely, you've been doing these:

- Switching between `src/Appointment.js` and `test/Appointment.test.js`
- Running `npm test`

To solve the first issue, you should use split-screen functionality in your editor. If you aren't already using that, then take this opportunity to learn how to do it. Load your production module on one side and the corresponding unit test file on the other. Here's a picture of my setup:

```
                                        1. tmux
 1 import React from 'react';                1 import React from 'react';
 2 import ReactDOM from 'react-dom';         2
 3 import { Appointment } from '../src/Appointment';  3 export const Appointment = ({ customer }) =>
 4                                            4    <div>{customer.firstName}</div>;
 5 describe('Appointment', () => {
 6   let container;
 7   let customer;
 8
 9   beforeEach(() => {
10     container = document.createElement('div');
11   });
12
13   const render = (component) =>
14     ReactDOM.render(component, container);
15
16   it('renders the customer first name', () => {
17     customer = { firstName: 'Ashley' };
18     render(<Appointment customer={customer} />);
19     expect(container.textContent).toMatch('Ashley');
20   });
21
22   it('renders another customer first name', () => {
23     customer = { firstName: 'Jordan' };
24     render(<Appointment customer={customer} />);
25     expect(container.textContent).toMatch('Jordan');
26   });
27 });
~
~
~
~
~
~
~
~
~
~
 N_    test/Appointment.test.js              4/27  src/Appointment.js                    4/4
---------------------------------------------------------------------------------------
  Appointment
    ✓ renders the customer first name (14ms)
    ✓ renders another customer first name (1ms)

Test Suites: 1 passed, 1 total
Tests:       2 passed, 2 total
Snapshots:   0 total
Time:        0.921s, estimated 1s
Ran all test suites.
~/work/appointments (master) $ █
```

You can see that I also have a little test window at the bottom for showing test output.

Jest can also watch your files and auto-run tests when they change. To enable this, change the test command in package.json to jest --watchAll. This reruns all of your tests when it detects any changes.

> Jest has an option to run only the tests in files that have changed, but you'll find that since your React app will be composed of many different files, each of which is interconnected, it's better to run everything, as breakages can happen in many modules.

Rendering lists and detail views

The Git tag for this section is `appointments-day-view`.

So far, we've seen a great deal of test-driven development, but not much of React. In this section, we'll take what we've learned about TDD and apply it to learning more React.

Our app at the moment just displays a single thing—a customer's name. Now, we'll extend it so that we have a view of all appointments that are happening today.

Let's do a little more up-front design. We've got an `Appointment` component that takes an appointment and displays it. We can build an `AppointmentsDayView` component around it that takes an array of appointment objects and displays them as a list. It also displays a single `Appointment` component at any one time, whichever appointment is currently selected. The user can click on an `Appointment` and it will open up that appointment for viewing:

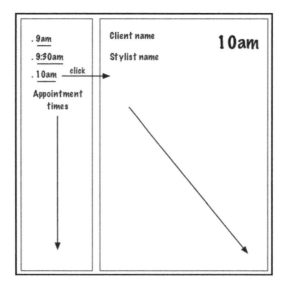

Rendering the list of appointments

We'll add our new component into the same file we've been using already because there's not much code in there so far.

We don't always need a new file for each component, particularly when the components are short functional components, such as our `Appointment` component (a one-line function). It can help to group related components or small sub-trees of components in one place.

In `test/Appointment.test.js`, create a new `describe` block under the first one, with a single test, as follows. This test checks that we render a `div` with a particular ID. That's important in this case because we load a CSS file that looks for this element. The expectations in this test use the DOM method, `querySelector`. This searches the DOM tree for a single element with the tag provided:

```
describe('AppointmentsDayView', () => {
  let container;

  beforeEach(() => {
    container = document.createElement('div');
  });

  const render = component =>
    ReactDOM.render(component, container);

  it('renders a div with the right id', () => {
    render(<AppointmentsDayView appointments={[]} />);
expect(container.querySelector('div#appointmentsDayView')).not.toBeNull();
  });
});
```

It isn't always necessary to wrap your component in a `div` with an ID or a class. I tend to do it when I have CSS that I want to attach to the entire group of HTML elements that will be rendered by the component, which, as you'll see later, is the case for `AppointmentsDayView`.

This test uses the exact same `render` function from the first `describe` block, as well as the same `let container` declaration and `beforeEach` block. In other words, we've introduced duplicated code. By duplicating code from our first test suite, we're making a mess straight after cleaning up our code! Well, we're allowed to do it when we're in the first stage of the TDD cycle. Once we've got the test passing, we can think about the right structure for the code.

Run `npm test` and let's look at the output:

```
FAIL test/Appointment.test.js
  Appointment
    ✓ renders the customer first name (18ms)
    ✓ renders another customer first name (2ms)
  AppointmentsDayView
    ✗ renders a div with the right id (7ms)

  ● AppointmentsDayView › renders a div with the right id

    ReferenceError: AppointmentsDayView is not defined
```

Let's work on getting this test to pass!

1. To fix this, change the last `import` in your test file to read as follows:

    ```
    import {
      Appointment,
      AppointmentsDayView
    } from '../src/Appointment';
    ```

2. In `src/Appointment.js`, add this functional component below `Appointment`:

    ```
    export const AppointmentsDayView = () => null;
    ```

When we first defined our `Appointment` component earlier, we didn't return null. In fact, we didn't return anything. React then gave us a test error that we needed to fix before we got to a helpful test failure. So, returning `null` allows us to *skip past* the error from React and will bring us directly to a test failure. I'll generally begin all my components in this way—with a `null` value.

3. Run your tests again:

> ● AppointmentsDayView › renders a div with the right id
>
> expect(received).not.toBeNull()
>
> Received: null
>
> ```
>   47 |   it('renders a div with the right id', () => {
>   48 |     render(<AppointmentsDayView appointments={[]} />);
> > 49 |
> expect(container.querySelector('div#appointmentsDayView')).not.toBe
> Null();
>      |
> ^
>   50 |   });
> ```

4. Finally, a test failure! Let's get that `div` in place:

```
export const AppointmentsDayView = () =>
  <div id="appointmentsDayView"></div>;
```

5. Your test should now be passing. Let's move on to the next test. Add the following text, just below the last test in `test/Appointment.test.js`, still inside the `AppointmentsDayView` describe block:

```
it('renders multiple appointments in an ol element', () => {
  const today = new Date();
  const appointments = [
    { startsAt: today.setHours(12, 0) },
    { startsAt: today.setHours(13, 0) }
  ];
  render(<AppointmentsDayView appointments={appointments} />);
  expect(container.querySelector('ol')).not.toBeNull();
  expect(
    container.querySelector('ol').children
  ).toHaveLength(2);
});
```

6. Run your tests:

> expect(received).not.toBeNull()
>
> Received: null
>
> ```
>   57 |     ];
>   58 |     render(<AppointmentsDayView appointments={appointments}
> />);
> ```

```
> 59 |        expect(container.querySelector('ol')).not.toBeNull();
     |                                                    ^
  60 |
expect(container.querySelector('ol').children).toHaveLength(2);
  61 |   });
  62 | });

   at Object.toBeNull (test/Appointment.test.js:48:47)
```

In the test, the `today` constant is defined to be `new Date()`. Each of the two records then uses this as a kind of "base" date to work its own time off. Whenever we're dealing with dates, it's important that we base all events on the same moment in time, rather than asking the system for the current time more than once. Doing that is a subtle bug waiting to happen.

7. Let's add the `ol` element. Remember not to jump ahead; at this point, we just need `ol` to be there, not including the two items:

```
export const AppointmentsDayView = () => (
  <div id="appointmentsDayView">
    <ol />
  </div>
);
```

8. Run `npm test` again. The test output is now as follows:

```
Expected length: 2
Received length: 0
Received object: []

  47 |        render(<Appointments appointments={appointments} />);
  48 |        expect(container.querySelector('ol')).not.toBeNull();
> 49 |
expect(container.querySelector('ol').children).toHaveLength(2);
     |                                                    ^
  50 |   });
  51 | });
  52 |
```

9. Since we've got multiple expectations in this test, the stack trace is essential in highlighting which expectation failed. This time, it's the second expectation: we've got zero children in the `ol` element but we want two. To fix this, as always, we'll do the simplest thing that will possibly work, as follows:

```
export const AppointmentsDayView = ({ appointments }) => (
  <div id="appointmentsDayView">
```

```
      <ol>
        {appointments.map(() => (
          <div />
        ))}
      </ol>
    </div>
  );
```

The `map` function will provide a single argument to the function passed to it. Since we don't use the argument (yet), we don't need to assign it in the function signature—we can just pretend that our function has no arguments instead, hence the empty brackets. Don't worry, we'll need the argument for a subsequent test and we'll add it in then.

10. If we're being strict, this isn't quite right: `ol` elements should not have `div` elements for children. But, that's all we should need to pass the test. We can use the next test to make sure the children are `li` elements. Let's see what Jest says; run `npm test` again:

```
PASS test/Appointment.test.js
  Appointment
    ✓ renders the customer first name (19ms)
    ✓ renders another customer first name (2ms)
  AppointmentsDayView
    ✓ renders a div with the right id (7ms)
    ✓ renders multiple appointments in an ol element (16ms)

  console.error node_modules/react/cjs/react.development.js:217
  Warning: Each child in an array or iterator should have a unique
  "key" prop.
```

11. Our test passed, but we got a warning from React. It's telling us to set a key value on each `li` element. We can use `startsAt` as a key:

```
<ol>
  {appointments.map(appointment => (
    <div key={appointment.startsAt} />
  ))}
</ol>
```

Unfortunately there's no easy way for us test key values in React. To do it, we'd need to rely on internal React properties, which would make our tests at risk of breaking if the React team were to ever change those properties.

The best we can do is set a key to get rid of this warning message. Any value will do: unfortunately we can't use TDD to specify how keys are formed.

In this case, I'd quite like a test that uses the startsAt timestamp for each li key. Let's just imagine that we have that test in place.

Specifying list items

Now, let's fill in the list items for the ol element we just rendered.

1. Create a third test in the new describe block, with this content:

```
it('renders each appointment in an li', () => {
  const today = new Date();
  const appointments = [
    { startsAt: today.setHours(12, 0) },
    { startsAt: today.setHours(13, 0) }
  ];
  render(<AppointmentsDayView appointments={appointments} />);
  expect(container.querySelectorAll('li')).toHaveLength(2);
  expect(
    container.querySelectorAll('li')[0].textContent
  ).toEqual('12:00');
  expect(
    container.querySelectorAll('li')[1].textContent
  ).toEqual('13:00');
});
```

Jest will show the following error:

```
Expected length: 2
Received length: 0
Received object: []

  58 |  render(<Appointments appointments={appointments} />);
  59 |  expect(container.querySelectorAll('li')).toHaveLength(2);
> 60 |                                          ^
```

2. Change that `div` element into an `li` element:

```
<ol>
  {appointments.map(appointment => (
    <li key={appointment.startsAt} />
  ))}
</ol>
```

3. You'll see the following error from Jest:

```
expect(received).toEqual(expected)

Difference:

- Expected
+ Received

- 12:00
+

  59 | expect(container.querySelectorAll('li')[0].textContent)
> 60 |    .toEqual('12:00');
     |         ^
  61 | expect(container.querySelectorAll('li')[1].textContent)
  62 |    .toEqual('13:00');
  63 | });
```

4. Add the following function to `src/Appointment.js` that converts a Unix timestamp (which we get from the return value from `setHours`) into a time of day. It doesn't matter where in the file you put it; I usually like to define constants before I use them, so this would go at the top of the file:

```
const appointmentTimeOfDay = startsAt => {
  const [h, m] = new Date(startsAt).toTimeString().split(':');
  return `${h}:${m}`;
}
```

This uses the destructuring assignment and template literals, which are both space-saving features that you should start using if they aren't already part of your toolbox.

TDD can help us to overcome the fear of using complicated language features. If we're ever unsure what production code does, we can simply look at the tests to tell us.

5. Use the previous function to update `AppointmentsDayView`, as follows:

```
<ol>
  {appointments.map(appointment => (
    <li key={appointment.startsAt}>
      {appointmentTimeOfDay(appointment.startsAt)}
    </li>
  ))}
</ol>
```

6. Running tests should show everything as green:

```
PASS test/Appointment.test.js
  Appointment
    ✓ renders the customer first name (19ms)
    ✓ renders another customer first name (2ms)
  AppointmentsDayView
    ✓ renders a div with the right id (7ms)
    ✓ renders multiple appointments in an ol element (13ms)
    ✓ renders each appointment in an li (4ms)
```

7. This is a great chance to refactor. Both of our `AppointmentsDayView` tests use the same datasets. These can be lifted out into the `describe` scope, the same way we did with `customer` in the `Appointment` tests. This time, however, they can remain as `const` declarations as they never change.

   To do that, move the `today` and `appointments` definitions from one of the tests to the top of the `describe` block, above `beforeEach`. Then, delete the definitions from both tests.

Selecting data to view

Let's add in some dynamic behavior to our page. We'll make each of the list items a link that the user can click on to view that appointment.

Thinking through our design a little, there are a few pieces we'll need:

- A `button` element within our `li`
- An `onClick` handler that is attached to that `button` element
- A component state to record which appointment is currently being viewed

When we test React actions, we do it by observing the consequences of those actions. In this case, we can click on a button and then check that its corresponding appointment is now rendered on screen.

Initial selection of data

Let's start by asserting that each `li` element has a `button` element:

1. First up, let's display a message to the user if there are no appointments scheduled for today. In the `AppointmentsDayView` `describe` block, add this test:

```
it('initially shows a message saying there are no appointments
today', () => {
  render(<AppointmentsDayView appointments={[]} />);
  expect(container.textContent).toMatch(
    'There are no appointments scheduled for today.'
  );
});
```

2. Make that pass by adding in a message at the bottom of rendered output. We don't need a check for an empty appointments array just yet; we'll need another test to triangulate to that:

```
return (
  <div id="appointmentsDayView">
    ...
    <p>There are no appointments scheduled for today.</p>
  </div>
);
```

3. If there are appointments scheduled, then we start off by showing the first one of the day. We can check for a rendered customer `firstName` to determine whether the right customer is shown:

```
it('selects the first appointment by default', () => {
  render(<AppointmentsDayView appointments={appointments} />);
  expect(container.textContent).toMatch('Ashley');
});
```

4. Since we're looking for the customer name, we'll need to make sure that's available in the `appointments` array. Update it now to include the customer `firstName`:

```
const appointments = [
  {
    startsAt: today.setHours(12, 0),
    customer: { firstName: 'Ashley' }
  },
  {
    startsAt: today.setHours(13, 0),
    customer: { firstName: 'Jordan' }
  }
];
```

5. Let's make that pass by using our `Appointment` component. Modify the last line of the `div` component to read as follows:

```
<div id="appointmentsDayView">
  // ... existing code here ...
  {appointments.length === 0 ? (
    <p>There are no appointments scheduled for today.</p>
  ) : (
    <Appointment {...appointments[0]} />
  )}
</div>
```

Now, we're ready to let the user make a selection.

Adding events to a functional component

We're about to add *state* to our component. The component will show a button for each appointment. When the button is clicked, the component stores the array index of the appointment that it refers to. To do that, we'll use the `useState` hook.

Hooks are a feature of React that manage various non-rendering related operations. The `useState` hook stores data across multiple renders of your function. The call to `useState` returns you both the current value in storage and a setter function that allows it to be set.

If you're new to hooks, check out the *Further learning* section at the end of this chapter. Alternatively, you could just follow along and see how much you can pick up just by reading the tests!

Let's start by asserting that each `li` element has a `button` element:

1. Add the following test, just below the last one you added. The second
    expectation is a little peculiar in that it is checking the type of the button to be
    `button`. If you haven't seen this before, it's idiomatic when using `button`
    elements to define its role by setting the `type` attribute, as I'm doing here:

    ```
    it('has a button element in each li', () => {
      render(<AppointmentsDayView appointments={appointments} />);
      expect(
        container.querySelectorAll('li > button')
      ).toHaveLength(2);
      expect(
        container.querySelectorAll('li > button')[0].type
      ).toEqual('button');
    });
    ```

    We don't need to be pedantic about checking the content or placement of
    the `button` element within its parent. For example, this test would pass if
    we put an empty `button` child at the end of `li`. But, thankfully, doing the
    right thing is just as simple as doing the wrong thing, so we can opt to do
    the right thing instead. All we need to do to make this pass is wrap the
    existing content in the new tag.

2. Make this test pass by modifying the `AppointmentsDayView` return value, as
    shown:

    ```
    <ol>
      {appointments.map(appointment => (
        <li key={appointment.startsAt}>
          <button type="button">
            {appointmentTimeOfDay(appointment.startsAt)}
          </button>
        </li>))}
    </ol>;
    ```

3. We can now test what happens when the button is clicked. Back in
    `test/Appointment.test.js`, add the following as the next test. This uses the
    `ReactTestUtils.Simulate.click` function to perform the click action:

    ```
    it('renders another appointment when selected', () => {
      render(<AppointmentsDayView appointments={appointments} />);
      const button = container.querySelectorAll('button')[1];
      ReactTestUtils.Simulate.click(button);
      expect(container.textContent).toMatch('Jordan');
    });
    ```

React components respond to what it calls **synthetic** events. React uses these to mask browser discrepancies in the DOM event model. That means we can't raise standard events that we'd fire through JSDOM. Instead, we use the `ReactTestUtils.Simulate` object to raise events.

4. Include the following import at the top of `test/Appointment.test.js`:

```
import ReactTestUtils from 'react-dom/test-utils';
```

5. Go ahead and run the test:

```
 ● AppointmentsDayView › renders appointment when selected

expect(received).toMatch(expected)

Expected value to match:
  "Jordan"
Received:
  "12:0013:00Ashley"
```

We're getting all of the list content dumped out too, because we've used `container.textContent` in our expectation rather than something more specific.

At this stage, I'm not too bothered about where the customer name appears on screen. Testing `container.textContent` is like saying *I want this text to appear somewhere, but I don't care where.* Later on, we'll see techniques for expecting text in specific places.

There's a lot we now need to get in place in order to make the test pass: we need to introduce state and we need to add the handler. But, first, we'll need to modify our definition to use a block with a return statement:

1. Set the last test to skip, using `it.skip`.

We never refactor on red. It's against the rules! But if you're on red, you can cheat a little by rewinding to green by skipping the test that you've just written.

It may seem a little pedantic to do that for the very tiny change we're about to make, but it's good practice.

2. Wrap the constant definition in curly braces, and then return the existing value. Once you've made this change, run your tests and check you're all green:

```
export const AppointmentsDayView = ({ appointments }) => {
  return (
    <div id="appointmentsDayView">
      <ol>
      {appointments.map(appointment => (
        <li key={appointment.startsAt}>
          <button type="button">
            {appointmentTimeOfDay(appointment)}
          </button>
        </li>))}
      </ol>
      <Appointment customer={appointments[0].customer} />
    </div>
  );
};
```

3. Unskip the latest test by changing `it.skip` to `it`, and let's get to work on making it pass.

4. Update the import at the top of the file to pull in the `useState` function:

```
import React, { useState } from 'react';
```

5. Add the following line above the return statement:

```
const [selectedAppointment, setSelectedAppointment] = useState(
  0
);
```

6. We can now use this `selectedAppointment` rather than hard-coding an index selecting the right appointment. Change the return value to use this new state value when selecting an appointment:

```
<div id="appointmentsDayView">
  ...
  <Appointment {...appointments[selectedAppointment]} />
</div>
```

7. Then, change the `map` call to include an index in its arguments. Let's just name that `i`:

```
{appointments.map((appointment, i) => (
  <li key={appointment.startsAt}>
    <button type="button">
      {appointmentTimeOfDay(appointment.startsAt)}
```

```
      </button>
    </li>
  ))}
```

8. Now call `setSelectedAppointment` from within the `onClick` handler on the `button` element:

```
<button
  type="button"
  onClick={() => setSelectedAppointment(i)}>
```

9. Run your tests, and you should find they're all green:

```
PASS test/Appointment.test.js
  Appointment
    ✓ renders the customer first name (18ms)
    ✓ renders another customer first name (2ms)
  AppointmentsDayView
    ✓ renders a div with the right id (7ms)
    ✓ renders multiple appointments in an ol element (16ms)
    ✓ renders each appointment in an li (4ms)
    ✓ initially shows a message saying there are no appointments
today (6ms)
    ✓ selects the first element by default (2ms)
    ✓ has a button element in each li (2ms)
    ✓ renders another appointment when selected (3ms)
```

Our component is now complete and ready to be used in the rest of our application. That is, once we've *built* the rest of the application!

Manually testing our changes

 The Git tag for this section is `entrypoint`.

The words *manual testing* should strike fear into the heart of every TDDer. Manual testing takes up *so* much time. I usually avoid it if I can. That being said, even if we wanted to manually test, we couldn't as we can't yet run our app. To do that, we'll need to add an entrypoint.

Adding an entrypoint

React applications are composed of a hierarchy of components that are rendered at the root. Our application entrypoint should render this root component.

I tend to *not* test-drive my entrypoint, because any test that loads our entire application can become quite brittle as we add in more and more dependencies into it. In Section 4, *Acceptance Testing with BDD*, we'll look at using acceptance tests to write some tests that *will* cover the entrypoint.

Since we aren't test-driving it, we follow a couple of general rules:

- Keep it as brief as possible

- Only use it to instantiate dependencies for your root component, and to call ReactDOM.render.

Before we run our app, we'll need some sample data. Create a file named src/sampleData.js and fill it with the following:

```
const today = new Date();

const at = hours => today.setHours(hours, 0);

export const sampleAppointments = [
  { startsAt: at(9), customer: { firstName: 'Charlie' } },
  { startsAt: at(10), customer: { firstName: 'Frankie' } },
  { startsAt: at(11), customer: { firstName: 'Casey' } },
  { startsAt: at(12), customer: { firstName: 'Ashley' } },
  { startsAt: at(13), customer: { firstName: 'Jordan' } },
  { startsAt: at(14), customer: { firstName: 'Jay' } },
  { startsAt: at(15), customer: { firstName: 'Alex' } },
  { startsAt: at(16), customer: { firstName: 'Jules' } },
  { startsAt: at(17), customer: { firstName: 'Stevie' } }
];
```

The GitHub repository contains a more complete set of sample data. You can use this by pulling the same file, src/sampleData.js, from the tag extracting-helpers.

This list also doesn't need to be test-driven, for a couple of reasons:

- It's a list of static data with no behavior.
- This module will be removed once we begin using our back-end API to pull data.

 Test-driven development is often a pragmatic choice. Sometimes, *not* test-driving is the right thing to do.

Create a new file `src/index.js` and enter the following:

```
import React from 'react';
import ReactDOM from 'react-dom';
import { AppointmentsDayView } from './Appointment';
import { sampleAppointments } from './sampleData';

ReactDOM.render(
  <AppointmentsDayView appointments={sampleAppointments} />,
  document.getElementById('root')
);
```

That's all you'll need.

Putting it all together with Webpack

Jest includes Babel, which transpiles all our code when it's run in the test environment. But what about when we're serving our code via our website? Jest won't be able to help us there.

That's where Webpack comes in, and we can introduce it now to help us, do a quick manual test:

1. Install Webpack using the following command:

   ```
   npm install --save-dev webpack webpack-cli babel-loader
   ```

2. Add the following to the scripts section of your `package.json`:

   ```
   "build": "webpack",
   ```

3. You'll also need to set some configuration for Webpack. Create
   the `webpack.config.js` file in your project root directory with the following
   content:

```
const path = require("path");
const webpack = require("webpack");

module.exports = {
 mode: "development",
 module: {
   rules: [{
     test: /\.(js|jsx)$/,
     exclude: /node_modules/,
     loader: 'babel-loader'}]}
};
```

This configuration works for Webpack in development mode. Consult the
Webpack documentation for information on setting up production builds.

4. In your source directory, run the following commands:

```
mkdir dist
touch dist/index.html
```

5. Add the following content to the file you just created:

```
<!DOCTYPE html>
<html>
  <head>
    <title>Appointments</title>
  </head>
  <body>
    <div id="root"></div>
    <script src="main.js"></script>
  </body>
</html>
```

6. You're now ready to run the build:

```
npm run build
```

You should see a bunch of output like this:

```
    Asset Size Chunks Chunk Names
main.js 764 KiB main [emitted] main
Entrypoint main = main.js
[./src/Appointment.js] 4.67 KiB {main} [built]
```

```
[./src/index.js] 544 bytes {main} [built]
[./src/sampleData.js] 726 bytes {main} [built]
 + 11 hidden modules
```

7. Open `index.html` in your browser and behold your creation:

The following screenshot shows the application once the *Exercises* are completed, and with added CSS and extended sample data. To include the CSS, you'll need to pull `dist/index.html` and `dist/styles.css` from the `chapter-2` tag. The sample data can be found in `src/sampleData.js`, within the same tag. If you're choosing not to complete the Exercises, you can skip to that tag now.

As you can see, we've only got a little part of the way to fully building our application. The first few tests of any application are always the hardest and take the longest to write. We are now over that hurdle, so we'll move quicker from here onward.

Before you check in...

Make sure to add `dist/main.js` to your `.gitignore` file. This file is generated by Webpack, and as with every generated file, you shouldn't check it in.

You may also want to add a `README.md` at this point, to remind yourself how to run tests and how to build the application.

Summary

One of the many wonderful things about test-driven development is that it's teachable. Tests act like a safety harness in our learning: we can build little blocks of understanding, building on top of each other, up and up to ever-greater heights, without fear of falling.

In this chapter, you've learned a lot of the test-driven development experience: the red-green-refactor cycle, triangulation, and *Arrange, Act, Assert*. You've also learned some design principles such as DRY and YAGNI.

While this is a great start, the journey has only just begun. Coming up next, we'll look at test-driving React forms and building complex user interface designs with our tests acting as scaffold.

Exercises

The Git tag for this section is `chapter-1-exercises`.

- Rename `Appointment.js` and `Appointment.test.js` to `AppointmentsDayView.js` and `AppointmentsDayView.test.js`. While it's fine to include multiple components in one file if they form a hierarchy, you should always name the file after the root component for that hierarchy.
- Complete the `Appointment` component by displaying the following fields on the page. You should use a `table` HTML element to give the data some visual structure. This shouldn't affect how you write your tests:
    - Customer last name, using the `lastName` field
    - Customer telephone number, using the `phoneNumber` field
    - Stylist name, using the `stylist` field
    - Salon service, using the `service` field
    - Appointment notes, using the `notes` field

- Add a heading to `Appointment` to make it clear which appointment time is being viewed.
- There is some repeated sample data. We've used sample data in our tests and we also have `sampleAppointments` in `src/sampleData.js`, which we used to manually test our application. Do you think it is worth drying this up? If so, why? If not, why not?

Further learning

- Node.js: `https://nodejs.org/en/`
- Correctly configuring the Babel `env` preset: `https://babeljs.io/docs/en/babel-preset-env`
- Jest documentation on the `watch` tool: `https://jestjs.io/docs/en/cli#watch`
- Hooks at a Glance: `https://reactjs.org/docs/hooks-overview.html`

2
Test-driving Data Input with React

In this chapter, we'll explore React forms and controlled components. We'll work with textboxes, select boxes, and radio buttons to build out these forms:

- `CustomerForm`, which is used when adding or modifying customers, with three fields: first name, last name, and phone number
- `AppointmentForm`, for adding and modifying appointments, which contains two fields for choosing a salon service and an appointment time

In the process of building these forms, we'll dig deeper into testing complex DOM trees.

The following topics will be covered in this chapter:

- Extracting a test helper
- Adding a form element
- Accepting text input
- Selecting from a dropdown
- Making a choice from radio buttons

But, first, we will start with a little tidy-up.

Extracting a test helper

The Git tag for this section is `extracting-helpers`. It contains solutions to the exercises from the previous chapter, so if you haven't completed the *Exercises* section yourself, then you should move to this tag now so that you're up to date.

For more detailed instructions, see the *To get the most out of this book* section in the `Preface`.

In the first chapter, our test suites shared common code for constructing a DOM container element before each test. This element was used as the React root element. By doing this for each test, we avoided modifying global state. Let's extract that code so that we can re-use it across all of our test suites.

The shared code can be split into four parts:

- A common declaration of `container` in the `describe` block, accessible by all tests
- A `beforeEach` call to set `container` to a newly constructed container element
- A `render` function to insert DOM elements into the container
- Various expectations on the container to verify its content

At first glance, it might seem difficult to extract this logic since the `container` variable is manipulated in both a `beforeEach` block and each of our test functions. However, it's possible if we use a higher-order function that encapsulates its own state.

Create a new file `test/domManipulators.js`, and add the following content:

```
import ReactDOM from 'react-dom';

export const createContainer = () => {
  const container = document.createElement('div');

  return {
    render: component => ReactDOM.render(component, container),
    container
  };
};
```

Calling `domManipulators` creates an empty DOM element, `container`, and then returns an object with two properties: `render` and `container`. We'll see how these can be used in the next section.

Adding a form element

Let's create our first form:

1. Create a new file called `test/CustomerForm.test.js` and add the following:

```
import React from 'react';
import { createContainer } from './domManipulators';
import { CustomerForm } from '../src/CustomerForm';

describe('CustomerForm', () => {
  let render, container;

  beforeEach(() => {
    ({ render, container } = createContainer());
  });
});
```

 The call in the `beforeEach` block looks a little odd; it's a destructuring assignment where the variables have already been declared. The declaration and assignment are split in this way because the variables must be accessible within the scope of the `describe` block, but they must also be reassigned for each and every test. Each test gets its own container, independent of the other tests.

2. Add the following test into the `describe` block:

```
it('renders a form', () => {
  render(<CustomerForm />);
  expect(
    container.querySelector('form[id="customer"]')
  ).not.toBeNull();
});
```

3. We have a complete test, so let's run it and see what happens:

```
FAIL test/CustomerForm.test.js
  ● Test suite failed to run

    Cannot find module '../src/CustomerForm' from
'CustomerForm.test.js'
```

4. Go ahead and create `src/CustomerForm.js`. Running your test again should give you the following output:

```
FAIL test/CustomerForm.test.js
 ● CustomerForm › renders a label for the first name field

  Invariant Violation: Element type is invalid: expected a string
  (for built-in components) or a class/function (for composite
  components) but got: object. You likely forgot to export your
  component from the file it's defined in, or you might have mixed up
  default and named imports.

     10 |
   > 11 |    render: component => ReactDOM.render(component,
  container),
        |
     12 |    container
     13 | };
```

5. One issue with our `domManipulators` code is that Jest's stack trace points to a failure within our helper code, not the test itself. Thankfully, the error message is helpful enough; we need to add an export that matches the import we wrote at the top of our test file. Add the following line to `src/CustomerForm.js`:

```
export const CustomerForm = () => null;
```

6. Running tests gives another failure:

```
Invariant Violation: CustomerForm(...): Nothing was returned from
render. This usually means a return statement is missing. Or, to
render nothing, return null.
```

7. Fix that by making the component return something:

```
import React from 'react';

export const CustomerForm = () => <form id="customer" />;
```

This passes our tests.

Asserting on DOM IDs

We've given this form an ID and that our test looks specifically for that ID in its expectation. This protects us from **brittle tests**. For example, if our test just looked for *any* form, then it could break if we design our page to include *two* forms rather than just this one.

Extracting a form-finder method

We'll be writing quite a few tests for this form, so let's extract the call to `querySelector` into an arrow function. Add this just below the `beforeEach` definition:

```
const form = id => container.querySelector(`form[id="${id}"]`);
```

The expectation in your test then becomes this:

```
expect(form('customer')).not.toBeNull();
```

This is much more readable, because the CSS selector is abstracted away behind the function call. I'd encourage you to repeat that pattern in your tests. CSS selectors are a useful tool, but they detract from the "plain English" that you should be aiming for in your tests.

Accepting text input

The Git tag for this section is `accepting-text-input`.

Let's render an HTML text input field onto the page. Add the following test to `test/CustomerForm.test.js`:

```
it('renders the first name field as a text box', () => {
  render(<CustomerForm />);
  const field = form('customer').elements.firstName;
  expect(field).not.toBeNull();
  expect(field.tagName).toEqual('INPUT');
  expect(field.type).toEqual('text');
});
```

This test makes use of the DOM form API: any form allows access to all of its input elements using the elements indexer. This is a simpler way of accessing form fields than CSS selectors, so I prefer to use it when it's an option.

There are three expectations in this test:

- For there to be a form element with the name `firstName`
- For it to be an `input` element
- For it to have a type of `text`

Let's make them all pass. Update `CustomerForm` to include a single input field, as shown:

```
export const CustomerForm = () => (
  <form id="customer">
    <input
      type="text"
      name="firstName"
    />
  </form>
);
```

Extracting an expectation group function

The three expectations in this test will be needed every time we define a new text field. A simple way to avoid repeating each expectation is to extract an arrow function that runs all three as a group:

```
const expectToBeInputFieldOfTypeText = formElement => {
  expect(formElement).not.toBeNull();
  expect(formElement.tagName).toEqual('INPUT');
  expect(formElement.type).toEqual('text');
};
```

Define this function above your test and replace the expectations in your test with a call to this function.

In the next chapter, we'll build a Jest matcher that performs a similar function, but for a different use case.

Passing in an existing value

Since this form will be used when modifying existing customers as well as adding new ones, we must set the text field's initial value to the existing first name if set:

```
it('includes the existing value for the first name', () => {
  render(<CustomerForm firstName="Ashley" />);
  const field = form('customer').elements.firstName;
  expect(field.value).toEqual('Ashley');
});
```

To make this test pass, change the component definition to the following. We use a prop to pass in the previous first name value:

```
export const CustomerForm = ({ firstName }) => (
  <form id="customer">
    <input
      type="text"
      name="firstName"
      value={firstName}
    />
  </form>
);
```

Running tests again, you'll see that the test passes, but with a warning:

```
PASS test/CustomerForm.test.js
  ● Console
    console.error node_modules/prop-types/checkPropTypes.js:19
      Warning: Failed prop type: You provided a `value` prop to a form
field without an `onChange` handler. This will render a read-only field. If
the field should be mutable use `defaultValue`. Otherwise, set either
`onChange` or `readOnly`.
        in input (created by CustomerForm)
        in form (created by CustomerForm)
        in CustomerForm
```

To get rid of the warning, add the word `readOnly` to the input tag. You might be thinking: surely, we don't want a read-only field? You're right, but we need a further test, for modifying the input value, before we can avoid using the `readOnly` keyword. We'll add that test a little further on.

> Always consider React warnings to be a test failure. Don't proceed without first fixing the warning.

Extracting out a field-finder function

Both of our tests include the following line, which reaches inside the form to pull out the firstName field:

```
const field = form('customer').elements.firstName;
```

This DOM manipulation is not related to what we're testing: while we care about the value of field, we are not interested in how the DOM API works.

We can improve the readability of our tests by keeping code within tests at a high level of abstraction, and extracting lower-level logic into helper methods. Since our tests are passing at the moment, now is a great opportunity to refactor.

Extract this field variable into a new function called firstNameField, as shown:

```
const firstNameField = () => form('customer').elements.firstName;
```

In the process of converting this variable into a function, we renamed it from field to firstNameField. A short, generic variable name such as field is fine inside the short scope of a single test. But once you pull the variable up into the describe scope, you need to be more specific in your naming.

The last test we wrote now simplifies to this:

```
it('includes the existing value for the first name', () => {
  render(<CustomerForm firstName="Ashley" />);
  expect(firstNameField().value).toEqual('Ashley');
});
```

Update the first test in the same way:

```
it('renders as a text box', () => {
  render(<CustomerForm />);
  expectToBeInputFieldOfTypeText(firstNameField());
});
```

It's worth pointing out here that, if we hadn't extracted the three expectations into this function, we could have called this new function three times, rather than calling it once and saving that value in a variable. I probably wouldn't do this in my production code, but it's fine in tests; readability is more important than minimizing computation:

```
expect(firstNameField()).not.toBeNull();
expect(firstNameField()).toEqual('INPUT');
expect(firstNameField()).toEqual('text');
```

Labeling the field

Let's add a label to the field so the user knows what they are typing in:

```
const labelFor = formElement =>
  container.querySelector(`label[for="${formElement}"]`);

it('renders a label for the first name field', () => {
  render(<CustomerForm />);
  expect(labelFor('firstName')).not.toBeNull();
  expect(labelFor('firstName').textContent).toEqual('First name');
});
```

Make this pass by changing the JSX fragment to read as follows:

```
<form id="customer">
  <label htmlFor="firstName">First name</label>
  <input
    type="text"
    name="firstName"
    value={firstName}
    readOnly
  />
</form>
```

 The JSX `htmlFor` attribute sets the HTML `for` attribute. `for` couldn't be used in JSX because it is a reserved JavaScript keyword. The attribute is used to signify that the label matches a form element with the given ID, in this case, `firstName`.

Now we need to ensure that our input has that same id, so that they match up. Add the following next test:

```
it('assigns an id that matches the label id to the first name field', () =>
{
  render(<CustomerForm />);
  expect(firstNameField().id).toEqual('firstName');
});
```

Making that pass is as simple as adding in the new attribute:

```
<form id="customer">
  <label htmlFor="firstName">First name</label>
  <input
    type="text"
    name="firstName"
    id="firstName"
    value={firstName}
    readOnly
  />
</form>
```

Checking for null or not

There is a school of thought that checking for `null` in tests is redundant and can be removed all together. In other words, the second-to-last test we wrote would become this:

```
it('renders a label for the first name field', () => {
  render();
  expect(labelFor('firstName').textContent).toEqual('First name');
});
```

In the original test, the first `not null` expectation is a *guard* expectation. The test will still function even without this line, since the second expectation will throw an exception if the value of label is `null`.

The run-time difference between the two variants of the test is subtle. The original test will fail with a test failure, not an exception. In this second version, your test will fail with an exception, not a test failure.

In some languages and test environments, exceptions can be more painful than test failures. Ultimately, which style you choose is a matter of personal preference. In this book, I'll continue to use guard expectations for completeness, but I'd encourage you to experiment with both styles.

Saving the customer information

The Git tag for this section is `saving-form-data`.

To save and submit form data, we'll convert our component into a React-controlled component. We will use the component state to save the current values of input fields.

Submitting a form with data

The next test introduces some new concepts, so we'll break it down into its component parts. To start, add `ReactTestUtils` to your list of imports in `test/CustomerForm.test.js`:

```
import ReactTestUtils from 'react-dom/test-utils';
```

Then, begin your test with the following outline:

```
it('saves existing first name when submitted', async () => {
  expect.hasAssertions();
});
```

There are two new pieces of functionality here.

The `async` keyword appears on the first line, just before our test function definition. This tells Jest that the test will return a promise, and that the test runner should wait for that promise to resolve before reporting on the success or failure of the test.

The `hasAssertions` expectation tells Jest that it should expect at least one assertion to occur. Without this line, Jest could happily pass your test if the task queue clears but your event handler was never executed. We'll see how this might occur once the test is completed.

Now, add the next part of the test into the outline, below the `hasAssertions` call:

```
render(
  <CustomerForm
    firstName="Ashley"
    onSubmit={({ firstName }) =>
      expect(firstName).toEqual('Ashley')
    }
  />
);
```

This function call is a mix of *Arrange* and *Assert* phases in one. The *Arrange* phase is the `render` call itself. In previous tests, `render` has been the *Act* phase of our test. That means we've already tested that the form renders successfully in other tests, so we're permitted to use that functionality now as part of the *Arrange* phase.

The *Assert* phase of this code is the onSubmit handler. This is the handler that we want React to call on form submission. By defining onSubmit as a prop on the CustomerForm component, we are delegating responsibility for handling the submitted data. All the form has to do is batch up the updated data into an object and pass it on.

You'll see that there's an expectation within our handler. This is why we need the call to hasAssertions. Without the hasAssertions expectation, Jest will happily pass your test even if onSubmit never gets called: no expectation was ever run in order for your test to fail.

Finish off the test by adding in this line just below the call to render:

```
await ReactTestUtils.Simulate.submit(form('customer'));
```

The call to Simulate.submit places a React submit event on the task queue, as if a submit button had been pressed. Since this is handled asynchronously, we need to use the await keyword to ensure Jest waits before continuing to look for assertions. Once the event has been dispatched and handled, Jest will decide on the pass/fail status of the test.

We don't need a submit button on the page for this to work; raising the event is enough. Later on, we'll use another test to add the submit button.

 This test is slightly confused: our render call is both the *Arrange* phase and the *Assert* phase. In the next chapter, we'll use **test doubles** to separate out these test phases. The method we're using here is a perfectly valid TDD practice; it's just a little messy.

Let's work on making the new test pass. This is simple despite the test itself being complicated. Change the component definition to read as follows:

```
export const CustomerForm = ({ firstName, onSubmit }) => {
  const customer = { firstName };
  return <form id="customer" onSubmit={() => onSubmit(customer)}>
    <label htmlFor="firstName">First name</label>
    <input
      type="text"
      name="firstName"
      id="firstName"
      value={firstName}
      readOnly
    />
  </form>;
};
```

This hooks up the form's onSubmit handler to the onSubmit function that we passed into the component, and passes it a new customer object, which includes firstName. Don't miss out the return statement and the extra curly braces that now need to be added!

Run your tests and ensure they are all passing.

Using state instead of props

It's finally time to introduce some state into our component. Add the following test, which what should happen when the text field value changes:

```
it('saves new first name when submitted', async () => {
  expect.hasAssertions();
  render(
    <CustomerForm
      firstName="Ashley"
      onSubmit={({ firstName }) =>
        expect(firstName).toEqual('Jamie')
      }
    />
  );
  await ReactTestUtils.Simulate.change( firstNameField(), {
    target: { value: 'Jamie' }
  });
  await ReactTestUtils.Simulate.submit(form('customer'));
});
```

The call to Simulate.change dispatches a React onChange event to the field. The event object sends the value of the text field to the event handler, which we'll use to set state.

> In the browser, this event would be dispatched after every keystroke; however, in our test, we simulate just the final change event. That's enough because we'll write our event handler to always overwrite previous changes. In other words, only the last change matters.

Follow these steps to make this pass:

1. Import useState into the module by modifying the existing React import:

```
import React, { useState } from 'react';
```

2. Change the customer constant definition to be assigned via a call to useState. The default state is the original value of customer. Note the relationship between the two pieces of code. This is an example of how we can "upgrade" existing code from one level of complexity to another—in this case, from a constant definition to a state variable:

```
const [ customer, setCustomer ] = useState({ firstName });
```

3. Create a new arrow function that will act as our event handler. This uses the form of setCustomer that takes a function. Using this form ensures that we correctly apply updates in the right order:

```
const handleChangeFirstName = ({ target }) =>
  setCustomer(customer => ({
    ...customer,
    firstName: target.value
  }));
```

4. In the returned JSX, modify the input element as shown. We replace the readOnly property with an onChange property, hooking it up to the handler we just created:

```
<input
  type="text"
  name="firstName"
  id="firstName"
  value={firstName}
  onChange={handleChangeFirstName}
/>
```

Duplicating fields

 The Git tag for this section is duplicating-fields.

We've written a set of tests that fully define the firstName text field. We now want to add two more fields, which are essentially the same as the firstName field but with different id and labels.

Before you reach for the copy and paste, stop and think about the duplication you could be about to add to both your tests and your production code. We have six tests that define the first name. We'll end up with 18 tests to define three fields. That's a lot of tests without any kind of grouping or abstraction.

So, let's do both. Let's group our tests and abstract out a function that generates our tests for us.

Nesting describe blocks

We can nest describe blocks to break similar tests up into logical contexts. We can invent our own convention for how to name these describe blocks. Whereas the top level is named after the form itself, the second-level describe blocks are named after the form fields.

Here's how we'd like them to end up:

```
describe('CustomerForm', () => {
  describe('first name field', () => {
    // ... tests ...
  };
  describe('last name field', () => {
    // ... tests ...
  };
  describe('phone number field', () => {
    // ... tests ...
  };
});
```

With this structure in place, you can simplify the it descriptive text by removing the name of the field. For example, 'renders the first name field as a text box' becomes 'renders as a text box', because it has already been scoped by the 'first name field' describe block. Because of the way Jest displays describe block names before test names in test output, each of these still reads like a plain-English sentence, but without the verbiage. In the example just given, Jest will show us: *CustomerForm first name field renders as a text box*.

Let's do that now for the first name field. Wrap the six existing tests in a `describe` block, and then rename the tests, as shown:

```
describe('first name field', () => {
  it('renders as a text box' ... );

  it('includes the existing value' ... );

  it('renders a label' ... );

  it('assigns an id that matches the label id' ... );

  it('saves existing value when submitted' ... );

  it('saves new value when submitted' ... );
});
```

Generating parameterized tests

Some programming languages, such as Java and C#, require special framework support to build parameterized tests. But in JavaScript, we can very easily roll our own parameterization because our test definitions are just function calls. We can use this to our advantage by pulling out each of the existing six tests as functions taking parameter values.

This kind of change requires some diligent refactoring. We'll do the first two tests together, and then you can either repeat for the remaining five tests or jump ahead to the next tag in the Git repository:

1. Our existing tests use a function named `firstNameField`. Create a generic version of function that will work for any field, as shown next. It takes a `name` parameter that must be passed in by the caller to specify which field is being accessed:

   ```
   const field = name => form('customer').elements[name];
   ```

2. Replace each occurrence of `firstNameField()` with `field('firstName')`. You can use **find** and **replace** for this.
3. Run all tests and ensure they are still passing. At this point, you should have 28 passing tests.
4. Delete the `firstNameField` function.

5. Starting with `renders as a text box`, wrap the entirety of the `it` call in an arrow function, and then call that function straight after, as shown:

```
const itRendersAsATextBox = () =>
  it('renders as a text box', () => {
    render(<CustomerForm />);
    expectToBeInputFieldOfTypeText(field('firstName'));
  });

itRendersAsATextBox();
```

6. Verify that you still have 28 passing tests.

7. Parameterize this function by promoting the `firstName` string to a function parameter. You'll then need to pass in the `firstName` string into the function call itself, as shown here:

```
const itRendersAsATextBox = (fieldName) =>
  it('renders as a text box', () => {
    render(<CustomerForm />);
    expectToBeInputFieldOfTypeText(field(fieldName));
  });

itRendersAsATextBox('firstName');
```

8. Again verify that your tests are passing.

9. Push the `itRendersAsATextBox` function up one level, and its dependent function, `expectToBeInputFieldOfTypeText`, into the parent `describe` scope. That will allow us to use it in subsequent `describe` blocks.

10. For the next test, `includes the existing value`, we can use the same procedure, but this time rather than promoting the string value, `Ashley` to a parameter, we'll simply replace it with a more generic value. We can do that because the value isn't really important to the test:

 We pass in the prop in a generic fashion, using the `[fieldName]:` syntax to specify the key. This is about as difficult as JSX can get!

```
const itIncludesTheExistingValue = (fieldName) =>
  it('includes the existing value', () => {
    render(<CustomerForm { ...{[fieldName]: 'value'} } />);
    expect(field(fieldName).value).toEqual('value');
  });

itIncludesTheExistingValue('firstName');
```

11. Verify your tests are passing and then push `itIncludesTheExistingValue` up one level, into the parent describe scope.

12. Repeat steps 5-9 for the remaining four tests. As a hint, the next test for the label will need a second parameter for the label text, and the two tests for submitting existing values and new values will need a second parameter, for the value. For reference, here's how the final test might end up looking:

```
const itSubmitsNewValue = (fieldName, value) =>
  it('saves new value when submitted', async () => {
    expect.hasAssertions();
    render(
      <CustomerForm
        { ...{[fieldName]: 'existingValue'} }
        onSubmit={props =>
          expect(props[fieldName]).toEqual(value)
        }
      />);
    await ReactTestUtils.Simulate.change(field(fieldName), {
      target: { value }
    });
    await ReactTestUtils.Simulate.submit(form('customer'));
  });

itSubmitsNewValue('firstName', 'firstName');
```

With all that done, your `describe` block will now quite succinctly describe what the first name field does:

```
describe('first name field', () => {
  itRendersAsATextBox('firstName');
  itIncludesTheExistingValue('firstName');
  itRendersALabel('firstName', 'First name');
  itAssignsAnIdThatMatchesTheLabelId('firstName');
  itSubmitsExistingValue('firstName', 'firstName');
  itSubmitsNewValue('firstName', 'anotherFirstName');
});
```

Solving a batch of tests

We want to now duplicate those six tests for the last-name field. But how do we approach this? Well, we do it test-by-test, just as we did with the first name field. Only this time, we should go much faster as our tests are one-liners and the production code is a copy and paste job.

So, for example, the first test will be this:

```
describe('last name field', () => {
  itRendersAsATextBox('lastName');
});
```

That can be made to pass by adding the following line to our JSX, just below the first-name input field:

```
<input
  type="text"
  name="lastName"
/>
```

This is just the start for the input field: you'll need to complete it as you add in the next tests.

Go ahead and add the remaining five tests together with their implementation. Then, repeat the process for the phone number field. When adding the submit tests for the phone number, make sure to provide a string value made up of numbers, such as `'012345'`. Later in this book, we'll add validations to this field that will fail if you don't use the right values now.

> You might be tempted to try to solve all 12 new tests at once. If you're feeling confident, go for it!

If you want to see a listing of all tests in a file, you need to invoke Jest with just a single file. Run the `npm test test/CustomerForm.test.js` command to see what that looks like. Alternatively, you can run `npx jest --verbose` to run all tests with full test listings:

```
PASS test/CustomerForm.test.js
  CustomerForm
    ✓ renders a form (28ms)
    first name field
      ✓ renders as a text box (4ms)
      ✓ includes the existing value (3ms)
      ✓ renders a label (2ms)
      ✓ saves existing value when submitted (4ms)
      ✓ saves new value when submitted (5ms)
    last name field
      ✓ renders as a text box (3ms)
      ✓ includes the existing value (2ms)
      ✓ renders a label (6ms)
      ✓ saves existing value when submitted (2ms)
```

```
    ✓ saves new value when submitted (3ms)
  phone number field
    ✓ renders as a text box (2ms)
    ✓ includes the existing value (2ms)
    ✓ renders a label (2ms)
    ✓ saves existing value when submitted (3ms)
    ✓ saves new value when submitted (2ms)
```

Modifying handleChange to work with multiple fields

 The Git tag for this section is `handle-change`.

After adding all three fields, you will have ended up with three very similar `onChange` event handlers:

```
const handleChangeFirstName = ({ target }) =>
  setCustomer(customer => ({
    ...customer,
    firstName: target.value
  }));

const handleChangeLastName = ({ target }) =>
  setCustomer(customer => ({
    ...customer,
    lastName: target.value
  }));

const handleChangePhoneNumber = ({ target }) =>
  setCustomer(customer => ({
    ...customer,
    phoneNumber: target.value
  }));
```

You can simplify these down into one function, but you'll need to modify your tests first. The calls to `ReactTestUtils.Simulate.change` needs some extra data to be passed: the target's `name`. At runtime, this property is passed to all event handlers by React.

Add that in now, as shown:

```
const itSubmitsNewValue = (fieldName) =>
  it('saves new value when submitted', async () => {
    ...
```

```
await ReactTestUtils.Simulate.change(field(fieldName), {
  target: { value: 'newValue', name: fieldName }
});
...
});
```

Test data should always be as simple as possible, by only including what's relevant for the test to pass. We omitted the `name` property initially because we didn't need it to make our tests pass. Now, we have an opportunity to simplify our production code, so we can include it.

Since the name of our fields is the same as the name of our customer properties, we can now destructure the event to pull out the target name, merging our event handlers into one, as shown. This uses the *computed property name* feature of ES6:

```
const handleChange = ({ target }) =>
  setCustomer(customer => ({
    ...customer,
    [target.name]: target.value
  }));
```

Finishing off the form with a submit button

It's a good time to add a `submit` button and perform a manual test to check what you've created. A `submit` button test is relatively simple. Add the following test to your test file:

```
it('has a submit button', () => {
  render(<CustomerForm />);
  const submitButton = container.querySelector(
    'input[type="submit"]'
  );
  expect(submitButton).not.toBeNull();
});
```

Then, make that pass by adding in your submit button into the form, at the bottom:

```
<form id="customer" onSubmit={handleSubmit}>
  ...
  <input type="submit" value="Add" />
</form>
```

Update your entrypoint in `src/index.js` to render a new `CustomerForm` instance, rather than an `AppointmentsDayView`, and you should be ready to manually test:

Selecting from a dropdown

 The Git tag for this section is `appointment-form`.

Let's move on to creating our appointment form. This form is used to book an appointment for a customer. The first field is the service the customer requires: cut, color, blow-dry, and so on:

1. Create a new file, `test/AppointmentForm.test.js`, with the following test and setup:

```
import React from 'react';
import { createContainer } from './domManipulators';
import { AppointmentForm } from '../src/AppointmentForm';

describe('AppointmentForm', () => {
  let render, container;

  beforeEach(() => {
    ({ render, container } = createContainer());
  });

  const form = id =>
    container.querySelector(`form[id="${id}"]`);

  it('renders a form', () => {
```

```
      render(<AppointmentForm />);
      expect(form('appointment')).not.toBeNull();
    });
  });
```

2. Fix this test by implementing the production code in
   src/AppointmentForm.js, as shown:

   ```
   import React from 'react';

   export const AppointmentForm = () => <form id="appointment" />;
   ```

3. Create a nested describe block for the service field. We do this right away
   because we know this form will have multiple fields:

   ```
   describe('service field', () => {
   });
   ```

4. Add the following test in the describe block:

   ```
   it('renders as a select box', () => {
     render(<AppointmentForm />);
     expect(form('appointment').elements.service)
       .not.toBeNull();
     expect(form('appointment').elements.service.tagName)
       .toEqual('SELECT');
   });
   ```

5. To make this test pass, modify the AppointmentForm component as follows:

   ```
   export const AppointmentForm = () => (
     <form id="appointment">
       <select name="service" />
     </form>
   );
   ```

6. Run tests and ensure all are passing.

7. Simplify the test code by extracting a function for retrieving the service field. The
   function is essentially the same as the field function from the CustomerForm
   tests, the only difference being the form that it accesses:

   ```
   const field = name => form('appointment').elements[name];

   it('renders as a select box') {
     expect(field('service')).not.toBeNull();
     expect(field('service').tagName).toEqual('SELECT');
   });
   ```

Providing options to a dropdown

 The Git tag for this section is `providing-options`.

The first option in our dropdown should be an empty value. This is the value that's initially selected when the user creates a new appointment: no option is selected. Let's write that test now:

```
it('initially has a blank value chosen', () => {
  render(<AppointmentForm />);
  const firstNode = field('service').childNodes[0];
  expect(firstNode.value).toEqual('');
  expect(firstNode.selected).toBeTruthy();
});
```

Make that pass by adding in an empty option into the top of the select:

```
export const AppointmentForm = () => (
  <form id="appointment">
    <select name="service">
      <option />
    </select>
  </form>
);
```

In the first chapter, you saw the importance of keeping test data simple. Our tests reference just what we need to exercise the test, and nothing more. We have to be very careful of noise, and we aim to keep our tests as concise as possible.

Now, we'll apply that principle to a larger set of data.

Our salon provides a whole range of services and we'd like to ensure that they are all listed in the app. We could start our test by defining our expectations like this:

```
it('lists all salon services', () => {
  const selectableServices = [
    'Cut',
    'Blow-dry',
    'Cut & color',
    'Beard trim',
    'Cut & beard trim',
    'Extensions' ];
```

As it turns out, there's a simpler way. We want to prove that our code can take an array and list each array item within the dropdown. We can do this with just *two* items in our array. Any more is overkill.

But how do we use only two items in our test when we need six items for the production code?

We do that by passing in our array as a prop to the component, rather than hard-coding it within the component itself. We can then provide a two-item array for our tests and the full list when we hook the AppointmentForm up in our application entrypoint.

Add the following test:

```
it('lists all salon services', () => {
  const selectableServices = ['Cut', 'Blow-dry'];
  render(
    <AppointmentForm
      selectableServices={selectableServices}
    />
  );
  const optionNodes = Array.from(
    field('service').childNodes
  );
  const renderedServices = optionNodes.map(
    node => node.textContent
  );
  expect(renderedServices).toEqual(
    expect.arrayContaining(selectableServices)
  );
});
```

The expectations here are more complicated than we've seen before. The Array.from method takes childNodes, which is a NodeList, and produces a standard JavaScript array with the same nodes. We then use the Array.map function to pull out the textContent of these nodes and check that it matches our original array.

 NodeList objects are "live" in that they automatically update when the DOM changes. By calling Array.from, we are taking a snapshot of the values within it at a particular moment in time.

The toEqual matcher, when applied to arrays, will check that each array has the same number of elements and that each element appears in the same place.

I've used "real"-like data for my expected services: cut and blow-dry. It's also fine to use non-real names such as Service A and Service B. Often, that can be more descriptive. Both are valid approaches.

Let's make this pass. Change the component definition, as follows:

```
export const AppointmentForm = ({ selectableServices }) => (
  <form id="appointment">
    <select name="service">
      <option />
      {selectableServices.map(s => (
        <option key={s}>{s}</option>
      ))}
    </select>
  </form>
);
```

The latest test should now pass, but our earlier tests break because of the introduction of the new prop. We could update our tests to explicitly pass a `selectableServices` prop into `AppointmentForm`. We could also change our production code to use a default array if `selectableServices` isn't defined.

But there's another way, which is also conveniently how we'll get our real data into the application.

Utilizing defaultProps to specify real data

React offers a mechanism for setting default prop values, `defaultProps`, which will be used when required props are not explicitly provided.

Just below the definition of the `AppointmentForm` function in `src/AppointmentForm.js`, add the following:

```
AppointmentForm.defaultProps = {
  selectableServices: [
    'Cut',
    'Blow-dry',
    'Cut & color',
    'Beard trim',
    'Cut & beard trim',
    'Extensions']
};
```

We didn't write a test for this code. Doesn't this break our rule of never writing code without first having a failing test? No. In our unit tests, we only test-drive *behavior*, not static data. A test to prove that `defaultProps` has the values we expect would simply be duplicating the array list.

Testing static data does happen, just not within our unit tests. One place that can be tested is within acceptance tests, which we'll look at in Section 4, *Acceptance testing with BDD*.

Pre-selecting a value

Before we write out next test, define a `findOption` arrow function at the top of the `describe` block:

```
const findOption = (dropdownNode, textContent) => {
  const options = Array.from(dropdownNode.childNodes);
  return options.find(
    option => option.textContent === textContent
  );
};
```

This function searches the DOM tree for a particular text node. We can find that node and then check that it is selected:

```
it('pre-selects the existing value', () => {
  const services = ['Cut', 'Blow-dry'];
  render(
    <AppointmentForm
      selectableServices={services}
      service="Blow-dry"
    />
  );
  const option = findOption(
    field('service'),
    'Blow-dry'
  );
  expect(option.selected).toBeTruthy();
});
```

To make this pass, we set the value property on the root `select` tag:

```
<select
  name="service"
  value={service}
  readOnly>
```

You'll also need to change your component props to include the new `service` prop:

```
export const AppointmentForm = ({
  selectableServices,
  service
}) =>
```

Remember to run your tests and check they are passing before continuing.

Completing the remaining tests for the select box

For labeling and handling state changes, the dropdown behaves just like a text field. Go ahead and write the following remaining tests:

- Renders a label
- Assigns an ID that matches the label ID
- Saves existing value when submitted
- Saves new value when submitted

To make these pass you'll need to define a `handleChange` event handler in the same way you did for the input field, this time setting the `onChange` prop on the `select` field.

Although you can use `CustomerForm` as a guide, you shouldn't worry about building parameterized versions of these test. Just write out the plain ol' `it` calls. Our parameterized versions from `CustomerForm` aren't quite usable, as they are hard-coded to render the `CustomerForm`. We'd need to do extra work to make these functions usable in both files.

An important skill for TDD practitioners is knowing which battles to pick. Although we want our code to be clean and concise, we need stay focused on the task in hand. Although we have a sense that there is repeated code between the two test suites, it's hard to immediately see a clear path. Therefore, it's better to defer and keep working, until a path *does* become clear. It will eventually.

Making a choice from radio buttons

The Git tag for this section is `time-slot-table`.

It's time to apply what we've learn to a more complicated HTML setup. In this section, we'll test-drive a whole bunch of interconnected elements. To make things harder, we'll also be manipulating times and dates using the standard JavaScript `Date` object. As you'll soon see, our tests give us a structure to our work that makes even complicated scenarios straightforward.

We'd like to display available time slots over the next seven days as a grid, with columns representing days and rows representing 30-minute time slots, just like a standard calendar view. The user will be able to quickly find a time slot that works for them and then select the right radio button before submitting the form:

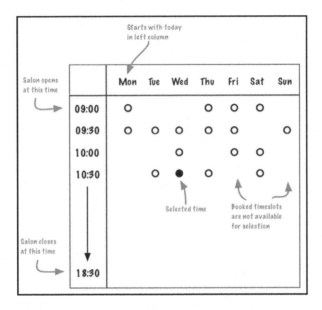

Here's an example of the HTML structure that we're aiming to build. We can use this as a guide as we write out our React component:

```
<table id="time-slots">
  <thead>
    <tr>
      <th></th>
      <th>Oct 11</th>
      <th>Oct 12</th>
      <th>Oct 13</th>
    </tr>
  </thead>
  <tbody>
    <tr>
      <th>9:00</th>
```

```
    <td><input type="option" name="timeSlot" value="1234567" /></td>
  </tr>
  <!-- ... two more cells ... -->
</tbody>
</table>
```

Constructing a calendar view

We can now begin our table:

1. Create a nested `describe` block with a new test at the bottom of
   `test/AppointmentForm.test.js`. This time, we'll use the `querySelector`
   function rather than the DOM form API. The `querySelector` function is more
   appropriate here because we're interested in testing the layout than the radio
   buttons themselves:

   ```
   describe('time slot table', () => {
     it('renders a table for time slots', () => {
       render(<AppointmentForm />);
       expect(
         container.querySelector('table#time-slots')
       ).not.toBeNull();
     });
   });
   ```

2. Define a new `TimeSlotTable` component, above the definition of
   `AppointmentForm`. We don't need to mark this one as an export as it will only be
   referenced by `AppointmentForm`:

   ```
   const TimeSlotTable = () => <table id="time-slots" />;
   ```

3. Add this component to your `AppointmentForm` JSX, just below the `select` tag:

   ```
   return <form
     id="appointment"
     onSubmit={() => onSubmit(appointment)}>
     <label htmlFor="service">Salon service</label>
     <select
       name="service"
       id="service"
       value={service}
       onChange={handleServiceChange}>
       <option />
       {selectableServices.map(s => (
   ```

```
              <option key={s}>{s}</option>
          ))}
      </select>
      <TimeSlotTable />
    </form>;
```

4. Run tests and verify that they are all passing.

5. Before moving on, extract out that `querySelector` call into a function named `timeSlotTable`. Make sure to update your test afterward to use this new helper:

```
const timeSlotTable = () =>
    container.querySelector('table#time-slots');
```

For the next test, we'll test the left-hand header column that displays a list of times. This is the first test to use `salonOpensAt` and `salonClosesAt`, which inform the component of which time period to show each day:

```
it('renders a time slot for every half an hour between open and close
times', () => {
  render(
    <AppointmentForm salonOpensAt={9} salonClosesAt={11} />
  );
  const timesOfDay = timeSlotTable().querySelectorAll(
    'tbody >* th'
  );
  expect(timesOfDay).toHaveLength(4);
  expect(timesOfDay[0].textContent).toEqual('09:00');
  expect(timesOfDay[1].textContent).toEqual('09:30');
  expect(timesOfDay[3].textContent).toEqual('10:30');
});
```

Asserting on arrays of data

In this example, we check the `textContent` on *three* array entries, even though there are four entries in the array.

Properties that are the same for all array entries only need to be tested on one entry. Properties that vary per entry, such as `textContent`, need to be tested on two or three entries, depending on how many you need to test a pattern.

For this test, I want to test that it starts and ends at the right time, and that each time slot increases by 30 minutes. I can do that with assertions on array entries 0, 1, and 3.

Let's make this pass:

1. Add the following function, above the `TimeSlotTable` component, that calculates the list of daily time slots:

```
const dailyTimeSlots = (salonOpensAt, salonClosesAt) => {
  const totalSlots = (salonClosesAt - salonOpensAt) * 2;
  const startTime = new Date().setHours(salonOpensAt, 0, 0, 0);
  const increment = 30 * 60 * 1000;
  return Array(totalSlots)
    .fill([startTime])
    .reduce((acc, _, i) =>
      acc.concat([startTime + (i * increment)])
    );
};
```

2. In the JSX for `AppointmentForm`, pass the `salonOpensAt` and `salonClosesAt` props to `TimeSlotTable`:

```
export const AppointmentForm = ({
  selectableServices,
  service,
  onSubmit,
  salonOpensAt,
  salonClosesAt
}) => {
  ...
  return <form ...>
    ...
    <TimeSlotTable
      salonOpensAt={salonOpensAt}
      salonClosesAt={salonClosesAt} />
  </form>;
};
```

3. Define the `toTimeValue` function as follows:

```
const toTimeValue = timestamp =>
  new Date(timestamp).toTimeString().substring(0, 5);
```

4. Update `TimeSlotTable` to read as follows:

```
const TimeSlotTable = ({
  salonOpensAt,
  salonClosesAt
}) => {
  const timeSlots = dailyTimeSlots(
    salonOpensAt,
    salonClosesAt);
  return (
    <table id="time-slots">
      <tbody>
        {timeSlots.map(timeSlot => (
          <tr key={timeSlot}>
            <th>{toTimeValue(timeSlot)}</th>
          </tr>
        ))}
      </tbody>
    </table>
  );
};
```

5. Fill in `defaultProps` for both `salonOpensAt` and `salonsCloseAt`:

```
AppointmentForm.defaultProps = {
  salonOpensAt: 9,
  salonClosesAt: 19,
  selectableServices: [ ... ]
};
```

6. Run tests and ensure everything is passing.

We've now got the row headings sorted about. But what about the column headings? We'll create a new top row that contains these cells, starting with an empty cell in the top-left corner, since the left column contains the time headings and not data:

```
it('renders an empty cell at the start of the header row', () => {
  render(<AppointmentForm />);
  const headerRow = timeSlotTable().querySelector(
    'thead > tr'
  );
  expect(headerRow.firstChild.textContent).toEqual('');
});
```

Making this pass is straightforward. Modify the table JSX to include a new table row:

```
<table id="time-slots">
  <thead>
    <tr>
      <th />
    </tr>
  </thead>
  <tbody>
    ...
  </tbody>
</table>
```

For the rest of the header row, we'll show the seven days starting from today. `AppointmentForm` will need to take a new prop, `today`, which is the first day to display within the table:

```
it('renders a week of available dates', () => {
  const today = new Date(2018, 11, 1);
  render(<AppointmentForm today={today} />);
  const dates = timeSlotTable().querySelectorAll(
    'thead >* th:not(:first-child)'
  );
  expect(dates).toHaveLength(7);
  expect(dates[0].textContent).toEqual('Sat 01');
  expect(dates[1].textContent).toEqual('Sun 02');
  expect(dates[6].textContent).toEqual('Fri 07');
});
```

Now let's make that pass:

1. Create a function to list the seven days we're after, in the same way we did with time slots:

```
const weeklyDateValues = (startDate) => {
  const midnight = new Date(startDate).setHours(0, 0, 0, 0);
  const increment = 24 * 60 * 60 * 1000;
  return Array(7)
    .fill([midnight])
    .reduce((acc, _, i) =>
      acc.concat([midnight + (i * increment)])
    );
};
```

2. Within `AppointmentForm`, **pass the** `today` **prop from** `AppointmentForm` into `TimeSlotTable`:

```
export const AppointmentForm = ({
  selectableServices,
  service,
  onSubmit,
  salonOpensAt,
  salonClosesAt,
  today
}) => {
  ...
  return <form ...>
    <TimeSlotTable
      ...
      salonOpensAt={salonOpensAt}
      salonClosesAt={salonClosesAt}
      today={today}
    />
  </form>;
};
```

3. Modify `TimeSlotTable` to take that prop and to use the previous function:

```
const TimeSlotTable = ({
  salonOpensAt,
  salonClosesAt,
  today
}) => {
  const dates = weeklyDateValues(today);
  ...
}
```

4. Define the function `toShortDate`, which formats our date as a short string:

```
const toShortDate = timestamp => {
  const [day, , dayOfMonth] = new Date(timestamp)
    .toDateString()
    .split(' ');
  return `${day} ${dayOfMonth}`;
};
```

5. Map over those dates in the existing JSX, to fill out the rest of the values:

```
<thead>
  <tr>
```

```
        <th />
        {dates.map(d => (
          <th key={d}>{toShortDate(d)}</th>
        ))}
      </tr>
    </thead>
```

6. Add a `defaultProp` for `today`. Set it to the current date by calling the `Date` constructor:

```
AppointmentForm.defaultProps = {
  today: new Date(),
  // ... previous props ...
}
```

7. Run tests. They should be all green.

8. It's time to refactor. You'll notice that `dailyTimeSlots` and `weeklyDateValues` share some code. Dry up your test file by extracting the shared code into a function named `timeIncrements`, which is shown here:

```
const timeIncrements = (numTimes, startTime, increment) =>
  Array(numTimes)
    .fill([startTime])
    .reduce((acc, _, i) =>
      acc.concat([startTime + (i * increment)]));
```

Displaying radio buttons for available appointments

 The Git tag for this section is `adding-radio-buttons`.

Now that we have our table with headings in place, it's time to add in radio buttons into each of the table cells. Not all cells will have radio buttons: only those that represent an available time slot will have a radio button.

That means we'll need to pass in another new prop to `AppointmentForm` that will help us to determine which time slots to show. That prop is `availableTimeSlots`, which is an array of objects that list times that are still available.

Add this next test, which uses that prop:

```
it('renders a radio button for each time slot', () => {
  const today = new Date();
  const availableTimeSlots = [
      { startsAt: today.setHours(9, 0, 0, 0) },
      { startsAt: today.setHours(9, 30, 0, 0) }
  ];
  render(
    <AppointmentForm
      availableTimeSlots={availableTimeSlots}
      today={today}
    />
  );
  const cells = timeSlotTable().querySelectorAll('td');
  expect(
    cells[0].querySelector('input[type="radio"]')
  ).not.toBeNull();
  expect(
    cells[7].querySelector('input[type="radio"]')
  ).not.toBeNull();
});
```

This test checks that there are radio buttons in the first two time slots for today. These will be in cells 0 and 7, since `querySelectorAll` returns matching elements in page order. We can make this test pass very simply, by adding the following in our `AppointmentForm` render method, just below `th` within each `tr`:

```
{timeSlots.map(timeSlot =>
  <tr key={timeSlot}>
    <th>{toTimeValue(timeSlot)}</th>
    {dates.map(date => (
      <td key={date}>
        <input type="radio" />
      </td>
    ))}
  </tr>
)}
```

At this point, your test will be passing. We didn't actually need to use `availableTimeSlots` in our production code, even though our tests requires it! This occasionally happens with TDD. We need to fully specify the test with the design that we want, but the first test may not appear to need all of the setup within it.

Once we add the second test, which will block out radio buttons for times that aren't available, and the extra set up will suddenly become necessary. Without it, our first test would begin failing once we'd made the second test pass.

It's time to triangulate.

Hiding input controls

How can we get to the right implementation? We do that by testing that having no available time slots renders no radio buttons at all:

1. Add the following test:

   ```
   it('does not render radio buttons for unavailable time slots', ()
   => {
     render(<AppointmentForm availableTimeSlots={[]} />);
     const timesOfDay = timeSlotTable().querySelectorAll(
       'input'
     );
     expect(timesOfDay).toHaveLength(0);
   });
   ```

2. Define the `mergeDateAndTime` function above the `TimeSlotTable` component. This takes the date from a column header together with a time from a row header and converts them into a timestamp that we can then use to compare against the `startsAt` fields in `availableTimeSlots`:

   ```
   const mergeDateAndTime = (date, timeSlot) => {
     const time = new Date(timeSlot);
     return new Date(date).setHours(
       time.getHours(),
       time.getMinutes(),
       time.getSeconds(),
       time.getMilliseconds()
     );
   };
   ```

3. Update `TimeSlotTable` to take the new `availableTimeSlots` prop:

   ```
   const TimeSlotTable = ({
     salonOpensAt,
     salonClosesAt,
     today,
     availableTimeSlots
   }) => {
   ```

```
      ...
    };
```

4. Also, update `AppointmentForm` to take the new prop, and then pass it through to `TimeSlotTable`:

```
export const AppointmentForm = ({
  selectableServices,
  service,
  onSubmit,
  salonOpensAt,
  salonClosesAt,
  today,
  availableTimeSlots
}) => {
  ...
  return (
    <form
      id="appointment"
      onSubmit={() => onSubmit(appointment)}>
      ...
      <TimeSlotTable
        salonOpensAt={salonOpensAt}
        salonClosesAt={salonClosesAt}
        today={today}
        availableTimeSlots={availableTimeSlots} />
    </form>
  );
};
```

5. Replace the existing radio button element in `TimeSlotTable` with a JSX conditional:

```
{dates.map(date =>
  <td key={date}>
    {availableTimeSlots.some(availableTimeSlot =>
      availableTimeSlot.startsAt === mergeDateAndTime(date,
timeSlot)
    )
     ? <input type="radio" />
     : null
    }
  </td>
)}
```

6. Finally, make sure to add a new `defaultProp` for `availableTimeSlots`, with a value of `[]`. After this change, your tests should all be green:

```
AppointmentForm.defaultProps = {
  availableTimeSlots: [],
  ...
};
```

7. Let's continue with the next test. We need to ensure each radio button has the correct value. We'll use the `startsAt` value for each radio button's value. Note that radio button values are strings, but `startsAt` is a number. We'll need to be careful of that later on:

```
it('sets radio button values to the index of the corresponding
appointment', () => {
  const today = new Date();
  const availableTimeSlots = [
    { startsAt: today.setHours(9, 0, 0, 0) },
    { startsAt: today.setHours(9, 30, 0, 0) }
  ];
  render(
    <AppointmentForm
      availableTimeSlots={availableTimeSlots}
      today={today}
    />);
  expect(startsAtField(0).value).toEqual(
    availableTimeSlots[0].startsAt.toString()
  );
  expect(startsAtField(1).value).toEqual(
    availableTimeSlots[1].startsAt.toString()
  );
});
```

8. That test uses a new `startsAtField` function. Define that now at the top of the `describe` block:

```
const startsAtField = index =>
  container.querySelectorAll(`input[name="startsAt"]`)[
    index
  ];
```

9. Pull out the ternary that contained the original call to `mergeDateAndTime` into a new component. Take care to add in the new `name` and `value` attributes on the `input` element:

```
const RadioButtonIfAvailable = ({
  availableTimeSlots,
```

```
        date,
        timeSlot
    }) => {
      const startsAt = mergeDateAndTime(date, timeSlot);
      if (
        availableTimeSlots.some(availableTimeSlot =>
          availableTimeSlot.startsAt === startsAt
        )
      ) {
        return (
          <input
            name="startsAt"
            type="radio"
            value={startsAt}
          />;
      }
      return null;
    };
```

10. You can now use this within `TimeSlotTable`, replacing the existing ternary with an instance of this functional component. After this, your tests should be passing:

```
{dates.map(date =>
  <td key={date}>
    <RadioButtonIfAvailable
      availableTimeSlots={availableTimeSlots}
      date={date}
      timeSlot={timeSlot}
    />
  </td>
)}
```

Finishing it off

 The Git tag for this section is `submitting-radio-buttons`.

The next few tests are tests you've seen before:

- Pre-selects the existing value
- Saves existing value when submitted
- Saves new value when submitted

For the first of these, to ensure a radio button is checked, add `checked={true}` to the JSX `input` element. Your code will look like this:

```
const isChecked = startsAt === checkedTimeSlot;
return (
  <input
    name="startsAt"
    type="radio"
    checked={isChecked}
    readOnly
  />
);
```

In the previous example, `checkedTimeSlot` is the `startsAt` value that is currently selected, and would be a prop passed into `RadioButtonIfAvailable`.

 The prop passed into `AppointmentForm` should be called `timeSlot`. To improve clarity within the `RadioButtonIfAvailable` component, it's better to rename it to a more specific name such as `checkedTimeSlot`.

Rather than look at that first test in detail, we'll skip to looking at the last of the three tests. The first two are very similar to the tests for the previous fields, but the last test is different enough that we should walk through it.

You can go ahead and implement the first two tests now, or skip to the `submitting-radio-buttons` tag where they are already implemented. Once you're done, add the following test:

```
it('saves new value when submitted', () => {
  expect.hasAssertions();
  const today = new Date();
  const availableTimeSlots = [
    { startsAt: today.setHours(9, 0, 0, 0) },
    { startsAt: today.setHours(9, 30, 0, 0) }
  ];
  render(
    <AppointmentForm
      availableTimeSlots={availableTimeSlots}
      today={today}
      startsAt={availableTimeSlots[0].startsAt}
      onSubmit={({ startsAt }) =>
        expect(startsAt).toEqual(availableTimeSlots[1].startsAt)
      }
    />
  );
```

```
ReactTestUtils.Simulate.change(startsAtField(1), {
  target: {
    value: availableTimeSlots[1].startsAt.toString(),
    name: 'startsAt'
  }
});
ReactTestUtils.Simulate.submit(form('appointment'));
});
```

The call to `ReactTestUtils.Simulate.change` finds a field with the right index, and passes back its own value. At run time, React will provide the value and name for us, based on whatever those props are set to on the input element, so really we are repeating ourselves with this code. In the next chapter, we'll improve on this.

We'll give every radio button the same name of `startsAt`. That means they are *grouped*: checking one radio button will uncheck which radio button is currently checked, if there is one.

To solve this test, there are two pieces we need to do the following:

- Pass through an event handler from the parent component, through the child components and assign it to the `input` button.
- Convert the radio button string value back into an integer.

Let's define the event handler. We'll define it in `AppointmentForm`, since that holds the state, and pass it through `TimeSlotTable` and `RadioButtonIfAvailable`. Since we're passing it through our own components, we need to make sure that we memoize it using `useCallback`.

Add that to your list of imports at the top of the file:

```
import React, { useState, useCallback } from 'react';
```

Now, you can use this to define `handleStartsAtChange`. In addition to wrapping the `setAppointment` call in a `useCallback` hook, we call `parseInt` on the value to make sure we save a numeric version of the radio button value:

```
const handleStartsAtChange = useCallback(
  ({ target: { value } }) =>
    setAppointment(appointment => ({
      ...appointment,
      startsAt: parseInt(value)
    })),
  []
);
```

The `useCallback` hook returns a memoized callback. That means you always get the same reference back each time it's called, rather than a new constant with a new reference. Without this, child components that are passed the callback as a prop (such as `TimeSlotTable`) would re-render each time the parent re-renders, because the different reference would cause it to believe that a re-render was required.

Event handlers on input elements don't need to use `useCallback` because event handler props are handled centrally; changes to those props do not require re-renders.

The second parameter to `useCallback` is the set of dependencies that will cause `useCallback` to update. In this case, it's `[]`, an empty array, because it isn't dependent on any props or other functions that may change. Parameters to the function such as `target` don't count, and `setAppointment` is a function that is guaranteed to remain constant across re-renders.

See the *Further learning* section at the end of the book for a link to more information on `useCallback`.

Then, pass that through to `TimeSlotTable`:

```
<TimeSlotTable
  salonOpensAt={salonOpensAt}
  salonClosesAt={salonClosesAt}
  today={today}
  availableTimeSlots={availableTimeSlots}
  checkedTimeSlot={appointment.startsAt}
  handleChange={handleStartsAtChange}
/>
```

From there, pass it through to `RadioButtonIfAvailable`:

```
const TimeSlotTable = ({
  salonOpensAt,
  salonClosesAt,
  today,
  availableTimeSlots,
  checkedTimeSlot,
  handleChange }) => {
  ...
  <RadioButtonIfAvailable
    availableTimeSlots={availableTimeSlots}
```

```
      date={date}
      timeSlot={timeSlot}
      checkedTimeSlot={checkedTimeSlot}
      handleChange={handleChange} />
    ...
};
```

And finally, in `RadioButtonIfAvailable`, remove the `readOnly` property on the input field and set `onChange` in its place:

```
const RadioButtonIfAvailable = ({
  availableTimeSlots,
  date,
  timeSlot,
  checkedTimeSlot,
  handleChange
}) => {
  ...
  return (
    <input
      name="startsAt"
      type="radio"
      value={startsAt}
      checked={isChecked}
      onChange={handleChange}
    />
  );
  ...
};
```

At this point, your test should be passing. For completeness, you could also add in the following assertion into the test:

```
expect(timeSlotField(0).checked).toEqual(false);
```

This verifies that your radio buttons are grouped, but assuming you made the last expectation pass using the simplest possible method—by adding `name="startsAt"` to every radio button—then this expectation will already be passing.

Manually testing your solution

The Git tag for this section is `submit-application-form`.

It's time to see what you've created. You should first add a `submit` button just as you did for `CustomerForm`. Change your `src/index.js` to instantiate a new `AppointmentForm` component. You'll need to pass in some example `availableTimeSlots`: in my own implementation I've added code to `src/sampleData.js` to generate 50 random available time slots, as you can see next:

Check out the `chapter-2-exercises` tag if you'd like to see the sample code described.

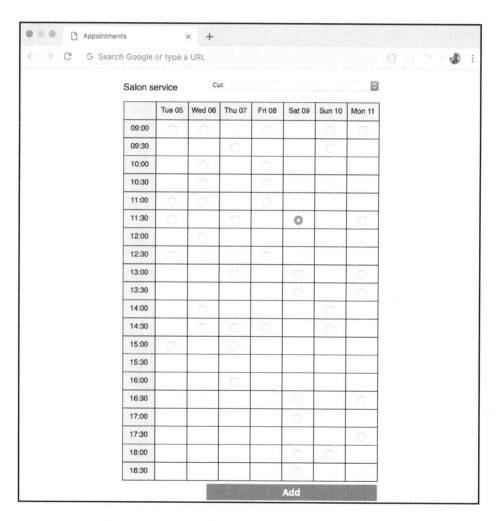

Summary

This chapter has covered usage of four HTML form elements: textboxes, selects, radio buttons, and, of course, labels.

Although these controls are basic, we've used this opportunity to dig much deeper into test-driven React. We've built controlled components, used `defaultProps`, and split our top-level component into a hierarchy of smaller components and plain JavaScript functions.

We've also gone much further with Jest. We extracted common test logic into modules, used nested `describe` blocks, and built assertions using the `document.form` property and CSS selectors.

In `Chapter 3`, *Exploring Test Doubles*, we'll discover how to get data into and out of our components using the fetch API.

Exercises

The Git tag for this section is `chapter-2-exercises`.

- Add the ability to choose a stylist before choosing a time slot. This should be a dropdown that filters based on the service required, as not all stylists will be qualified to provide all services. You'll need to decide on a suitable data structure to hold this data. Modify `availableTimeSlots` to list which stylists are available at each time, and update the table to reflect which stylist has been chosen and their availability during the week.

Further learning

- Supported React events that can be simulated: `https://reactjs.org/docs/events.html#form-events`
- `useCallback` hook: `https://reactjs.org/docs/hooks-reference.html#usecallback`

3
Exploring Test Doubles

In this chapter, we'll look at the most involved piece of the TDD puzzle: test doubles.

The *unit* in unit testing refers to the single function or component that we focus on for the duration of that test. The *Act* phase of a test should involve just one action on one unit. But units don't act in isolation: functions and components *collaborate* and *depend on* other units. Your application can be thought of as a web of dependencies, and test doubles help us to design and test those dependencies.

The following topics will be covered in this chapter:

- What is a test double?
- Submitting forms using spies
- Stubbing the fetch API
- Extracting test helpers

What is a test double?

When we're writing tests, we **isolate** the unit under test. Sometimes (but not always) that means we avoid exercising any of the **collaborating objects**. That can be for a number of reasons: sometimes it helps us work toward our goal of independent tests, and sometimes it's because those collaborating objects have side-effects that would complicate our tests.

For example, with React components we sometimes want to avoid rendering child components because they perform network requests when they are mounted.

A **test double** is an object that acts in place of a collaborating object. In Chapter 2, *Test-driving Data Input with React*, you saw an example of a collaborator: the onSubmit function, which is a prop passed to both CustomerForm and AppointmentForm. We can use a test double in place of the real function to help us define the relationship between the two.

Although we aim to isolate single units in our tests, there is no rule that says we must have one test file per one production file, one component, or one anything. Sometimes we do end up testing clumps of components in one test file. This primarily occurs when we have a **component tree**, where a root object is composed of other smaller units. In this case, the dependency relationships are well defined as parent-child, and they only occur in this one tree.

You saw this when we split out functional components in `AppointmentForm`. Our tests applied at the root object, the `AppointmentForm` component. But the child components, such as `TimeSlotTable`, were all tested implicitly without being mentioned at all in our tests. This makes sense because `AppointmentForm` and its child components make one logical unit. Splitting these tests into one file per component would be a great deal of extra work for no real benefit.

The most important place to use test doubles is at the edges of our system, when our code interacts with the outside world. Any kind of operating system resource is a candidate: filesystem access, network access, sockets, HTTP calls, and so on.

Test doubles are categorized into a number of different types: spies, stubs, mocks, dummies, and fakes. We normally only use the first two, and that's what we'll concentrate on in this chapter.

Learning to avoid fakes

A **fake** is any test double that has any kind of logic or control structure within it, such as conditional statements or loops. Other types of test object, such as spies and stubs, are made up entirely of variable assignments and function calls.

One type of fake you'll see is the in-memory repository. You can use these in place of SQL data stores, message brokers, and other complex sources of data.

Fakes are useful when testing complex collaborations between two units. We'll often start by using spies and stubs and then refactor to a fake once the code starts to feel unwieldy. A single fake can cover a whole set of tests, which is simpler than maintaining a whole bunch of spies and stubs.

We avoid fakes for these reasons:

- Any logic requires tests, which means we must write tests for fakes, even though they are part of the test code. Spies and stubs don't require tests.
- Often spies and stubs work in place of fakes. Only a small category of testing is simpler when we use fakes.
- Fakes increase test brittleness because they are shared between tests, unlike other test doubles.

Submitting forms using spies

The Git tag for this section is `adding-spies`. It contains solutions to the exercises from the previous chapter, so if you haven't completed the Exercises section yourself, then you should move to this tag now so that you're up to date.

For more detailed instructions, see the *To get the most out of this book* section in the `Preface`.

In `Chapter 2`, *Test-driving Data Input with React*, we wrote some tests that didn't use the normal *Arrange-Act-Assert* test format. Here's a reminder of how one of those tests looked, from the `CustomerForm` test suite:

```
it('saves existing value when submitted', async () => {
  expect.hasAssertions();

  render(
    <CustomerForm
      firstName="Ashley"
      onSubmit={customer =>
        expect(customer.firstName).toEqual('Ashley')
      }
    />
  );

  ReactTestUtils.Simulate.submit(form('customer'));
});
```

There are a couple of issues with this code:

- The *Assert* phase of the test—the expectation—appears wrapped within the *Act* phase. That makes the test difficult to read and understand.
- The call to `expect.hasAssertions` is ugly and is only there because our expectation is called as part of the `onSubmit` function, which may or may not be called.

We can fix this by building a spy.

 A **spy** is a test double that records the arguments it is called with so that those values can be inspected later on.

Untangling Arrange-Act-Assert

To move the expectation under the *Act* phase of the test, we can introduce a variable to store the `firstName` that's passed into the `onSubmit` function. We then write the expectation against that stored value.

Let's do that now. Modify the `saves existing value when submitted` test-generator function in `test/CustomerForm.test.js`:

```
const itSubmitsExistingValue = fieldName =>
  it('saves existing value when submitted', async () => {
    let submitArg;

    render(<CustomerForm
      { ...{[fieldName]: 'value'} }
      onSubmit={customer => submitArg = customer}
    />);
    ReactTestUtils.Simulate.submit(form('customer'));

    expect(submitArg[fieldName]).toEqual('value');
  });
```

The `submitArg` variable is assigned within our `onSubmit` handler, and then asserted in the very last line of the test. This fixes both the issues we had with the first test: our test is back in *Arrange-Act-Assert* order and we got rid of the ugly `expect.hasAssertions()` call.

Watching it fail

If you run your tests now, they should be green. However, any time you refactor tests in this way, you should verify that you're still testing the right thing by unwinding the production code and watching the test fail. It's all too easy to build tests that produce **false positives**, which are tests that pass when they shouldn't.

To check that our tests still work, locate this line in `src/CustomerForm.js`:

```
<form id="customer" onSubmit={() => onSubmit(customer)}>
```

Remove the `onSubmit` prop entirely:

```
<form id="customer">
```

If you run tests now, you'll get multiple test failures from various different tests. However, we're only interested in this one test generator, so update its declaration to `it.only` rather than `it`:

```
it.only('saves existing value when submitted', async () => {
```

Running the tests now should give three failures, one for each of the fields that uses this generator function. That's a good sign; any fewer and we would have been generating false positives:

```
FAIL test/CustomerForm.test.js
  ● CustomerForm › first name field › saves existing value when submitted

    TypeError: Cannot read property 'firstName' of undefined
      63 |         ReactTestUtils.Simulate.submit(form('customer'));
      64 |
    > 65 |         expect(submitArg[fieldName]).toEqual('value');
         |                                       ^
      66 |       });
```

This is a test exception rather than a test failure. Since we prefer to see test failures over exceptions, we can introduce the following expectation before the one we already have:

```
expect(submitArg).toBeDefined();
```

Running the tests now gives the following:

```
FAIL test/CustomerForm.test.js
  ● CustomerForm › first name field › saves existing value when submitted
    expect(received).toBeDefined()
    Received: undefined
      64 |
```

```
> 65 |          expect(submitArg).toBeDefined();
     |                          ^
  66 |          expect(submitArg[fieldName]).toEqual('value');
  67 |        });
  68 |    };
```

We've proved the test works, so you can go ahead and change the it.only back to it, and re-insert the onSubmit prop that you removed in CustomerForm.js.

Congratulations, you've hand-rolled your first spy.

Making spies reusable

We know that we have another bunch of tests within CustomerForm, and we have similar tests for AppointmentForm. How can we reuse what we've built in this one test across everything else? We can create a generalized spy function that can be used any time we want spy functionality.

 Using hand-rolled test doubles is perfectly acceptable; you shouldn't feel the need to always generalize as we're about to do.

Let's start by defining a function that can stand in for any single-argument function, such as the event handlers we would pass to the onSubmit form prop:

1. Define the following function at the top of test/CustomerForm.test.js:

```
const singleArgumentSpy = () => {
  let receivedArgument;
  return {
    fn: arg => (receivedArgument = arg),
    receivedArgument: () => receivedArgument
  };
};
```

2. Rewrite your test generator to use this function. Although your tests should still pass, remember to watch your tests fail by unwinding the production code:

```
const itSubmitsExistingValue = fieldName =>
  it('saves existing value when submitted', async () => {
    const submitSpy = singleArgumentSpy();

    render(
      <CustomerForm
```

```
    {...{ [fieldName]: 'value' }}
    onSubmit={submitSpy.fn}
  />
);
ReactTestUtils.Simulate.submit(form('customer'));

expect(submitSpy.receivedArgument()).toBeDefined();
expect(
  submitSpy.receivedArgument()[fieldName]
).toEqual('value');
});
```

3. Let's go a little further and make our spy function work for functions with any number of arguments. Replace singleArgumentSpy with the following function:

```
const spy = () => {
  let receivedArguments;
  return {
    fn: (...args) => (receivedArguments = args),
    receivedArguments: () => receivedArguments,
    receivedArgument: n => receivedArguments[n]
  };
};
```

4. This uses parameter destructuring to save an entire array of parameters. We can use receivedArguments to return that array, or use receivedArgument(n) to retrieve the nth argument.

5. Update your test code to use this new function:

```
const itSubmitsExistingValue = fieldName =>
  it('saves existing value when submitted', async () => {
    const submitSpy = spy();

    render(
      <CustomerForm
        {...{ [fieldName]: 'value' }}
        onSubmit={submitSpy.fn}
      />
    );
    ReactTestUtils.Simulate.submit(form('customer'));

    expect(submitSpy.receivedArguments()).toBeDefined();
    expect(
      submitSpy.receivedArgument(0)[fieldName]
```

```
        ).toEqual('value');
    });
```

Using a Jest matcher to simplify expectations

Wouldn't it be great if we could write this? Check it out:

```
expect(submitSpy).toHaveBeenCalled();
```

This is more descriptive than using a `toBeDefined()` argument on the matcher. It also encapsulates the notion that if `receivedArguments` hasn't been set, then it hasn't been called.

Let's write our first Jest matcher.

We'll **spike** this code—in other words, not write tests. That's for two reasons: for brevity, and because soon we'll replace this with Jest's own built-in spy functionality. However, I'd encourage you to write tests around all matchers that you use in your code.

All matchers and the test "helper" code that you write should be fully test-driven. Just like fakes, they contain logic and need to be tested too.

A good rule of thumb is that if it contains any kind of branching logic or looping, it requires a test.

Add the following just under your spy function:

```
expect.extend({
  toHaveBeenCalled(received) {
    if (received.receivedArguments() === undefined) {
      return {
        pass: false,
        message: () => 'Spy was not called.'
      };
    }
    return { pass: true, message: () => 'Spy was called.' };
  }
});
```

This adds a new matcher, called `toHaveBeenCalled`, that you can now use within your test:

```
...
expect(submitSpy).toHaveBeenCalled();
```

```
expect(
  submitSpy.receivedArgument(0)[fieldName]
).toEqual('value');
```

All Jest matchers must return an object with a `pass` property, which is either `true` or `false`, and a `message` property, which is a function that returns a string.

If you've test-driven this matcher, two tests should have been enough to cover it, since it consists of a single conditional. Any time you see a conditional in the production code, that automatically means you need two tests to ensure it's fully covered.

The preceding example is about as simple as a matcher can get, since it has no arguments passed to it. Matchers such as `toEqual` and `toMatch` take an argument to the matcher. As soon as you involve arguments in your matchers, you'll find they become a big nest of `if` statements.

Stubbing the fetch API

The Git tag for this section is `stubbing-fetch`.

In this section, we'll use the fetch API to send customer data to our backend service. When the form is submitted, instead of directly calling the `onSubmit` prop, we'll send a POST HTTP request via the fetch API. If it returns a successful result, we'll call the `onSubmit` prop.

Add this next test in `test/CustomerForm.test.js`, right after the `has a submit button` test. This test is going to check that when we call `fetch`, we pass in the right arguments. In the *Arrange* phase of the test, we pass a new prop, `fetch`, to `CustomerForm`. This prop will eventually replace the `onSubmit` prop:

```
it('calls fetch with the right properties when submitting data', async ()
=> {
  const fetchSpy = spy();
  render(
    <CustomerForm fetch={fetchSpy.fn} onSubmit={() => {}} />
  );
  ReactTestUtils.Simulate.submit(form('customer'));
  expect(fetchSpy).toHaveBeenCalled();
```

```
expect(fetchSpy.receivedArgument(0)).toEqual('/customers');

const fetchOpts = fetchSpy.receivedArgument(1);
expect(fetchOpts.method).toEqual('POST');
expect(fetchOpts.credentials).toEqual('same-origin');
expect(fetchOpts.headers).toEqual({
  'Content-Type': 'application/json'
});
});
```

 We'll build a **side-by-side implementation**. This means we leave the existing implementation in place, and just write the new code under it. That's why we still have the `onSubmit` prop in place, even though it has a dummy value. It allows our existing implementation to stay in place while we perfect the new implementation. We'll delete this prop later, along with the rest of the old implementation, once our new implementation is finished.

This asserts on three individual properties of the fetch options: `method`, `credentials`, and `headers`. There's one more property that we're interested in, and that's `body`. The contents of `body` varies depending on the form fields that are passed across, so we'll test that value within each of the nested describe blocks for each form field.

Let's make this test pass:

1. Add the following fetch prop to the `CustomerForm` function definition:

```
export const CustomerForm = ({
  firstName,
  lastName,
  phoneNumber,
  onSubmit,
  fetch
}) => {
  ...
}
```

2. Define a new `handleSubmit` event handler in `CustomerForm`, with the side-by-side implementation of both `onSubmit` and `fetch` being called. Notice that this isn't functionally complete yet; our test doesn't make any mention of the body of the POST request. We'll add that in later:

```
const handleSubmit = () => {
  onSubmit(customer);
  fetch('/customers', {
    method: 'POST',
```

```
    credentials: 'same-origin',
    headers: { 'Content-Type': 'application/json' }
  });
};
```

3. Update the returned JSX by changing the form declaration to read as follows:

```
<form id="customer" onSubmit={handleSubmit}>
```

4. Run your tests. The test you've just written should now be passing, but you'll get a lot of failures saying that `fetch is not a function`.

5. Add `CustomerForm.defaultProps`, just beneath the `CustomerForm` function. This is marked `async` to mimic the fetch API:

```
CustomerForm.defaultProps = {
  fetch: async () => {}
};
```

6. Run tests; they should now be passing.

7. Let's move back to the test generator we were working on earlier in the chapter, in the section *Untangling Arrange-Act-Assert*. Change it to use the new `fetch` prop:

```
const itSubmitsExistingValue = fieldName =>
  it('saves existing value when submitted', async () => {
    const fetchSpy = spy();

    render(
      <CustomerForm
        {...{ [fieldName]: 'value' }}
        fetch={fetchSpy.fn}
        onSubmit={() => {}}
      />
    );
    ReactTestUtils.Simulate.submit(form('customer'));

    const fetchOpts = fetchSpy.receivedArgument(1);
    expect(JSON.parse(fetchOpts.body)[fieldName]).toEqual(
      'value'
    );
  });
```

8. Run tests. Your test will give you a strange error from `JSON.parse`:

```
Unexpected token u in JSON as position 0
```

9. This error occurs because the call to JSON.parse is attempting to parse the word undefined. The body property of the fetch call hasn't been set yet. In the handleSubmit event handler, add the following property into the object passed to the fetch call:

```
body: JSON.stringify(customer)
```

10. Update the second test generator function that calls submit, as shown. After this change, your tests should pass without needing any further changes to the implementation:

```
const itSubmitsNewValue = fieldName =>
  it('saves new value when submitted', async () => {
    const fetchSpy = spy();

    render(
      <CustomerForm
        {...{ [fieldName]: 'existingValue' }}
        fetch={fetchSpy.fn}
        onSubmit={() => {}}
      />
    );
    ReactTestUtils.Simulate.change(field(fieldName), {
      target: { value: 'newValue', name: fieldName }
    });
    ReactTestUtils.Simulate.submit(form('customer'));

    const fetchOpts = fetchSpy.receivedArgument(1);
    expect(JSON.parse(fetchOpts.body)[fieldName]).toEqual(
      'newValue'
    );
  });
```

11. Remove the onSubmit prop from each of the tests.

12. Remove the call to onSubmit in the handleSubmit method.

13. Remove the onSubmit prop from the CustomerForm component definition. Your tests should still be passing.

Replacing global variables with spies

You may be scratching your head wondering why we passed in fetch as a prop when it's available as a global variable. In the browser, we can simply call window.fetch when we need it.

That's where we'll eventually end up, but we've split that goal up into two subgoals. We started by taking the smallest step possible to move away from using `onSubmit`. Now let's take the next step to using `window.fetch`.

The easy way to do this would be to simply update your `defaultProp` to point to `window.fetch`, and that would be it. This is a perfectly valid approach, but it produces more production code than necessary due to the extra prop. Let's just get rid of the prop entirely.

We'll need to overwrite the value of `window.fetch` with your spy function, like this:

```
window.fetch = fetchSpy.fn;
```

However, before you dive in and update all your tests, let's simplify it a little. Since `fetch` is a required dependency of your component—in other words, it won't function without it—we can set a default spy in our `beforeEach` block that can be used by all our tests. This saves us having to instantiate a spy in each and every test that uses it. And, as you'll see in the next section, *Acting on return values with stubs*, it also helps us set default return values from our spy functions.

> It's common practice to set up test doubles from within your `beforeEach` blocks.

Follow these steps to set a default spy on `window.fetch`:

1. Add the following declarations to the outer `describe` block in `test/CustomerForm.test.js`:

```
const originalFetch = window.fetch;
let fetchSpy;
```

2. You already have a `beforeEach` that calls `createContainer`. Change it to read as follows:

```
beforeEach(() => {
  ({ render, container } = createContainer());
  fetchSpy = spy();
  window.fetch = fetchSpy.fn;
});
```

3. Add an `afterEach` block to unset your mock:

```
afterEach(() => {
  window.fetch = originalFetch;
});
```

 It's important to reset any global variables that you replace with spies. This is a common cause of test interdependence that can cause a lot of hair-pulling if not noticed. You may find tests break because some other test failed to reset its spies.

4. Delete all the `fetchSpy` definitions from within your tests—just the top line which declares the `fetchSpy` variable. These will now use the `fetchSpy` variable from the describe scope instead. Your tests should still be passing at this point.

Now let's get rid of the `fetch` prop entirely:

1. In `CustomerForm`, change the function call in `handleSubmit` from `fetch` to `window.fetch`:

```
const handleSubmit = () => {
  window.fetch(...);
};
```

2. Remove the `fetch` prop that is passed into the `CustomerForm` component in each of these tests.
3. Remove `CustomerForm.defaultProps`.

You should now be on green.

Systematic refactoring

 You may be wondering why we are going through this strange process of adding props just to delete them again. It seems to be a lot of extra work. The important thing to remember is that we are finding the smallest steps that we can take toward our final goal. At each step, our tests should be green and our product still works. Breaking work down in this way reduces the risk of getting lost in a huge refactor. It helps reduce fear of change.

The process can seem convoluted at first, but with practice, you'll get used to it. Soon you'll find it hard to live without building software this way.

Installing the window.fetch polyfill

For this to work in the browser, you will most likely need to install a fetch polyfill. The standard way to do this is using the `whatwg-fetch` packages, which you can install using the following command:

```
npm install --save whatwg-fetch
```

In `src/index.js`, add the following line to install a real implementation of `window.fetch`:

```
import 'whatwg-fetch';
```

You don't need to import this into your test modules.

Acting on return values with stubs

The Git tag for this section is `fetch-result`.

Previously, we had an `onSubmit` prop that we've removed in favor of calling `window.fetch`. Now let's add that prop back in! But this time, it will do something else: it will be used to notify its parent component when the form data has been saved successfully. So instead of `onSubmit`, let's call it `onSave`, just to show that it's doing something different.

When a new customer is saved, `CustomerForm` needs to return the new customer object. This will be the same data we submitted, but in addition, it will contain an ID that the server assigns to the customer.

To achieve this, we can ask our `fetchSpy` to return a value whenever it is called. This is known as a stub.

A **stub** is a test double that always returns the same value when it is invoked. You decide what this value is when you construct the stub.

Let's convert our `spy` function to also have the ability to stub:

1. Change the `spy` function to include the following new variable declaration at the top. This variable will store the value, ready to be returned by our function:

   ```
   let returnValue;
   ```

2. Change the `fn` definition to the following:

   ```
   fn: (...args) => {
     receivedArguments = args;
     return returnValue;
   },
   ```

3. Add this new function to your spy object, which sets the `returnValue`:

   ```
   stubReturnValue: value => returnValue = value
   ```

Acting on the fetch response

So far, our submit button causes a fetch request to be made, but it doesn't do anything with the response. In particular, it doesn't *wait* for the response; the fetch API is asynchronous and returns a promise. Once that promise resolves, we can do something with the data that's returned.

The next tests we'll write will specify what our component should do with the resolved data.

In order to write these tests, we'll need to use a React function named `act`. We're required to use this function when our actions perform any kind of side-effects that happen outside the synchronous flow of our components, including resolving promises.

There are two forms of `act`: a synchronous form and an asynchronous form. We'll be using the asynchronous form in this section. It looks like this:

```
await act(async () => { performSomeReactAction() });
```

The action may be a button click, form submission, or any kind of input field event. It could also be a render itself, in which we'd be expecting the `useEffect` handler to perform some side-effects.

So what does `act` do for us? First, it defers state updates until the entirety of the function passed to `act` has completed. That helps to avoid timing issues when multiple state setters are running at once and could potentially clobber each other. Second, it waits for any `useEffect` hook functions to complete.

Additionally, the asynchronous version will wait for the runtime's task queue to complete execution. This means that anything that occurs as a separate asynchronous task, such as a fetch request invoked from a `useEffect` hook, is guaranteed to have completed by the time your expectations happen.

In the days before `act` was available, we would have done this ourselves by calling `await new Promise(setTimeout)`. That is fairly ugly, non-descriptive, and not at all obvious. Thankfully the React `act` function is much better.

When you're writing your tests, you'll know that you need to use `act` if you see this warning:

```
Warning: An update to null inside a test was not wrapped in act(...).

When testing, code that causes React state updates should be wrapped into
act(...):
```

As we walk through the following sections, if you see this warning, look at the last test and try to spot whether you missed any `async` or `await` keywords. We will eventually hide `act` behind our own helper methods but you'll still need to make liberal use of `async` and `await` within the tests themselves.

As usual, we start with the test:

1. Define a test helper function in `test/CustomerForm.test.js` that builds you a type of `Response` object to mimic what would be returned from the fetch API. That means it returns a Promise with an `ok` property with a value of `true`, and a `json` function that returns *another* Promise that, when resolved, returns the JSON we pass in. You can define this just under your `spy` function:

```
const fetchResponseOk = body =>
  Promise.resolve({
    ok: true,
    json: () => Promise.resolve(body)
  });
```

The `ok` property returns `true` if the HTTP response status code was in the 2xx range. Any other kind of response, such as a `404` or `500`, will cause `ok` to be `false`.

2. Modify the import for `ReactTestUtils` to include the `act` function:

```
import ReactTestUtils, { act } from 'react-dom/test-utils';
```

3. The new test checks that the `onSave` prop function is called when the user submits the form, and passes back the customer object. I placed this test under the `calls fetch with the right properties when submitting data` test:

```
it('notifies onSave when form is submitted', async () => {
  const customer = { id: 123 };
  fetchSpy.stubReturnValue(fetchResponseOk(customer));
  const saveSpy = spy();

  render(<CustomerForm onSave={saveSpy.fn} />);
  await act(async () => {
    ReactTestUtils.Simulate.submit(form('customer'));
  });

  expect(saveSpy).toHaveBeenCalled();
  expect(saveSpy.receivedArgument(0)).toEqual(customer);
});
```

4. To make this pass, start by defining the new `onSave` prop for `CustomerForm`, in `src/CustomerForm.js`:

```
export const CustomerForm = ({
  firstName,
  lastName,
  phoneNumber,
  onSave
}) => {
  ...
};
```

5. Add the following code at the end of `handleSubmit`. The function is now declared as `async` and uses `await` to unwrap the promise returned from `window.fetch`:

```
const handleSubmit = async () => {
  const result = await window.fetch(...);
```

```
    const customerWithId = await result.json();
    onSave(customerWithId);
};
```

6. If you run tests, you'll notice that although your latest test passes, your previous test fails and there's a whole bunch of unhandled promise exceptions. In fact, anything that submits the form will fail, because they use the `fetchSpy` that's initialized in the `beforeEach` block, and this is not a stub. It's just a plain old spy. Fix that now by giving the spy a return value, within `beforeEach`. In this case, we don't need to give it a customer; an empty object will do:

```
beforeEach(() => {
  ({ render, container } = createContainer());
  fetchSpy = spy();
  window.fetch = fetchSpy.fn;
  fetchSpy.stubReturnValue(fetchResponseOk({}));
});
```

When stubbing out global functions such as `window.fetch`, always set a default dummy value within your `beforeEach` block and then override it in individual tests.

In fact, if you do this for all your test suites that use global variables, you can often avoid the unmocking step in the `afterEach` block. This is a risky approach but it will reduce the amount of test setup that's required.

7. Run the tests and you'll notice that the same test still fails! And you'll *still* get a lot of unhandled promise rejections. These are now due to `onSave` being called but not being defined. To fix these, add in a `defaultProp` for `CustomerForm`, at the bottom of `src/CustomerForm.js`. After this change your tests should be passing without any warnings:

```
CustomerForm.defaultProps = {
  onSave: () => {}
};
```

8. Add another test to ensure that we only call `onSave` when the fetch response has an OK status. Start by defining another helper, `fetchResponseError`, right under `fetchResponseOk`. This one doesn't need a body as we aren't interested in it just yet:

```
const fetchResponseError = () =>
  Promise.resolve({ ok: false });
```

9. Use the new function in the next test:

```
it('does not notify onSave if the POST request returns an error',
async () => {
  fetchSpy.stubReturnValue(fetchResponseError());
  const saveSpy = spy();

  render(<CustomerForm onSave={saveSpy.fn} />);
  await act(async () => {
    ReactTestUtils.Simulate.submit(form('customer'));
  });

  expect(saveSpy).not.toHaveBeenCalled();
});
```

10. To make this pass, move the `onSave` call into a new conditional in `handleSubmit`:

```
const handleSubmit = async () => {
  const result = ...;
  if (result.ok) {
    const customerWithId = await result.json();
    onSave(customerWithId);
  }
};
```

11. There's one final thing we need to do. Since this form will take part in a workflow all within a single page, we need to stop the page from refreshing when we submit the form. We can do that by passing a spy in using an object that mimics the structure of the `Event` object that would be passed to the form. Add the following test to your code:

```
it('prevents the default action when submitting the form', async ()
=> {
  const preventDefaultSpy = spy();

  render(<CustomerForm />);
  await act(async () => {
    ReactTestUtils.Simulate.submit(form('customer'), {
      preventDefault: preventDefaultSpy.fn
    });
  });

  expect(preventDefaultSpy).toHaveBeenCalled();
});
```

12. Making this pass is straightforward. Add the event as a parameter to `handleSubmit` and then call `preventDefault` on it. After this change, your test should be passing:

```
const handleSubmit = async e => {
  e.preventDefault();
  ...
};
```

If, after writing out this code, you see an error about e being undefined, check that your form element has `onSubmit={handleSubmit}` and not `onSubmit={() = handleSubmit()}`.

You might have expected all our other submission tests to fail now, because we aren't passing the event object to `ReactTestUtils.Simulate.submit`. Thankfully, that isn't the case because React provides a default event stub when we don't provide one ourselves.

Displaying errors to the user

Let's display an error to the user if the fetch returns an `ok` value of false. This would occur if the HTTP status code returned was in the 400 or 500 range, although for our tests we won't need to worry about the specific status code. Follow these steps:

1. Add the following test in `test/CustomerForm.test.js`:

```
it('renders error message when fetch call fails', async () => {
  fetchSpy.stubReturnValue(Promise.resolve({ ok: false }));

  render(<CustomerForm />);
  await act(async () => {
    ReactTestUtils.Simulate.submit(form('customer'));
  });

  const errorElement = container.querySelector('.error');
  expect(errorElement).not.toBeNull();
  expect(errorElement.textContent).toMatch('error occurred');
});
```

2. To make this pass, introduce a new `error` variable at the top of the `CustomerForm` definition:

```
const [error, setError] = useState(false);
```

3. Change the `handleSubmit` function:

```
const handleSubmit = async () => {
  ...
  if (result.ok) {
    ...
  } else {
    setError(true);
  }
}
```

4. In the component's JSX, add the following line as the first child of your form element:

```
{ error ? <Error /> : null }
```

5. All that remains is to define the `Error` component. You can place this definition in the same file, before or after the `CustomerForm` component:

```
const Error = () => (
  <div className="error">An error occurred during save.</div>
);
```

Extracting test helpers

 The Git tag for this section is `extracting-test-helpers`.

It's time to dry up our code. We'll do this in two ways:

- Replace our stub and spy with Jest's built-in spy functionality
- Extract repeated test code into their own files that can be reused across test suites

Using Jest to spy and stub

So far in this chapter you've built a usable set of spy and stub functions. Jest has built-in functionality that does the same thing but works slightly differently.

Here's a rundown of Jest test double support and how it compares to what you've built. We'll convert our `CustomerForm` tests to use these new functions in just a moment:

- To create a new spy, call `jest.fn()`. For example, you might write `const fetchSpy = jest.fn()`.
- To override an existing property, call `jest.spyOn(object, property)`.
- To set a return value, call `spy.mockReturnValue()`. You can also pass this value directly to the `jest.fn()` call.
- You can set multiple return values by chaining calls to `spy.mockReturnValueOnce()`.
- To check that your spy was called, use `expect(spy).toHaveBeenCalled()`.
- To check the arguments passed to your spy, you can use `expect(spy).toHaveBeenCalledWith(arguments)`. Or, if your spy is called multiple times and want to check the last time it was called, you can use `expect(spy).toHaveLastBeenCalledWith(arguments)`.
- Calling `spy.mockReset()` removes all the mocked implementations, return values, and existing call history from a spy.
- Calling `spy.mockRestore()` will remove the mock and give you back the original implementation.
- When using `toHaveBeenCalledWith`, you can pass an argument value of `expect.anything()` to say that you don't care what the value of that argument is.
- You can use `expect.objectMatching(object)` to check that an argument has all the properties of the object you pass in, rather than being exactly equal to the object.
- When your spy is called multiple times, you can check the parameters passed to specific calls by using `spy.mock.calls[n]` where n is the call number (for example, `calls[0]` will return the arguments for the first time it was called).
- If you need to perform complex matching on a specific argument, you can use `spy.mock.calls[0][n]` where n is in the argument number.
- You can stub out and spy on entire modules using the `jest.mock()` function.

When your production code imports an object from another package, you will not be able to simply reassign its global value. You'll need to use `jest.mock` for that purpose. We'll see this in Chapter 9, *Test-driving GraphQL*.

The `window.fetch` call doesn't need this because it's a globally available browser API function. In a moment we'll see how we can use `jest.spyOn` to overwrite a polyfilled function like this.

There's a lot more available with the Jest API but these are the core features and should cover most of your test-driven use cases.

Let's convert our `CustomerForm` tests to use Jest's mocks. In some ways, we shot ourselves in the foot with this one: the `fetchSpy` variable is defined in the `beforeEach` block and used for *all* of our tests. Once we change its value, *all* our tests will break. Rather than push it back down into each of the individual tests, let's just be careful about how we use copy and paste. Follow these steps:

1. Update the test with `preventDefaultSpy` first. Change `preventDefaultSpy` to call `jest.fn()` and then pass that object to the submit event. Make sure you remove `.fn` when passing the `preventDefault` prop. The result of calling `jest.fn()` is a spy function ready to be used as-is, unlike our version which had its own `fn` property:

```
it('prevents the default action when submitting the form', async ()
=> {
  const preventDefaultSpy = jest.fn();

  render(<CustomerForm />);
  await act(async () => {
    ReactTestUtils.Simulate.submit(form('customer'), {
      preventDefault: preventDefaultSpy
    });
  });

  expect(preventDefaultSpy).toHaveBeenCalled();
});
```

2. Delete the Jest matcher, which was defined with `expect.extend`.

3. All your other tests that depend on `toHaveBeenCalled` have been broken, so if you want to test this one test, set it to `it.only` and run it. You should find it passes.

4. Remove the `.only` and then update the `beforeEach` block as follows:

```
beforeEach(() => {
  ({ render, container } = createContainer());
  fetchSpy = jest.fn(() => fetchResponseOk({}));
  window.fetch = fetchSpy;
});
```

5. Search and replace across the whole file, finding the `stubReturnValue` function name and replacing it with `mockReturnValue`.

6. Let's go through the tests one by one, and update them in the same way we did with the `prevents the default action...` test. The first test is `calls fetch with the right properties when submitting data`. Update it to match the following code. This is about as complicated as expectations get:

```
it('calls fetch with the right properties when submitting data',
async () => {
  render(<CustomerForm />);
  ReactTestUtils.Simulate.submit(form('customer'));

  expect(fetchSpy).toHaveBeenCalledWith(
    '/customers',
    expect.objectContaining({
      method: 'POST',
      credentials: 'same-origin',
      headers: { 'Content-Type': 'application/json' }
    }));
});
```

This uses the `objectContaining` matcher that passes if the object contains each of the listed key-value pairs. The object under test can also contain other keys too and the matcher won't care. In our case, the fetch options will include the `body` key-value pair which we aren't interested in testing within this test.

7. For the next test, `notifies onSave when form is submitted`, we've got an additional spy, `saveSpy`, that we can update to use `jest.fn`. Don't forget to change `saveSpy.fn` to `saveSpy` in the prop passed to `CustomerForm`:

```
it('notifies onSave when form is submitted', async () => {
  const customer = { id: 123 };
  fetchSpy.mockReturnValue(fetchResponseOk(customer));
  const saveSpy = jest.fn();

  render(<CustomerForm onSave={saveSpy} />);
  await act(async () => {
```

```
                ReactTestUtils.Simulate.submit(form('customer'));
            });

            expect(saveSpy).toHaveBeenCalledWith(customer);
        });
```

8. Moving on to the next test, we update `saveSpy` in a similar way. The actual expectation stays the same this time:

```
it('does not notify onSave if the POST request returns an error',
async () => {
  fetchSpy.mockReturnValue(fetchResponseError());
  const saveSpy = jest.fn();

  render(<CustomerForm onSave={saveSpy} />);
  await act(async () => {
    ReactTestUtils.Simulate.submit(form('customer'));
  });

  expect(saveSpy).not.toHaveBeenCalled();
});
```

9. Now to test the request body. We need to fall back to the `.mock.calls` variant so that we can reach inside the second argument to fetch, call `JSON.parse` on it, and then assert on just part of the object. Since this is something that we'll make use of in *two* tests, define it as a helper at the top of your file:

```
const fetchRequestBody = () =>
  JSON.parse(fetchSpy.mock.calls[0][1].body);
```

10. Update the two test-generator functions to use this new function:

```
const itSubmitsExistingValue = fieldName =>
  it('saves existing value when submitted', async () => {
    render(<CustomerForm {...{ [fieldName]: 'value' }} />);

    ReactTestUtils.Simulate.submit(form('customer'));

    expect(fetchRequestBody()).toMatchObject({
      [fieldName]: 'value'
    });
  });

const itSubmitsNewValue = fieldName =>
  it('saves new value when submitted', async () => {
    render(
      <CustomerForm {...{ [fieldName]: 'existingValue' }} />
```

```
    );
    ReactTestUtils.Simulate.change(field(fieldName), {
      target: { value: 'newValue', name: fieldName }
    });
    ReactTestUtils.Simulate.submit(form('customer'));

    expect(fetchRequestBody()).toMatchObject({
      [fieldName]: 'newValue'
    });
  });
```

11. Move to the top of the file and delete the spy function. Run all your tests and, with any luck, they are all passing!

Extracting spy helpers

CustomerForm is not the only component we'll use that will call fetch. In fact, the fetch tests we've written in this chapter will be a common occurrence in our code base. It makes sense to reuse the common code we've used, by pulling it out into its own module:

1. Create a test/spyHelpers.js file and add the following two function definitions, which are exactly the same as what you have at the top of test/CustomerForm.test.js, except this time they're exports:

```
export const fetchResponseOk = body =>
  Promise.resolve({
    ok: true,
    json: () => Promise.resolve(body)
  });

export const fetchResponseError = () =>
  Promise.resolve({ ok: false });
```

2. Delete those two definitions from within test/CustomerForm.test.js, and replace them with an import. After this change, run your tests and check they are still passing:

```
import { fetchResponseOk, fetchResponseError } from './spyHelpers';
```

3. Let's look at the `fetchRequestBody` function. This is slightly more difficult as it uses the `fetchSpy` variable, which is only accessible within the describe block. That's a simple one to fix; we can pass it in as a parameter. Update the two tests that call `fetchRequestBody`, passing in `fetchSpy` as a parameter. Your tests should still pass after making this change:

```
expect(fetchRequestBody(fetchSpy)).toMatchObject(...);
```

4. Update the function to use the new `fetchSpy` parameter:

```
const fetchRequestBody = fetchSpy =>
    JSON.parse(fetchSpy.mock.calls[0][1].body);
```

5. Copy the function into `test/spyHelpers.js`, and mark it with the `export` keyword.

6. In `test/CustomerForm.test.js`, delete the existing function you just copied. Update the import to include the function:

```
import {
    fetchResponseOk,
    fetchResponseError,
    fetchRequestBody
} from './spyHelpers';
```

7. Let's update the name. The word *fetch* is now repeated so we can remove that and make it slightly more readable by appending `Of` to the end of it. You can do a search and replace it across your code base to make this change. Here's how it should look in your expectations—much more readable:

```
expect(requestBodyOf(fetchSpy)).toMatchObject(...);
```

Ensure you've run all tests and you're on green before continuing.

Using jest.spyOn to spy on module mocks

There's one more thing we can do to simplify our spies.

When we stubbed out `window.fetch`, we saved the original value in a variable named `originalFetch`. We then reset `window.fetch` to use that value in `afterEach`. Jest can simplify this for us with the `jest.spyOn` function. It stores the old value within Jest so we don't need to define the additional `originalFetch` variable.

The only complication of using this function is that the value we're mocking needs to already exist as a function. No big deal you might think. But if you remember, `window.fetch` isn't ever defined in our test module because we polyfilled it in `src/index.js` and that file is never imported.

So you can decide which you prefer: either an extra variable in the describe block, or an extra import at the top of your file. I'm going to opt for the extra import, and here's how to do that if you're following along:

1. Pull `whatwg-fetch` into `test/CustomerForm.test.js`:

   ```
   import 'whatwg-fetch';
   ```

2. Update your `beforeEach` block as follows:

   ```
   beforeEach(() => {
     ...
     jest
       .spyOn(window, 'fetch')
       .mockReturnValue(fetchResponseOk({}));
   });
   ```

3. Add the `afterEach` block, as shown. This uses the `mockRestore()` function that's set up for us by `spyOn`. It removes the mock from `window.fetch` and returns the original value, just as our old code did:

   ```
   afterEach(() => {
     window.fetch.mockRestore();
   });
   ```

4. Delete the `originalFetch` constant from the top of the describe block.
5. Since `fetchSpy` is gone, you'll need to refer directly to `window.fetch` instead. Perform a search in your file for all occurrences of `fetchSpy` and replace them with `window.fetch`. Here's an example of one of our expectations after the change:

   ```
   expect(window.fetch).toHaveBeenCalledWith(
     '/customers',
     expect.objectContaining({
       method: 'POST',
       credentials: 'same-origin',
       headers: { 'Content-Type': 'application/json' }
     })
   );
   ```

That's it. Remember to run tests and check that everything is passing.

Drying up DOM queries

Why stop now when we're on a roll? There's *loads* more we can extract!

In `test/CustomerForm.test.js`, we also have definitions for `form`, `field`, and `labelFor`. As it turns out, these are exactly the same as our definitions in `test/AppointmentForm.test.js`, so that's a great signal that we should extract them.

Since they all refer to a container, we have the same problem as we had with `fetchRequestBody`. However, rather than solving it by passing in a container reference, let's solve it by adding these functions to the object returned by the `createContainer` call.

In addition, the `field` function refers to fields within the customer form, so let's modify that to work for *any* form before extracting the function out of the test suite:

1. In `test/CustomerForm.test.js`, search for all usages of the `field` function and then add in a new first parameter of `'customer'`. For example, `itRendersAsATextBox` becomes this:

    ```
    it('renders as a text box', () => {
      render(<CustomerForm />);
      expectToBeInputFieldOfTypeText(field('customer', fieldName));
    });
    ```

2. Modify the `field` function to use this parameter value in order to find the right form:

    ```
    const field = (formId, name) => form(formId).elements[name];
    ```

3. Open `test/domManipulators.js` and copy across the three functions, just under the definition of `container`, as shown:

    ```
    export const createContainer = () => {
      const container = document.createElement('div');

      const form = id =>
        container.querySelector(`form[id="${id}"]`);
      const field = (formId, name) => form(formId).elements[name];
      const labelFor = formElement =>
        container.querySelector(`label[for="${formElement}"]`);

      return {
        render: component => ReactDOM.render(component, container),
        container
      };
    };
    ```

4. Add those definitions into the returned object:

```
return {
  render: component => ReactDOM.render(component, container),
  container,
  form,
  field,
  labelFor
};
```

5. Back in `test/CustomerForm.test.js`, modify the `createContainer` call to save the three new fields. Your tests should still be passing after this:

```
let render, container, form, field, labelFor;

beforeEach(() => {
  ({
    render,
    container,
    form,
    field,
    labelFor
  } = createContainer());
  ...
});
```

6. Let's extract the `container.querySelector()` function. We'll take what you learned from renaming `fetchRequestBody` to make something more readable. We can call this one `element`. Create the following function in `test/domManipulators.js`:

```
const element = selector =>
  container.querySelector(selector);

return {
  element,
  ...
};
```

To see why `element` makes sense as a name, consider this current set of expectations:

```
const errorElement = container.querySelector('.error');
expect(errorElement).not.toBeNull();
expect(errorElement.textContent).toMatch('error
occurred');
```

Look at how the preceding code compares to this:

```
expect(element('.error')).not.toBeNull();
expect(element('.error').textContent).toMatch('error
occurred');
```

The new version is genericised in that it works for any element, but it contains all the same textual elements (error, element, textContent and so on) so there's no loss of information.

7. Back in test/CustomerForm.js, add element to the list of functions returned from createContainer:

```
let render, container, form, field, labelFor, element;

beforeEach(() => {
  ({
    render,
    container,
    form,
    field,
    labelFor,
    element
  } = createContainer());
});
```

8. Perform a search in test/CustomerForm.js, finding all occurrences of container.querySelector and replacing them with element.
9. Find the test that uses the errorElement constant and inline it, as shown in the Tip box in step 6.

Extracting container.querySelectorAll

The exercises for this chapter ask you to use your new domManipulator functions within your other test files.

If you're doing the exercises, you'll see that our other tests make use of the querySelectorAll DOM function. You can build a helper for this with the name elements. You should also wrap the Array.from call when you define this function, as shown:

```
const elements = selector =>
  Array.from(container.querySelectorAll);
```

The call to `Array.from` is noise when it's held within your tests. Pushing it into the helper function allows the test reader to not have to worry about what it does or why it's there.

Drying up DOM events

There's *still* more that we can do. Those `ReactTestUtils.Simulate.*` calls can be shortened and made a little easier to read.

If you do a search in the code base for these calls (for example, by running `git grep ReactTestUtils.Simulate` on the command line), you'll see that we use three functions on the `Simulate` object: `click`, `change`, and `submit`. We can deal with these by adding new properties onto the returned value from `createContainer`.

The first two functions, `click` and `change`, will be simple pass-throughs to the `ReactTestUtils.Simulate` call of the same name. We'll pull out a helper function, named `simulateEvent`, that we can re-use for each of the events.

The third function, `submit`, needs a little extra work. All our calls to `submit` have been wrapped in the `await act(async () ...)` pattern, so we'll need to pull that code in now. We use a second helper, `simulateEventAndWait`, to do that.

Follow these steps to define these new functions:

1. Add an import at the top of `test/domManipulators.js`, to pull in `ReactTestUtils`:

```
import ReactTestUtils, { act } from 'react-dom/test-utils';
```

2. Define the following functions within `createContainer`, just before the returned object value:

```
const simulateEvent = eventName => (element, eventData) =>
  ReactTestUtils.Simulate[eventName](element, eventData);

const simulateEventAndWait = eventName => async (
  element,
  eventData
) =>
  await act(async () =>
    ReactTestUtils.Simulate[eventName](element, eventData)
  );
```

3. Use those new helper functions to add new function properties to the object that
   createContainer returns:

```
return {
  click: simulateEvent('click'),
  change: simulateEvent('change'),
  submit: simulateEventAndWait('submit'),
  ...
};
```

4. In test/CustomerForm.js, modify the createContainer call to assign values
   to change and submit (the click function isn't used in this file; you'll need it
   when solving the *Exercises*):

```
let render,
  container,
  form,
  field,
  labelFor,
  element,
  change,
  submit;
let fetchSpy;

beforeEach(() => {
  ({
    render,
    container,
    form,
    field,
    labelFor,
    element,
    change,
    submit
  } = createContainer());
```

5. Remove all occurrences of ReactTestUtils.Simulate.; don't forget the
   trailing dot!
6. Delete the act import at the top of test/CustomerForm.test.js.

There's *one* more thing we can do. The change function takes event data, which looks like
this:

```
{
  target: { value: 'newValue', name: fieldName }
}
```

Defining this object within our tests seems like a little too much detail for our tests, and detracts from the overall intention of the test code. Let's define a new helper to solve that, by hiding the object structure behind a function with a descriptive name. This time, it doesn't need to be part of your `createContainer` function, it can simply be a top-level export in `test/domManipulators.js`:

```
export const withEvent = (name, value) => ({
  target: { name, value }
});
```

You can then update the `CustomerForm` test suite to use it, like this:

```
change(
  field(fieldName),
  withEvent(fieldName, 'newValue')
);
```

Summary

In this chapter, we explored test doubles and how they are used to verify interactions with collaborating objects. We looked in detail at spies and stubs, the two main types of doubles you'll use. As we went through, we used a couple of additional testing techniques: we built a Jest matcher, and we built a side-by-side implementation that helped us keep most of our existing tests green as we reworked our component.

Then we removed our hand-rolled code in favor of Jest's own built-in functionality, which helped to dry up our tests.

We also extracted a bunch of helper code into modules that made our tests more readable, because they are shorter and clearer about their intent.

In the next chapter, we'll tie each of our components together into an application with a working data flow.

Exercises

 The Git tag for this section is `chapter-3-exercises`.

- Add a test to `CustomerForm` which specifies that the error state is cleared when the form is submitted again.
- Update the `AppointmentForm` tests to use `jest.fn()`, `jest.spyOn()`, and all of the new helpers in `domManipulators.js` and `spyHelpers.js`.
- Extend `AppointmentForm` so that it submits an appointment using a `POST` request to `/appointments`. Unlike with `CustomerForm`, you don't need to call `json` on the result body, or send back any parameters to `onSave`. The `/appointments` endpoint returns a 201 Created status without any body.
- Update the tests in `AppointmentsDayView` to use the new helpers from `test/domManipulators.js`.

Further learning

Check out the following resources for more information on the topics covered in this chapter:

- A good introduction to the different kinds of test doubles: `https://martinfowler.com/articles/mocksArentStubs.html`
- Jest mock functions: `https://jestjs.io/docs/en/mock-functions.html`
- An introduction to using the Fetch API: `https://github.github.io/fetch`

4
Creating a User Interface

The components we've built so far have been isolated: they don't fit together, and there's no sequence of events for the user. In this chapter, we'll tie all those components into a functioning system. Here's how we'll do it.

When the user navigates to the app, they will see a list of today's appointments using the `AppointmentsDayView` component. That appointment data will be loaded from the server. In addition to the list, the user will see a button labeled **Add customer and appointment**. Clicking that button makes the `CustomerForm` appear. When the form is filled out and the submit button is clicked, the user is then shown the `AppointmentForm` and can add a new appointment for that customer, as shown below:

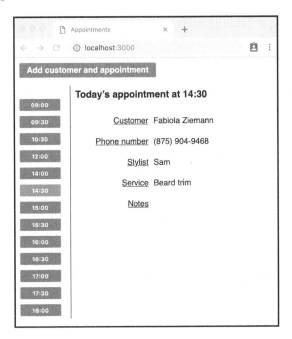

The Appointments system showing the new button in the upper-left corner

Once they've added the appointment they'll be taken back to the `AppointmentsDayView`.

This orchestration between `AppointmentsDayView`, `CustomerForm`, and `AppointmentForm` will be performed by a new `App` component, which will know where the user is at in the workflow.

This is a very simple workflow that supports just one use case: adding a new customer and an appointment at the same time. Later on, we'll add support for creating appointments for existing customers.

To make all that happen, we'll cover the following topics:

- Fetching data on load with `useEffect`
- Using props within `useEffect`
- Passing customer data through to `AppointmentForm`
- Using shallow rendering to build a root component

Fetching data on load with useEffect

The Git tag for this section is `load-available-time-slots`. It contains solutions to the exercises from the previous chapter, so if you haven't completed the *Exercises* section yourself, then you should move to this tag now so that you're up to date.

For more detailed instructions, see the *To get the most out of this book* section in the `Preface`.

When we built our `AppointmentForm` component, we passed in `availableTimeSlots` as a prop. We passed sample data to check that our form was displaying those time slots correctly.

Our server offers an endpoint that returns us this week's available time slots:

```
GET /availableTimeSlots
```

In this section, we'll make a fetch request to the endpoint when our application first loads. As we saw in the previous chapter, each time we use fetch to pull data, we need at least two tests: one to check that we make the call to fetch, and one to make sure that we use the data correctly.

We'll do this using a **container component**. This is a component whose purpose is simply to pull data together and pass it on to another component. In this case, we'll create an `AppointmentFormLoader` that will find all the `availableTimeSlots` and then pass them on to `AppointmentForm` as a prop.

I prefer to suffix my container components with the word `Loader` rather than `Container`. `Container` is a "nothing" word that has very little meaning, a bit like manager and utility! Avoid it!

Why use a container component?

Instead of creating a new component, we could add a `useEffect` hook straight into `AppointmentForm`. But if we did that, we'd then have *two* methods for setting `availableTimeSlots`: the original prop and the new fetch call. Aligning the two adds complication. Do we set the initial value to the prop and then overwrite it with the data from fetch? Or perhaps we should get rid of the prop entirely, in which case we'll need to rewrite our tests to use a stubbed fetch response to set `availableTimeSlots`.

That's a whole bunch of complexity and uncertainty. By splitting apart the rendering of data from fetching of data, we can avoid questions like these, and our existing tests remain as they are.

Let's begin by creating the new test suite:

1. Create a new test file, `test/AppointmentFormLoader.test.js`, with the following imports and describe block. This setup is slightly different from the tests in the previous chapter, because our fetch spy is set up to return an array of items rather than a single object:

```
import React from 'react';
import 'whatwg-fetch';
import { createContainer } from './domManipulators';
import { fetchResponseOk } from './spyHelpers';
import {
  AppointmentFormLoader
} from '../src/AppointmentFormLoader';

describe('AppointmentFormLoader', () => {
  let render, container;

  const today = new Date();
  const availableTimeSlots = [
```

```
      { startsAt: today.setHours(9, 0, 0, 0) }
  ];

  beforeEach(() => {
    ({ render, container } = createContainer());
    jest
      .spyOn(window, 'fetch')
      .mockReturnValue(fetchResponseOk(availableTimeSlots));
  });

  afterEach(() => {
    window.fetch.mockRestore();
  });
});
```

2. Add the first test, as shown in the following code. There's nothing out of the ordinary here, but what is different is that we're expecting fetch to have been called, even though all we've done is render the component:

```
it('fetches data when component is mounted', () => {
  render(<AppointmentFormLoader />);

  expect(window.fetch).toHaveBeenCalledWith(
    '/availableTimeSlots',
    expect.objectContaining({
      method: 'GET',
      credentials: 'same-origin',
      headers: { 'Content-Type': 'application/json' }
    })
  );
});
```

3. To make that happen, we need the useEffect hook. Create a new file, src/AppointmentFormLoader.js, and add just enough code to make this test pass, as follows:

```
import React, { useEffect } from 'react';

export const AppointmentFormLoader = () => {

  useEffect(() => {
    const fetchAvailableTimeSlots = () => {
      window.fetch('/availableTimeSlots', {
        method: 'GET',
        credentials: 'same-origin',
        headers: { 'Content-Type': 'application/json' }
      });
```

```
    };

    fetchAvailableTimeSlots();
  }, []);

  return null;
};
```

The useEffect hook has a lot of subtleties that can make it hard to implement it correctly. There are some conventions you have to follow, even though it may seem like your tests don't require them.

For example, in the previous code snippet, the second argument to useEffect is the empty array, []. This is the hook's dependency list, and determines when the effect should be restarted. We'll explore the meaning of an empty dependency list in the next section, *Using props within useEffect*.

Another subtlety is defining a fetchAvailableTimeSlots function rather than simply calling window.fetch directly, and why that function is defined within the scope of the useEffect hook. From a test perspective, if you were to call window.fetch directly from within the useEffect hook you'd receive a warning from the React runtime when you run your tests. It would alert you that the useEffect hook should not return a promise. That's because the return value of the useEffect hook should be a function that performs teardown each time the hook is restarted. Restarting a hook involves tearing it down and then launching the same hook code again.

We'll explore this return function in detail in Chapter 11, *Adding Animation*.

 To learn more about useEffect subtleties, check out the *Further learning* section at the end of this chapter.

4. If you run this now, you'll see that the test doesn't pass yet. That's because your useEffect hook is placed onto the runtime task queue and will not be executed synchronously: your test expectations will be executed before your hook gets a chance to run. To make this work, we need to update our render helper to use the synchronous form of the act function.

Open `test/domManipulators.js` and modify the definition of `render` to look as follows. The test should pass after this change:

```
render: component =>
  act(() => {
    ReactDOM.render(component, container);
  }),
```

The synchronous form of `act` does two things: first, it calls all `useEffect` hooks after it has rendered the provided component. Second, it defers any state setters until after all effects have executed. We are using the first behavior here. The second behavior isn't covered in this book, but is a helpful "guard rail" for subtle timing bugs that can be difficult to pick up in tests, when multiple state updates fire at once and end up overwriting each other's updates.

5. Let's add a test to get an `AppointmentForm` rendered on the page. Before we pass our fetched data to it, however, let's write a test for how it will be rendered before the data is retrieved. Our component will, after all, render for a split second before the network call resolves.

   We want to render an `AppointmentForm` with the `availableTimeSlots` prop set. To test that prop, we'll need to spy on `AppointmentForm`, just like we did with `window.fetch`. Yes, components can be stubbed too!

   Start by adding this export at the top of your test file. It looks different from the imports we've seen already; we'll look at it in detail once we're done with this test:

   ```
   import * as AppointmentFormExports from '../src/AppointmentForm';
   ```

6. Stub out `AppointmentForm` in the `beforeEach` block, since we'll want the stub so that we can apply it to all the tests in this test suite. While you're here, restore the mock in the `afterEach` block:

   ```
   beforeEach(() => {
     ({ render, container } = createContainer());
     jest
       .spyOn(window, 'fetch')
       .mockReturnValue(fetchResponseOk(availableTimeSlots));
     jest
       .spyOn(AppointmentFormExports, 'AppointmentForm')
       .mockReturnValue(null);
   });
   ```

```
afterEach(() => {
  window.fetch.mockRestore();
  AppointmentFormExports.AppointmentForm.mockRestore();
});
```

7. Add the following test. It simply checks that we pass an empty array, [], to `AppointmentForm`:

```
it('initially passes no data to AppointmentForm', () => {
  render(<AppointmentFormLoader />);

  expect(
    AppointmentFormExports.AppointmentForm
  ).toHaveBeenCalledWith(
    { availableTimeSlots: [] },
    expect.anything()
  );
});
```

8. To make that pass, add an import for `AppointmentForm` at the top of `src/AppointmentFormLoader.js`:

```
import { AppointmentForm } from './AppointmentForm';
```

9. Render an instance of this component with its prop set. Your test should now be green:

```
return (
  <AppointmentForm availableTimeSlots={[]} />
);
```

10. Let's add in the fetched data. When we've received data, we want to render an `AppointmentForm` with the `availableTimeSlots` prop set to the received data. By the time our expectations have run in this test, `AppointmentForm` will actually have been rendered twice: the first time with an empty array, and the second time with our data. Therefore, we can be specific here by using the `toHaveBeenLastCalledWith` matcher:

```
it('displays time slots that are fetched on mount', async () => {
  render(<AppointmentFormLoader />);

  expect(
    AppointmentFormExports.AppointmentForm
  ).toHaveBeenLastCalledWith(
    {
      availableTimeSlots
    },
```

```
      expect.anything()
    );
  });
```

11. To make this pass, first import the `useState` hook into
    `src/AppointmentFormLoader.js`:

    ```
    import React, { useEffect, useState } from 'react';
    ```

12. Then, define a new state variable at the top of the `AppointmentFormLoader`
    component. Its initial value is the empty array, `[]`, which we'll use to make sure
    that our previous test still passes:

    ```
    const [ availableTimeSlots, setAvailableTimeSlots ] = useState(
      []
    );
    ```

13. Update your `useEffect` hook to set that value:

    ```
    useEffect(() => {
      const fetchAvailableTimeSlots = async () => {
        const result = await window.fetch('/availableTimeSlots', {
          method: 'GET',
          credentials: 'same-origin',
          headers: { 'Content-Type': 'application/json' }
        });
        setAvailableTimeSlots(await result.json());
      };

      fetchAvailableTimeSlots();
    }, []);
    ```

React guarantees that setters such as `setAvailableTimeSlots` remain
static. That means they don't need to appear in the `useEffect`
dependency list.

14. Set the prop on your `AppointmentForm` instance:

    ```
    return (
      <AppointmentForm availableTimeSlots={availableTimeSlots} />
    );
    ```

15. Running tests now will show you that the test still doesn't pass, and additionally we now have a bunch of warnings about `act` not being used correctly. The issue is that we've triggered an asynchronous action in `useEffect`, and React doesn't like it. It wants us to use the asynchronous form of `act`. We'll build a new `renderAndWait` function for this purpose. Open `test/domManipulators.js` and add the following new property to the `createContainer` return object:

```
renderAndWait: async component =>
  await act(async () => ReactDOM.render(component, container)),
```

 The `async` form of `act` does the same two things that the `sync` form does, but it also flushes the current runtime task queue. For those of you who have been doing this manually before React 16.9, this is equivalent to calling `await new Promise(setTimeout)`.

16. Back in `test/AppointmentFormLoader.test.js`, assign a new `renderAndWait` constant that refers to the function you've just defined:

```
let renderAndWait, render, container;

. . .

beforeEach(() => {
  ({ renderAndWait, render, container } = createContainer());
  . . .
});
```

17. Update your test in `test/AppointmentFormLoader.test.js` to use this new function:

```
it('displays time slots that are fetched on mount', async () => {
  await renderAndWait(<AppointmentFormLoader />);

  expect(
    AppointmentFormExports.AppointmentForm
  ).toHaveBeenLastCalledWith(
    {
      availableTimeSlots
    },
    expect.anything()
  );
});
```

18. Your test should now pass, but there are two large, ugly warnings coming from React. This is because of the two previous tests we wrote in this test suite. Both of them now need to be updated to use `renderAndWait` too. Update them as follows. The warnings will have disappeared:

```
it('fetches data when component is mounted', async () => {
  await renderAndWait(<AppointmentFormLoader />);

  ...
});

it('initially passes no data to AppointmentForm', async () => {
  await renderAndWait(<AppointmentFormLoader />);

  ...
});
```

19. Before moving on, delete the `render` constant and assignment from the top of the test suite. We're now exclusively using `renderAndWait` in this file, and `render` is no longer needed.

In the preceding code, we stubbed out `AppointmentForm` so that we could check props that are passed to the component. Later on, we'll stub out components for another reason, which is when child components have their own `useEffect` hooks that we don't want to run.

Stubbing exported constants

Our components are defined using `const`, which theoretically means we can't change their value. For example:

```
export const AppointmentForm = ...
```

So, how can we stub a value that shouldn't change? There's a simple trick to stubbing these kinds of components. We need to import them differently. Usually, we would do this:

```
import { AppointmentForm } from '../src/AppointmentForm';
```

Instead, we will use a **namespace import**:

```
import * as AppointmentFormExports from '../src/AppointmentForm';
```

What we get from this is an object, `AppointmentFormExports`, with
an `AppointmentForm` property is safe to reassign, as you'll see in the following test.

This technique won't work for modules from other packages. For that, you'll need to use
`jest.mock`, which we'll cover later in this book.

Using props within useEffect

The Git tag for this section is `fetching-todays-appointments`.

In this section, we'll repeat almost the same thing. We'll load data into our
`AppointmentsDayView` component so that the user can view a list of appointments
occurring today. However, the endpoint for retrieving appointments is more complicated
than `/availableTimeSlots`: this time, we need to pass in a time range:

```
GET /appointments/<from>-<to>
```

We'll do that by building a new component, `AppointmentsDayViewLoader`. Follow these
steps to get started:

1. Create a new file, `test/AppointmentsDayViewLoader.test.js`. Start by
   adding the imports:

   ```
   import React from 'react';
   import 'whatwg-fetch';
   import { createContainer } from './domManipulators';
   import { fetchResponseOk } from './spyHelpers';
   import {
     AppointmentsDayViewLoader
   } from '../src/AppointmentsDayViewLoader';
   import * as AppointmentsDayViewExports
     from '../src/AppointmentsDayView';
   ```

It's perfectly normal to find container components that are very similar in nature, like `AppointmentsDayViewLoader` and `AppointmentFormLoader`. When you build new container components, don't be afraid to copy and paste code and then alter it as necessary. You should always use existing tests to help you speed up your test development.

2. Add in a describe block with `beforeEach` and `afterEach`. We're jumping ahead here a little because, strictly speaking, the stub setup isn't needed for the first test. However, we know what's coming because we just did the same thing for `AppointmentFormLoader`, so we can get our test setup in the correct shape initially rather than getting part of the way and having to jump back to it later. In addition, I'm also jumping ahead with `renderAndWait`, which is unnecessary for our first test, but we may as well cheat now and begin using it since we know we'll need to refactor it later.

The data we're sending back from the endpoint is an array of two appointments, occurring today at 9:00 and 10:00:

```
describe('AppointmentsDayViewLoader', () => {
  let renderAndWait, container;

  const today = new Date();
  const appointments = [
    { startsAt: today.setHours(9, 0, 0, 0) },
    { startsAt: today.setHours(10, 0, 0, 0) }
  ];

  beforeEach(() => {
    ({ renderAndWait, container } = createContainer());
    jest
      .spyOn(window, 'fetch')
      .mockReturnValue(fetchResponseOk(appointments));
    jest
      .spyOn(AppointmentsDayViewExports, 'AppointmentsDayView')
      .mockReturnValue(null);
  });

  afterEach(() => {
    window.fetch.mockRestore();
    AppointmentsDayViewExports.AppointmentsDayView.mockRestore();
  });
});
```

3. Add the first test. We'll pass in a prop of `today` so that the component can calculate the right `from` and `to` times. The component's calculation should match our test's calculation:

```
it('fetches appointments happening today when component is
mounted', async () => {
  const from = today.setHours(0, 0, 0, 0);
  const to = today.setHours(23, 59, 59, 999);

  await renderAndWait(
    <AppointmentsDayViewLoader today={today} />
  );

  expect(window.fetch).toHaveBeenCalledWith(
    `/appointments/${from}-${to}`,
    expect.objectContaining({
      method: 'GET',
      credentials: 'same-origin',
      headers: { 'Content-Type': 'application/json' }
    })
  );
});
```

Our test calculates `from` and `to`, but doesn't send those values through to `AppointmentsDayViewLoader`. The component will need to do exactly the same calculation. This kind of duplication is often necessary with test-driven development. It's not a bad thing; in fact, it's perfectly normal. Our test clearly specifies what's necessary from the component.

We could argue about the design – is this really as simple as it could be? Should we introduce a new type to represent a time range so that neither the test nor `AppointmentsDayViewLoader` needs to perform this calculation? That discussion is a useful one to have, but I leave it to you to decide your preference.

4. To pass this test, create a new file, `src/AppointmentsDayViewLoader.js`, and add the following code:

```
import React, { useEffect } from 'react';

export const AppointmentsDayViewLoader = ({ today }) => {
  useEffect(() => {
    const from = today.setHours(0, 0, 0, 0);
    const to = today.setHours(23, 59, 59, 999);
```

```
        const fetchAppointments = () => {
          window.fetch(`/appointments/${from}-${to}`, {
            method: 'GET',
            credentials: 'same-origin',
            headers: { 'Content-Type': 'application/json' }
          });
        };

        fetchAppointments();
      }, [from, to]);

      return null;
    };
```

5. The next test is essentially the same as we've seen for `AppointmentForm`. We don't pass in a `today` prop this time; we want to set that in `defaultProps` instead:

```
    it('initially passes no data to AppointmentsDayView', async () => {
      await renderAndWait(<AppointmentsDayViewLoader />);

      expect(
        AppointmentsDayViewExports.AppointmentsDayView
      ).toHaveBeenCalledWith(
        { appointments: [] },
        expect.anything()
      );
    });
```

6. Now, add in `defaultProps`:

```
    AppointmentsDayViewLoader.defaultProps = {
      today: new Date()
    };
```

7. Make that pass by introducing the `AppointmentsDayView` into the imports:

```
    import { AppointmentsDayView } from './AppointmentsDayView';
```

8. Then, return a new `AppointmentsDayView`:

```
    return <AppointmentsDayView appointments={[]} />;
```

9. The next test is also pretty similar to `AppointmentsDayView`:

```
    it('displays time slots that are fetched on mount', async () => {
      await renderAndWait(<AppointmentsDayViewLoader />);
```

```
      expect(
        AppointmentsDayViewExports.AppointmentsDayView
      ).toHaveBeenLastCalledWith(
        {
          appointments
        },
        expect.anything()
      );
    });
```

10. Make that pass by first importing the `useState` function:

```
import React, { useEffect, useState } from 'react';
```

11. Save the appointments that are brought back by the endpoint:

```
const [appointments, setAppointments] = useState([]);

useEffect(() => {
  ...
  const fetchAppointments = async () => {
    const result = await window.fetch(
      `/appointments/${from}-${to}`,
      {
        method: 'GET',
        credentials: 'same-origin',
        headers: { 'Content-Type': 'application/json' }
      }
    );
    setAppointments(await result.json());
  };

  fetchAppointments();
}, []);

return <AppointmentsDayView appointments={appointments} />;
```

12. When we built `AppointmentFormLoader`, we stopped here. Unfortunately, we're not quite done for this component. What happens when we update today? Write out the following test. You'll find that it fails. The issue is that `useEffect` only runs on the initial component mount, not when props change:

```
it('re-requests appointment when today prop changes', async () => {
  const tomorrow = new Date(today);
  tomorrow.setHours(24);
  const from = tomorrow.setHours(0, 0, 0, 0);
  const to = tomorrow.setHours(23, 59, 59, 999);
```

```
    await renderAndWait(
      <AppointmentsDayViewLoader today={today} />
    );
    await renderAndWait(
      <AppointmentsDayViewLoader today={tomorrow} />
    );

    expect(window.fetch).toHaveBeenLastCalledWith(
      `/appointments/${from}-${to}`,
      expect.anything());
  });
```

13. Making it pass, however, is very straightforward. We just need to pass the prop into the second argument that's passed to `useEffect`:

```
useEffect(() => {
  ...
}, [today]);
```

It's important to write tests that accurately reflect the contract of whichever hook we're working against. The `useEffect` hook is a particularly tricky customer. Don't take anything for granted when dealing with it!

In fact, if we were being pedantic, we could have actually tested *more* than we have done. To see why, consider the difference between these two calls:

```
useEffect(() => { ... });
useEffect(() => { ... }, []);
```

The first of these calls will rerun the effect every time the component is re-rendered, which includes whenever props or state are modified. The second only runs once, when the component first mounts.

For `AppointmentsDayViewLoader`, we do not want to rerun the effect unless props change. We could have written this test to prove it:

```
it('calls window.fetch just once', async () => {
  await renderAndWait(<AppointmentsDayViewLoader />);
  await renderAndWait(<AppointmentsDayViewLoader />);
  expect(window.fetch.mock.calls.length).toBe(1);
});
```

The same idea applies to `AppointmentFormLoader`, too.

Whether or not you wish to be pedantic is entirely up to you. Some parts of the React API are highly conventional, and that may mean you do things subconsciously, or through habit, such as always starting a `useEffect` hook with an empty array for the second parameter. Writing out explicit tests can help challenge your assumptions and can help document those unwritten habits for team members who may be new to React programming.

Passing customer data through to AppointmentForm

The Git tag for this section is `passing-data-through-loader`.

In this section, we'll build an `AppointmentForm` so that it's ready for use in our new workflow. The main requirement here is that our `App` component can pass the `customer` prop through the `AppointmentFormLoader` and into `AppointmentForm`, and that the customer ID is submitted to the server when an appointment is saved. We'll split that work into two parts.

Passing through props to the child component

This requires two new tests, one in each of `AppointmentFormLoader` and `AppointmentForm`, and updating existing tests in `AppointmentForm` to provide a default value of the prop:

1. Add the following test in `test/AppointmentFormLoader.js`. What's of interest here is that we test *any* props that are passed through, not just a customer prop. I find this a useful habit for all components of this nature: it makes them less brittle because what you're passing through is not their concern. The primary concern of this component should be loading data. I'm using a prop named `testProp` just to signify that the identity of the prop isn't important: *every* prop should be passed through:

   ```
   it('passes props through to children', async () => {
     await renderAndWait(<AppointmentFormLoader testProp={123} />);
   ```

```
    expect (
      AppointmentFormExports.AppointmentForm
    ).toHaveBeenCalledWith (
      expect.objectContaining({ testProp: 123 }),
      expect.anything()
    );
  });
```

2. Update the `AppointmentFormLoader` component to take the new props parameter, and then pass it to `AppointmentForm`:

```
export const AppointmentFormLoader = props => {
  ...
  return (
    <AppointmentForm
      {...props}
      availableTimeSlots={availableTimeSlots}
    />;
};
```

3. Moving on to `AppointmentForm`, add the following test to `test/AppointmentForm.test.js`, which checks that we pass the customer ID through to the `/appointments` endpoint:

```
it('passes the customer id to fetch when submitting', async () => {
  const customer = { id: 123 };
  render(<AppointmentForm customer={customer} />);
  await submit(form('appointment'));
  expect(requestBodyOf(window.fetch)).toMatchObject({
    customer: customer.id
  });
});
```

4. Add in the prop to the definition of `AppointmentForm` in `src/AppointmentForm.js`:

```
export const AppointmentForm = ({
  customer,
  ...
}) => {
```

5. Then, set the customer ID on the object. Running tests after this step will show a whole bunch of errors, so you may want to single out the test we've just written with `.only` to prove to yourself that it works. Then, move on to fixing the rest of the tests:

```
const result = await window.fetch('/appointments', {
  method: 'POST',
  credentials: 'same-origin',
  headers: { 'Content-Type': 'application/json' },
  body: JSON.stringify({
    ...appointment,
    customer: customer.id
  })
});
```

6. Any test that causes a submit to occur will now be broken due to the `customer.id` access. To fix your tests, first pull up the definition of the `customer` constant from the test you just wrote and into the outer describe block. Then duplicate the definition at the higher scope and finally delete it from the original location. This way, we can use it across all our other tests:

```
describe('AppointmentForm', () => {
  const customer = { id: 123 };
  ...
});
```

7. Update any of the failing tests so that they pass through `customer={customer}` to the `AppointmentForm`. Here's an example of how to change one of the tests. Go through the rest of your failures and update the tests in the same way:

```
it('saves existing value when submitted', async () => {
  render(
    <AppointmentForm
      customer={customer}
      availableTimeSlots={availableTimeSlots}
      today={today}
      startsAt={availableTimeSlots[0].startsAt}
    />
  );
  await submit(form('appointment'));

  expect(requestBodyOf(window.fetch)).toMatchObject({
    startsAt: availableTimeSlots[0].startsAt
  });
});
```

After all that, we're ready to begin work on App. But first, we need to learn about shallow rendering and beef up what React offers us.

Working with the shallow renderer

You've already seen one technique for testing child components that perform side effects. We can stub out those components and uses spies to assert that they were instantiated with the right props.

There's another technique that we can use to test components, and we'll use it for building App. It's *shallow rendering,* and it essentially builds us a tree of React component instances, but stops at all custom components. All primitives, such as div, ol, and table, will be rendered along with their children. Since all of the components that we've written in the book are custom components, none of them will be rendered.

The root component itself will have all of its hooks and side effects run, so we can continue to test any kind of life cycle, and we'll use that to test-drive App.

So, what does this tree of component instances look like? Here's an example of the output of <div id="test"><p>Hello, world!</p></div>:

```
{ '$$typeof': Symbol(react.element),
    type: 'div',
    key: null,
    ref: null,
    props:
     { id: 'test',
       children:
        { '$$typeof': Symbol(react.element),
          type: 'p',
          key: null,
          ref: null,
          props:  { children: 'Hello, world!' },
          _owner: null,
          _store: {} } },
    _owner: null,
    _store: {} }
```

These objects are essentially the same objects that are returned by compiling your JSX.

When it comes to testing a shallow rendered component, we can make our lives easier by building an API to work more easily with returned component instance graphs. That's what we'll do in this section. We'll build out the following functions:

- `childrenOf(element)`, which returns the list of direct children of an element, by inspecting and sanitizing the `props.children` property
- `render(element)`, which encapsulates the shallow renderer inside a function, just like we did with `domManipulators`
- `child(n)`, which returns the *n*th direct child of the root component instance rendered by render
- `elementsMatching(matcherFn)`, which returns an array of children across the entire tree that match the given function
- `elementMatching(matcherFn)`, which returns the first element of the `elementsMatching` array and a set of matcher functions

Almost all of this will be test-driven. Yes, we will be test-driving our test code!

> This is the reason that some people find TDD a little over the top. Test-driving test code? Why would we want to do that? Well, the answer is that these helpers will not just be one-liners, as we've encountered before. They will contain a whole bunch of conditional and recursive logic.

> In addition, working with raw React instances like this is *not* straightforward. There are a whole bunch of gotchas waiting for us, in particular the fact that `props.children` can have many different types: it can be an object, a string value, an array, or it can even just not be defined at all. By having clear examples in the form of tests, we can document these gotchas and save our future selves a lot of head-scratching.

To put all of this into context, here are some example expectations that we'll be able to write with this API. We'll get to the actual tests in the next section. With any luck, you can guess what these expectations do just from reading them. They are designed to be readable:

```
expect(elementMatching(type(AppointmentsDayViewLoader))).toBeDefined();

expect(child(0).type).toEqual('div');

const buttons = childrenOf(elementMatching(className('button-bar')));
expect(buttons[0].type).toEqual('button');
expect(buttons[0].props.children).toEqual('Add customer and appointment');
```

Understanding the importance of spiking

Before we embark on building this all-singing, all-dancing shallow renderer helper library, I want to get across the importance of *spiking* and how I came up with the approach you're about to follow.

It would be wrong to think that I sat down and planned out this code in a linear progression from A to B, just as shown in this books. That is absolutely *not* what I did. When I started, I first had to explore with a lot of trial and error. Of course, all programmers should know how to *explore* a codebase, but in the TDD process, it's given a special significance.

The process for me looked a little like this:

1. Write a test that looked *kind of* how I wanted it to look, by making a guess
2. Write some production code
3. Watch it fail in ways I didn't expect
4. Use `console.log` to view the output of the shallow renderer to figure out what was going on
5. Fix the test code
6. Write another test, then adjust the API to make it more cohesive across all tests
7. Repeat

It would take up too much space in this book if I were to show you all of this process, so what you see is just the end result. Hopefully, it's a clean and understandable API for working more easily with the shallow renderer, but it look a lot of trial and error to get there.

That is what spiking is all about. It's an integral part of the TDD process.

Building shallow renderer helpers

 The Git tag for this section is `shallow-rendering`.

We'll create a new module for testing shallow components. Both it and its tests will live in the `test` directory.

Listing element children

Let's begin by building out the `childrenOf` function, which lists all the direct children of a component instance:

1. Create a new file named `test/shallowHelpers.test.js` and add the following test for `childrenOf`. It's a simple one to get us started. We pass in JSX directly to it; there's no mention of the shallow renderer yet. At this stage, it would be essentially the same output, except that the shallow renderer won't run on primitives such as `div`. When we do eventually bring in the shallow renderer, we'll use `childrenOf` on the rendered output:

    ```
    import React from 'react';
    import { childrenOf } from './shallowHelpers';

    describe('childrenOf', () => {
      it('returns no children', () => {
        expect(childrenOf(<div />)).toEqual([]);
      });
    });
    ```

    If you were to run `console.log(<div />)`, you'd see this:

    ```
    {
      '$$typeof': Symbol(react.element),
      type: 'div',
      key: null,
      ref: null,
      props: {},
      _owner: null,
      _store: {}
    }
    ```

    From this, we can tell that when there are no children, the children property of `props` is not yet defined, so that's what we need to code up for our test to pass.

2. Create a new file named `test/shallowHelpers.js`, and make the preceding test pass with the following code. Make sure to add this in the `test` directory, not the `src` directory:

    ```
    import React from 'react';

    export const childrenOf = element => ([]);
    ```

3. Next, we need to triangulate, of course. Add the following test:

```
it('returns direct children', () => {
  expect(
    childrenOf(
      <div>
        <p>A</p>
        <p>B</p>
      </div>
    )
  ).toEqual([<p>A</p>, <p>B</p>]);
});
```

4. We can make that pass by checking for an undefined value. If we get undefined, we return an empty array:

```
export const childrenOf = element => {
  if (!element.props.children) {
    return [];
  }
  return element.props.children;
};
```

One of the simplest ways to make your code overly complex is to have a varying return type of the same property. As we'll find out, `props.children` can be either `undefined`, an array, an object, or a string. All of that adds a stunning level of complexity to our test code, which can tell us the number of `if` statements in our code base.

The presence of the humble `if` is often a design smell. In this case, it most certainly is! Think about that as we go through the rest of these tests.

5. Add the next test: what happens if the child is text itself?

```
it('returns text as an array of one item', () => {
  expect(childrenOf(<div>text</div>)).toEqual(['text']);
});
```

6. In this case, we have to deal with a string value. Modify `childrenOf` so that it looks as follows:

```
export const childrenOf = element => {
  if (!element.props.children) {
    return [];
  }
  if (typeof element.props.children === 'string') {
    return [element.props.children];
```

```
    }
    return element.props.children;
};
```

7. Next up, what happens if the element itself is a string? This is not an obvious test case, but this is an important edge case for our elementsMatching function, which we'll come to soon:

```
it('returns no children for text', () => {
    expect(childrenOf('text')).toEqual([]);
});
```

 You could argue that this check should live in elementsMatching; I've introduced a stronger coupling between these two functions than could otherwise be necessary. Feel free to play around with the API if you wish.

8. Make that pass with the following change to childrenOf:

```
export const childrenOf = element => {
    if (typeof element === 'string') {
        return [];
    }
    ...
};
```

9. What happens when we have just one child of the parent? In this case, React returns an object and not an array, so we need to cater for that:

```
it('returns array of children for elements with one child', () => {
    expect(
        childrenOf(
            <div>
                <p>A</p>
            </div>
        )
    ).toEqual([<p>A</p>]);
});
```

10. Make that pass with the following code; we've now arrived at our final implementation of childrenOf:

```
export const childrenOf = element => {
    if (typeof element === 'string') {
        return [];
    }
    const {
```

```
      props: { children }
    } = element;
    if (!children) {
      return [];
    }
    if (typeof children === 'string') {
      return [children];
    }
    if (Array.isArray(children)) {
      return children;
    }
    return [children];
  };
```

Encapsulating render output to dry up tests

Now, let's wrap up `childrenOf` so that our helpers "match" what we built in `domManipulators`. We'll build a render function that will call the shallow renderer, and then we'll build a `child` function that calls `childrenOf` on the result of that render. The test code will never need to manipulate the result object directly:

1. In `test/shallowHelpers.test.js`, change the import to bring in the new function that we're about to build, `createShallowRenderer`:

   ```
   import {
     createShallowRenderer,
     childrenOf
   } from './shallowHelpers';
   ```

2. Add the following `describe` block to `test/shallowHelpers.test.js`. This should be outside of the previous `describe` block, not nested within it. This also defines a new `TestComponent` component; we need this because the shallow renderer will complain if we give it a primitive component type. It doesn't do anything except render its children:

   ```
   const TestComponent = ({ children }) => (
     <React.Fragment>{children}</React.Fragment>
   );

   describe('child', () => {
     let render, child;

     beforeEach(() => {
       ({ render, child } = createShallowRenderer());
     });
   ```

```
    it('returns undefined if the child does not exist', () => {
      render(<TestComponent />);
      expect(child(0)).not.toBeDefined();
    });
  });
```

The `React.Fragment` element provides a way to wrap child elements without introducing an extra element into the rendered DOM tree. It's generally used when you want to wrap multiple elements where React expects only one, such as the root element returned from a component. However, `React.Fragment` *will* appear in the shallow rendered element tree, and I'm making use of that characteristic here to represent it as a parent element. See *Further learning* if you'd like to learn more.

3. Install the test renderer:

   npm install --save-dev react-test-renderer

4. In `test/shallowHelpers.js`, import the renderer:

   ```
   import ShallowRenderer from 'react-test-renderer/shallow';
   ```

5. Now, add the following definition for `createShallowRender`, which includes definitions for render and child that will make this test pass. This is equivalent to how we built `domManipulators`, except this time we're using the shallow renderer:

   ```
   export const createShallowRenderer = () => {
     let renderer = new ShallowRenderer();

     return {
       render: component => renderer.render(component),
       child: n => undefined
     };
   };
   ```

6. For the next test, we'll triangulate to get to the real implementation of `child`:

   ```
   it('returns child of rendered element', () => {
     render(
       <TestComponent>
         <p>A</p>
         <p>B</p>
       </TestComponent>
     );
     expect(child(1)).toEqual(<p>B</p>);
   });
   ```

7. Make that pass by modifying `child`, as follows:

```
child: n => childrenOf(renderer.getRenderOutput())[n]
```

8. We're ready for the biggest chunk of work: the `elementsMatching` function. This recursively searches through the tree and returns all elements that match the matcher function. If an element matches, we stop searching and don't look at that element's children, although our implementation doesn't have a specific test to prove that:

```
const type = typeName => element => element.type === typeName;

describe('elementsMatching', () => {
  let render, elementsMatching;

  beforeEach(() => {
    ({ render, elementsMatching } = createShallowRenderer());
  });

  it('finds multiple direct children', () => {
    render(
      <TestComponent>
        <p>A</p>
        <p>B</p>
      </TestComponent>
    );
    expect(elementsMatching(type('p'))).toEqual([
      <p>A</p>,
      <p>B</p>
    ]);
  });
});
```

As I mentioned in the preceding section, *Understanding the importance of spiking,* this design of the `elementsMatching` function that takes a matcher took a lot of trial and error to find the "right" design. If it seems overly complicated right now, take a look at the expectation of this test: I've tried to come up with something that is both readable and flexible enough to be used across multiple types of test.
The `elementsMatching` function can be used with many different matchers, as we'll see when we code the `App` component.

9. To make that pass, first add this new `elementsMatching` function to `test/shallowHelpers.js`:

```
const elementsMatching = (element, matcherFn) =>
  childrenOf(element).filter(matcherFn);
```

10. Tie it to the `createShallowRenderer` function. We pass in the render output as the `element` argument for `elementsMatching`:

```
export const createShallowRenderer = () => {
  let renderer = new ShallowRenderer();

  return {
    render: component => renderer.render(component),
    elementsMatching: matcherFn =>
      elementsMatching(renderer.getRenderOutput(), matcherFn),
    child: n => childrenOf(renderer.getRenderOutput())[n]
  };
};
```

11. The following test brings in the recursive nature of the function:

```
it('finds indirect children', () => {
  render(
    <TestComponent>
      <div>
        <p>A</p>
      </div>
    </TestComponent>
  );
  expect(elementsMatching(type('p'))).toEqual([<p>A</p>]);
});
```

12. Make that pass by modifying `elementsMatching` as follows; this is a bit of a **big bang**. Big bangs are sometimes unavoidable. We use `childrenOf` to find all children of the current element, and use `reduce` to recursively call `elementsMatching` for each of those child elements. Our terminating condition is if `matcherFn` returns `true` when called with the element; in addition, if there are no children for the given element, `reduce` will simply return an empty array:

```
const elementsMatching = (element, matcherFn) => {
  if (matcherFn(element)) {
    return [element];
  }
  return childrenOf(element).reduce(
    (acc, child) => [
      ...acc,
```

```
      ...elementsMatching(child, matcherFn)
    ],
    []
  );
};
```

13. Finally, let's build a useful extension of that. The `elementMatching` function will return the first matching element:

```
describe('elementMatching', () => {
  let render, elementMatching;

  beforeEach(() => {
    ({ render, elementMatching } = createShallowRenderer());
  });

  it('finds first direct child', () => {
    render(
      <TestComponent>
      <p>A</p>
      <p>B</p>
      </TestComponent>
    );
    expect(elementMatching(type('p'))).toEqual(<p>A</p>);
  });
});
```

14. To make that pass, update `createShallowRenderer` with the new function:

```
export const createShallowRenderer = () => {
  let renderer = new ShallowRenderer();

  return {
    render: component => renderer.render(component),
    elementMatching: matcherFn =>
      elementsMatching(renderer.getRenderOutput(), matcherFn)[0],
    elementsMatching: matcherFn =>
      elementsMatching(renderer.getRenderOutput(), matcherFn),
    child: n => childrenOf(renderer.getRenderOutput())[n]
  };
};
```

15. We're *almost* done: to clean up, move across the definition of type into
    `test/shallowHelpers.js`. We aren't going to test this, since it's a straight one-
    liner. The pragmatist in me avoids writing tests for anything this simple:

    ```
    const type = typeName => element => element.type === typeName;
    ```

16. Delete the definition from `test/shallowHelpers.test.js`, and import it
    instead:

    ```
    import {
      createShallowRenderer,
      childrenOf,
      type
    } from './shallowHelpers';
    ```

17. Then, define two more helpers in `test/shallowHelpers.js`:

    ```
    export const id = id => element =>
      element.props && element.props.id === id;
    export const className = className => element =>
      element.props.className === className;
    ```

18. As a final flourish, define a `click` function in `test/shallowHelpers.js`,
    which will pull out the `onClick` prop and invoke it. We'll use this and
    everything else we've built in the next section:

    ```
    export const click = element => element.props.onClick();
    ```

And there we have it: a complete `shallowHelpers` module that we can use to build our
entrypoint component, `App`.

Building a new root component

 The Git tag for this section is `root-component`.

After all that setup, we're now ready to build `App`, the component that ties everything else together. As a reminder, this component will implement our workflow, switching between three screens:

- Initially, it will show the `AppointmentsDayViewLoader`, along with a button
- If the user clicks the button, they will be shown the `CustomerForm`
- Once they've completed that form and submitted the customer to the server, the user will be shown the `AppointmentFormLoader` and can then book an appointment
- Once the appointment has been booked, the user is taken back to viewing the `AppointmentsDayViewLoader`

Let's get started:

1. Create a new file, `test/App.test.js`, with the following setup and the first test:

```
import React from 'react';
import {
  createShallowRenderer,
  type
} from './shallowHelpers';
import { App } from '../src/App';
import { AppointmentsDayViewLoader } from
'../src/AppointmentsDayViewLoader';

describe('App', () => {
  let render, elementMatching;

  beforeEach(() => {
    ({ render, elementMatching } = createShallowRenderer());
  });

  it('initially shows the AppointmentDayViewLoader', () => {
    render(<App />);
    expect(
      elementMatching(type(AppointmentsDayViewLoader))
    ).toBeDefined();
  });
});
```

2. Make that pass by adding the following to a new file, `src/App.js`:

```
import React from 'react';
import ReactDOM from 'react-dom';
import { AppointmentsDayViewLoader } from
```

```
'./AppointmentsDayViewLoader';

export const App = () => (
  <React.Fragment>
    <AppointmentsDayViewLoader />
  </React.Fragment>
);
```

3. For the second test, we'll add a button bar to the top of the page. For this, we'll use the new `child` function, so add that now:

```
import {
  child,
  createShallowRenderer,
  type
} from './shallowHelpers';
```

4. Now add that second test:

```
it('has a button bar as the first child', () => {
  render(<App />);
  expect(child(0).type).toEqual('div');
  expect(child(0).props.className).toEqual('button-bar');
});
```

5. To make that pass, change the `App` component, as follows:

```
<React.Fragment>
  <div className="button-bar" />
  <AppointmentsDayViewLoader />
</React.Fragment>
```

6. Now, we want to display a button on the page that, when clicked, will move to the `CustomerForm`. First, add an import for the `className` matcher:

```
import {
  className,
  child,
  createShallowRenderer,
  type
} from './shallowHelpers';
```

7. Time to add the test. We will look for a specific ID of `addCustomer` because we'll add other buttons in later:

```
it('has a button to initiate add customer and appointment action',
() => {
```

```
render(<App />);
const buttons = childrenOf(
  elementMatching(className('button-bar'))
);
expect(buttons[0].type).toEqual('button');
expect(buttons[0].props.children).toEqual(
  'Add customer and appointment'
);
});
```

8. To make that pass, change the button-bar `div` in the `App` component to the following:

```
<div className="button-bar">
  <button type="button" id="addCustomer">
    Add customer and appointment
  </button>
</div>
```

9. For the next test, we need to check that clicking the button renders the `CustomerForm`. We'll need to add that as a child component. First, import `CustomerForm` into the file:

```
import { CustomerForm } from '../src/CustomerForm';
```

10. Bring in the `click` function:

```
import {
  click,
  className,
  child,
  createShallowRenderer,
  type
} from './shallowHelpers';
```

11. Now add the test. This includes a helper function, `beginAddingCustomerAndAppointment`, that we'll use in all of the remaining tests:

```
const beginAddingCustomerAndAppointment = () => {
  render(<App />);
  click(elementMatching(id('addCustomer')));
};

it('displays the CustomerForm when button is clicked', async () =>
{
  beginAddingCustomerAndAppointment();
```

```
    expect(elementMatching(type(CustomerForm))).toBeDefined();
  });
```

12. Making this pass involves adding state to track that we've clicked the button. Since we know we'll have three different views ultimately, it makes sense to use a variable, `view`, that records which view we're on. Start by importing the two hooks we'll need, and the `CustomerForm` too:

```
import React, { useState, useCallback } from 'react';
import { CustomerForm } from './CustomerForm';
```

13. In the `App` component, define the new view state variable and initialize it to `dayView`, which we'll use to represent the `AppointmentsDayViewLoader`:

```
const [view, setView] = useState('dayView');
```

14. Then, add the new `transitionToAddCustomer` callback, which we'll attach to the button's `onClick` handler:

```
const transitionToAddCustomer = useCallback(
  () => setView('addCustomer'),
  []
);
```

15. Plug that in to the `onClick` prop of the button:

```
<button
  type="button"
  id="addCustomer"
  onClick={transitionToAddCustomer}>
  Add customer and appointment
</button>
```

16. To make the test pass, add the following code to your rendered JSX, just after the button bar. After doing this your tests should be passing. It's important not to jump ahead at this point: we don't need to switch between views just yet. The simplest way to make the test pass is with the following code:

```
return (
  <React.Fragment>
    . . .
    { view === 'addCustomer' ? <CustomerForm /> : null }
  </React.Fragment>
);
```

Strictly speaking, this *isn't* the simplest way to make this pass. We could make this pass by *always* rendering a `CustomerForm`. We should add a test to prove that we initially do *not* show a `CustomerForm`. I'm skipping that step for brevity, but feel free to add it in if you prefer.

17. Next, add the following test to hide the `AppointmentsDayViewLoader` when a customer is being added:

```
it('hides the AppointmentDayViewLoader when button is clicked',
async () => {
  beginAddingCustomerAndAppointment();
  expect(
    elementMatching(type(AppointmentsDayViewLoader))
  ).not.toBeDefined();
});
```

18. Now, all we need to do is suck the `AppointmentsDayViewLoader` into that ternary, in place of the null:

```
{ view === 'addCustomer' ? (
  <CustomerForm />
) : (
  <AppointmentsDayViewLoader />
) }
```

19. Let's hide the button bar, too:

```
it('hides the button bar when CustomerForm is being displayed',
async () => {
  beginAddingCustomerAndAppointment();
  expect(wrapper.find('.button-bar').exists()).not.toBeTruthy();
});
```

20. To solve that one, we need to lift the ternary out of the JSX entirely, as shown in the following code. This is messy, but we'll fix it in the next step:

```
return view === 'addCustomer' ? <CustomerForm /> :
  (<React.Fragment>
    <div className="button-bar">...</div>
    <AppointmentsDayViewLoader />
  </React.Fragment>);
```

21. This is where things start to get interesting. We need to test that `AppointmentsFormLoader` is displayed once the `CustomerForm` is submitted:

```
const saveCustomer = customer =>
  elementMatching(type(CustomerForm)).props.onSave(customer);
```

```
it('displays the AppointmentFormLoader after the CustomerForm is
submitted', async () => {
  beginAddingCustomerAndAppointment();
  saveCustomer();

  expect(
    elementMatching(type(AppointmentFormLoader))
  ).toBeDefined();
});
```

22. Making this pass will involve adding a new value to `view`. Our ternary is no longer fit for purpose, since it can only handle two possible values of `view`. So, before we continue with making this pass, let's refactor that ternary to use a `switch`. Skip the test you just wrote using `it.skip`.

23. Replace the return statement of your component with the following. It's another big bang, unfortunately:

```
switch (view) {
  case 'addCustomer':
    return (
      <CustomerForm />
    );
  default:
    return (
      <React.Fragment>
        <div className="button-bar">
          <button
            type="button"
            id="addCustomer"
            onClick={transitionToAddCustomer}>
            Add customer and appointment
          </button>
        </div>
        <AppointmentsDayViewLoader today={today} />
      </React.Fragment>
    );
}
```

24. Once you've verified that your tests still pass, unskip your latest test by changing `it.skip` back to `it`.

25. Making this test pass will involve setting the `onSave` prop of the `CustomerForm`. Add a new handler for displaying the appointment. We'll hook this up to the `CustomerForm` `onSave` prop. Interestingly, the `CustomerForm` component will invoke our callback with a `customer` object, but we don't need that for this test so we don't need to reference it in our code:

```
const transitionToAddAppointment = useCallback(() =>
  setView('addAppointment'),
[]);
```

26. Modify the `CustomerForm` to take this as a prop:

```
<CustomerForm onSave={transitionToAddAppointment} />
```

27. Hook up the new `addAppointment` view by adding the following case statement into the `switch`:

```
case 'addAppointment':
  return (
    <AppointmentFormLoader />
  );
```

28. Almost there; just two tests left. The following test ensures that we pass the saved customer object to the form:

```
it('passes the customer to the AppointmentForm', async () => {
  const customer = { id: 123 };

  beginAddingCustomerAndAppointment();
  saveCustomer(customer);

  expect(
    elementMatching(type(AppointmentFormLoader)).props
      .customer
  ).toBe(customer);
});
```

29. We'll need to add a state variable for `customer`. Add the following at the top of the `App` component:

```
const [customer, setCustomer] = useState();
```

30. Modify `transitionToAddAppointment` to now take the `onSave` argument we left off before, and save it into the state:

```
const transitionToAddAppointment = useCallback(customer => {
  setCustomer(customer);
  setView('addAppointment');
}, []);
```

31. Then, pass that into `AppointmentFormLoader`, at which point your test should be passing:

```
case 'addAppointment':
  return (
    <AppointmentFormLoader
      customer={customer}
    />
  );
```

32. Write the final test for this component. This one tests that once we've saved an appointment, we go back to showing the appointments day view:

```
const saveAppointment = () =>
  elementMatching(
    type(AppointmentFormLoader)
  ).props.onSave();

it('renders AppointmentDayViewLoader after AppointmentForm is
submitted', async () => {
  beginAddingCustomerAndAppointment();
  saveCustomer();
  saveAppointment();

  expect(
    elementMatching(type(AppointmentsDayViewLoader))
  ).toBeDefined();
});
```

33. Define a new function to set the state back to the day view:

```
const transitionToDayView = useCallback(
  () => setView('dayView'),
  []
);
```

34. Finally, pass this function to `AppointmentsFormLoader` to ensure it's called when the appointment is saved. After this your tests are complete and all should be passing:

```
case 'addAppointment':
  return (
    <AppointmentFormLoader
      customer={customer}
      onSave={transitionToDayView}
    />
  );
```

That was our trickiest component yet, but we're done! Now all that's left is `src/index.js`, which launches this root component. Then you can manually test this to check out your handiwork.

Here's `src/index.js` in its entirety. It's short; that's how it should be, since this is untested code:

```
import 'whatwg-fetch';
import React from 'react';
import ReactDOM from 'react-dom';
import { App } from './app';

ReactDOM.render(
  <App />,
  document.getElementById('root'));
```

If you're using the GitHub code repository for this book, consult the `README.md` file for instructions on running this code against a pre-built server.

Summary

We've covered a huge amount of ground in this chapter. We've stubbed out our own components in order to verify that our loader components correctly instantiate our rendering components. In addition, we've not just learned about shallow rendering, but also built our own set of helpers that aid us in building concise, readable test suites.

One of the major reasons for stubbing and spying on our child components is so that we can avoid running their side effects, such as fetch requests. Spying on them also allows us to easily assert that we set their `props` correctly.

In the next chapter, we'll make our forms more usable by adding validation and status messages.

Further learning

- A Complete Guide to `useEffect`: `https://overreacted.io/a-complete-guide-to-useeffect`
- React fragments: `https://reactjs.org/docs/fragments.html`
- React shallow renderer documentation: `https://reactjs.org/docs/shallow-renderer.html`

Section 2: Building a Single-Page Application

In this section, we'll expand on the work we've done by moving beyond the realms of simple React tasks. We'll build complex components and integrate three libraries: React Router, Redux, and Relay. By the end of the section, you'll have seen how to tackle some of the most challenging aspects of the test-driven approach.

This section includes the following chapters:

5
Humanizing Forms

It's virtually impossible to build a modern web application without having some kind of form validation. Normally with React, you'll reach for a ready-made validation library that does this for you. You might by now realize that this isn't the choice I'll make, at least not for this book.

Writing your own validation logic from scratch will help you understand what those other validation libraries are doing, and it will help you uncover an important architectural principle when dealing with frameworks like React: moving business logic out of framework-controlled components as soon as possible.

This chapter covers the following topics:

- Performing client-side validation
- Handling server errors
- Indicating that the form has been submitted

Performing client-side validation

The Git tag for this section is client-side-validation.

As our users fill out our forms, we want to alert them to any issues as soon as possible. We'll alert the user to any validation issues once the focus is no longer on the text field, using the blur event.

We will represent validation errors as strings within a `validationErrors` object that's stored as component state. We can use this object to help us validate each field within the form. Each field has a key in the object. An undefined value (or absence of a value) represents no validation error, and a string value represents an error. Here's an example:

```
{
  validationErrors: {
    firstName: 'First name is required',
    lastName: undefined,
    phoneNumber: 'Phone number must contain only numbers, spaces, and any
of the following: + - ( ) .'
  }
}
```

Validation errors displayed to the user

Let's get started by showing validation errors for the first name field:

1. We'll start by adding a new `blur` helper that our tests will invoke to trigger validation. In `test/domManipulators.js`, add the following new property to the return object of `createContainer`:

   ```
   blur: simulateEvent('blur')
   ```

2. In `test/CustomerForm.test.js`, modify the variables within the top-level `describe` and the `beforeEach` block to pull in the new `blur` function:

   ```
   let render,
     ...,
     blur;
   ```

```
beforeEach(() => {
  ({
    render,
    ...,
    blur
  } = createContainer());
  ...
});
```

3. Add the following new test at the bottom of the file. For this to run, you may need to move the `firstNameField` function to the top of the outer describe block, depending on where you originally placed it. Mine was inside the `firstNameField` describe block, so I needed to pull it up to use it here:

```
it('displays error after blur when first name field is blank', ()
=> {
  render(<CustomerForm />);

  blur(
    field('customer', 'firstName'),
    withEvent('firstName', ' ')
  );
  expect(element('.error')).not.toBeNull();
  expect(element('.error').textContent).toMatch(
    'First name is required'
  );
});
```

This test is actually related to `firstNameField`, which already has its own describe block nearer the top of the file. In this case, however, I think a separate validation describe block is a more natural grouping for this test and for the subsequent tests we'll write.

4. To make this pass, start by adding the following inline function definition at the top of `src/CustomerForm.js`, just below the imports but above the `CustomerForm` component definition:

```
const required = value =>
  !value || value.trim() === ''
    ? 'First name is required'
    : undefined;
```

5. Within `CustomerForm`, define a `validationErrors` state variable, initially set to an empty object:

```
const [validationErrors, setValidationErrors] = useState({});
```

6. Create a handler function inside `CustomerForm` that can be used when the user switches focus away from the first name field. It runs the required validation we defined in the first step, and then saves the response in the `errors` state object:

```
const handleBlur = ({ target }) => {
  const result = required(target.value);
  setValidationErrors({
    ...validationErrors,
    firstName: result
  });
};
```

7. Create a method to render an error if one exists. To aid with readability, I've pulled out a helper function, `hasFirstNameError`:

```
const hasFirstNameError = () =>
  validationErrors.firstName !== undefined;

const renderFirstNameError = () => {
  if (hasFirstNameError()) {
    return (
      <span className="error">
        {validationErrors.firstName}
      </span>
    );
  }
};
```

8. All that's left is to modify our JSX. Use the snippet below to set the `onBlur` handler on the existing `input` field for `firstName` and to render the error text just after it. After this change, your test should be passing:

```
<input
  type="text"
  name="firstName"
  id="firstName"
  value={firstName}
  onChange={handleChange}
  onBlur={handleBlur}
/>
{renderFirstNameError()}
```

For the next test, we have a few options for what to implement. Here are some ideas:

- Add required validation to the last name and phone number fields
- Add further validations, such as min or max length, for the first name field
- Prohibit form submission when there are validation errors

I'm going to go with the first option, of supporting more fields.

 Often, we find ourselves with many choices for which test to write next. It can be hard to choose between them. In this case, I've chosen multiple fields because I prefer to cover *breadth* of feature before *depth*. In this case, I'd rather see the existing validation functionality extend to work for the entire form than continue on the first name field, or switch to thinking about submission logic.

Since we're on green, we can refactor our existing code *before* we write the next test. The code we've written is very much about the first name field: we pull out that specific value from `validationErrors`, and we even have functions, `hasFirstNameError` and `renderFirstNameError`, that are named after the first name field. These can be refactored so that the field name is passed through as a parameter.

This will be an exercise in systematic refactoring: breaking the refactoring down into small steps, and, after each step, we're aiming for our tests to still be green:

1. Start with the outermost point where we mention first name. That's in our JSX, where we call `renderFirstNameError`. We can add a new parameter value into this call, and then refactor the function to use it. JavaScript being as awesome as it is, our code still happily works even if our function isn't expecting a parameter. Add the new parameter value:

   ```
   {renderFirstNameError('firstName')}
   ```

2. Rewrite the `renderFirstNameError` function as follows, using the new `fieldName` parameter:

   ```
   const renderFirstNameError = fieldName => {
     if (hasFirstNameError(fieldName)) {
       return (
         <span className="error">
           {validationErrors[fieldName]}
         </span>
       );
     }
   };
   ```

Even though this function now works for more than just the first name, we won't rename it just yet. Renaming is the last step of our refactoring. I always like to leave naming (or renaming) as late as possible, so I can wait to see what the function ends up doing before I spend time thinking of a name.

3. Add the `fieldName` parameter to `hasFirstNameError` and modify the function body to use the parameter in place of the `firstName` error property:

```
const hasFirstNameError = fieldName =>
  validationErrors[fieldName] !== undefined;
```

Remember to run your tests afterward and ensure they're still passing.

4. At this stage, you're ready to rename the functions, so go ahead and do that by removing "FirstName" from both functions: `renderFirstNameError` becomes `renderError`, and `hasFirstName Error` becomes `hasError`.

Your IDE may have renaming support built in. If it does, you should use it. It lessens the risk of human error.

5. Let's tackle `handleBlur`. This is slightly more complicated because the concept of validating `firstName` is baked in to the method. We can use `target.name`, which is the input field name, to key into a map that then tells us which validator to perform for each field:

```
const handleBlur = ({ target }) => {
  const validators = {
    firstName: required
  };
  const result = validators[target.name](target.value);
  setValidationErrors({
    ...validationErrors,
    [target.name]: result
  });
};
```

You can see the first half of the function (the definition of validators) is now static data that defines how the validation should happen for firstName. This can be extended with more fields. The second half is generic and will work for any input field that's passed in, so long as a validator exists for that field.

6. The required validator is hardcoded with the first name description. Let's pull out the entire message as a variable. We can create a higher-order function that returns a validation function that uses this message. Modify required to look as shown:

```
const required = description => value =>
  !value || value.trim() === '' ? description : undefined;
```

7. Finally, update the validator to call this new required function:

```
const validators = {
  firstName: required('First name is required')
};
```

At this point, your tests should be passing.

We didn't need a test to triangulate this functionality. There *is* a conditional in the functionality: if there's an error then render some text; otherwise, don't render anything. That would indeed suggest we need to triangulate. However, if you try to pass the test without the if statement—always rendering an error—you'll find one of our previous tests begins to fail. So we have some kind of safety net already, by virtue of our existing tests.

This should make you think that the existing test is serving a dual purpose, and could be refactored to make that clear. This is left as an exercise for you!

8. Let's move on to adding a required field test for the last name field. Add the following test into the validation describe block in test/CustomerForm.test.js:

```
it('displays error after blur when last name field is blank', () =>
{
  act(() => {
    render(<CustomerForm />);

    blur(
      field('customer', 'lastName'),
      withEvent('lastName', ' ')
```

```
    );
  });

  expect(element('.error')).not.toBeNull();
  expect(element('.error').textContent).toMatch(
    'Last name is required'
  );
});
```

9. To make that pass, add a new validator for the `lastName` field:

```
const validators = {
  firstName: required('First name is required'),
  lastName: required('Last name is required')
};
```

10. Add the `onBlur` handler to the input field and render the last name errors. Your test should be passing after this change:

```
<label htmlFor="lastName">Last name</label>
<input
  type="text"
  name="lastName"
  id="lastName"
  value={lastName}
  onChange={handleChange}
  onBlur={handleBlur}
/>
{renderError('lastName')}
```

11. Before we move on to the next test, let's stop to think about our tests. Can we dry them up? We've just written two tests that are *exactly* the same except for the field they mention. We can extract out the commonality into a method that uses parameters, just as we've done with our production code.

   Here's a function that generates a test for us. Given a field with a name and a value, it asserts that an error is displayed when the field loses focus, and that the error matches the description given. This can be used not just for required field validation, but for *any* field validation.

   Add this to the bottom of your test file, inside the validation describe block:

```
const itInvalidatesFieldWithValue = (
  fieldName,
  value,
  description
```

```
) => {
  it(`displays error after blur when ${fieldName} field is
'${value}'`, () => {
    render(<CustomerForm />);

    blur(
      field('customer', fieldName),
      withEvent(fieldName, value)
    );

    expect(element('.error')).not.toBeNull();
    expect(element('.error').textContent).toMatch(
      description
    );
  });
}
```

12. Rewrite the existing two tests to use that function, as follows. You'll need to place these *after* the arrow function definition. Make sure you run tests and verify that this still works, and you still have the same number of tests:

```
itInvalidatesFieldWithValue(
  'firstName',
  ' ',
  'First name is required'
);
itInvalidatesFieldWithValue(
  'lastName',
  ' ',
  'Last name is required'
);
```

This testing technique of build test generator functions is not universally liked. If you think it's horrendous, then feel free to not do this. Conversely, if you love it, then feel free to refactor the existing tests in a similar fashion.

There is a downside to this approach: you won't be able to use `it.only` or `it.skip` on individual tests.

13. Add the next test, which is for the last name field. It's now just one line, as follows:

```
itInvalidatesFieldWithValue(
  'phoneNumber',
  ' ',
  'Phone number is required'
);
```

14. Make this pass by following the preceding steps 1 and 2 for the `lastName` field, but this time for the `phoneNumber` field.

Since we're working with the phone number field validation, let's add another validation there. We want to ensure the phone number only contains numbers and a few special characters: brackets, dashes, spaces, and pluses.

Let's work to add that second validation:

1. Add this new test:

```
itInvalidatesFieldWithValue(
  'phoneNumber',
  'invalid',
  'Only numbers, spaces and these symbols are allowed: ( ) + -'
);
```

2. We'll solve this by introducing two new validators. So far, we've just used one: the `required` validator. Now we'll introduce a `match` validator that can perform the phone number matching we need, and also a `list` validator that composes validations.

   Let's start with `match`. Add the following definition at the top of `src/CustomerForm.js`. This expects a regular expression, `re`, which can then be matched against:

```
const match = (re, description) => value =>
  !value.match(re) ? description : undefined;
```

Regular expressions are a flexible mechanism for matching string formats. If you're uncomfortable with using them, check out the *Further learning* section at the end of the chapter.

3. Now let's go for the `list` function. This is quite a dense piece of code that returns a short-circuiting validator. It runs each validator that it's given until it finds one that returns a string, and then returns that string. Add this just below the definition for `match`:

```
const list = (...validators) => value =>
  validators.reduce(
    (result, validator) => result || validator(value),
    undefined
  );
```

4. Time to use these new validations. Replace the existing `phoneNumber` validation in the `handleBlur` function with the following one:

```
validations = {
  ...
  phoneNumber: list(
    required('Phone number is required'),
    match(
      /^[0-9+()\- ]*$/,
      'Only numbers, spaces and these symbols are allowed: ( ) + -'
    )
  )
};
```

5. Your test should now be passing. However, it doesn't quite prove that we have the right regular expression: we could pass `/^$/` as the first parameter to `match`, meaning we can only pass if the string is empty, and the test would pass. We need a kind of "inverse" test to check that any combination of characters works. This is a type of triangulation. You can add this in; it should already pass if you used the preceding regular expression:

```
it('accepts standard phone number characters when validating', ()
=> {
  render(<CustomerForm />);

  blur(
    element("[name='phoneNumber']"),
    withEvent('phoneNumber', '0123456789+()- ')
  );
  expect(element('.error')).toBeNull();
});
```

Submitting the form

 The Git tag for this section is `submitting-with-validations`.

What should happen when we submit the form? Well, for a start, in this application we'll let the user hit the submit button at any time—we won't disable it. Instead, if they happen to hit it while the form isn't complete, the submission should be canceled and all fields should display their validation errors at once.

We can do this with two tests: one to check that the form isn't submitted while there are errors, and the second to check that all fields are showing errors.

Before we do that, we'll need to update our existing tests that submit the form, as they all assume that the form has been filled in correctly. We need to ensure that we pass valid customer data in first that can be overridden in each test.

Let's get to work on the `CustomerForm` test suite:

1. At the top of `test/CustomerForm.test.js`, define the following object:

   ```
   const validCustomer = {
     firstName: 'first',
     lastName: 'last',
     phoneNumber: '123456789'
   };
   ```

2. Starting at the top, modify each test that simulates a submit event. Each should be mounted with this new `validCustomer` object:

   ```
   render(<CustomerForm {...validCustomer} />);
   ```

3. If the test has its own props, then make sure to pass in `validCustomer` *before* any overriding props, for example:

   ```
   render(
     <CustomerForm
       {...validCustomer}
       {...{ [fieldName]: 'value' }}
     />
   );
   ```

4. Check your tests are still passing.

5. Add a new test for submitting the form. This can go alongside the other submit tests, rather than in the validation block:

```
it('does not submit the form when there are validation errors',
async () => {
  render(<CustomerForm />);

  await submit(form('customer'));
  expect(window.fetch).not.toHaveBeenCalled();
});
```

6. To make this pass, first define the following `validateMany` function inside the `CustomerForm` component. Its job is to validate many fields at once. It takes a single parameter, `fields`, which is an object of the field values we care about. That's actually a subset of the component state, and we'll create it during the next step:

```
const validateMany = fields =>
  Object.entries(fields).reduce(
    (result, [name, value]) => ({
      ...result,
      [name]: validators[name](value)
    }),
    {}
  );
```

7. Since this references the `validators` variable, pull that constant up out of the `handleBlur` function and into the `App` component scope so that it's visible to `validateMany`.

8. We'll need a function to return `true` if we had any errors at all, and `false` otherwise. That's `anyErrors`; add that now, as shown:

```
const anyErrors = errors =>
  Object.values(errors).some(error => error !== undefined);
```

9. Now we can use `validateMany` and `anyErrors` in our `handleSubmit` function, as shown. Your test should be passing after adding this code:

```
const handleSubmit = async e {
  e.preventDefault();
  const validationResult = validateMany(customer);
  if (!anyErrors(validationResult)) {

    ...
  }
}
```

10. Let's move on to the next test; we want to check that any errors appear on screen:

```
it('renders validation errors after submission fails', async () =>
{
  render(<CustomerForm />);
  await submit(form('customer'));
  expect(window.fetch).not.toHaveBeenCalled();
  expect(element('.error')).not.toBeNull();
});
```

11. This one is easy to pass; we simply need to call `setValidationErrors` with `validationResult` when `anyErrors` returns false:

```
if (!anyErrors(validationResult)) {
  ...
} else {
  setValidationErrors(validationResult);
}
```

Extracting non-React functionality into a new module

 The Git tag for this section is `out-of-react`.

One of the major rules of good architectural design is that you get out of framework land as soon as possible. You want to be dealing with plain old JavaScript objects as often as possible. Any kind of "business logic" should be extracted out as soon as possible.

The same rule applies here. We want to get out of "React land" as often as we can. There are a few different reasons for that. First, testing components is harder than testing plain objects. Second, the framework changes at breakneck speed, but JavaScript itself doesn't. Keeping our code bases up to date with the latest React trends is a large-scale task *if* our code base is first and foremost a React code base. If we keep React at bay, our lives will be simpler in the longer term. So, we always prefer plain JavaScript when it's an option.

Our validation code is a great example of this. We have a number of functions that do not care about React at all:

- The validators: `required`, `match`, and `list`
- `hasError` and `anyErrors`
- `validateMany`
- Some of the code in `handleBlur`, which is like a single-entry equivalent of `validateMany`

Let's pull all of these out into their own namespace called `formValidation`:

1. Create a new file called `src/formValidation.js`.
2. Move across the function definitions for `required`, `match`, and `list` from the top of `CustomerForm`. Make sure to delete the old definitions!
3. Add the word `export` to the front of each definition in the new module.
4. Add the following import to the top of `CustomerForm`, and then check that your tests are still passing:

   ```
   import { required, match, list } from './formValidation';
   ```

5. In `src/CustomerForm.js`, change `renderError` to pass in the errors from state into `hasError`:

   ```
   const renderError = fieldName => {
     if (hasError(validationErrors, fieldName)) {
       return <span className="error">
         {validationErrors[fieldName]}
       </span>;
     }
   }
   ```

6. Update `hasError` to include the new `validationErrors` argument, and use that rather than state:

   ```
   const hasError = (validationErrors, fieldName) =>
     validationErrors[fieldName] !== undefined;
   ```

7. Update `validateMany` to pass in the list of validators as its first argument, rather than using component state:

   ```
   const validateMany = (validators, fields) =>
     Object.entries(fields).reduce(
       (result, [name, value]) => ({
         ...result,
   ```

```
        [name]: validators[name](value)
    }),
    {}
);
```

8. Update `handleBlur` to use `validateMany`, as follows:

```
const handleBlur = ({ target }) => {
  const result = validateMany(validators, {
    [target.name] : target.value
  });
  setValidationErrors({ ...validationErrors, ...result});
}
```

9. Update `handleSubmit` to pass validators to `validateMany`:

```
const validationResult = validateMany(validators, customer);
```

10. Move across `hasError`, `validateMany`, and `anyErrors` into `src/formValidation.js`, ensuring you delete the functions from the `CustomerForm` component.

11. Add the word `export` in front of each of these definitions.

12. Update the import to pull in these functions:

```
import {
  required,
  match,
  list,
  hasError,
  validateMany,
  anyErrors
} from './formValidation';
```

Although this is enough to extract the code out of React-land, we've only just made a start. There is plenty of room for improvement on this API. There are a couple of different approaches that you could take here. The exercises for this chapter have some suggestions of how to do that.

You may be thinking, do these functions now need tests? And do I need to update the tests in `CustomerForm`?

In this case, I would probably write a few tests for `formValidation`, just to make it clear how each of the functions should be used. This isn't test-driving since you already have the code, but you can still mimic the experience by writing tests as you would normally.

When extracting functionality from components like this, it often makes sense to update the original components to simplify and perhaps move across tests. In this particular instance, I wouldn't bother. The tests are high-level enough that they make sense regardless of how the code is organized internally.

Handling server errors

The Git tag for this section is `handle-server-errors`.

The `/customers` endpoint may return a `422 Unprocessable Entity` error if the customer data failed validation. That could happen if, for example, the phone number already exists within the system. If this happens, we want to withhold calling the `onSave` callback and instead display the errors to the user and give them the chance to correct them.

The body of the response will contain error data very similar to the data we've built for the validation framework. Here's an example of the JSON that would be received:

```
{
  "errors": {
    "phoneNumber": "Phone number already exists in the system"
  }
}
```

We'll update our code to display these errors in the same way our client errors appeared. Since we already handle errors for `CustomerForm`, we'll need to adjust our tests in addition to the existing `CustomerForm` code.

Our code to date has made use of the `ok` property returned from fetch. This property returns true if the HTTP status code is 200, and false otherwise. Now we need to be more specific. For a status code of 422, we want to display new errors, and for anything else (such as a 500 error) we want to fall back to the existing behavior.

Let's add support for those additional status codes:

1. Before we write a new test, update the `fetchResponseError` method in `test/spyHelpers.js`, as shown:

```
const fetchResponseError = (status = 500, body = {}) =>
  Promise.resolve({
    ok: false,
    status,
    json: () => Promise.resolve(body)
  });
```

If you'd prefer to give names to your error codes, please go ahead and do that. I've omitted them for brevity.

2. Write a test for 422 errors in `test/CustomerForm.test.js`. I've placed this toward the top of the file, next to the other tests that manipulate the HTTP response:

```
it('renders field validation errors from server', async () => {
  const errors = {
    phoneNumber: 'Phone number already exists in the system'
  };
  window.fetch.mockReturnValue(
    fetchResponseError(422, { errors })
  );
  render(<CustomerForm {...validCustomer} />);
  await submit(form('customer'));
  expect(element('.error').textContent).toMatch(
    errors.phoneNumber
  );
});
```

3. To make that pass, add a new branch to the nested conditional statement in `handleSubmit`, which handles the response of the fetch request:

```
if (result.ok) {
  setError(false);
  const customerWithId = await result.json();
```

```
    onSave(customerWithId);
  } else if (result.status === 422) {
    const response = await result.json();
    setValidationErrors(response.errors);
  } else {
    setError(true);
  }
```

Your tests should now be passing.

Indicating that the form has been submitted

It'd be great if we could indicate to the user that their form data is being sent to our application servers. The GitHub repository for this book contains a spinner graphic and some **Cascading Style Sheets (CSS)** that we can use. All that our React component needs to do is display span with a class name of submittingIndicator.

Before we write out the tests, let's look at how the production code will work. We will introduce a new submitting boolean state variable that is used to toggle between states. It will be toggled to true just before we perform the fetch request, and toggled to false once the request completes. Here's how we'll modify handleSubmit:

```
const handleSubmit = async e => {
  e.preventDefault();
  const validationResult = validateMany(validators, customer);
  if (!anyErrors(validationResult)) {
    setSubmitting(true);
    const result = await window.fetch(...);
    setSubmitting(false);
    ...
  } else {
    setValidationErrors(validationResult);
  }
};
```

If submitting is set to true then we render the spinner graphic. Otherwise, we render nothing.

Let's write a few tests for this new feature.

The first test avoids the `submit` helper we've been using up until now. It's defined in terms of the `submitAndWait` function. As a reminder, here's what that looks like:

```
const simulateEventAndWait = eventName => async (
  element,
  eventData
) =>
  await act(async () =>
    ReactTestUtils.Simulate[eventName](element, eventData)
  );
```

The `submit` helper uses the async form of the `act` function to ensure that all promises (such as fetch requests) have run by the time the call completes. That's usually fine when we want to test anything once the submit handler has completed. But it's not fine when we have state such as `submitting` which is toggled from `false` to `true` and then back to `false` all within the handler. There will be no observable difference to the value of `submitting` once the handler has run fully.

What the test should do instead is use the *synchronous* form of `act`, which will return *before* the task queue completes, in other words, before the `fetch` call returns any results.

However, we still need to include the async `act` form *somewhere* in our test. React knows the submit handler returns a promise and it expects us to wait for its execution via a call to async `act`. We need to do that after we've checked the toggle value of `submitting`, not before.

Let's build that test now:

1. Add `ReactTestUtils` and `act` as imports into `test/CustomerForm.test.js`:

   ```
   import ReactTestUtils, { act } from 'react-dom/test-utils';
   ```

2. Create a new nested describe block at the bottom of the `CustomerForm` describe block, just below the existing form submission tests. This submits the call itself within a synchronous `act`, as explained previously. We then wrap the expectation in an async `act` call that suppresses any warnings or errors from React:

   ```
   it('displays indicator when form is submitting', async () => {
     render(<CustomerForm {...validCustomer} />);
     act(() => {
       ReactTestUtils.Simulate.submit(form('customer'));
     });
     await act(async() => {
       expect(element('span.submittingIndicator')).not.toBeNull();
   ```

```
  });
});
```

3. To make this pass, we just need to show that `span` within the JSX. Place that just after the `submit` button, as follows:

```
return (
  <form id="customer" onSubmit={handleSubmit}>
    ...
    <input type="submit" value="Add" />
    <span className="submittingIndicator" />
  </form>
);
```

4. Now we need to triangulate, to ensure the indicator only shows when the form has been submitted and not before:

```
it('initially does not display the submitting indicator', () => {
  render(<CustomerForm {...validCustomer} />);
  expect(element('.submittingIndicator')).toBeNull();
});
```

5. We can make this pass by using a flag called `submitting`. It should be set to `false` when the indicator is disabled, and `true` when it's enabled. Add the following state variable to the top of the `CustomerForm` component:

```
const [submitting, setSubmitting] = useState(false);
```

6. Change the submitting indicator span to read as follows:

```
{ submitting ? <span className="submittingIndicator" /> : null }
```

7. The new test will now be passing, but the original test will be failing. We had to switch `submittingIndicator` to `true` just before we call `fetch`. In `handleSubmit`, add this line just above the call to `fetch`. After adding this code, your test should be passing:

```
if (!anyErrors(validationResult)) {
  setSubmitting(true);
  const result = await window.fetch(/* ... */);
  ...
}
```

8. Add this final test, which checks that the indicator disappears once the response has been received. This test is very similar to our first test for the submitting indicator:

```
it('hides indicator when form has submitted', async () => {
  render(<CustomerForm {...validCustomer} />);
  await submit(form('customer'));
  expect(element('.submittingIndicator')).toBeNull();
});
```

9. This time, we need to add in a setSubmitting call *after* the fetch.

```
if (!anyErrors(validationResult)) {
  setSubmitting(true);
  const result = await window.fetch(/* ... */);
  setSubmitting(false);
  ...
}
```

That's everything; your tests should all be passing.

Refactoring long methods

After this, our handleSubmit function is a huge mess. I have counted 23 lines in my method; in the test-driven world, that is *very* long. Anything over five lines should be refactored (excluding our render function, which, for some reason, is generally accepted as long by default).

Refactoring handleSubmit into smaller methods is an exercise left for you; see the *Exercises* section. But here are some hints for how you can go about that systematically:

- Extract blocks into methods; in this case, that means the contents of if statements. For example, if there are no validation errors, you could call out to a performSubmit method, which actually does the submission.
- Look for temporal coupling and see if there are other ways to format that code. In this case, we have the submitting state variable that is set to true before the fetch call, and then false after. This could be done differently.

Summary

This chapter has shown you some techniques for making your forms more humane. We show validation errors at an appropriate moment: when fields lose focus and when forms are submitted. We display a loading indicator to show the user that data is in the process of being saved.

We've also seen how to pull code out of our React components to make them more easily testable and to protect them from the fast-changing React landscape. That being said, we didn't actually add those tests to our non-React code: that's left as an exercise!

In the next chapter, we'll add a new use case to our system, allowing users to create appointments for existing customers by using a snazzy search interface.

Exercises

 The Git tag for this section is `chapter-5-exercises`.

- Add a feature to clear any validation errors when the user corrects them. Use the `onChange` handler for this rather than `onBlur`, since we want to let the user know as soon as they've corrected the error.
- Add a feature that disables the **Submit** button once the form has been submitted.
- Write tests for each of the functions within the `formValidation` module.
- The `handleSubmit` function is long. Extract a `doSave` function that pulls out the main body of the `if` statement.

Further learning

- Spread operator: `https://developer.mozilla.org/en-US/docs/Web/JavaScript/Reference/Operators/Spread_syntax`
- Guide to regular expressions: `https://developer.mozilla.org/en-US/docs/Web/JavaScript/Guide/Regular_Expressions`
- JSX spread attributes: `https://reactjs.org/docs/jsx-in-depth.html#spread-attributes`
- Using reduce effectively: `https://developer.mozilla.org/en-US/docs/Web/JavaScript/Reference/Global_Objects/Array/reduce`

6
Filtering and Searching Data

In previous chapters, we built up a single workflow. Application users can add new customers and then add an appointment for that customer. In this chapter, we'll expand on that by allowing them to choose an existing customer before adding an appointment.

The system that we're building has thousands of customers, so a simple dropdown won't cut it. Instead, we'll build a new component, `CustomerSearch`, which will allow our users to page through a dataset.

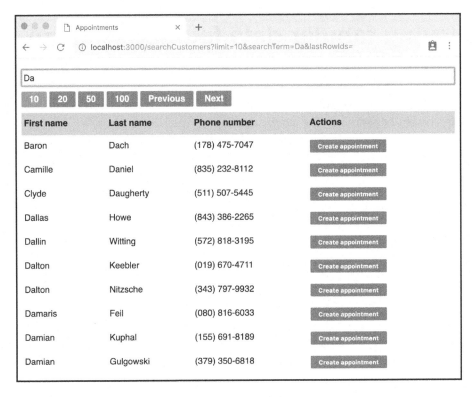

The new CustomerSearch component

The server API we'll be working against supports a basic form of paging data that will allow us to build a search facility which can page back and forth between pages without having to load the entire dataset up front.

As we go through this process, we'll simulate the unwanted but common behavior of *making a design mistake*. We will then fix that mistake by reworking our design. **Test-driven development (TDD)** really helps us when we trip up like this because it removes the fear of changing code. We'll use our tests to change how our implementation works without needing to run a manual test.

In this chapter, you'll learn about the following:

- Displaying tabular data fetched from an endpoint
- Paging through a large data set
- Filtering data
- Adding table row action

Displaying tabular data fetched from an endpoint

The Git tag for this section is `search-table`. It contains new code that wasn't covered in the previous chapter, including a new `CustomerSearch` component. You should either move to this tag now or merge the changes into your own branch.

For more detailed instructions, see the *To get the most out of this book* section in the `Preface`.

Our server responds to `GET` requests to the `/customers` endpoint. There are a whole bunch of parameters, such as `after` and `searchTerm`, which can be passed to it and determine the customer records it should return. We'll cover these parameters later on in the chapter. The response is an array of customers:

```
[{ id: 123, firstName: 'Ashley'}, ... ]
```

At its most basic level, sending a request to `/customers` with no parameters will return the first 10 of our customers, in alphabetical order by first name.

This gives us a good place to start. When the component mounts, we'll perform this basic search and display the results in a table:

1. Start with the following test in `test/CustomerSearch.test.js`:

```
it('renders a table with four headings', async () => {
  await renderAndWait(<CustomerSearch />);
  const headings = elements('table th');
  expect(headings.map(h => h.textContent)).toEqual([
    'First name', 'Last name', 'Phone number', 'Actions'
  ]);
});
```

2. That test should be simple to pass with the following definition for `CustomerSearch` in `src/CustomerSearch.js`:

```
export const CustomerSearch = () => {
  return (
    <table>
      <thead>
        <tr>
          <th>First name</th>
          <th>Last name</th>
          <th>Phone number</th>
          <th>Actions</th>
        </tr>
      </thead>
    </table>
  );
};
```

3. In order to display data, the component will need to make a GET request. Write out this next test, which specifies that behavior:

```
it('fetches all customer data when component mounts', async () => {
  await renderAndWait(<CustomerSearch />);
  expect(window.fetch).toHaveBeenCalledWith('/customers', {
    method: 'GET',
    credentials: 'same-origin',
    headers: { 'Content-Type': 'application/json' }
  });
});
```

4. To make this pass, first import `useEffect` into `src/CustomerSearch.js`:

```
import React, { useEffect } from 'react';
```

5. Then add a `useEffect` hook into the component that performs the search. We need to use the same `useEffect` ceremony that we've seen before, using an inline function to ensure we don't return a value to `useEffect`, and passing an empty array to ensure the effect only runs when the component is first mounted:

```
useEffect(() => {
  const fetchData = () =>
    window.fetch('/customers', {
      method: 'GET',
      credentials: 'same-origin',
      headers: { 'Content-Type': 'application/json' }
    });

  fetchData();
}, []);
```

6. Add the following as the next test, which verifies that the component displays all the customer data for a single customer row. Add the definition of `oneCustomer` at the top of the file (it can even be outside of the `describe` block). Then add the test at the bottom of the describe block:

```
const oneCustomer = [
  { id: 1, firstName: 'A', lastName: 'B', phoneNumber: '1' },
];

it('renders all customer data in a table row', async () => {
  window.fetch.mockReturnValue(fetchResponseOk(oneCustomer));
  await renderAndWait(<CustomerSearch />);
  const rows = elements('table tbody td');
  expect(columns[0].textContent).toEqual('A');
  expect(columns[1].textContent).toEqual('B');
  expect(columns[2].textContent).toEqual('1');
});
```

7. To make this pass, we'll need to use component state to pass data back from the `useEffect` hook into the next render cycle. Import `useState` now, before we define our new state variable in the next step:

```
import React, { useEffect, useState } from 'react';
```

8. Create a new state variable, `customers`, which has an initial value of the empty array (`[]`):

```
const [customers, setCustomers] = useState([]);
```

9. Save the results of the search into `customers` by modifying the definition of `useEffect`, as shown here. Don't forget the `async` keyword in front of the function name:

```
const fetchData = async () => {
  const result = await window.fetch(...);
  setCustomers(await result.json());
};
```

10. Define the following component to display a single row of customer information. The final column is left blank because it doesn't hold customer information. Instead, it will hold action buttons that perform various operations on the specific customer record. We'll use a separate test later on to fill out that functionality:

```
const CustomerRow = ({ customer }) => (
  <tr>
    <td>{customer.firstName}</td>
    <td>{customer.lastName}</td>
    <td>{customer.phoneNumber}</td>
    <td />
  </tr>
);
```

11. All that's left is to make use of this new component in `render`. Add the following `tbody`, which renders `CustomerRow` for the first customer, if it exists. After adding this code, your test should now be passing:

```
return (
  <table>
    <thead>
      ...
    </thead>
    <tbody>
      {customers[0] ? (
        <CustomerRow customer={customers[0]} />
      ) : null}
    </tbody>
  </table>
);
```

12. For the final test in this section, let's add a test to show that this works for multiple customers. The definition of `twoCustomers` can be placed at the top of the file, next to `oneCustomer`:

```
const twoCustomers = [
  { id: 1, firstName: 'A', lastName: 'B', phoneNumber: '1' },
  { id: 2, firstName: 'C', lastName: 'D', phoneNumber: '2' }];

it('renders multiple customer rows', async () => {
  window.fetch.mockReturnValue(fetchResponseOk(twoCustomers));
  await renderAndWait(<CustomerSearch />);
  const rows = elements('table tbody tr');
  expect(rows[1].childNodes[0].textContent).toEqual('C');
});
```

13. Making this pass is a one-liner; change the JSX to map over each customer, instead of pulling out just the first customer:

```
<tbody>
  {customers.map(customer => (
    <CustomerRow customer={customer} key={customer.id} />
  ))}
</tbody>
```

14. This gives us a great base to build on for the remaining functionality we'll build in this chapter.

Paging through a large data set

The Git tag for this section is `paging`.

Our endpoint, by default, returns at most 10 records. To get more than that, we can page through the result set by using the `after` parameter, which takes a customer ID. The server will skip through results until it finds that ID and returns the one after it.

Remember that customers are in alphabetical order by first name, so their IDs most likely won't be in order. But we can still use `after` because searches should be mostly stable between calls.

We'll add **Next** and **Previous** buttons that will help us move between search results. Clicking **Next** will take the ID of the last customer record currently shown on the page, and send it as the `after` parameter to the next search request.

To support **Previous**, we'll need to maintain a stack of `after` IDs that we can pop each time the user clicks **Previous**.

Adding a next page button

Let's start with the **Next** button, which the user can click to bring them to the next page of results:

1. Write the following test, which will let us get a **Next** button onto the page:

```
it('has a next button', async () => {
  await renderAndWait(<CustomerSearch />);
  expect(element('button#next-page')).not.toBeNull();
});
```

2. Create a `SearchButtons` component which renders the **Next** button in a `button-bar` div, just as we did in `App`. I've chosen to extract this into its own component because we'll be expanding on it soon, when we add a **Previous** button:

```
const SearchButtons = () => (
  <div className="button-bar">
    <button role="button" id="next-page">
      Next
    </button>
  </div>
);
```

3. Use that within `render`. We'll need to wrap the existing table in a `React.Fragment`, and then call the new function just above the table:

```
return (
  <React.Fragment>
    <SearchButtons />
    <table>
      ...
    </table>
  </React.Fragment>
);
```

4. Before we get on to writing the test, we need to create ourselves a new helper. We'll call this new helper `clickAndWait`, and it will be exactly like our `submitAndWait` function in the sense that it's a `ReactTestUtil.Simulate` call wrapped in an async `act`. We'll need this, since clicking the **Next** button will cause an asynchronous fetch request to occur, pulling in the next page of data from the server. In `test/domManipulators.js`, add the following function to the object returned from `createContainer`.

```
clickAndWait: simulateEventAndWait('click'),
```

5. Back in `test/CustomerSearch.test.js`, add `clickAndWait` to the functions assigned from the `createContainer` call.

```
let renderAndWait,
  container,
  element,
  elements,
  clickAndWait;

beforeEach(() => {
  ({
    renderAndWait,
    container,
    element,
    elements,
    clickAndWait
  } = createContainer());
  ...
});
```

6. Write out the following test, which checks that we make a new GET request with the appropriate ID when we click the **Next** button. The first line is slightly complex: it generates a list of customers with different IDs. It's really only the last one we're interested in—the one with ID 9. You should place the definition of `tenCustomers` at the top of the file, next to your other customer definitions. Take care to call `toHaveBeen*Last*CalledWith` rather than `toHaveBeenCalledWith`:

```
const tenCustomers = Array.from('0123456789', id => ({ id }));

it('requests next page of data when next button is clicked', async
() => {
  window.fetch.mockReturnValue(fetchResponseOk(tenCustomers));
  await renderAndWait(<CustomerSearch />);
  await clickAndWait(element('button#next-page'));
```

```
expect(window.fetch).toHaveBeenLastCalledWith(
  '/customers?after=9',
  expect.anything()
);
});
```

 The mock expectation matcher `toHaveBeenLastCalledWith` is an important tool when you have multiple calls to your spy. We aren't interested in the first call to `window.fetch` as we've tested that in previous tests. We're just interested in the very last one that occurred, which should be in response to the action we performed in the test.

7. To make this pass, we'll need to do another search. Since that will be a function passed through to `SearchButtons`, we need to wrap it in a `useCallback` hook. Import that now:

```
import React, { useEffect, useState, useCallback } from 'react';
```

8. Define the handler for the **Next** button. It calculates `after`, which is the last ID in the current customer list. Then it calls `fetch` with this parameter placed into the URL that's fetched:

```
const handleNext = useCallback(() => {
  const after = customers[customers.length - 1].id;
  const url = `/customers?after=${after}`;
  window.fetch(url, {
    method: 'GET',
    credentials: 'same-origin',
    headers: { 'Content-Type': 'application/json' }
  });
}, [customers]);
```

9. Give `SearchButtons` a `handleNext` prop and set that as the `onClick` handler on the button:

```
const SearchButtons = ({ handleNext }) => (
  <div className="button-bar">
    <button role="button" id="next-page" onClick={handleNext}>
      Next
    </button>
  </div>
);
```

10. Hook the handler up to `SearchButtons`. After this change, your test should be passing:

```
<SearchButtons handleNext={handleNext} />
```

 Although this test is passing, we have some repeated code in here: there are two places where `window.fetch` gets called. However, this isn't a good point to refactor as the **Next** button isn't functionality complete as yet. We still have one more test to do. After that, we can dry up our code.

11. Add the following test. It sets up *two* responses to the fetch spy, using a sequence of `mockReturnValueOnce` followed by `mockReturnValue`. The second response only contains one record. After the button has been clicked, we assert that this record is displayed by checking the first cell's value:

```
it('displays next page of data when next button is clicked', async
() => {
  const nextCustomer = [{ id: 'next', firstName: 'Next' }];
  window.fetch
    .mockReturnValueOnce(fetchResponseOk(tenCustomers))
    .mockReturnValue(fetchResponseOk(nextCustomer));
  await renderAndWait(<CustomerSearch />);
  await clickAndWait(element('button#next-page'));
  expect(elements('tbody tr').length).toEqual(1);
  expect(elements('td')[0].textContent).toEqual('Next');
});
```

12. To make this pass, we need to modify `handleNext` to save its response into the `customers` variable. After this, the test should be passing:

```
const handleNext = useCallback(async () => {
  ...
  const result = await window.fetch(...);
  setCustomers(await result.json());
}, [customers]);
```

13. Look at the similarities between the `handleNext` and `fetchData` functions. In fact, they are almost identical; the only place they differ is in the first parameter to the `fetch` call. Each passes a slightly different URL. `handleNext` passes `/customers?after=<after>` and `fetchData` passes `/customers`. You might think we should extract `fetchData` so that `handleNext` can call it. Well, we could do that, but, in this case, we can take advantage of the `useEffect` hook's ability to re-run when the state changes. We can introduce a new state variable, `queryString`, which `handleNext` will update and `useEffect` will listen for. In this case, it would be quite nice to leave the prefix of `/customers` and pass in only the query string.

14. Add that new variable now at the top of the `CustomerSearch` component, as shown:

    ```
    const [queryString, setQueryString] = useState('');
    ```

15. Replace `handleNext` with the following function. The value of `newQueryString` will not include the `/customers` path name as that's constant for this component:

    ```
    const handleNext = useCallback(() => {
      const after = customers[customers.length - 1].id;
      const newQueryString = `?after=${after}`;
      setQueryString(newQueryString);
    }, [customers]);
    ```

16. Update `useEffect` with the following definition. Your tests should still be passing at this point:

    ```
    useEffect(() => {
      const fetchData = async () => {
        const result = await window.fetch(
          '/customers${queryString}`',
          {
            method: 'GET',
            credentials: 'same-origin',
            headers: { 'Content-Type': 'application/json' }
          }
        );
        setCustomers(await result.json());
      };

      fetchData();
    }, [queryString]);
    ```

That's it for the **Next** button.

Adding a previous page button

Let's move on to the **Previous** button:

1. Write out the following test:

```
it('has a previous button', async () => {
  await renderAndWait(<CustomerSearch />);
  expect(element('button#previous-page')).not.toBeNull();
});
```

2. Make that pass by modifying `SearchButtons` to include the following button, just before the **Next** button:

```
<button role="button" id="previous-page">
  Previous
</button>
```

3. Write out the following test, which mounts the component, clicks **Next**, and then clicks **Previous**. It expects another call to the endpoint to have been made, but this time identical to the initial page—in other words, with no query string:

```
it('moves back to first page when previous button is clicked',
async () => {
  window.fetch.mockReturnValue(fetchResponseOk(tenCustomers));
  await renderAndWait(<CustomerSearch />);
  await clickAndWait(element('button#next-page'));
  await clickAndWait(element('button#previous-page'));
  expect(window.fetch).toHaveBeenLastCalledWith(
    '/customers',
    expect.anything()
  );
});
```

4. To make this pass, define the `handlePrevious` function:

```
const handlePrevious = useCallback(() => setQueryString(''), []);
```

> This causes the `useEffect` handler to move back a page, so we get some behavior "for free." We don't need to write a test to prove that the customer table is updated with the returned records. If we wrote that test, it would automatically pass.

5. Modify `SearchButtons` to take a new `handlePrevious` prop, and set that as the `onClick` handler on the new button:

```
const SearchButtons = ({ handleNext, handlePrevious }) => (
  <div className="button-bar">
    <button
      role="button"
      id="previous-page"
      onClick={handlePrevious}>
      Previous
    </button>
    <button role="button" id="next-page" onClick={handleNext}>
      Next
    </button>
  </div>
);
```

6. Hook up the handler to `SearchButtons`:

```
<SearchButtons
  handleNext={handleNext}
  handlePrevious={handlePrevious}
/>
```

7. Add the next test, which is the one that'll require us to do some thinking. It simulates clicking **Next** twice, then clicking **Previous** once. This should bring us back to the second page. You should place `anotherTenCustomers` just after the definition of `tenCustomers`:

```
const anotherTenCustomers = Array.from('ABCDEFGHIJ', id => ({ id
}));

it('moves back one page when clicking previous after multiple
clicks of the next button', async () => {
  window.fetch
    .mockReturnValueOnce(fetchResponseOk(tenCustomers))
    .mockReturnValue(fetchResponseOk(anotherTenCustomers));
  await renderAndWait(<CustomerSearch />);
  await clickAndWait(element('button#next-page'));
  await clickAndWait(element('button#next-page'));
  await clickAndWait(element('button#previous-page'));
  expect(window.fetch).toHaveBeenLastCalledWith(
    '/customers?after=9',
    expect.anything());
});
```

8. We'll make this pass by maintaining a record of the query strings that were passed to the endpoint. For this specific test, we only need to know what the *previous* query string was. Add a new state variable to record that:

```
const [previousQueryString, setPreviousQueryString] = useState('');
```

9. Change `handleNext` to save the previous query string, making sure that this happens before the call to `setQueryString`. Include `queryString` in the array passed to the second parameter of `useCallback`, so that this callback is regenerated each time the value of `queryString` changes:

```
const handleNext = useCallback(queryString => {
  ...
  setPreviousQueryString(queryString);
  setQueryString(newQueryString);
}, [queryString]);
```

10. Now `handlePrevious` can use this value as the query string to pass to `fetchData`. Your test should be passing at this point:

```
const handlePrevious = useCallback(async () =>
  setQueryString(previousQueryString)
, [previousQueryString]);
```

11. For the next test, we'll make sure that **Previous** works for multiple clicks, since right now it will only work for a single press. Write out the following test:

```
it('moves back multiple pages', async () => {
  window.fetch
    .mockReturnValueOnce(fetchResponseOk(tenCustomers))
    .mockReturnValue(fetchResponseOk(anotherTenCustomers));
  await renderAndWait(<CustomerSearch />);
  await clickAndWait(element('button#next-page'));
  await clickAndWait(element('button#next-page'));
  await clickAndWait(element('button#previous-page'));
  await clickAndWait(element('button#previous-page'));
  expect(window.fetch).toHaveBeenLastCalledWith(
    '/customers',
    expect.anything()
  );
});
```

12. We'll make use of a stack to make this pass. To do that, we merge the two variables we have back into one, but this time it's an array called `queryStrings`. Start by adding a new `queryStrings` state variable, deleting `queryString` and `previousQueryStrings`:

```
const [queryStrings, setQueryStrings] = useState([]);
```

I'm not using a side-by-side implementation here, but, if you'd like to practice that technique, then feel free to go ahead and do that.

13. Change `fetchData` as follows. If there are entries in the `queryStrings` array, it sets `queryString` to the last entry, and that value is then passed to the fetch call. If there's nothing in the array, then `queryString` will be the empty string:

```
useEffect(() => {
  const fetchData = async () => {
    let queryString = '';
    if (queryStrings.length > 0)
      queryString = queryStrings[queryStrings.length - 1];

    const result = await window.fetch(
      '/customers${queryString}`',
      {
        method: 'GET',
        credentials: 'same-origin',
        headers: { 'Content-Type': 'application/json' }
      }
    );
    setCustomers(await result.json());
  };

  fetchData();
}, [queryStrings]);
```

14. Change `handleNext` as follows. It now *appends* the current query string to the previous query strings:

```
const handleNext = useCallback(() => {
  const after = customers[customers.length - 1].id;
  const queryString = `?after=${after}`;
  setQueryStrings([...queryStrings, queryString]);
}, [customers, queryStrings]);
```

15. Change `handlePrevious` as follows. This *pops* the last value off the query string stack:

```
const handlePrevious = useCallback(() => {
  setQueryStrings(queryStrings.slice(0, -1));
} [queryStrings]);
```

There is more work to do on these buttons—disabling them, for example, when there are no further records in either direction. See the *Exercises* at the end of the chapter for suggestions on further tests that could be added.

Filtering data

 The Git tag for this section is `filtering`.

Let's add a textbox that the user can use to filter names. Each character that the user types into the search field will cause a new fetch request to be made to the server. That request will contain the new search term as provided by the search box.

The `/customers` endpoint supports a parameter named `searchTerm`, which filters search results using those terms. Adding this functionality will highlight the design mistake we made earlier:

1. For this feature, we'll hook on to the change event handler for the input box. Since it will cause an asynchronous fetch request, we know we'll need to use async `act` to wait for this to happen. Let's build `changeAndWait` now; add the following to the return object of `createContainer` in `test/domManipulators.js`:

   ```
   changeAndWait: simulateEvent('change'),
   ```

2. Add the new function in to the assignments at the top of the `CustomerSearch` describe block:

   ```
   let renderAndWait,
     container,
     element,
     elements,
     clickAndWait,
     changeAndWait;
   ```

```
beforeEach(() => {
  ({
    renderAndWait,
    container,
    element,
    elements,
    clickAndWait,
    changeAndWait
  } = createContainer());
  ...
});
```

3. Before we make use of `changeAndWait`, we need to ensure that there is an input field on the page, ready for our input. Insert that as the next test:

```
it('has a search input field with a placeholder', async () => {
  await renderAndWait(<CustomerSearch />);
  expect(element('input')).not.toBeNull();
  expect(element('input').getAttribute('placeholder')).toEqual(
    'Enter filter text'
  );
});
```

4. It's a one-liner to make that test pass; insert the following in the JSX, right at the top of the fragment, above the search buttons:

```
<input placeholder="Enter filter text" />
```

5. Let's make it do something. Each time a new character is entered into the search box, we should perform a new search with whatever text is entered in the textbox. Add the following test:

```
it('performs search when search term is changed', async () => {
  await renderAndWait(<CustomerSearch />);
  await changeAndWait(
    element('input'),
    withEvent('input', 'name')
  );
  expect(window.fetch).toHaveBeenLastCalledWith(
    '/customers?searchTerm=name',
    expect.anything()
  );
});
```

6. Define the new `searchTerm` variable:

```
const [searchTerm, setSearchTerm] = useState('');
```

7. Add a new handler, `handleSearchTextChanged`. It stores the search term in the state because we'll need to pull it back when moving between pages:

```
const handleSearchTextChanged = ( { target: { value } }) =>
  setSearchTerm(value);
```

8. Hook it up to the input element:

```
<input
  value={searchTerm}
  onChange={handleSearchTextChanged}
  placeholder="Enter filter text"
/>
```

9. Now we can use this in `fetchData`:

```
const fetchData = async () => {
  let queryString = '';
  if (searchTerm !== '') {
    queryString = `?searchTerm=${searchTerm}`;
  } else if (queryStrings.length > 0) {
    queryString = queryStrings[queryStrings.length - 1];
  }
  ...
};
```

In this implementation, searching with a new search term will also wipe out the previous query strings, meaning our search will reset to the first page. That may or may not be the desired behavior; if we wanted to retain existing `queryStrings` we'd need to add another test to account for that.

10. Finally, we need to modify `useEffect` by adding `searchTerm` into the array, passed as the second parameter to `useEffect`. After this, the test should be passing:

```
useEffect(() => {
  const fetchData = {
    ...
  };
  fetchData();
}, [queryStrings, searchTerm]);
```

11. We need to ensure that hitting the **Next** button will maintain our search term. Right now, it won't. We can use the following test to fix that:

```
it('includes search term when moving to next page', async () => {
  window.fetch.mockReturnValue(fetchResponseOk(tenCustomers));
```

```
    await renderAndWait(<CustomerSearch />);
    await changeAndWait(
      element('input'),
      withEvent('input', 'name')
    );
    await clickAndWait(element('button#next-page'));
    expect(window.fetch).toHaveBeenLastCalledWith(
      '/customers?after=9&searchTerm=name',
      expect.anything());
  });
```

12. To make this pass, let's force the behavior into `fetchData` with an addition to the `if` statement:

```
const fetchData = async () => {
  let queryString;
  if (queryStrings.length > 0 && searchTerm !== '') {
    queryString = queryStrings[queryStrings.length - 1]
      + '&searchTerm=' + searchTerm;
  } else if (searchTerm !== '') {
    queryString = '?searchTerm=' + searchTerm;
  } else if (queryStrings.length > 0) {
    queryString = queryStrings[queryStrings.length - 1];
  }
  ...
};
```

We've made this test pass... but at what cost? This `if` statement really *smells*—meaning it's easy to see from a glance that it can be improved. Any `if` statement with so many moving parts (variables, operators, conditions, and so on) is a signal that the design isn't correct. All `if` statements like this one become vortexes for bad code. Let's fix it.

Refactoring to simplify component design

The issue, as I see it, is that we've made our primary data structure `queryString`. We constructed it in multiple methods and even stored an array of past query strings. There are (at least) a couple of issues with this:

- Strings are difficult to manipulate once created, as we've seen. What if we wanted to add a *third* parameter? We'd possibly end up parsing the string and reconstructing it! Oh dear.
- In addition, the `queryString` itself is related *only* to the `fetch` request. Nothing else cares about this string format.

Splitting apart the problem like this helps us see a solution. How about we just pass through the *original data* instead—in other words the ID of the customer in the last table row? Then we can construct the queryString immediately before fetching.

Let's plan out our refactor. At each of these stages, our tests should still be passing, giving us confidence that we're still on the right path:

- We'll move the query string building logic from handleNext into fetchData, changing the values that are stored in queryStrings from query strings to customer IDs in the process
- We'll change the names of those variables, using search and replace
- We'll simplify the logic in fetchData

Doesn't sound so hard, does it? Let's begin:

1. At the top of the component, replace the queryStrings variable with this new one:

   ```
   const [lastRowIds, setLastRowIds] = useState([]);
   ```

2. Use your editor's search and replace functionality to change all occurrences of queryStrings to lastRowIds.
3. Likewise, change the call to setQueryStrings to a call to setLastRowIds. Your tests should still be passing at this point.
4. Delete the following line from handleNext:

   ```
   const newQueryString = `?after=${after}`;
   ```

5. On the line below that, change the call to fetchData to pass in after instead of the now-deleted newQueryString:

   ```
   const handleNext = useCallback(() => {
     const after = customers[customers.length - 1].id;
     setLastRowIds([...lastRowIds, after]);
   }, [customers, lastRowIds]);
   ```

6. In the same function, rename after to currentLastRowId. Your tests should still be passing at this point.

7. It's time to simplify the logic within `fetchData`. **Create a** `searchParams` function, which will generate the search params for us given values for `after` and `searchTerm`. This can be defined outside of your component:

```
const searchParams = (after, searchTerm) => {
  let pairs = [];
  if (after) { pairs.push(`after=${after}`); }
  if (searchTerm) { pairs.push(`searchTerm=${searchTerm}`); }
  if (pairs.length > 0) {
    return `?${pairs.join('&')}`;
  }
  return '';
};
```

8. Finally, update `fetchData` to use this new function in place of the existing query string logic. At this point, your tests should be passing, but with a vastly simpler and easier-to-understand implementation:

```
const fetchData = async () => {
  let after;
  if (lastRowIds.length > 0)
    after = lastRowIds[lastRowIds.length - 1];
  const queryString = searchParams(after, searchTerm);
  const response = await window.fetch(...);
};
```

The `searchParams` function we've defined is a suggestion of a component-agnostic functionality that could be reused in other places. Check out the *Exercises* section for specific guidance on how to build on what we've developed in this section.

Adding table row actions

 The Git tag for this section is `table-row-actions`.

The final thing we need to do is display actions that the user can choose to take for each customer. For now, we'll need just one action: *Create appointment*. When the user has found the customer they are searching for, they can move on to creating an appointment for that customer by clicking a button.

We'll display these actions by using a render prop, `renderCustomerActions`, which is passed to `CustomerSearch`. This enables the component to be agnostic of which actions can be performed; the client needs to specify what those are.

 I've chosen to go with a render prop simply to show you how to test that approach. In the real world, I may not have chosen to do this as it's something of a premature generalization. A perfectly reasonable approach would be to hard-code the actions in place until the point that `CustomerSearch` needs to support some other use case.

1. In `test/CustomerSearch.test.js`, write the following test:

```
it('displays provided action buttons for each customer', async ()
=> {
  const actionSpy = jest.fn();
  actionSpy.mockReturnValue('actions');
  window.fetch.mockReturnValue(fetchResponseOk(oneCustomer));
  await renderAndWait(<CustomerSearch
renderCustomerActions={actionSpy} />);
  const rows = elements('table tbody td');
  expect(rows[rows.length-1].textContent).toEqual('actions');
});
```

2. Set a default `renderCustomerActions` prop so that our existing tests won't start failing when we begin using the new prop. This goes at the bottom of `src/CustomerSearch.js`:

```
CustomerSearch.defaultProps = {
  renderCustomerActions: () => {}
};
```

3. Destructure that prop in the top line of the `CustomerSearch` component:

```
export const CustomerSearch = ({ renderCustomerActions }) => {
  ...
};
```

4. Pass it through to `CustomerRow`:

```
<CustomerRow
  customer={customer}
  key={customer.id}
  renderCustomerActions={renderCustomerActions}
/>
```

5. In `CustomerRow`, update the fourth `td` cell to call this new prop:

```
const CustomerRow = ({ customer, renderCustomerActions }) => (
 <tr>
   <td>{customer.firstName}</td>
   <td>{customer.lastName}</td>
   <td>{customer.phoneNumber}</td>
   <td>{renderCustomerActions()}</td>
 </tr>
);
```

6. For the last test, we want to check that this render prop receives the specific customer record that applies to that row:

```
it('passes customer to the renderCustomerActions prop', async () =>
{
  const actionSpy = jest.fn();
  actionSpy.mockReturnValue('actions');
  window.fetch.mockReturnValue(fetchResponseOk(oneCustomer));
  await renderAndWait(<CustomerSearch
renderCustomerActions={actionSpy} />);
  expect(actionSpy).toHaveBeenCalledWith(oneCustomer[0]);
});
```

7. To make this pass, all you have to do is update the JSX call that you just wrote to include the customer as a parameter:

```
<td>{renderCustomerActions(customer)}</td>
```

Specifying the render prop in App

It's the `App` component that will pass `renderCustomerActions` to `CustomerSearch`, so let's build that:

1. In `test/App.test.js`, add the following test inside the `search customers` describe block. It defines a helper, `renderSearchActionsForCustomer`, which navigates until the relevant search actions have been rendered. The test then looks for the first child in these search actions. We'll add a second button later on in the book:

```
const renderSearchActionsForCustomer = customer => {
  searchCustomers();
  const customerSearch = elementMatching(type(CustomerSearch));
  const searchActionsComponent =
    customerSearch.props.renderCustomerActions;
```

```
    return searchActionsComponent(customer);
};

it('passes a button to the CustomerSearch named Create
appointment', async () => {
  const button = childrenOf(
    renderSearchActionsForCustomer()
  )[0];
  expect(button).toBeDefined();
  expect(button.type).toEqual('button');
  expect(button.props.role).toEqual('button');
  expect(button.props.children).toEqual('Create appointment');
});
```

2. In `src/App.js`, add the following function just above the returned JSX:

```
const searchActions = () => (
  <React.Fragment>
    <button role="button">Create appointment</button>
  </React.Fragment>
);
```

3. Set the prop on `CustomerSearch`:

```
case 'searchCustomers':
  return (
    <CustomerSearch renderCustomerActions={searchActions} />
  );
```

4. Back in `test/CustomerSearch.test.js`, add the next test. This uses the same helper function, but this time clicks the button and verifies that the `AppointmentFormLoader` was shown with the correct customer ID:

```
it('clicking appointment button shows the appointment form for that
customer', async () => {
  const customer = { id: 123 };
  const button = childrenOf(
    renderSearchActionsForCustomer(customer)
  )[0];
  click(button);
  expect(
    elementMatching(type(AppointmentFormLoader))
  ).not.toBeNull();
  expect(
    elementMatching(type(AppointmentFormLoader)).props.customer
  ).toBe(customer);
});
```

5. To make that pass, update `searchActions` in `src/App.js` to use the customer parameter that will be passed to it by `CustomerSearch`:

```
const searchActions = customer => (
  <React.Fragment>
    <button
      role="button"
      onClick={() => transitionToAddAppointment(customer)}>
      Create appointment
    </button>
  </React.Fragment>
);
```

That's it! Everything is now complete; go ahead and manually test if you'd like to see it all in action.

Summary

This chapter has explored building out a component with some complex user interactions between the user interface and an API.

The shape that our code takes is often dependent on the order in which we add features. In our case, that ultimately took us down the "wrong" path with the design that we had corrected. Thankfully, our tests helped us do that without fear of functional regression.

Making the "wrong" decisions is a normal part of coding, and it's important we notice when it's time to try a different approach. Our tests help us admit when we're doing the wrong thing, rather than being stuck with our poor choices.

In the next chapter, we'll use tests to integrate React Router into our application. We'll revisit our `CustomerSearch` component by adding the ability to use the browser location bar to specify search criteria. That will set us up nicely for introducing Redux in GraphQL later on.

Exercises

- Disable the **Previous** button if the user is on the first page, and disable the **Next** button if the current listing has fewer than 10 records on display.
- Extract the `searchParams` function into a separate module that handles any number of parameters and uses the `encodeURIComponent` JavaScript function to ensure the values are encoded correctly.
- The `/customers` endpoint supports a `limit` parameter, which allows you to specify the number of records that are returned. Provide a mechanism for the user to change the number of records returned on each page.

Test-driving React Router

7

React Router is a popular library that provides navigational components that integrate with the browser's own navigation system. For example, it can update the current page location that appears in the address bar, and it will make the back button work within your single-page application.

The beauty of React Router is that it can help simplify a great deal of code in addition to adding new functionality. In our example Appointments system, it can be used to simplify our user workflow in the App component. We can also use it to upgrade our CustomerSearch component to store its current search parameters as part of the URL query string. That allows our users to bookmark and share particular searches that they've performed.

In this chapter, rather than walking through a refactor of our codebase, we'll look at specific examples of React Router components and their corresponding tests. The refactor has already been done in the Git repository that accompanies the book. So, in this chapter, we'll just look at some of the more interesting pieces of code.

This chapter covers:

- General rules for test-driving React Router
- Building a root component
- Using the location query string to store component state

General rules for test-driving React Router

React Router is the kind of library that can cause people to "forget about" testing. Although the library itself is simple to use—it's just a collection of Router, Route, and Link components—testing can prove tricky once you get past the simple examples and into the real world.

When people hit difficulty in real-world scenarios, sometimes their response is to give up on the tests and perhaps come back to them later. Unfortunately, having holes in your test coverage can severely impact the confidence you have in your test suite, so it's important to resist that impulse to move on to the next thing.

With a little bit of perseverance and some critical thinking, testing React Router is quite feasible, as you're about to find out. In this section, I'll give you some general guidance, which you should use when you write any React Router component.

Using shallow rendering for the simplest results

We can test React Router using either full rendering or shallow rendering. In this book, I'll use shallow rendering, for a couple of reasons.

The first reason is that by shallow rendering we don't need to test the *effects* of the React Router. We don't need to assert that our browser "navigates" and that the browser location changes. This is good because those side effects are nuanced and not straightforward to test. So, if we wanted to verify that a Link actually "works," we'd have a lot of different things to verify.

Contrast this with the tests we've written up until now, where we full-rendered buttons and happily clicked them. Why is this any different? Well, the DOM is a very well-understood API, and is relatively simple. Clicking a button generally has only one effect: it fires a React event that then calls any attached event handler. That's it. Writing tests against this is straightforward.

What's more, at the time of writing, the JSDOM environment doesn't have a fully-fledged history API, so building the right assertions in a non-browser environment can be challenging.

With shallow rendering, we assume that Link and Route do what the library authors intended them to do. Instead, we simply verify that the Link and Route components exist, where and when we expect them to exist, and that they have the right props set.

If we were to full render, we would lose information about which components were originally Link components and which were originally Route components. Instead, we'd simply see clickable DOM elements, so we couldn't even assert that the right elements were displayed.

The second reason that I prefer shallow rendering is that you don't need to wrap your component under test in a Router. This is a requirement of the Link, Route, and Switch components. While that is a wonderful feature at runtime, in our tests it's simply noise.

Sometimes, we have components that we *need* to use full rendering on, because we want to run useEffect hooks. And sometimes, those same components have React Router requirements. In fact, we have one in our very codebase: the CustomerSearch component. In this scenario, the best thing to do is to introduce an intermediate component that you can stub out. This is what I've done with the SearchButtons component. CustomerSearch is responsible for running side effects, and SearchButtons is responsible for rendering links.

You could even stub out Link and Route themselves, if you wanted.

Let's take a look at an example of shallow rendering.

Here's the RouterButton component, which is used to render both the **Next** and **Previous** buttons in the SearchButtons component. RouterButton does a few different things, but probably the most interesting is that it converts an object of query parameters (queryParams) into a search string, such as ?limit=20&searchTerm=Ba, using the objectToQueryString function from the last chapter:

```
import React from 'react';
import { objectToQueryString } from '../objectToQueryString';
import { Link } from 'react-router-dom';

export const RouterButton = ({
  queryParams,
  pathname,
  children,
  disabled
}) => {
  let className = 'button';
  if (disabled) {
    className += ' disabled';
  }
  return (
    <Link
      className={className}
      to={{
        pathname: pathname,
        search: objectToQueryString(queryParams)
      }}>
      {children}
    </Link>
  );
};
```

To test that the `Link` is displayed, we simply use shallow rendering, as shown:

```
describe('RouterButton', () => {
  const pathname = '/path';
  const queryParams = { a: '123', b: '234' };
  let render, elementMatching, root;

  beforeEach(() => {
    ({ render, elementMatching, root } = createShallowRenderer());
  });

  it('renders a Link', () => {
    render(
      <RouterButton
        pathname={pathname}
        queryParams={queryParams}
      />
    );
    expect(root().type).toEqual(Link);
    expect(root().props.className).toContain('button');
    expect(root().props.to).toEqual({
      pathname: '/path',
      search: '?a=123&b=234'
    });
  });
});
```

Passing React Router props down through your components

In the last example, we passed the `pathname` prop to `RouterButton`. Aside from the non-camelCase name, what's different about this prop? Well, it comes from React Router's current page location, which is a prop that we receive from the Router.

Here's the render hierarchy from `App`, through `CustomerSearch` and right down to the `Link` from the previous example. I have highlighted three props that React Router provides us: `history`, `location`, and `match`:

```
<Router>
  <App>
    <Switch>
      <Route
        path="/searchCustomers"
        render={({history, location, match}) => { ... }}>
        <CustomerSearchRoute history={...} location={...} match={...}>
```

```
<CustomerSearch
  history={...}
  location={...}
  match={...}
  searchTerm={...}
  limit={...}
  lastRowIds={...}>
  <SearchButtons pathname={location.pathname}>
    <RouterButton pathname={...}>
      <Link to={...}>
```

Each of the three props has different uses:

- `history` gives us the `push` function that allows us to modify the current page location
- `location` gives us the `pathname` property that tells us what page we're currently on
- `match` gives us any groups that matched the Route location pattern

The simplest and most explicit way we can access these props is by passing them through our components, as shown previously. Let's look at how that happens in `CustomerSearch`. Here's how it passes the current window location to `SearchButtons`:

```
export const CustomerSearch = ({
  renderCustomerActions,
  lastRowIds,
  searchTerm,
  limit,
  history,
  location
}) => {
  // ... other code here ...
  return (
    <React.Fragment>
      <SearchButtons
        customers={customers}
        searchTerm={searchTerm}
        limit={limit}
        lastRowIds={lastRowIds}
        pathname={location.pathname}
      />
    </React.Fragment>
  );
  // ... other code here ...
};
```

`SearchButtons` doesn't need the entire location object, so we pass only the part it needs: the `pathname`. This is good programming practice—only pass components exactly what they need to do their job and nothing more.

Avoiding withRouter

Passing down these props into your components should be your default method of accessing React Router state. You could use the `withRouter` higher-order component to avoid passing props, but that adds a significant amount of complexity to your code, including your tests.

Why can props be a problem? Well, let's look at an example from our codebase. There are actually a whole bunch of `RouterButton` elements in the button bar. They all get passed the same `pathname` prop:

```
<ToggleRouterButton id="limit-10" ... pathname={pathname}>
  10
</ToggleRouterButton>
<ToggleRouterButton id="limit-20" ... pathname={pathname}>
  20
</ToggleRouterButton>
<ToggleRouterButton id="limit-50" ... pathname={pathname}>
  50
</ToggleRouterButton>
<ToggleRouterButton id="limit-100" ... pathname={pathname}>
  100
</ToggleRouterButton>
<RouterButton id="previous-page" ... pathname={pathname}>
  Previous
</RouterButton>
<RouterButton id="next-page" ... pathname={pathname}>
  Next
</RouterButton>
```

Passing the same prop over and over again is noisy. The `withRouter` higher-order component offers a potential solution; it wraps each component in a call that grabs the relevant information out of context and passes it as a prop. If `RouterButton` and `ToggleRouterButton` were wrapped in `withRouter`, we'd avoid having to write out this prop each time.

Unfortunately, by doing this, you've traded brevity for ease of comprehension and ease of testing. Shallow rendering will be more difficult because you now have an extra layer to work through. That leads to developers testing the unwrapped component and leaving the wrapped component untested. This introduces a whole other level of complexity into your codebase.

Building a root component

In this section, we'll look at some specific tests from the App component once it has been reworked to use React Router. There are a few key points:

- The initial screen, which contains a button bar and the AppointmentsDayViewLoader, needs to be wrapped in a single component so that we can pass it to the component prop of Route.
- The Switch component is used to decide which high-level component should be shown. This replaces our own switch.
- The non-default Route component instances uses a render function to display their components, because they require specific props to be passed in. We'll look at how to avoid this in the next chapter when we introduce Redux.

Using the Router Switch component

In the App component we created, we had three components on the main page: two navigation buttons and an AppointmentsDayViewLoader instance. Both the Router code and our test code becomes simpler if we batch those up into one component.

Here's what an extracted MainScreen component looks like:

```
export const MainScreen = () => (
  <React.Fragment>
    <div className="button-bar">
      <Link to="/addCustomer" className="button">
        Add customer and appointment
      </Link>
      <Link to="/searchCustomers" className="button">
        Search customers
      </Link>
    </div>
    <AppointmentsDayViewLoader />
  </React.Fragment>
);
```

Of course, this needs tests itself, which is why it's exported. Once you've test-driven that component, it can be used in App as shown. We pass it straight into the component prop of the final Route:

```
return (
  <Switch>
    <Route path="/addCustomer" render={...} />
    <Route path="/addAppointment" render={...} />
    <Route path="/searchCustomers" render={...} />
    <Route component={MainScreen} />
  </Switch>
);
```

Testing the default route

A Switch component lists a number of routes, only one of which will be rendered at a time. The last Route listed in a Switch will be the one used if nothing else matches, just as a switch statement in most programming languages makes the last clause its default clause.

Here's a test to verify that the last route renders what we expect. The name of the test is important; it explicitly mentions that this is the default route:

```
it('renders the MainScreen as the default route', () => {
  render(<App />);
  const routes = childRoutes();
  const lastRoute = routes[routes.length - 1];
  expect(lastRoute.props.component).toEqual(MainScreen);
});
```

The test succinctly encodes the notion of a default route into our tests, which is useful in documenting the React Router API. That will be of help to anyone reading your code who isn't already familiar with React Router.

Invoking render functions and inspecting their properties

The other routes in App aren't so simple. They require the use of state and props. For example, here's how we rendered AppointmentFormLoader before, which needs to be passed a customer object and an onSave handler:

```
switch(view) {
  case 'addAppointment':
```

```
    return <AppointmentFormLoader
      customer={customer}
      onSave={transitionToDayView} />;
```

To do the same with React Router, we need to use the render prop on a `Route`:

```
<Route
  path="/addAppointment"
  render={() => (
    <AppointmentFormLoader
      customer={customer}
      onSave={transitionToDayView} />
  )}
/>
```

This render prop poses a problem. How can we verify that the `AppointmentFormLoader` was passed the right props?

We need to **invoke** the render function, but not **mount** it. (For a component like `AppointmentFormLoader`, mounting would run its lifecycle methods, which we don't want to do since that causes a network request to occur.) By invoking it, we construct the React element so that we can inspect its properties, just as we did when we built our shallow rendering helpers.

There are at least three tests required for this route: one to check the element type is indeed `AppointmentFormLoader`, one to check that `customer` was passed correctly, and another to test what happens when `onSave` is called. Let's start with testing the type:

```
const childRoutes = () =>
  childrenOf(elementMatching(type(Switch)));

const routeFor = path => childRoutes().find(prop('path', path));

it('renders AppointmentFormLoader at /addAppointment', () => {
  render(<App />);
  expect(
    routeFor('/addAppointment').props.render().type
  ).toEqual(AppointmentFormLoader);
});
```

I've pulled out a `routeFor` helper which makes clever use of our shallow helpers to find the right Route. It then invokes the render function (using `.props.render()`) before checking its type.

The other two tests are similar. With the test for onSave, we need to invoke that property too:

```
it('navigates to / when AppointmentFormLoader is saved', () => {
  render(<App history={{ push: historySpy }} />);
  const onSave = routeFor('/addAppointment').props.render().props
    .onSave;
  onSave();
  expect(historySpy).toHaveBeenCalledWith('/');
});
```

Invoking render functions in this fashion is about as complicated as our tests can get. Here's another example, where I pulled out a helper method and gave it a reasonable name to aid in keeping the test short and keeping it in the realms of human understanding:

```
const customer = { id: 123 };

const renderSearchActionsForCustomer = customer => {
  render(<App history={{ push: historySpy }} />);
  const customerSearch =
    routeFor('/searchCustomers').props.render();
  const searchActionsComponent =
    customerSearch.props.renderCustomerActions;
  return searchActionsComponent(customer);
};

it('passes saved customer to AppointmentFormLoader when clicking the Create
appointment button', () => {
  const button = childrenOf(
    renderSearchActionsForCustomer(customer)
  )[0];
  click(button);
  const appointmentForm =
    routeFor('/addAppointment').props.render();
  expect(appointmentForm.props.customer).toEqual(customer);
});
```

The test first follows the /searchCustomers route, and then mimics the UI by invoking the renderCustomerActions prop with the provided customer object. We then reach inside the rendered component instance and pull out its first button, which we then click on. This will save the customer object ready for use in AppointmentFormLoader.

However, because we're shallow rendering, React Router won't update the displayed route automatically for us when we click the button. So, the second-to-last line of the test does our navigation for us, almost like a second *Arrange* phase. This is complex and pretty nasty, but it's the price we have to pay for using shallow rendering. Thankfully, these kinds of tests are relatively rare.

Changing location using history.push

Link components are one way to cause a URL change, but clearly, they require the user to click on them. To programmatically change a URL, we need to use the history prop that React Router gives us. This has a push function, which we can test using a standard spy.

In the test that follows, App is passed a history object, which replicates the object that a Router component would give us:

```
describe('App', () => {
  let historySpy;

  beforeEach(() => {
    historySpy = jest.fn();
  });

  it('navigates to / when AppointmentFormLoader is saved', () => {
    render(<App history={{ push: historySpy }} />);
    const onSave = routeFor('/addAppointment').props.render().props.onSave;
    onSave();
    expect(historySpy).toHaveBeenCalledWith('/');
  });
});
```

In the last section, we saw that the AppointmentFormLoader onSave prop was hooked up to the transitionToDayView function. To make the preceding test pass, we can call history.push within that function:

```
const transitionToDayView = useCallback(
  () => history.push('/'),
  [history]
);
```

The spy doesn't actually trigger a page change. Just as we saw in the previous section, when we use shallow rendering, a Switch component won't do any routing at all. We have to mimic that in our tests.

If you really want to see the Switch in action, you'll need to use mount to render your component. In our application, this is possible as long as you don't render a route that causes a network request when it is mounted, such as /addAppointment.

The simpler approach is to test that the root component contains a Switch component with a bunch of routes, and assume that Switch actually does its job.

Using the location query string to store component state

In the current implementation of CustomerSearch, we save the search configuration—the search term, the row limit, and the last row IDs—in a component state. But if we move the search configuration to the browser's query string, the user will be able to bookmark search pages, or share them with colleagues.

A search URL might look as follows:

```
/searchCustomers?searchTerm=An&limit=20&previousRowIds=20
```

What will need to change in our implementation to support this design change?

We'll replace onClick handlers with Link components. That skips the need to use the useState hook. Our search parameters will be passed back into our component when React Router re-renders the component with new props values.

One unfortunate thing about URLs as states, is that they tend to have a longer life than component states, for example if the user bookmarks the page. That means these searches may become "stale" as customer records are added, updated, and deleted.

Replacing onClick handlers with Link components

The RouterButton component we saw earlier renders a Link, which is given an object that should be serialized into a query string. When the user clicks this link, React Router will navigate to a new location.

One of the buttons on the page is the **Next** button, which moves to the next page of results. Let's look at how the **Next** button is tested:

```
const renderSearchButtons = props =>
  render(
    <SearchButtons
      pathname="/path"
      lastRowIds={['123']}
      searchTerm="term"
      customers={tenCustomers}
      {...props}
    />
  );

describe('next button', () => {
  it('renders', () => {
    renderSearchButtons();
    const button = elementMatching(id('next-page'));
    expect(button).toBeDefined();
    expect(button.type).toEqual(RouterButton);
    expect(button.props.children).toEqual('Next');
    expect(button.props.pathname).toEqual('/path');
    expect(button.props.disabled).toBeFalsy();
  });
});
```

The test isn't a complete definition of the `RouterButton`. We still need to specify a `queryParams` prop, which is the object to be "saved" in the query string. Two of these query params will be `limit` and `searchTerm`. These don't change when **Next** is called. We simply use the same values that are passed in as props:

```
it('includes limit and search term in queryParams prop', () => {
  renderSearchButtons({ limit: 20, searchTerm: 'name' });
  const button = elementMatching(id('previous-page'));
  expect(button.props.queryParams).toMatchObject({
    limit: 20,
    searchTerm: 'name'
  });
});
```

In this test, the props are passed into `CustomerSearch`. But where do these props come from? React Router doesn't parse the query string for us; we need to do that ourselves.

Using a parent component to convert a query string to props

Now that we are setting up the query string correctly, we need to get the data back out of it. We can do that by defining a new component called `CustomerSearchRoute`, which has the single responsibility of converting the query string to props that are then passed to `CustomerSearch`:

```
import React from 'react';
import { createShallowRenderer, type } from './shallowHelpers';
import { CustomerSearchRoute } from '../src/CustomerSearchRoute';
import { CustomerSearch } from '../src/CustomerSearch/CustomerSearch';

describe('CustomerSearchRoute', () => {
  let render, elementMatching;

  beforeEach(() => {
    ({ render, elementMatching } = createShallowRenderer());
  });

  it('parses searchTerm from query string', () => {
    const location = { search: '?searchTerm=abc' };
    render(<CustomerSearchRoute location={location} />);
    expect(
      elementMatching(type(CustomerSearch)).props.searchTerm
    ).toEqual('abc');
  });
});
```

`CustomerSearchRoute` has a whole bunch of tests like this. The implementation of the component itself is straightforward. It uses a `convertParams` function, which is like the opposite of our `objectToQueryString` function, taking a query string and converting it into an object:

```
export const CustomerSearchRoute = props => (
  <CustomerSearch
    {...props}
    {...convertParams(props.location.search)}
  />
);
```

You can find the code for `convertParams` in the Git repository.

Following is the route that launches `CustomerSearchRoute`, as defined in the `App` component. This makes use of the entire set of props that the `Route` component gives us, passing it directly to the component.

Even though `CustomerSearchRoute` itself only uses one of these props (`location`), it's important that we pass all the props, as `CustomerSearch` makes use of all three Router props: `location`, `history`, and `match`. You could be explicit about this if you preferred:

```
<Route
  path="/searchCustomers"
  render={props => (
    <CustomerSearchRoute
      {...props}
      renderCustomerActions={searchActions}
    />
  )}
/>
```

Replacing onChange handlers with history.push

Let's take a closer look at `CustomerSearch`. We'll look at the example of entering a search term. This uses a textbox with an `onChange` handler. Each new character causes a new search to occur, and that should be reflected in the browser's location.

We need to use `history.push` to programmatically update the API, just as we did in `App`.

Of interest in this example is that `CustomerSearch` is actually being full rendered here, because it has a `useEffect` hook, which many of the tests need to run. But this doesn't affect our tests—we've simply stubbed out `SearchButtons` so that none of the `Link` components are rendered:

```
const renderCustomerSearch = props =>
  renderAndWait(
    <CustomerSearch
      {...props}
      history={{ push: historySpy }}
      renderCustomerActions={actionSpy}
      location={{ pathname: '/path' }}
    />
```

```
  );

it('changes location when search term is changed', async () => {
  await renderCustomerSearch();
  change(element('input'), withEvent('input', 'name'));
  expect(historySpy).toHaveBeenCalledWith(
    '/path?searchTerm=name'
  );
});
```

Notice that we've given CustomerSearch access to both history and location props. The test can then be made to pass with a simple call to history.push, as shown in the handleSearchTextChanged handler here:

```
const handleSearchTextChanged = ({ target: { value } }) => {
  const params = { limit, searchTerm: value };
  history.push(location.pathname + objectToQueryString(params));
};
```

Summary

This chapter has shown you how to introduce React Router in a testable fashion. We made extensive use of shallow rendering, and you've seen how to use both routing and query string in place of states.

Now that we've successfully refactored to one library, the next one shouldn't be too tricky, right? In the next chapter, we'll apply all the skills we've learned in this chapter in another context. We'll refactor our codebase to use what's arguably the most cryptic of React libraries: Redux.

Exercises

The Git tag for this section is `react-router`. It contains solutions to the exercises from the previous chapter, so if you haven't completed the *Exercises* section yourself, then you should move to this tag now so that you're up to date.

For more detailed instructions, see the *To get the most out of this book* section in the `Preface`.

If you'd like to use this chapter as a reference, you can view my version in `react-router-complete`.

- Attempt the refactor to React Router yourself. Try to keep as many tests as possible green while you work by making use of side-by-side implementations.
- Refactor `convertParams` to be a generalized function that works for all parameters. You will need to think of a set of rules under which values should be converted to different data types. Both integer and array conversion should be supported, as in our version.
- Move the new `convertParams` function to the `objectToQueryString` module. Now that it has two functions, can you think of a better name for this module?

Further learning

- React Router documentation: `https://reacttraining.com/react-router/`

8
Test-driving Redux

Redux is a **predictable state container**. To the uninitiated, these words mean very little. But Redux doesn't have to be scary. In fact, TDD can help us understand how to implement and reason about our Redux application architecture.

Refactoring to Redux is a common operation. Many React projects will begin without Redux in place but then grow to need it. Teams will adopt Redux when they start to feel the pain of managing an application state across multiple components. TDD can help us refactor in a safe way.

Designing a Redux system is not straightforward. Although Redux is simple at its core, that simplicity leaves the integrator with many decisions to make. Redux isn't very opinionated about how it should be used. That being said, my focus in this chapter is on teaching you how to test-drive Redux, not how to model state in Redux. "Eloquent" use of Redux is a huge topic in itself, and one that I gladly side-step.

So, it's worth saying that although you will learn *some* aspects of Redux by reading this chapter, it's really just an introduction.

In addition to Redux itself, we'll use `redux-saga` as a means of performing asynchronous actions (in other words, `fetch` requests). Using this library means the code to submit a `fetch` request will look almost identical to the code we've already written. We'll essentially be transplanting it out of React and into Redux.

We'll also use `expect-redux` to test Redux interactions. This allows us to write tests that are not tied to `redux-saga`. Being independent of libraries is a great way of ensuring that your tests are not brittle and are resilient to change. By using `expect-redux`, we can write our tests without any reference to `redux-saga`. This is a good thing! You could replace `redux-saga` with `redux-thunk` and your tests would still work.

In the previous chapter, we took the opposite approach: our tests were highly dependent on React Router. They checked for the presence of `Link` and `Route` components rather than manipulating and asserting on the browser history API. We did that in part because JSDOM doesn't have great support for the browser history API. If its support was better, we may have made a different choice. Ultimately, you should pick whichever solution provides you wish the simplest, most resilient tests.

In this chapter `expect-redux` really saves the day by providing a very simple mechanism for testing Redux interactions.

This chapter covers the following topics:

- Test-driving a Redux saga
- Making asynchronous requests with sagas
- Switching out component state for Redux state
- Shifting workflow to Redux

Prerequisites

The Git tag for this section is `add-redux`. It contains solutions to the exercises from the previous chapter, so if you haven't completed the *Exercises* section yourself, then you should move to this tag now so that you're up to date.

For more detailed instructions, see the *To get the most out of this book* section in the `Preface`.

This chapter uses *four* libraries: `redux`, `react-redux`, `redux-saga`, and our test library, `expect-redux`. You should install these now using the following commands:

```
npm install --save redux react-redux redux-saga
npm install --save-dev expect-redux
```

Test-driving a Redux saga

This chapter focuses on modifying `CustomerForm` to submit its data to a Redux store, which then in turn submits the data to our server with a `fetch` call. In other words, we are introducing a level of indirection between our component and the fetch API. One reason you might want to do this in your own app is that network code can quickly become complicated and you may want to keep it all in one place where it is more easily reasoned about.

We'll explore other use cases of Redux later in the book.

Designing the state object

It's now time for some up-front design.

A Redux store is simply an object of data with some restrictions on how it is accessed. So, how do we expect our store data to look? Here's what we'll aim for. The object encodes all the information that `CustomerForm` already uses about a `fetch` request to save customer data:

```
{
  addCustomer: {
    status: SUBMITTING | FAILED | VALIDATION_FAILED | SUCCESSFUL,

    // only present if the customer was saved successfully
    customer: { id: 123, firstName: 'Ashley' ... },

    // only present if the server returned validation errors
    validationErrors: { phoneNumber: '...' },

    // only present if the server returned an error other than validation
    error: true | false
  }
}
```

We save the `customer` in the Redux store so that components that are rendered later on in the workflow process, such as `AppointmentForm`, can read it straight away without needing to awkwardly pass it through a parent component, such as `App`. `App` could also use the `status` to help with navigation, by checking whether the customer submission was successful rather than waiting for its `onSave` handler to be called.

Scaffolding the saga and reducer

There are two new types of function: **sagas** and **reducers**. They work in tandem with each other. The approach we'll use in this section is to build a single Redux action that works its way through both a saga and a reducer. We will "scaffold" barebones implementation for both, for that single action, before fleshing out the functions with more detail.

For reference, here's the existing code that we'll be extracting from `CustomerForm`. It's all helpfully in one function, `doSave`, even though it is quite long:

```
const doSave = async () => {
  setSubmitting(true);
  const result = await window.fetch('/customers', {
    method: 'POST',
    credentials: 'same-origin',
    headers: { 'Content-Type': 'application/json' },
    body: JSON.stringify(customer)
  });
  setSubmitting(false);
  if (result.ok) {
    setError(false);
    const customerWithId = await result.json();
    onSave(customerWithId);
  } else if (result.status === 422) {
    const response = await result.json();
    setValidationErrors(response.errors);
  } else {
    setError(true);
  }
};
```

This does a bunch of different things, such as toggling the submitting variable, calling `window.fetch`, dealing with errors, and calling the `onSave` prop when submission succeeds.

We'll start by building a saga that initiates a save action. It listens for an
ADD_CUSTOMER_REQUEST action to the Redux store. The generator function we're about to
write, named addCustomer, is then invoked when that action is received:

1. Create two new directories: test/sagas and src/sagas. This is where our saga definitions will live.

2. Create a new file named test/sagas/customer.test.js and add the following code. Usually, I would pair this with a first test, but there's enough new content in just the test setup that it's worth breaking apart. In this part, we're setting up a store variable that both our sagas and our test expectations will configureStore function is something we'll write ourselves; storeSpy is a core part of expect-redux:

```
import { storeSpy, expectRedux } from 'expect-redux';
import { configureStore } from '../../src/store';

describe('addCustomer', () => {
  let store;

  beforeEach(() => {
    store = configureStore([ storeSpy ]);
  });
});
```

3. Create a new file, src/store.js, and add the following code, which builds our first generator function, rootSaga. Every project that uses Redux will have a store.js file or equivalent. There's plenty of interest in this file, such as the use of storeEnhancers, which allows us to pass in the storeSpy from expect-redux. For the most part, however, this file is simply boilerplate, so you can safely ignore it. There are parts we'll add to as we go through this chapter, but you'll soon learn which parts are relevant to your work, and which can be ignored:

Generator function syntax

The arrow function syntax that we've been using throughout the book does not work with generator functions, so we need to fall back to using "real" function definitions.

```
import { createStore, applyMiddleware, compose } from 'redux';
import createSagaMiddleware from 'redux-saga';

function* rootSaga() {
}
```

```
export const configureStore = (storeEnhancers = []) => {
  const sagaMiddleware = createSagaMiddleware();

  const store = createStore(
    (state, _) => state,
    compose(
      ...[applyMiddleware(sagaMiddleware), ...storeEnhancers]
    )
  );
  sagaMiddleware.run(rootSaga);

  return store;
};
```

 I tend to not test my `configureStore` definitions, since they generally change infrequently, and when they do, it's usually just to add in a reducer. However, it is possible to test-drive this function if you so desire.

4. Let's go back and fill out our test file. In `test/sagas/customer.test.js`, add the following helper function and test, just after the `beforeEach` block. The very first thing our saga should do is update our state to reflect that the form is submitting. We use `expect-redux` to ensure that we dispatch the right action:

```
const dispatchRequest = customer =>
  store.dispatch({
    type: 'ADD_CUSTOMER_REQUEST',
    customer
  });

it('sets current status to submitting', () => {
  dispatchRequest();

  return expectRedux(store)
    .toDispatchAnAction()
    .matching({ type: 'ADD_CUSTOMER_SUBMITTING' });
});
```

 This test returns a promise. This is a shortcut we can use instead of marking our test function as `async` and the expectation with `await`. Jest is smart enough to know to wait if the test function returns a promise.

5. For this to work, we'll need to implement the saga and also hook it into the store. Let's start with the saga implementation. Create a new directory, `src/sagas`, and then a new file, `src/sagas/customer.js`, with the following content:

```
import { put } from 'redux-saga/effects';

export function* addCustomer() {
  yield put({ type: 'ADD_CUSTOMER_SUBMITTING' });
}
```

6. Back in `src/store.js`, add an import for the saga, and the `takeLatest` effect:

```
import { takeLatest } from "redux-saga/effects";
import { addCustomer } from './sagas/customer';
```

7. Update the root saga as shown next. After this, your saga is complete, and your test should pass:

```
function* rootSaga() {
  yield takeLatest('ADD_CUSTOMER_REQUEST', addCustomer);
}
```

We now need to handle the `ADD_CUSTOMER_SUBMITTING` action. Since this will update state, it needs to be done in a reducer.

Scaffolding a reducer

Our saga file actually needs to contain two things: the saga that we've just scaffolded, and a reducer that we can use to make state changes. In this section, we'll make a start adding our first action, `ADD_CUSTOMER_SUBMITTING`. We'll complete it later in the chapter:

1. Stay in `test/sagas/customer.test.js`, and import the `reducer` function:

```
import { reducer } from '../../src/sagas/customer';
```

2. Add a new `describe` block to the bottom of the file (not nested within the first `describe` block). This shows that if the reducer is invoked with an unknown action, our reducer should return a `default` state for our object. This is a standard behavior for Redux reducers, so you should almost always start with a test like this for your reducer:

```
describe('reducer', () => {
  it('returns a default state for an undefined existing state', ()
  => {
```

```
        expect(reducer(undefined, {})).toEqual({
          customer: {},
          status: undefined,
          validationErrors: {},
          error: false
        });
      });
    });
```

3. In `src/sagas/customer.js`, let's add our `reducer` function, just after the `saga` function. The test should pass at this point:

```
const defaultState = {
  customer: {},
  status: undefined,
  validationErrors: {},
  error: false
};

export const reducer = (state = defaultState, action) => {
  return state;
};
```

4. Now let's hook this reducer into our state. For this, we'll use `combineReducers`. In `src/store.js`, update the two imports shown here:

```
import {
  createStore,
  applyMiddleware,
  compose,
  combineReducers
} from 'redux';
import {
  addCustomer,
  reducer as customerReducer
} from './sagas/customer';
```

5. Then update the first parameter to `createStore` to use these new reducers:

```
const store = createStore(
  combineReducers({ customer: customerReducer }),
  compose(
    ...[applyMiddleware(sagaMiddleware), ...storeEnhancers]
  )
);
```

6. Let's update the state when we receive an action with type ADD_CUSTOMER_SUBMITTING. Add the following nested describe block inside the reducer describe block. We're only going to write one test for now, but we'll have more tests later on:

```
describe('ADD_CUSTOMER_SUBMITTING action', () => {
  const action = { type: 'ADD_CUSTOMER_SUBMITTING' };

  it('sets status to SUBMITTING', () => {
    expect(reducer(undefined, action)).toMatchObject({
      status: 'SUBMITTING'
    });
  });
});
```

7. Make that pass by replacing the body of the reducer with the following code. We can jump directly to using a switch statement here (rather than an if) because we know for certain that we'll be filling out other action types:

```
switch(action.type) {
  case 'ADD_CUSTOMER_SUBMITTING':
    return { status: 'SUBMITTING' };
  default:
    return state;
}
```

We'll stop at this point. The functionality we've implemented shows how the saga and reducer work together, and gets all of the usual ceremony out of the way. The next two sections complete the implementations for these pieces, starting with the saga.

Setting up an entrypoint

Since we're done scaffolding, let's finally update src/index.js to load Redux at runtime.

Add the following two imports to the top of the file:

```
import { Provider } from 'react-redux';
import { configureStore } from './store';
```

Then wrap the existing JSX in a Provider component, as shown. This is how all our components will gain access to the Redux store. As we'll see later, when we test Redux-enabled components, we'll also need to wrap them in Provider components, within our test suites.

Within the production code, however, we just need one that wraps the root component:

```
ReactDOM.render(
  <Provider store={configureStore()}>
    <Router history={appHistory}>
      <Route path="/" component={App} />
    </Router>
  </Provider>,
  document.getElementById('root')
);
```

With that in place, we're ready to begin completing our Redux code around our scaffold.

Making asynchronous requests with sagas

The saga should perform all the same work as our existing `doSave`. That's what we'll build out in this section:

1. In the same test file, add the following test to the saga `describe` block (the one named `addCustomer`, not the second `reducer` block you've just been working on). It doesn't look too different from anything we've seen before:

   ```
   it('submits request to the fetch api', async () => {
     const inputCustomer = { firstName: 'Ashley' };
     dispatchRequest(inputCustomer);

     expect(window.fetch).toHaveBeenCalledWith('/customers', {
       body: JSON.stringify(inputCustomer),
       method: 'POST',
       credentials: 'same-origin',
       headers: { 'Content-Type': 'application/json' }
     });
   });
   ```

2. We'll need to define the spy on `window.fetch` for this to work. Change the `beforeEach` block as follows:

   ```
   beforeEach(() => {
     jest.spyOn(window, 'fetch');
     store = configureStore([ storeSpy ]);
   });
   ```

3. You'll also need to import `whatwg-fetch` so that `fetch` is defined:

   ```
   import 'whatwg-fetch';
   ```

4. Make this pass with the following code, in `src/sagas/customer.js`. I've chosen to extract a `fetch` function, for clarity. This helps to keep our saga function at the right level of abstraction. You'll see that we've replaced our `await` syntax with a `yield`, which doesn't look too different from what we're used to. At this point, the test should be passing:

```
const fetch = (url, data) =>
  window.fetch(url, {
    body: JSON.stringify(data),
    method: 'POST',
    credentials: 'same-origin',
    headers: { 'Content-Type': 'application/json' }
  });
export function* addCustomer({ customer }) {
 yield put({ type: 'ADD_CUSTOMER_SUBMITTING' });
 yield call(fetch, '/customers', customer);
}
```

5. The preceding code won't pass until you've imported the `call` function, so bring that in now:

```
import { put, call } from 'redux-saga/effects';
```

6. Let's carry on with this by determining what to do when we get a successful response back. Add the following test:

```
it('dispatches ADD_CUSTOMER_SUCCESSFUL on success', () => {
  dispatchRequest();

  return expectRedux(store)
    .toDispatchAnAction()
    .matching({ type: 'ADD_CUSTOMER_SUCCESSFUL', customer });
});
```

7. When we set up our fetch spy before, we didn't set a return value. We need to do that now, and we'll set it up to return the `returnCustomer` variable that is mentioned in the preceding test. Add the two highlighted lines to your `describe` block setup:

```
const customer = { id: 123 };

beforeEach(() => {
  fetchSpy = jest.fn();
  jest
    .spyOn(window, 'fetch')
    .mockReturnValue(fetchResponseOk(customer));
```

```
    store = configureStore([ storeSpy ]);
  });
```

8. Import `fetchResponseOk`. After this, you'll be able to run your test:

```
import { fetchResponseOk } from '../spyHelpers';
```

9. Now make the test pass by adding the two lines highlighted next into `addCustomer`:

```
export function* addCustomer({ customer }) {
  yield put({ type: 'ADD_CUSTOMER_SUBMITTING' });
  const result = yield call(fetch, '/customers', customer);
  const customerWithId = yield call([result, 'json']);
  yield put({
    type: 'ADD_CUSTOMER_SUCCESSFUL',
    customer: customerWithId
  });
}
```

10. What about if the call isn't successful, perhaps because of a network failure? Add a test for that:

```
it('dispatches ADD_CUSTOMER_FAILED on non-specific error', () => {
  window.fetch.mockReturnValue(fetchResponseError());
  dispatchRequest();

  return expectRedux(store)
    .toDispatchAnAction()
    .matching({ type: 'ADD_CUSTOMER_FAILED' });
});
```

11. That test makes use of `fetchReponseError`; import it now:

```
import {
  fetchResponseOk,
  fetchResponseError
} from '../spyHelpers';
```

12. Make the test pass by wrapping the existing code in an `if` statement with an `else` clause:

```
export function* addCustomer({ customer }) {
  yield put({ type: 'ADD_CUSTOMER_SUBMITTING' });
  const result = yield call(fetch, '/customers', customer);
  if(result.ok) {
    const customerWithId = yield call([result, 'json']);
    yield put({
```

```
    type: 'ADD_CUSTOMER_SUCCESSFUL',
    customer: customerWithId
  });
} else {
  yield put({ type: 'ADD_CUSTOMER_FAILED' });
}
}
```

13. Finally, let's add a test for a more specific type of failure: validation failures:

```
it('dispatches ADD_CUSTOMER_VALIDATION_FAILED if validation errors
were returned', () => {
  const errors = { field: 'field', description: 'error text' };
  window.fetch.mockReturnValue(
    fetchResponseError(422, { errors })
  );

  dispatchRequest();

  return expectRedux(store)
    .toDispatchAnAction()
    .matching({
      type: 'ADD_CUSTOMER_VALIDATION_FAILED',
      validationErrors: errors
    });
});
```

14. Make that pass with the following code:

```
export function* addCustomer({ customer }) {
  yield put({ type: 'ADD_CUSTOMER_SUBMITTING' });
  const result = yield call(fetch, '/customers', customer);
  if(result.ok) {
    const customerWithId = yield call([result, 'json']);
    yield put({
      type: 'ADD_CUSTOMER_SUCCESSFUL',
      customer: customerWithId
    });
  } else if (result.status === 422) {
    const response = yield call([result, 'json']);
    yield put({
      type: 'ADD_CUSTOMER_VALIDATION_FAILED',
      validationErrors: response.errors
    });
  } else {
    yield put({ type: 'ADD_CUSTOMER_FAILED', error: true });
  }
}
```

Compare this function to the function in `CustomerForm` that we're aiming to replace, `doSave`. The structure is identical. That's a good indicator that we're ready to work on removing `doSave` from `CustomerForm`.

Completing the reducer

 The Git tag for this section is `customer-reducer`.

We've completed our saga; now let's complete the reducer. It already partially handles the `ADD_CUSTOMER_SUBMITTING` action, but not quite. We'll start there and then move on to handling `ADD_CUSTOMER_FAILED`, `ADD_CUSTOMER_VALIDATION_FAILED`, and `ADD_CUSTOMER_SUCCESSFUL`:

1. Add this test to the `ADD_CUSTOMER_SUBMITTING actions` describe block. This test specifies typically expected behavior for reducer actions: any existing state should always be maintained:

   ```
   it('maintains existing state', () => {
     expect(reducer({ a: 123 }, action)).toMatchObject({
       a: 123
     });
   });
   ```

2. Make that pass by modifying the reducers as follows:

   ```
   export const reducer = (state = defaultState, action) => {
     switch (action.type) {
       case 'ADD_CUSTOMER_SUBMITTING':
         return { ...state, status: 'SUBMITTING' };
       default:
         return state;
     }
   };
   ```

3. It's time for the next action: `ADD_CUSTOMER_FAILED`. Here are the first two tests: I'm cheating a little by writing two out at once, but I'm feeling confident about these, probably because it's an almost exact replica of the two tests before it:

   ```
   describe('ADD_CUSTOMER_FAILED action', () => {
     const action = { type: 'ADD_CUSTOMER_FAILED' };
   ```

```
  it('sets status to FAILED', () => {
    expect(reducer(undefined, action)).toMatchObject({
      status: 'FAILED'
    });
  });

  it('maintains existing state', () => {
    expect(reducer({ a: 123 }, action)).toMatchObject({
      a: 123
    });
  });
});
```

4. Make those both passes by adding a new case statement to the `reducer` switch:

```
case 'ADD_CUSTOMER_FAILED':
  return { ...state, status: 'FAILED' };
```

5. We aren't quite done with `ADD_CUSTOMER_FAILED` just yet. In this case, we also want to set `error` to `true`. Recall that we used an error state variable in the `CustomerForm` component to mark when an unexplained error had occurred. We need to replicate that here. Add this third test to the describe block:

```
it('sets error to true', () => {
  expect(reducer(undefined, action)).toMatchObject({
    error: true
  });
});
```

6. Make that pass by modifying the case statement, as shown:

```
case 'ADD_CUSTOMER_FAILED':
  return { ...state, status: 'FAILED', error: true };
```

7. Add the next two tests in a similar fashion. The `ADD_CUSTOMER_VALIDATION_FAILED` action occurs if field validation failed:

```
describe('ADD_CUSTOMER_VALIDATION_FAILED action', () => {
  const validationErrors = { field: "error text" };
  const action = {
    type: 'ADD_CUSTOMER_VALIDATION_FAILED',
    validationErrors
  };

  it('sets status to VALIDATION_FAILED', () => {
    expect(reducer(undefined, action)).toMatchObject({
      status: 'VALIDATION_FAILED'
```

```
        });
      });

      it('maintains existing state', () => {
        expect(reducer({ a: 123 }, action)).toMatchObject({
          a: 123
        });
      });
    });
```

8. Again, make these tests pass with another case statement in the reducer:

```
case 'ADD_CUSTOMER_VALIDATION_FAILED':
  return { ...state, status: 'VALIDATION_FAILED' };
```

9. This action also needs a third test. This time, the action itself can include error information that we want to store. Add the following test:

```
it('sets validation errors to provided errors', () => {
  expect(reducer(undefined, action)).toMatchObject({
    validationErrors
  });
});
```

10. Make that pass with the change shown:

```
case 'ADD_CUSTOMER_VALIDATION_FAILED':
  return {
    ...state,
    status: 'VALIDATION_FAILED',
    validationErrors: action.validationErrors
  };
```

11. Finally, we need to handle the action ADD_CUSTOMER_SUCCESSFUL. Start with the two tests shown:

```
describe('ADD_CUSTOMER_SUCCESSFUL action', () => {
  const customer = { id: 123 };
  const action = {
    type: 'ADD_CUSTOMER_SUCCESSFUL',
    customer
  };

  it('sets status to SUCCESSFUL', () => {
    expect(reducer(undefined, action)).toMatchObject({
      status: 'SUCCESSFUL'
    });
  });
```

```
    it('maintains existing state', () => {
      expect(reducer({ a: 123 }, action)).toMatchObject({
        a: 123
      });
    });
  });
```

12. To make that pass, add the final case statement to your reducer:

```
case 'ADD_CUSTOMER_SUCCESSFUL':
  return { ...state, status: 'SUCCESSFUL' };
```

13. Add the final test. This time, the action provides the new customer object with its assigned ID. We'll certainly want to save that:

```
it('sets customer to provided customer', () => {
  expect(reducer(undefined, action)).toMatchObject({
    customer
  });
});
```

14. Make that pass by adding in the customer property:

```
case 'ADD_CUSTOMER_SUCCESSFUL':
  return {
    ...state,
    status: 'SUCCESSFUL',
    customer: action.customer
  };
```

That completes the reducer. But, before we use it, how about we dry these tests up a little?

Pulling out generator functions for reducer actions

The reducer tests we just wrote contain a lot of repetition. In fact, the majority of reducers will follow exactly the same pattern: each action will set some new data, and ensure that the existing state is not lost.

Let's write a couple of test generator functions to do that for us, to help us dry up our tests:

1. Create a new file, `test/reducerGenerators.js`, and add the following function:

```
export const itMaintainsExistingState = (reducer, action) => {
  it('maintains existing state', () => {
    const existing = { a: 123 };
    expect(reducer(existing, action)).toMatchObject(existing);
  });
};
```

2. Add the following import to the top of `src/sagas/customer.test.js`:

```
import { itMaintainsExistingState } from '../reducerGenerators';
```

3. Modify your tests to use this function, deleting the test in each `describe` block and replacing it with the following single line:

```
itMaintainsExistingState(reducer, action);
```

4. Back in `test/reducerGenerators.js`, define the following function:

```
export const itSetsStatus = (reducer, action, value) => {
  it(`sets status to ${value}`, () => {
    expect(reducer(undefined, action)).toMatchObject({
      status: value
    });
  });
};
```

5. In `test/sagas/customer.test.js`, modify the existing import to pull in the new function:

```
import {
  itMaintainsExistingState,
  itSetsStatus
} from '../reducerGenerators';
```

6. Modify your tests to use this function, just as you did before. Make sure you run your tests to prove they work! Your tests should now be much shorter. Here's an example of the describe block for ADD_CUSTOMER_SUCCESSFUL:

```
describe('ADD_CUSTOMER_SUBMITTING action', () => {
  const action = { type: 'ADD_CUSTOMER_SUBMITTING' };
```

```
        itMaintainsExistingState(reducer, action);
        itSetsStatus(reducer, action, 'SUBMITTING');
    });
```

We'll use these generator functions again in the next chapter.

Switching out component state for Redux state

The saga and reducer are now complete and ready to be used in the `CustomerForm` React component. This isn't a trivial exercise, so to warm up to it we'll start by building a helper that will mitigate the difficulty.

Building a helper function to render with store

Unlike with React Router, with Redux we generally prefer to use full rendering over shallow rendering. We prefer that approach for a couple of reasons:

- Unlike React Router, Redux isn't rendering components, so we don't need to assert that specific Redux components are part of the React component instance graph.
- Redux actions perform a variety of user-defined operations when they are dispatched. We'd like to be able to run them within our tests so that we can assert our interactions. This is different from the Router API, such as the `history` prop, which has fixed behavior.

To test our components, we need to render each component wrapped in a `Provider` component, as we saw earlier when we wrote out our `src/index.js` file. This needs to be passed a store, which we'll set up using `expect-saga` and our `configureStore` functions.

That's quite a lot of machinery, and we'll be using it in every component that interacts with Redux, so let's build a new helper function in `test/domManipulators.js` before we proceed:

1. Open `test/domManipulators.js` and add the following imports:

```
import { Provider } from 'react-redux';
import { storeSpy } from 'expect-redux';
import { configureStore } from '../src/store';
```

2. At the bottom of the file, add a new `createContainerWithStore` function, as shown. It decorates the `createContainer` function with two new properties: `store` and `renderWithStore`:

```
export const createContainerWithStore = () => {
  const store = configureStore([storeSpy]);

  const container = createContainer();
  return {
    ...container,
    store,
    renderWithStore: component => {
      act(() => {
        ReactDOM.render(
          <Provider store={store}>{component}</Provider>,
          container.container
        );
      });
    }
  };
};
```

We're ready to use this in our component.

Submitting a React form by dispatching a Redux action

 The Git tag for this section is `replace-state-with-redux`.

At the start of the chapter, we looked at how the purpose of this change was essentially a transplant of `CustomerForm`'s `doSave` function into a Redux action. So, our code is to replace that call with a dispatch of an ADD_CUSTOMER_REQUEST action to the Redux store.

The trickiest part of this is how we deal with submission errors. In the existing code, any errors that were caught in `doSave` were directly saved to the component state, which would then cause the component to re-render. With our new Redux setup, that component state has been promoted to props. A re-render still occurs, but it's done indirectly. Say, for example, a server validation occurs.

The saga will dispatch an ADD_CUSTOMER_VALIDATION_FAILED action to the store, which is then picked up by our reducer. That, in turn, updates the store state with validationErrors, which then causes our connected component to notice a change to its subscribed value, which finally then triggers a re-render of the CustomerForm component, with the new validationErrors value passed in.

Since most of this is done implicitly within the react-redux logic, our tests don't need to worry about it. We no longer need to check that we update the component state when a fetch request returns a 422. Instead, we can dispatch an ADD_CUSTOMER_VALIDATION_FAILED event and wait for the effects to trickle through to our component.

We'll start by making our component Redux-aware:

1. Add the following import to the top of test/CustomerForm.test.js:

```
import { expectRedux } from 'expect-redux';
```

2. Update the domManipulators import, pulling in createContainerWithStore rather than createContainer:

```
import {
  createContainerWithStore,
  withEvent
} from './domManipulators';
```

3. Modify the describe block setup to call createContainerWithStore rather than createContainer. Also, save off renderWithStore rather than render, and save off store too:

```
let renderWithStore,
  store,
  ...;

beforeEach(() => {
  ({
    renderWithStore,
    store,
    ...
  } = createContainerWithStore());
});
```

4. Replace all calls to render with renderWithStore. Be careful if you're doing a search and replace, as the word *render* appears in some of the test descriptions.

5. We're *almost* ready to update our production code to bring in Redux. But before we do that, let's rework a single test that will force us to dispatch that action. The test we'll replace is calls fetch with the right properties when submitting data. Change that test to the following. In addition to having different expectations, the test is no longer async; we can use the trick we used in the previous section to return the Promise to Jest, and make Jest wait for it instead:

```
it('dispatches ADD_CUSTOMER_REQUEST when submitting data', async ()
=> {
  renderWithStore(<CustomerForm {...validCustomer} />);
  await submit(form('customer'));
  return expectRedux(store)
    .toDispatchAnAction()
    .matching({
      type: 'ADD_CUSTOMER_REQUEST',
      customer: validCustomer
  });
});
```

6. To make this pass, we'll use a side-by-side implementation. In handleSubmit, add the highlighted line. This calls a new addCustomerRequest prop, which we haven't yet defined, but we will do so once we connect with Redux in the next step:

```
const handleSubmit = async e => {
  e.preventDefault();
  const validationResult = validateMany(validators, customer);
  if (!anyErrors(validationResult)) {
    await doSave();
    addCustomerRequest(customer);
  } else {
    setValidationErrors(validationResult);
  }
};
```

7. It's time to connect our component to Redux. To do that, we first need to define two objects: `mapStateToProps` and `mapDispatchToProps`; that tells Redux what state the component is interested in and what actions the component will dispatch. At the top of `src/CustomerForm.js`, add the following definitions. We'll pass these to the `connect` function:

```
const mapStateToProps = () => ({});
const mapDispatchToProps = {
  addCustomerRequest: customer => ({
    type: 'ADD_CUSTOMER_REQUEST',
    customer
  })
};
```

8. We'll use the `connect` function from `react-redux` to connect our component. Import that now, by adding the following line to the top of `src/CustomerForm.js`:

```
import { connect } from 'react-redux';
```

9. Now let's hook up `component`. We'll do this by wrapping the definition of `CustomerForm` in a `connect` call, and then add in the new `addCustomerRequest` prop. The `connect` call that wraps our function makes everything pretty ugly, but I promise you'll get used to it! Be careful not to miss out the closing bracket in the last line. After this change, your updated tests should pass:

```
export const CustomerForm = connect(
  mapStateToProps,
  mapDispatchToProps
)(
  ({
    firstName,
    lastName,
    phoneNumber,
    onSave,
    addCustomerRequest
  }) => {

    . . .

  }
);
```

The `connect` call returns a React element in place of your function. This changes the return type of your component and that can affect how you stub it out. See the following section, *Stubbing out components built with useMemo*, for more information.

At this point, your component is now Redux-aware, and it's dispatching the right action to Redux. The remaining work is to modify the component to deal with validation errors coming from Redux rather than the component state. It essentially means replacing a whole bunch of tests:

1. To start off, find the test named `renders error message when fetch call fails`. Replace it with the implementation shown. It's quite different; it simulates an `ADD_CUSTOMER_FAILED` action so that we make sure all the Redux wiring is correct. Don't forget to remove the `async` keyword from the test function:

```
it('renders error message when error prop is true', () => {
    renderWithStore(<CustomerForm {...validCustomer} />);
    store.dispatch({ type: 'ADD_CUSTOMER_FAILED' });
    expect(element('.error').textContent).toMatch('error occurred');
});
```

2. To make this pass, modify `mapStateToProps` to pull out `error` from the store:

```
const mapStateToProps = ({ customer: { error } }) => ({ error });
```

3. Now add that to the props passed into `CustomerForm`:

```
({
    firstName,
    lastName,
    phoneNumber,
    onSave,
    addCustomerRequest,
    error
}) => {
```

4. Delete the error state variable that's defined with a `useState` hook at the top of `CustomerForm`. (Your tests won't run until you do this, due to `error` being declared twice.)

5. Now you'll also need to delete any line where `setError` is called. There are two occurrences, both in `doSave`. Your tests should be passing at this stage.

6. The next test, `clears error message when fetch call succeeds`, can be deleted. The reducer, as it stands, doesn't actually do this; see the *Exercises* section.

7. The test `does not submit the form when there are validation errors` needs to be updated as follows. It should pass already:

```
it('does not submit the form when there are validation errors',
async () => {
  renderWithStore(<CustomerForm />);

  await submit(form('customer'));
  return expectRedux(store)
    .toNotDispatchAnAction(100)
    .ofType('ADD_CUSTOMER_REQUEST');
});
```

This test uses the `toNotDispatchAnAction` matcher, which should always be used with a timeout. Since it's hard to prove that something *doesn't* happen in an asynchronous environment, this matcher should be used judiciously. In this case, we're fine, as our code isn't performing any explicitly asynchronous work.

8. Let's move on to the next test, `renders field validation errors from server`. Replace the existing test with the next test, remembering to remove the `async` keyword from the function definition:

```
it('renders field validation errors from server', () => {
  const errors = {
    phoneNumber: 'Phone number already exists in the system'
  };
  renderWithStore(<CustomerForm {...validCustomer} />);
  store.dispatch({
    type: 'ADD_CUSTOMER_VALIDATION_FAILED',
    validationErrors: errors
  });
  expect(element('.error').textContent).toMatch(
    errors.phoneNumber
  );
});
```

9. To make this pass, start by modifying `mapStateToProps`. This is slightly different because our component already has a `validationErrors` state variable that covers *both* server and client validation errors. We can't replace it entirely, because it handles client errors in addition to server errors.

So, let's *rename* the prop we get back from the server:

```
const mapStateToProps = ({
  customer: { validationErrors, error }
}) => ({
  serverValidationErrors: validationErrors,
  error
});
```

This highlights a design issue in our original code.
The validationErrors state variable had *two* uses, which were mixed up, and now we have to correct for it.

10. Pull in the new prop into CustomerForm:

```
({
  firstName,
  lastName,
  phoneNumber,
  onSave,
  addCustomerRequest,
  error,
  serverValidationErrors
}) => {
```

11. Finally for this test, update the renderError function to render errors for both validationErrors (client-side validation) and serverValidationErrors (server-side validation):

```
const renderError = fieldName => {
  const allValidationErrors = {
    ...validationErrors,
    ...serverValidationErrors
  };
  if (hasError(allValidationErrors, fieldName)) {
    return (
      <span className="error">
        {allValidationErrors[fieldName]}
      </span>
    );
  }
};
```

12. The next tests we need to look at are for the `submitting` indicator. We'll update the tests to respond to store actions rather than form submission. Here's the first one:

```
it('displays indicator when form is submitting', () => {
  renderWithStore(<CustomerForm {...validCustomer} />);
  store.dispatch({ type: 'ADD_CUSTOMER_SUBMITTING' });
  expect(element('.submittingIndicator')).not.toBeNull();
});
```

13. To make this pass, start by adding `status` to `mapStateToProps`:

```
const mapStateToProps = ({
  customer: { validationErrors, error, status }
}) => ({
  serverValidationErrors: validationErrors,
  error,
  status
});
```

14. Add in the prop to `CustomerForm`:

```
({
  firstName,
  lastName,
  phoneNumber,
  onSave,
  addCustomerRequest,
  error,
  serverValidationErrors,
  status
}) => {
```

15. Delete the state variable for `submitting`, and replace it with this:

```
const submitting = status === 'SUBMITTING';
```

16. Delete anywhere that `setSubmitting` is called within this component. The test should now pass.

17. Then, update the `hides indicator when form has submitted` test. This test won't need any change to the production code:

```
it('hides indicator when form has submitted', () => {
  renderWithStore(<CustomerForm {...validCustomer} />);
  store.dispatch({ type: 'ADD_CUSTOMER_SUCCESSFUL' });
  expect(element('.submittingIndicator')).toBeNull();
});
```

18. Finally, find the test `disables the submit button when submitting` and modify it in the same way as *Step 12*. Note that you'll only have this test if you completed the exercises from Chapter 5, *Humanizing Forms*.

That's it for test changes, but there is now some code we need to delete, as our side-by-side implementation is complete. We want to strip out the `doSave` function.

There is, however, one part of that function that we haven't replaced yet: that's the invocation of `onSave`, which is how our form alerts its parent component that submission is complete. We'll come back to that in the next section.

For now, follow these steps to remove `doSave` entirely:

1. Start by deleting the following tests, which are no longer necessary:
   - `notifies onSave when form is submitted`
   - `does not notify onSave if the POST request returns an error`
2. Delete the function `onSave` from `CustomerForm`.
3. Remove the invocation of `onSave` from `handleSubmit`. This function no longer awaits anything, so you can safely remove `async` from the function definition.
4. Finally, delete `defaultProp` from `CustomerForm`.

Now it's time to figure out what to do about that `onSave` functionality that we just removed.

Protecting against silent breakages

Our `CustomerForm` component is now in the right shape we want in. If you run all tests now using `npm test`, you'll see that all your tests are passing.

But did you notice that we have, in fact, broken our application? Go ahead and manually test it: what happens when you try to save your customer? The customer saves, but the screen doesn't change.

By removing the `onSave` prop, we changed the public interface of the `CustomerForm` component. Unfortunately, no one told `App`, which is still expecting it to be notified via `onSave`.

This is a serious problem. Clearly, our tests have not given us 100% protection. What can we do about this?

You might be able to guess my answer already, but it is *not* to set `propTypes` or to introduce typing. The answer is to add *more* tests, just not the same kind of tests we've been writing so far. They will be end-to-end tests, and they have an advantage over types because they specify *why* props are needed rather than just *what* props are needed. They are also high-level enough that they won't refer directly to your component tree. Instead, they will refer to the DOM and user actions. That means they are not brittle and they resist design change, unlike `propTypes`.

 This is *not* a failure of test-driven development, nor is it "proof" that TDD doesn't work. Remember that TDD is about helping you design your application to a specification. It is not about protecting against regression, and that there's no such thing as 100% protection against error.

In this case, we would want a test that operates against `App` and performs the following actions. The test could be called something like *displays application form after adding a customer*:

- Navigates to the root page
- Clicks the **Add customer** button
- Fills in customer information and clicks **Submit**
- Asserts that the application form then appears on screen.

There's a difficulty here though. The last step mentions the application form. How do we know that it appears on the screen? Do we look for `ApplicationForm` and assert on that? Well, no, because that would require the use of shallow rendering in order to check for that specific type, and shallow rendering is limited in that we couldn't use it to fill out forms, to give just one example. OK, so what about assigning an `id` of `appointmentForm` to the root rendered element in the `ApplicationForm` component, and then looking for that? Well, we could, but we'll also need to add a test to `ApplicationForm` to assert that the ID is set. What's more, if we're going to do that, aren't we getting into the realm of end-to-end testing? Why not extend the scope of the test and fill in the application form too, submit that and check that we end up back at the root page?

`Section 4`, *Acceptance Testing with BDD*, covers **acceptance testing**, which is a form of end-to-end testing. While it's not the only way to do end-to-end testing, it would indeed help out with this scenario.

Traditionally in the TDD world there is a distinction between *classicist* and *mockist*. Mockists prefer to mock collaborators in an effort to keep units independent; classicists prefer to not mock and test logic through all collaborators. At this point a classicist will be saying "*I told you so!*" because it's the use of mocks that has caused this breakage. The reality however is that this distinction between classicist and mockist is a false dichotomy: both approaches are useful and you should know when and how to apply either approach.

Shifting workflow to Redux

The Git tag for this section is `redux-workflow`. This tag contains additional code since the last section, so you may wish to switch to it now, or add the differences yourself, which are described next.

For more detailed instructions, see the *To get the most out of this book* section in the `Preface`.

Putting aside the question of how to complete our test coverage, how can we fix the problem?

Let's see whether we can restate it. Previously, our `onSave` callback was used to notify `App` that a customer had been saved. That callback was passed a `customer` object, but now the callback is gone and the `customer` is safely tucked away in our Redux store.

We can split the problem into two distinct subproblems:

- How can we trigger workflow and render the `AppointmentForm`?
- How can we pull out the `customer` from Redux?

As we solve these problems, we have to keep in mind that there's a second route into `AppointmentForm`, which is via the `CustomerSearch` screen. We have to make sure that continues to work. (Wouldn't some end-to-end tests be great right now?)

The solution is two fold:

- Build a reducer for an appointment that responds to an action of `SET_CUSTOMER_FOR_APPOINTMENT` that stores a `customer` object. The `AppointmentForm` component can read `customer` from the store, rather than from a direct prop.

- Build a new saga that listens for an ADD_CUSTOMER_SUCCESSFUL request, dispatches a new SET_CUSTOMER_FOR_APPOINTMENT action, and then routes to /addAppointment.

The first part of these solutions has already been coded up for you in the redux-workflow tag, which we won't cover in detail as it's very similar to what we've seen before. There are two new files: src/reducers/appointment.js and test/reducers/appointment.test.js, and the AppointmentForm has been updated so that it is now connected to the Redux store. In addition, src/store.js has been updated to wire in the appointment reducer.

This section will concentrate on the second part of the solution, which we can split again into two more subproblems:

- Building a customerAdded saga that routes to /addAppointment
- Updating App to tie it all together

However, before we get on to doing those, let's focus in a subtle change that was made in that latest redux-workflow branch.

Stubbing out components built with useMemo

There is one aspect of the AppointmentForm change that is worth drawing attention to.

The AppointmentFormLoader test suite (in test/AppointmentFormLoader.test.js) has changed how it stubs out AppointmentForm. Previously, we used jest.spyOn to stub it out:

```
jest
  .spyOn(AppointmentFormExports, 'AppointmentForm')
  .mockReturnValue(null);
```

Unfortunately, spyOn does not work with functions that are wrapped with the connect function. connect doesn't return a function itself but instead, an object that React understands.

If that sounds a bit cryptic, think of it like this. If you were to run console.log(AppointmentForm) prior to changing it to use connect, you'd see this in your console output:

```
[Function: AppointmentForm2]
```

It's just a standard function. But if you log it out once it has been wrapped in `connect`, it'll look like this:

```
{ '$$typeof': Symbol(react.memo),
  type: [Function: ConnectFunction],
  compare: null,
  WrappedComponent: [Function],
  displayName: 'Connect(Component)'
  ...
}
```

It has returned you a React *element*, which is clearly an object, not a function. The `connect` function (from `react-redux` v7 onwards) uses the `useMemo` function as a performance optimization and so it returns a React element. Older versions of `connect` did in fact return functions.

`spyOn` can only stub out functions. In order to stub out the newly connected `AppointmentForm`, and in fact anything that uses `useMemo`, we need to revert to our pre-`spyOn` ways and just overwrite the value ourselves:

```
AppointmentFormExports.AppointmentForm = jest.fn(() => null);
```

This will change the type of `AppointmentForm` back from a React element to a function. When rendering, React accepts both and so we shouldn't expect anything to blow up due to this type change.

 If you wanted to express intent more clearly, you could move this code to a helper file with a name like `spyOnReactType` or something similar.

Navigating router history in a Redux saga

It's fairly simple to navigate router history within a saga. We just have to make sure that we can get hold of the same `history` object that is passed to our React components. Unfortunately, the React router doesn't come set up by default to make this easy for us.

The trick is to use `Router` rather than `BrowserRouter` in your application entrypoint. That allows you to pass in your own `history`, which you can then explicitly construct yourself.

This has already been done for you in the repo. Here's `src/history.js`:

```
import { createBrowserHistory } from 'history';

export const appHistory = createBrowserHistory();
```

This module is already imported into `src/index.js`, where `appHistory` is passed into a `Router` instance. We can now begin to use the same module in our saga:

1. Create the file `test/sagas/app.test.js` and add the following first test. It replaces `appHistory` with a `pushSpy` that we can then assert on:

```
import { storeSpy, expectRedux } from 'expect-redux';
import { configureStore } from '../../src/store';
import * as HistoryExports from '../../src/history';

describe('customerAdded', () => {
  let store, pushSpy;

  beforeEach(() => {
    pushSpy = jest.spyOn(HistoryExports.appHistory, 'push');
    store = configureStore([storeSpy]);
  });

  const dispatchRequest = customer =>
    store.dispatch({
      type: 'ADD_CUSTOMER_SUCCESSFUL',
      customer
    });

  it('pushes /addAppointment to history', () => {
    dispatchRequest();
    expect(pushSpy).toHaveBeenCalledWith('/addAppointment');
  });
});
```

2. To make that pass, we'll first need to implement a new saga and then add it into store. Create the file `src/sagas/app.js` and add the following generator function:

```
import { put } from 'redux-saga/effects';
import { appHistory } from '../history';

export function* customerAdded({ customer }) {
  appHistory.push('/addAppointment');
}
```

3. Open `src/store.js` and add the new `customerAdded` saga to the root saga. The test should pass after this change:

```
import { customerAdded } from './sagas/app';

function* rootSaga() {
  yield takeLatest('ADD_CUSTOMER_REQUEST', addCustomer);
  yield takeLatest('ADD_CUSTOMER_SUCCESSFUL', customerAdded);
}
```

4. We need to do just one more thing in this saga. We need to push the added `customer` into the `AppointmentForm` so that it's ready for use. Add the following test to `test/sagas/app.test.js`:

```
it('dispatches a SET_CUSTOMER_FOR_APPOINTMENT action', () => {
  const customer = { id: 123 };
  dispatchRequest(customer);
  return expectRedux(store)
    .toDispatchAnAction()
    .matching({
      type: 'SET_CUSTOMER_FOR_APPOINTMENT',
      customer
    });
});
```

That's all there is to it. This file can easily be expanded with more workflow actions as they are migrated out of `App`. See the *Exercises* section for more information on how to go about doing that.

Separating Redux connection from presentation

Our remaining task is to strip the `onSave` callback logic from `App`.

There is, however, one small issue. We still need to support the use case of loading `AppointmentFormLoader` when the user chooses a customer record from the *Customer search* screen. Since the search actions are held within `App`, we need to ensure `App` is able to dispatch actions to Redux.

We'll do this using a different technique than with `CustomerForm` and `AppointmentForm`. In those two components, we exported the Redux-connected component, like this:

```
export const CustomerForm = connect(
  mapStateToProps,
  mapDispatchToProps
)(
```

```
  // ... original CustomerForm component here ...
);
```

With this approach, all of the original tests needed to be modified to use `renderWithStore`. That function wraps our component under test in a `Provider` component that gives it access to the Redux store:

```
<Provider store={store}>
  {component}
</Provider>
```

This approach is fine for `CustomerForm` and `AppointmentForm` since they are fully rendered, but `App` uses shallow rendering. Shallow rendering doesn't support rendering hierarchies of custom components. In other words, this approach won't work for `App`.

What we can do instead is create a new component called `ConnectedApp` that wraps `App`. We leave our tests for `App` as they are, and either don't do any testing for `ConnectedApp` or very minimal testing if we do any.

Of course, since we want `App` to be able to dispatch to the Redux store, we'll need new tests for `App` but we can simply pass in a spy function in place of a "real" Redux dispatch function.

Let's get started by removing the `onSave` callback:

1. Open `test/App.test.js` and delete the following two tests:
    - `navigates to /addAppointment after the CustomerForm is submitted`
    - `passes saved customer to AppointmentFormLoader after the CustomerForm is submitted`

2. Locate the `renders CustomerForm at the /addCustomer endpoint` test. Modify it to read as follows. Since we're no longer passing any props to `CustomerForm`, we can replace the `render` prop with the simpler `component` variation of `Route`:

    ```
    it('renders CustomerForm at the /addCustomer endpoint', () => {
      render(<App />);
      expect(routeFor('/addCustomer').props.component).toEqual(
        CustomerForm
      );
    });
    ```

3. In `src/App.js`, modify the routes as follows:

```
<Route path="/addCustomer" component={CustomerForm} />
<Route
  path="/addAppointment"
  render={() => (
    <AppointmentFormLoader onSave={transitionToDayView} />
  )}
```

4. Let's proceed with ensuring that the search customer action dispatches the `SET_CUSTOMER_FOR_APPOINTMENT` action. Locate the `search customers` describe block and add the following setup to the top of it:

```
let dispatchSpy;

beforeEach(() => {
  dispatchSpy = jest.fn();
});
```

5. Modify the `renderSearchActionsForCustomer` to pass this spy in as a new prop, `setCustomerForAppointment`. In a later step, we'll connect this prop to Redux in a new `ConnectedApp` component:

```
const renderSearchActionsForCustomer = customer => {
  render(
    <App
      history={{ push: historySpy }}
      setCustomerForAppointment={dispatchSpy}
    />
  );
  const customerSearch = routeFor(
    '/searchCustomers'
  ).props.render();
  const searchActionsComponent =
    customerSearch.props.renderCustomerActions;
  return searchActionsComponent(customer);
};
```

6. Locate the test `passes saved customer to AppointmentFormLoader when clicking the Create appointment button`. Modify it as shown. It previously checked that `AppointmentFormLoader` was passed a customer prop. Now instead we need to check that we've dispatched that same customer to the Redux store:

```
it('dispatches SET_CUSTOMER_FOR_APPOINTMENT when clicking the
Create appointment button', async () => {
```

```
      const button = childrenOf(
        renderSearchActionsForCustomer(customer)
      )[0];
      click(button);
      expect(dispatchSpy).toHaveBeenCalledWith(customer);
    });
```

7. To make that pass, firstly add the new prop to App:

```
    export const App = ({ history, setCustomerForAppointment }) => {
      ...
    };
```

8. Update `transitionToAddAppointment` to call this rather than `setCustomer`:

```
    const transitionToAddAppointment = customer => {
      setCustomerForAppointment(customer);
      history.push('/addAppointment');
    };
```

9. You can now delete the `customer` state variable, and remove the `useState` import, since there's nothing using it.

10. That's all that remains for the test coverage. The final thing we need to do is build a new `ConnectedApp`. To start, add an import for the `connect` function at the top of `src/App.js`:

```
    import { connect } from 'react-redux';
```

11. At the bottom of the file, define a new `mapDispatchToProps` object and a new `ConnectedApp` component:

```
    const mapDispatchToProps = {
      setCustomerForAppointment: customer => ({
        type: 'SET_CUSTOMER_FOR_APPOINTMENT',
        customer
      })
    };

    export const ConnectedApp = connect(
      null,
      mapDispatchToProps
    )(App);
```

12. Finally, in `src/index.js`, update the `App` import to import `ConnectedApp` instead:

```
import { ConnectedApp } from './App';

ReactDOM.render(
  <Provider store={configureStore()}>
    <Router history={appHistory}>
      <Route path="/" component={ConnectedApp} />
    </Router>
  </Provider>,
  document.getElementById('root')
);
```

All being well, your app should now be running with Redux managing the workflow.

Summary

This has been a whirlwind tour of Redux and how to refactor your application to it, using TDD.

The process worked as follows: We chose a small piece of our application to work on first; then, we did some up-front design; we then built our saga and reducer, and finally we integrated it into our existing code.

In the next chapter, we'll add in yet another library: **GraphQL**.

Exercises

The work we started in this chapter is only the beginning of the refactor to Redux. I'd encourage you to continue the process in your own codebase, using the following exercises as a starting point:

- Modify the customer reducer to ensure that `error` is reset to `false` when the `ADD_CUSTOMER_SUCCESSFUL` action occurs.
- Update `AppointmentForm` to submit its data via Redux in the same way as we've done with `CustomerForm`. Pull out the history change from `App` into its own saga that is triggered when an action of type `ADD_APPOINTMENT_SUCCESSFUL` occurs.

- Repeat the process for `CustomerSearch`. This time, you can add to the existing customer reducer rather than create a new one.
- Now that you have Redux actions for `CustomerSearch`, remove the last of the transition logic from `App` and push it into a saga.

Further learning

- MDN documentation on generator functions: `https://developer.mozilla.org/en-US/docs/Web/JavaScript/Reference/Operators/function*`
- `expect-redux`: `https://github.com/rradczewski/expect-redux`

Test-driving GraphQL

9

GraphQL offers an alternative mechanism for fetching data, but it's not just a drop-in replacement for the `fetch` API. In providing a layer of abstraction above HTTP calls, it offers a whole bunch of additional features that can be added to all of your requests with little effort.

The system has a reputation for being advanced or complicated, but, as we'll see in this chapter, it's really nothing harder than the `fetch` API, particularly if you're following TDD.

We'll use the Relay library to connect to our backend. This is a bare-bones GraphQL implementation that does the job well and without too much magic. If you're using other GraphQL libraries in place of Relay, the techniques we'll explore in this chapter will also apply.

We're going to build a new `CustomerHistory` component that displays details of a customer, together with a list of their appointment history.

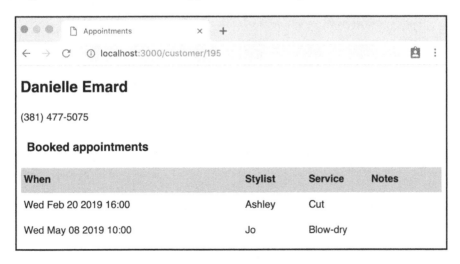

Showing customer history

There are three essential parts to this puzzle:

- The **Relay environment**, which describes how your GraphQL connection is built—for example, if it uses HTTP or WebSockets, and what caching strategy to apply
- A **data store**, which in our case will continue to be Redux
- The **React component**, which will connect with Redux in the usual way

This chapter covers the following topics:

- Installing Relay
- Test-driving the Relay environment
- Building the GraphQL reducer
- Building the `CustomerHistory` component

Installing Relay

The Git tag for this section is `relay-environment`. It contains solutions to the exercises from the previous chapter, so if you haven't completed the *Exercises* section yourself, then you should move to this tag now so that you're up to date.

For more detailed instructions, see the *To get the most out of this book* section in the `Preface`.

There are three parts to Relay that we'll need to install. Type the following at the command line:

```
npm install --save react-relay
npm install --save-dev babel-plugin-relay relay-compiler
```

You'll also need to update your `.babelrc` file to include the Babel plugin:

```
{
  "presets": ["@babel/env", "@babel/react"],
  "plugins": ["@babel/transform-runtime", "relay"]
}
```

Once you've done that, you're good to go.

The server you've been using already has a GraphQL endpoint set up in the /graphql endpoint. It uses the graphql NPM package to provide this functionality.

Testing the Relay environment

The core of Relay is the fetchQuery function. This function sends requests to your GraphQL endpoint. One of the parameters to the fetchQuery function is the *environment*, and we'll set this up in this section. This is an object of type Environment. We create it once and export it via a getEnvironment function, which our sagas will be able to call.

One of the arguments that the Environment object requires is a function that actually performs the fetch by calling window.fetch. We'll call this performFetch function and we'll start by building it first, and then move on to getEnvironment.

The Relay environment is an extension point for Relay, where all manner of functionality can be added. Data caching is one example. If you're interested in how to do that, check out the *Further learning* section at the end of this chapter.

The file that we'll build, src/relayEnvironment.js, is for the most part boilerplate code that you may be able to transfer between tests. It is feature agnostic—we only need to build it once and we're done.

Let's begin by creating our own performFetch function:

1. Create a new file, test/relayEnvironment.test.js, and add the following setup. This sets up our window.fetch spy in the same way as usual. There are two new constants here, text and variables, which we'll use in our first test:

```
import 'whatwg-fetch';
import { fetchResponseOk, fetchResponseError } from './spyHelpers';
import { performFetch } from '../src/relayEnvironment';

describe('performFetch', () => {
  let response = { data: { id: 123 } };
  const text = 'test';
  const variables = { a: 123 };

  beforeEach(() => {
    jest
```

```
      .spyOn(window, 'fetch')
      .mockReturnValue(fetchResponseOk(response));
  });
});
```

2. Add the first test, which checks that `performFetch` calls `window.fetch` with the right parameters:

```
it('calls window fetch', () => {
  performFetch({ text }, variables);
  expect(window.fetch).toHaveBeenCalledWith('/graphql', {
    method: 'POST',
    headers: {
      'Content-Type': 'application/json'
    },
    body: JSON.stringify({
      query: text,
      variables
    })
  });
});
```

3. Create a new file, `src/relayEnvironment.js`, and make the test pass with the following code:

```
export const performFetch = (operation, variables) =>
  window
    .fetch('/graphql', {
      method: 'POST',
      headers: { 'Content-Type': 'application/json' },
      body: JSON.stringify({
        query: operation.text,
        variables
      })
    });
```

4. The next test checks that we return the right data from the function. Relay expects our `performFetch` function to return a promise that will either resolve or reject. In this case, we're resolving it to the fetch response:

```
it('returns the request data', async () => {
  const result = await performFetch({ text }, variables);
  expect(result).toEqual(response);
});
```

5. Make that pass:

```
export const performFetch = (operation, variables) =>
  window
    .fetch('/graphql', ...)
    .then(result => result.json());
```

6. Now we need to handle the error cases. We need the promise to reject if an HTTP error occurred. We use a new form of `expect` that we haven't seen before; it takes a promise and expects it to reject:

```
it('rejects when the request fails', () => {
  window.fetch.mockReturnValue(fetchResponseError(500));
  return expect(performFetch({ text }, variables)).rejects.toEqual(
    new Error(500)
  );
});
```

7. In our production code, we'll test if the fetch response's `ok` property is `false`, and reject the promise if it is. Add the following function:

```
const verifyStatusOk = result => {
  if (!result.ok) {
    return Promise.reject(new Error(500));
  } else {
    return result;
  }
};
```

8. Call that function within your promise chain. After this, our `performFetch` function is complete:

```
export const performFetch = (operation, variables) =>
  window
    .fetch('/graphql', ...)
    .then(verifyStatusOk)
    .then(result => result.json());
```

9. Now let's test `getEnvironment`. Import that now at the top of `test/relayEnvironment.test.js`:

```
import {
  performFetch,
  getEnvironment
} from '../src/relayEnvironment';
```

10. The `getEnvironment` function will construct an `Environment` object, which, in turn, requires a whole bunch of other Relay types to be constructed. These types come directly from the `relay` package. In order to stub them out, we'll need to create a **module mock** with the `jest.mock` function. This function is special in that it is hoisted to the top of the file and will replace all functions and classes within that module before anything has a chance to load the file. At the same time, we also need to import all of the original functions ourselves so that we can spy on them in our tests. Add the following to the top of the file:

```
import {
  Environment,
  Network,
  Store,
  RecordSource
} from 'relay-runtime';
jest.mock('relay-runtime');
```

11. Let's start with a basic test. We want to test that the `Environment` constructor was called. Nothing more than that. The `getEnvironment` call actually happens in the `beforeAll` block; that's because, eventually, we'll memoize the value that's returned, and so only the first call to `getEnvironment` will trigger any of the mocks. That would make our tests misleading if we called `getEnvironment` in each test and then asserted on the mock values; only the first call to `getEnvironment` would have any impact, so it's better to call it just once from our tests:

```
describe('getEnvironment', () => {
  const environment = { a: 123 };

  beforeAll(() => {
    Environment.mockImplementation(() => environment);

    getEnvironment();
  });

  it('returns environment', () => {
    expect(getEnvironment()).toEqual(environment);
  });
});
```

12. To make that pass, start by adding all the imports in the production code. That's overkill for this test, but we'll use the rest of them in the next test:

```
import {
  Environment,
  Network,
  RecordSource,
  Store
} from 'relay-runtime';
```

13. Make it pass, very simply, by adding this code at the bottom of the file:

```
export const getEnvironment = () =>
  new Environment();
```

14. The next test makes sure we pass the right arguments to `Environment`. Its first argument is the result of calling `Network.create`, and the second argument is the result of constructing a `Store` object. The tests need to mock those out and then check the return values:

```
describe('getEnvironment', () => {
  const environment = { a: 123 };
  const network = { b: 234 };
  const store = { c: 345 };

  beforeAll(() => {
    Environment.mockImplementation(() => environment);
    Network.create.mockReturnValue(network);
    Store.mockImplementation(() => store);

    getEnvironment();
  });

  it('returns environment', () => {
    expect(getEnvironment()).toEqual(environment);
  });

  it('calls Environment with network and store', () => {
    expect(Environment).toHaveBeenCalledWith({ network, store });
  });
});
```

Note the difference in how we mock out constructors and functions calls. To mock out `new Store` and `new Environment`, we need to use `mockImplementation(fn)`. To mock out `Network.create` we need to use `mockReturnValue(returnValue)`.

15. Make it pass by updating the function to pass those arguments to the `Environment` constructor:

```
export const getEnvironment = () =>
  new Environment({
    network: Network.create(),
    store: new Store()
  });
```

16. Next up, we need to ensure that `Network.create` gets a reference to our `performFetch` function:

```
it('calls Network.create with performFetch', () => {
  expect(Network.create).toHaveBeenCalledWith(performFetch);
});
```

17. Make that pass by simply passing `performFetch` to the `Network.create` function:

```
export const environment = new Environment({
  network: Network.create(performFetch),
  store: new Store()
});
```

18. The `Store` constructor needs a `RecordSource` object. Add a new mock implementation for `RecordSource` in your test setup:

```
describe('getEnvironment', () => {
  ...
  const recordSource = { d: 456 };

  beforeAll(() => {
    ...
    RecordSource.mockImplementation(() => recordSource);

    getEnvironment();
  });
  ...
});
```

19. Add the following test to specify the behavior we want:

```
it('calls Store with RecordSource', () => {
  expect(Store).toHaveBeenCalledWith(recordSource);
});
```

20. Make that pass by constructing a new `RecordSource` object:

```
export const environment = new Environment({
  network: Network.create(performFetch),
  store: new Store(new RecordSource())
});
```

21. Finally, we need a test to ensure that the environment is only constructed once:

```
it('constructs the object only once', () => {
  getEnvironment();
  expect(Environment.mock.calls.length).toEqual(1);
});
```

22. Make that pass by introducing a top-level variable that can memoize the result of `getEnvironment` if it hasn't yet been called:

```
let environment = null;
export const getEnvironment = () =>
  environment ||
  (environment = new Environment({
    network: Network.create(performFetch),
    store: new Store(new RecordSource())
  }));
```

That's all for the boilerplate.

Building the GraphQL reducer

The Git tag for this section is `query-customer-reducer`.

Now that we have a Relay environment, we can begin to build out our feature. Recall from the introduction that we're going to build a new `CustomerHistory` component that displays customer details and a list of the customer's appointments. A GraphQL query to return this information already exists in our server, so we just need to call it in the right way. The query itself looks like this:

```
customer(id: $id) {
  id
  firstName
  lastName
```

```
      phoneNumber
      appointments {
        startsAt
        stylist
        service
        notes
      }
    }
  }
```

This essentially means we get a customer record for a given customer ID (specified by the $id parameter), together with a list of their appointments.

Since our application uses Redux for data access, we'll continue to use it in this section, and we'll use Relay directly within our reducer, not via React. We'll build a reducer and a saga that handles three states: submitting a request, retrieving a successful response, and failing with error.

This isn't the only way to do this: Relay provides a QueryRenderer component that can call your GraphQL endpoint directly, and can handle the same three cases using that component. This can sometimes be a simpler, less complicated way of handling your data than using Redux; however, it doesn't make sense for our application since we're already using Redux for all our data access.

QueryRenderer isn't covered in this book simply because we've covered all the TDD techniques you'll need elsewhere in the book. However, check out the *Further learning* section for a link to the documentation for that component.

Let's begin building our new reducer:

1. Create a new file named test/sagas/queryCustomer.test.js. Start with the same test that every reducer always starts with: that it returns a default state. In this case, the default state is no customer and no appointments, and an undefined status:

```
import { reducer } from '../../src/sagas/queryCustomer';

describe('reducer', () => {
  it('returns a default state for an undefined existing state', ()
=> {
    expect(reducer(undefined, {})).toEqual({
      customer: {},
      appointments: [],
      status: undefined
```

```
    });
  });
});
```

2. To make that pass, create a new file, `src/sagas/queryCustomer.js`, and add the following:

```
const defaultState = {
  customer: {},
  appointments: [],
  status: undefined
};

export const reducer = (state = defaultState, action) => {
  return state;
};
```

3. Next up, we'll check that, if we receive a `QUERY_CUSTOMER_SUBMITTING` event, then we set the status to `SUBMITTING`. Just like we did with the reducer in the last chapter, we'll build these two at a time. Start by importing the two generator functions we built for the last reducer:

```
import {
  itMaintainsExistingState,
  itSetsStatus
} from '../reducerGenerators';
```

4. Now go ahead and use them in your first describe block:

```
describe('QUERY_CUSTOMER_SUBMITTING action', () => {
  const action = { type: 'QUERY_CUSTOMER_SUBMITTING' };
  itSetsStatus(reducer, action, 'SUBMITTING');
  itMaintainsExistingState(reducer, action);
});
```

5. Make that pass with this code:

```
export const reducer = (state = defaultState, action) => {
  switch (action.type) {
    case 'QUERY_CUSTOMER_SUBMITTING':
      return { ...state, status: 'SUBMITTING' };
    default:
      return state;
  }
};
```

6. Next up, let's handle the failure case, which is pretty much identical to the last describe block:

```
describe('QUERY_CUSTOMER_FAILED action', () => {
  const action = { type: 'QUERY_CUSTOMER_FAILED' };
  itSetsStatus(reducer, action, 'FAILED');
  itMaintainsExistingState(reducer, action);
});
```

7. Make that pass by adding another `case` to the `switch`:

```
case 'QUERY_CUSTOMER_FAILED':
  return { ...state, status: 'FAILED' };
```

8. For the final action, `QUERY_CUSTOMER_SUCCESSFUL`, we'll start off with the same two tests:

```
describe('QUERY_CUSTOMER_SUCCESSFUL action', () => {
  const customer = { id: 123 };
  const appointments = [{ starts: 123 }];
  const action = {
    type: 'QUERY_CUSTOMER_SUCCESSFUL',
    customer,
    appointments
  };
  itSetsStatus(reducer, action, 'SUCCESSFUL');
  itMaintainsExistingState(reducer, action);
});
```

9. Make that pass with the usual `case` statement:

```
case 'QUERY_CUSTOMER_SUCCESSFUL':
  return { ...state, status: 'SUCCESSFUL' };
```

10. This action occurs when we receive a successful data response from the GraphQL query, so we'll need an additional third test that checks that we save the date into the store:

```
it('sets received customer and appointments', () => {
  expect(reducer(undefined, action)).toMatchObject({
    customer,
    appointments
  });
});
```

11. Make that pass by updating the `case` statement:

```
case 'QUERY_CUSTOMER_SUCCESSFUL':
  return {
    ...state,
    customer: action.customer,
    appointments: action.appointments,
    status: 'SUCCESSFUL'
  };
```

Now the tricky part; the saga itself:

1. Add some new imports at the top of `test/sagas/queryCustomer.test.js`.
   These are for `expect-redux` and our Redux store, and for Relay:

```
import { storeSpy, expectRedux } from 'expect-redux';
import { configureStore } from '../../src/store';
import { fetchQuery } from 'relay-runtime';
import { getEnvironment } from '../../src/relayEnvironment';
```

2. Update the existing import too. We'll pull in the saga generator function,
   `queryCustomer`, and also `query`, which is the GraphQL query itself:

```
import {
  query,
  queryCustomer,
  reducer
} from '../../src/sagas/queryCustomer';
```

3. Add in a module mock for `relay-runtime`. This is important because,
   otherwise, we can't spy on the `fetchQuery` function that we've imported. Add
   this line just below your imports:

```
jest.mock('relay-runtime');
```

4. Add a new describe block that sets up our Redux store and our `fetchQuery` spy:

```
describe('queryCustomer', () => {
  const appointments = [{ startsAt: '123' }];
  const customer = { id: 123, appointments };

  let store;

  beforeEach(() => {
    store = configureStore([storeSpy]);
    fetchQuery.mockReturnValue({ customer });
  });
```

```
      const dispatchRequest = () =>
        store.dispatch({ type: 'QUERY_CUSTOMER_REQUEST', id: 123 });
    });
```

5. Write the first test:

```
    it('calls fetchQuery', async () => {
      dispatchRequest();
      expect(fetchQuery).toHaveBeenCalledWith(
        getEnvironment(),
        query,
        { id: 123 });
    });
```

6. There's a bit of work we need to do to make that pass. First, define these new imports at the top of src/sagas/queryCustomer.js:

```
    import { call } from 'redux-saga/effects';
    import { fetchQuery, graphql } from 'relay-runtime';
    import { getEnvironment } from '../relayEnvironment';
```

7. Just below those, define the query we'll send to GraphQL. Don't miss the graphql tag in front of this string. This is how the Relay compiler finds this fragment.

```
    export const query = graphql`
      query queryCustomerQuery($id: ID!) {
        customer(id: $id) {
          id
          firstName
          lastName
          phoneNumber
          appointments {
            startsAt
            stylist
            service
            notes
          }
        }
      }
    `;
```

Yes, that's right: your queries need to be compiled by the Relay compiler before they will run. Thankfully, your tests will function perfectly fine without compilation. See the end of this section for information on how to run the compiler before you manually test your code.

8. Now, to define the generator function itself. Don't expect your test to pass after this—there's still one more step to go:

```
export function* queryCustomer({ id }) {
    yield call(fetchQuery, getnvironment(), query, { id });
}
```

9. Our code in `src/sagas/queryCustomer.js` is complete, but we need to hook this up to the store for the test to pass. Open `src/store.js` and add the following imports:

```
import {
  queryCustomer,
  reducer as queryCustomerReducer
} from './sagas/queryCustomer';
```

10. Then add the following to the root saga:

```
function* rootSaga() {
  ...
  yield takeLatest('QUERY_CUSTOMER_REQUEST', queryCustomer);
}
```

11. Finally, add your reducer to the `combineReducers` call. After this step, your test should be passing:

```
combineReducers({
  customer: customerReducer,
  appointment: appointmentReducer,
  queryCustomer: queryCustomerReducer
})
```

12. Add the next test, as shown:

```
it('sets status to submitting', () => {
  dispatchRequest();

  return expectRedux(store)
    .toDispatchAnAction()
    .matching({ type: 'QUERY_CUSTOMER_SUBMITTING' });
});
```

13. To fix that test, first add an import for the put function:

```
import { put, call } from 'redux-saga/effects';
```

14. The add this single line to your `queryCustomer` generator function. The test should pass once you're done:

```
export function* queryCustomer({ id }) {
  yield put({ type: 'QUERY_CUSTOMER_SUBMITTING' });
  yield call(fetchQuery, getEnvironment(), query, { id });
}
```

15. The next test checks that we dispatch an action to our reducer with the right data. This is slightly non-trivial as we'll split apart customers and appointments into their own separate state variables. Even more interesting, our GraphQL endpoint returns timestamps as strings, but we want to convert those values to integers before we save them into our store:

```
it('dispatches a SUCCESSFUL action when the call succeeds', async
() => {
  const appointmentsWithConvertedTimestamps = [
    { startsAt: 123 }
  ];
  dispatchRequest();

  return expectRedux(store)
    .toDispatchAnAction()
    .matching({
      type: 'QUERY_CUSTOMER_SUCCESSFUL',
      customer,
      appointments: appointmentsWithConvertedTimestamps
    });
});
```

16. Back in your production code, define a new function to do that conversion, and then dispatch a new action with that data:

```
const convertStartsAt = appointment => ({
  ...appointment,
  startsAt: Number(appointment.startsAt)
});

export function* queryCustomer({ id }) {
  yield put({ type: 'QUERY_CUSTOMER_SUBMITTING' });
  const { customer } = yield call(
    fetchQuery,
    getEnvironment(),
    query,
    { id }
  );
  yield put({
```

```
    type: 'QUERY_CUSTOMER_SUCCESSFUL',
    customer,
    appointments: customer.appointments.map(convertStartsAt)
  });
}
```

17. All that's left is a test to show what happens when our query fails. The `fetchQuery` should send a promise rejection:

```
it("dispatches a FAILED action when the call throws an error", ()
=> {
  fetchQuery.mockReturnValue(Promise.reject(new Error()));

  dispatchRequest();

  return expectRedux(store)
    .toDispatchAnAction()
    .matching({ type: 'QUERY_CUSTOMER_FAILED' });
});
```

18. We can handle this by using a standard try/catch block in the generator function:

```
export function* queryCustomer({ id }) {
  yield put({ type: 'QUERY_CUSTOMER_SUBMITTING' });
  try {
    const { customer } = yield call(
      fetchQuery,
      getEnvironment(),
      query,
      { id });
    yield put({
      type: 'QUERY_CUSTOMER_SUCCESSFUL',
      customer,
      appointments: customer.appointments.map(convertStartsAt)
    });
  } catch (e) {
    yield put({ type: 'QUERY_CUSTOMER_FAILED' });
  }
}
```

That completes the work on the saga. It's time for us to build our new React component.

Building the CustomerHistory component

The Git tag for this section is `customer-history-component`.

The tests we write in this section will exercise logic in both the component and our reducer, including the saga. This integrated approach allows us to view the React component itself as the highest level of computation within the application. The new tests build on what we've already tested, and, at the same time, each one will remain small and independent.

This isn't the only way to test. For example, we could build a `CustomerHistory` component without the connection to Redux, and test that in isolation before gluing it and Redux together in another component.

1. Create a new file, `test/CustomerHistory.test.js`, and add the following setup. We're going to break this setup into parts, as it's long! First up, our imports and our standard setup. We also mock `relay-runtime` again, since we'll be doing our usual trick of stubbing `fetchQuery`:

```
import React from 'react';
import { act } from 'react-dom/test-utils';
import { expectRedux } from 'expect-redux';;
import { createContainerWithStore } from './domManipulators';
import { fetchQuery } from 'relay-runtime';
import { CustomerHistory } from '../src/CustomerHistory';
jest.mock('relay-runtime');
```

2. Now let's define some sample data:

```
const date = new Date('February 16, 2019');

const appointments = [
  {
    startsAt: date.setHours(9, 0, 0, 0),
    stylist: 'Jo',
    service: 'Cut',
    notes: 'Note one'
  },
  {
    startsAt: date.setHours(10, 0, 0, 0),
    stylist: 'Stevie',
    service: 'Cut & color',
```

```
      notes: 'Note two'
    }
  ];

  const customer = {
    firstName: 'Ashley',
    lastName: 'Jones',
    phoneNumber: '123',
    appointments
  };
```

3. After all that, the first test! This uses the `beforeEach` to not only set up the store, but also to render the new component. That means each of our tests will contain assertions only:

```
describe('CustomerHistory', () => {
  let container, renderWithStore, store;

  beforeEach(() => {
    ({
      container,
      renderWithStore,
      store
    } = createContainerWithStore());
    fetchQuery.mockReturnValue({ customer });
    renderWithStore(<CustomerHistory id={123} />);
  });

  describe('successful', () => {
    it('dispatches queryCustomer on mount', () => {
      return expectRedux(store)
        .toDispatchAnAction()
        .matching({ type: 'QUERY_CUSTOMER_REQUEST', id: 123 });
    });
  });
});
```

4. Let's make that pass. Create a new file, `src/CustomerHistory.js`, and start it off with the following Redux connection code. Since all we're doing is dispatching an action, we don't need a definition of `mapStateToProps` right now, just `mapDispatchToProps`:

```
import React, { useEffect} from 'react';
import { connect } from 'react-redux';

const mapStateToProps = _ => ({});
const mapDispatchToProps = ({
```

```
queryCustomer: id => ({ type: 'QUERY_CUSTOMER_REQUEST', id })
});
```

5. Add the component, together with a `useEffect` hook:

```
export const CustomerHistory = connect(
  mapStateToProps,
  mapDispatchToProps
)(({ id, queryCustomer }) => {

  useEffect(() => {
    queryCustomer(id);
  }, [id, queryCustomer]);

  return null;
});
```

6. Now we can write a test to show what happens when we pull out some data:

```
it('renders the first name and last name together in a h2', () => {
  expect(container.querySelector('h2').textContent).toEqual(
    'Ashley Jones'
  );
});
```

7. To make that pass, we'll need to fill in `mapStateToProps`. Go back and change your definition of that to the following:

```
const mapStateToProps = ({ queryCustomer: { customer } }) => ({
  customer
});
```

8. Then, update your component to render that data, pulling in the customer prop:

```
export const CustomerHistory = connect(
  mapStateToProps,
  mapDispatchToProps
)(({ id, queryCustomer, customer }) => {
  useEffect(() => {
    queryCustomer(id);
  }, [id]);

  const { firstName, lastName } = customer;
  return (
    <div id="customer">
      <h2>
        {firstName} {lastName}
      </h2>
```

```
      </div>
   );
});
```

9. Time for the next test:

```
it('renders the phone number', () => {
   expect(container.textContent).toContain('123');
});
```

10. Make that pass by extending your JSX:

```
const { firstName, lastName, phoneNumber } = customer;
return (
   <div id="customer">
      <h2>
         {firstName} {lastName}
      </h2>
      <p>{phoneNumber}</p>
   </div>
);
```

11. Now let's get started on rendering the appointments:

```
it('renders a Booked appointments heading', () => {
   expect(container.querySelector('h3')).not.toBeNull();
   expect(container.querySelector('h3').textContent).toEqual(
      'Booked appointments'
   );
});
```

12. Add that heading into your JSX, after the phone number:

```
<h3>Booked appointments</h3>
```

13. We'll render a table for each of the appointments available:

```
it('renders a table with four column headings', () => {
   const headings = Array.from(
      container.querySelectorAll('table > thead > tr > th')
   ).map(th => th.textContent);
   expect(headings).toEqual([
      'When',
      'Stylist',
      'Service',
      'Notes'
   ]);
});
```

14. Add that table:

```
<table>
  <thead>
    <tr>
      <th>When</th>
      <th>Stylist</th>
      <th>Service</th>
      <th>Notes</th>
    </tr>
  </thead>
</table>
```

15. For the next set of tests, we'll use a `columnValues` helper, which will find a table and pull out an array of all the values in a column. We can use this to test that our code displays data for a list of appointments, rather than just one:

```
const columnValues = columnNumber =>
  Array.from(container.querySelectorAll('tbody > tr')).map(
    tr => tr.childNodes[columnNumber].textContent
  );

it('renders the start time of each appointment in the correct
format', () => {
  expect(columnValues(0)).toEqual([
    'Sat Feb 16 2019 09:00',
    'Sat Feb 16 2019 10:00'
  ]);
});
```

16. Let's start by pulling appointments out of the Redux store. Modify `mapStateToProps` as shown:

```
const mapStateToProps = ({
  queryCustomer: { customer, appointments }
}) => ({ customer, appointments });
```

17. Then, add that as a prop to the `CustomerHistory` component:

```
export const CustomerHistory = connect(
  mapStateToProps,
  mapDispatchToProps
)(({ id, queryCustomer, customer, appointments }) => {
```

18. Add a new `tbody` element here in the existing `CustomerHistory` JSX, just below the thead. This makes a reference to a new `AppointmentRow` component, which we haven't built yet, but we will do so in the next step:

```
<table>
  ...
  <tbody>
    {appointments.map((appointment, i) => (
      <AppointmentRow appointment={appointment} key={i} />
    ))}
  </tbody>
</table>
```

19. Now we need to define `AppointmentRow`. Add this above the `CustomerHistory` definition:

```
const toTimeString = startsAt =>
  new Date(startsAt).toString().substring(0, 21);

const AppointmentRow = ({ appointment }) => (
  <tr>
    <td>{toTimeString(appointment.startsAt)}</td>
  </tr>
);
```

20. Now that we've got the appointment time, let's add in the other columns. I'll list three tests as one here, to save space. You should, of course, write out and fix these tests one by one.

```
it('renders the stylist', () => {
  expect(columnValues(1)).toEqual(['Jo', 'Stevie']);
});

it('renders the service', () => {
  expect(columnValues(2)).toEqual(['Cut', 'Cut & color']);
});

it('renders notes', () => {
  expect(columnValues(3)).toEqual(['Note one', 'Note two']);
});
```

We're actually overtesting here. Since we've already got a test to prove that we display all appointments, we don't need to check multiple values here. We could get away with just checking the first row. However, I like the consistency and clarity of these tests—they are short and sharp, so I think, in this case, we're okay to overtest.

You may disagree with me, in which case, feel free to change the following tests to test only the first appointment row returned.

21. Make those pass by adding to your `AppointmentRow` JSX:

```
const AppointmentRow = ({ appointment }) => (
  <tr>
    <td>{toTimeString(appointment.startsAt)}</td>
    <td>{appointment.stylist}</td>
    <td>{appointment.service}</td>
    <td>{appointment.notes}</td>
  </tr>
);
```

22. We're almost done. Let's display a **Loading** message when the component is submitting. This should be a new nested `describe` block, just below the `successful` describe block that we've just completed:

```
describe('submitting', () => {
  it('displays a loading message', () => {
    renderWithStore(<CustomerHistory />);
    store.dispatch({ type: 'QUERY_CUSTOMER_SUBMITTING' });
    expect(container.firstChild.id).toEqual('loading');
    expect(container.textContent).toEqual('Loading');
  });
});
```

23. To make that pass, start by pulling out status from the store in `mapStateToProps`:

```
const mapStateToProps = ({
  queryCustomer: { customer, appointments, status }
}) => ({ customer, appointments, status });
```

24. Add it to the `CustomerHistory` component props:

```
export const CustomerHistory = connect(
  mapStateToProps,
  mapDispatchToProps
)(({ id, queryCustomer, customer, appointments, status }) => {
```

25. Add this code to `CustomerHistory`, above the existing return statement:

```
if (status === 'SUBMITTING')
  return <div id='loading'>Loading</div>;
```

26. For our final test, let's test what happens when an error occurs:

```
describe('failed', () => {
  it('displays an error message', () => {
    renderWithStore(<CustomerHistory />);
    store.dispatch({ type: 'QUERY_CUSTOMER_FAILED' });
    expect(container.firstChild.id).toEqual('error');
    expect(container.textContent).toEqual(
      'Sorry, an error occurred while pulling data from the
server.'
    );
  });
});
```

27. Make that pass with another return, just below the check you added for the SUBMITTING status:

```
if (status === 'FAILED')
  return (
    <div id='error'>
      Sorry, an error occurred while pulling data from the server.
    </div>
  );
```

Our component is now complete and ready for integration into our user workflow.

Tying it together in App

Bringing all of this chapter's work together involves adding a new route to App, and adding a new button to the search actions that are rendered by the `CustomerSearch` component:

1. Add this test to `test/App.test.js`, within the `search customers` nested describe block. It uses the `renderSearchActionsForCustomer` helper which was introduced in Chapter 6, *Filtering and Searching Data*. It clicks on the **Customer search** button, and then renders and returns the `searchActions` button bar component:

```
it('passes a button to the CustomerSearch named View history',
async () => {
  const button = childrenOf(
```

```
      renderSearchActionsForCustomer(customer)
    )[1];
    expect(button.type).toEqual('button');
    expect(button.props.role).toEqual('button');
    expect(button.props.children).toEqual('View history');
  });
```

2. Add the button:

```
const searchActions = customer => (
  <React.Fragment>
    <button
      role="button"
      onClick={() => transitionToAddAppointment(customer)}>
      Create appointment
    </button>
    <button role="button">View history</button>
  </React.Fragment>
);
```

3. Now we need a test to check what happens when we click the button:

```
it('navigates to /customer/:id when clicking the View history
button', async () => {
  const button = childrenOf(
    renderSearchActionsForCustomer(customer)
  )[1];
  click(button);
  expect(historySpy).toHaveBeenCalledWith('/customer/123');
});
```

4. Back in `src/App.js`, add a new handler:

```
const transitionToCustomerHistory = customer =>
  history.push(`/customer/${customer.id}`);
```

5. Now attach it to your button:

```
<button
  role="button"
  onClick={() => transitionToCustomerHistory(customer)}>
  View history
</button>
```

6. Finally, let's add a new route to display the `CustomerHistory` component. Start by adding a new import at the top of `test/App.test.js`:

```
import { CustomerHistory } from '../src/CustomerHistory';
```

7. Now add the test. This test does something interesting. It needs to provide a `match` prop to the Route. This mimics what React Router would do with the customer ID when it matches the URL:

```
it('renders CustomerHistory at /customer', async () => {
  render(<App />);
  const match = { params: { id: '123' } };
  const element = routeFor('/customer/:id').props.render({
    match
  });
  expect(element.type).toEqual(CustomerHistory);
  expect(element.props.id).toEqual('123');
});
```

8. Let's make that pass. In `src/App.js`, add a new import for the new component you've just built:

```
import { CustomerHistory } from './CustomerHistory';
```

9. Now create a new `Route` that instantiates the `CustomerHistory` component with the customer ID. After this, you're done:

```
<Route
  path="/customer/:id"
  render={({ match }) => <CustomerHistory id={match.params.id} />}
/>
```

Compiling Relay queries

There's just one more thing that needs to be done: Relay queries must be compiled before they can be used. To do that, add the following Relay command to your `package.json` so that it's easy to recompile when necessary:

```
"scripts": {
  "relay": "relay-compiler --src ./src --schema ./src/schema.graphql --
watchman false"
},
```

Now you can recompile by typing `npm run relay`.

Once you've done that, spin up the server with `npm run serve`, add some appointments for a customer, and then hit the **View history** button to check out your work.

You will most likely want to explore other, less manual ways of compiling your queries. Check out the *Further learning* section for more information.

Summary

This chapter has explored how to test drive the integration of a not-so-simple package, Relay. We encountered something new in the use of `jest.mock` so that we could stub and spy on types coming from an external module. We also used our previously built knowledge to create tests that instrumented multiple modules, all in the name of expressive testing.

We've now explored about as much as this code base can usefully offer us.

In `Section 3`, *Interactivity*, we'll begin work in a new code base that will allow us to explore more complex use cases involving undo/redo, animation, and WebSocket manipulation.

In `Chapter 10`, *Building a Logo interpreter*, we'll begin by writing new Redux middleware to handle undo/redo behavior.

Exercises

- Convert the remaining fetch calls to use their GraphQL counterparts.

Further learning

- Relay environment documentation: `https://facebook.github.io/relay/docs/en/relay-environment.html`
- QueryRenderer component documentation: `https://facebook.github.io/relay/docs/en/query-renderer.html`
- Installing the Relay Compiler: `https://facebook.github.io/relay/docs/en/installation-and-setup.html#set-up-relay-compiler`

Section 3: Interactivity

3

In this section, we take a deep-dive into three more involved aspects of React development: Redux middleware, animation, and WebSocket integration. It demonstrates how, with enough effort, even the most involved parts of our code bases can be test-driven.

This section includes the following chapters:

- Chapter 10, *Building a Logo Interpreter*
- Chapter 11, *Adding Animation*
- Chapter 12, *Working with WebSockets*

10
Building a Logo Interpreter

Logo is a programming language that was created in the 1960s. It was, for many decades, a popular way to teach children how to code. I have fond memories of writing Logo programs back in high school. What better way to relive my childhood than by building a Logo interpreter with React?

The application we'll build is called **Spec Logo**. The code for the interpreter and the barebones UI have already been written. In the following three chapters, we'll bolt on additional features to this codebase.

This chapter covers the following topics:

- Studying the *Spec Logo* user interface
- Undoing and redoing user actions in Redux
- Saving to `LocalStorage` via Redux middleware
- Changing keyboard focus

Of course, we'll be doing all of this with a test-first approach.

 This chapter uses a different codebase from the previous chapters. You can find the starting point by switching to the `undo-redo` tag. You will need to switch to the `spec-logo` directory, and you will want to create a new branch for your work.

For more detailed instructions, see the *To get the most out of this book* section in the `Preface`.

Studying the Spec Logo user interface

The interface is fairly simple: it contains a drawing on the left pane, which is where the output from the Logo script appears. On the right side is a prompt where the user can edit instructions:

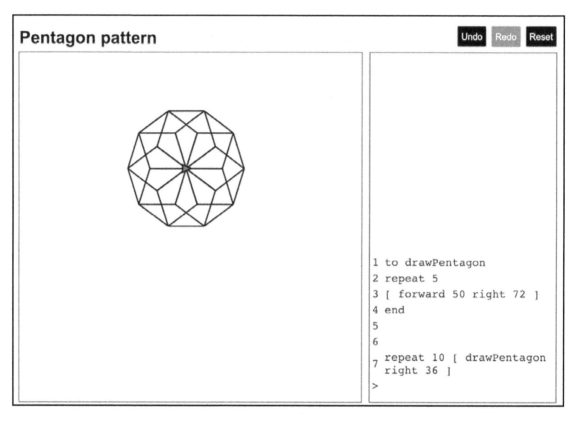

Take a look at the screenshot. You can see the following:

- The **script name** in the top-left corner. This is a text field that the user can click on to change the name of the current script.
- A **menu bar** in the top-right corner, containing **Undo**, **Redo**, and **Reset** buttons. This is the menu bar that we will build in this chapter. The starting point has a `MenuButtons` component with a **Reset** button. We'll add the other two.
- The **display**, which shows script output on the left-hand side of the page. You can see a shape has been drawn here, which is the result of the Logo statements entered at the prompt.

- The **turtle** is shown in the middle of the screen. This is a little green triangle that marks where drawing commands originate. The turtle has an *x* and *y* position, starting at 0,0 which is the middle of the screen. The viewable drawing is 600x600, and the turtle can move throughout this area (although there is nothing stopping it going off screen.) The turtle also has an angle, initially zero, which is pointing directly right.
- The **prompt** is in the bottom right-hand corner, and is marked with a > symbol. This is where you enter your statements, which can be multiline. Hitting *Enter* will send the current prompt text to the interpreter. If it makes a complete statement, it will be executed and the prompt cleared ready for your next statement.
- The **statement history** is above the prompt and lists all the previously executed statements. Each is given a number so you can refer back to the statement.
- **Errors** can appear just below the prompt if they occur. This might happen if you misspell a command name or do not provide enough parameters.

Although we won't be writing any Logo code in this chapter, it's worth spending some time playing around and making your own drawings with the interpreter. Here's a list of instructions that you can use:

Statement	Alias	Description
forward *d*	fd	Move the turtle forward a distance of *d* pixels
backward *d*	bd	Move the turtle backward a distance of *d* pixels
right *a*	rt	Rotate the turtle *a* degrees clockwise
left *a*	lt	Rotate the turtle *a* degrees anti-clockwise
to *fn* <*args*> <*instructions*> end		Defines a function named *fn* with the arguments *args* and instructions *instructions*
repeat *n* [<*instructions*>]		Repeats the provided *instructions* n times

If you're interested in learning more about Logo, check out the *Further learning* section at the end of this chapter.

Looking through the codebase

It would help you to get acquainted with the codebase before we begin.

The file `src/parser.js` and the directory `src/language` contain the Logo interpreter. There are also corresponding test files in the `test` directory. We won't be modifying these files, but you may be interested in seeing how I've test-driven this functionality.

There is a single Redux reducer in `src/reducers/script.js`. You should take a look at this, particularly `defaultState`, which shows how we store states in Redux. Almost all of the React components use this state in some way.

We'll be adding two more reducers into this directory: one for undo/redo and one for prompt focus.

The files `src/index.js` and `src/store.js` are untested and contain the minimal amount of code required to render the `App` component and to configure the store.

The remaining files are all React components, and each has an individual test file: `App`, `Display`, `MenuButtons`, `Prompt`, `PromptError`, `ScriptName`, and `StatementHistory`. In this chapter, we'll be making modifications to `MenuButtons`, `Prompt`, and `ScriptName`.

We'll be making a start by building undo/redo functionality around the script reducer in `src/reducers/script.js`, so that the reducer is the most important thing to understand right now.

Undoing and redoing user actions in Redux

 The Git tag for this section is `undo-redo`. If you haven't already, please move to that tag now.

In this section, we'll add undo and redo buttons at the top of the page, which allow the user to undo statements that they've previously run. They'll work like this:

1. Initially, both buttons will be disabled.
2. Once the user executes a statement, the **Undo** button will become enabled.
3. When the user clicks the **Undo** button, the last statement will be undone.
4. At that point, the **Redo** button becomes available and the user can choose to redo the last statement.
5. Multiple actions can be undone and then redone, in sequence.
6. If the user performs a new action while **Redo** is available, the redo sequence is cleared and the **Redo** button becomes unavailable again.

Aside from the buttons, the work involved here is building a new reducer, `withUndoRedo`, which will decorate the `script` reducer. This reducer will return the same state as the `script` reducer, but with two additional properties: `canUndo` and `canRedo`. In addition, the reducer stores `past` and `future` arrays within it, which store past and future states. These will never be returned to the user, just stored, available to be used should the user choose to undo or redo.

Building the reducer

Before we begin building the reducer, let's think about what we're going to build.

The reducer will be a higher-order function which, when called with an existing reducer, returns a new reducer that returns the state we're expecting. In our production code, we'll replace this store code:

```
combineReducers({
    script: scriptReducer
})
```

With this "decorated" reducer, which takes exactly the same reducer and wraps it in the `withUndoRedo` reducer that we'll build in this section:

```
combineReducers({
    script: withUndoRedo(scriptReducer)
})
```

To test this, we'll need to use a spy to act in place of the script reducer, which we'll call the `decoratedReducerSpy`.

Setting the initial state

Let's make a start by building the reducer itself, before adding buttons to exercise the new functionality:

1. Open a new file named `test/reducers/withUndoRedo.test.js` and add the following setup and test, which specifies what should happen when we pass an `undefined` state to the reducer. This is equivalent to how we began testing our other reducers, but in this case, we pass the call through to the decorated reducer:

   ```
   import { withUndoRedo } from '../../src/reducers/withUndoRedo';

   describe('withUndoRedo', () => {
     let decoratedReducerSpy;
   ```

```
    let reducer;

    beforeEach(() => {
      decoratedReducerSpy = jest.fn();
      reducer = withUndoRedo(decoratedReducerSpy);
    });

    describe('when initializing state', () => {
      it('calls the decorated reducers with undefined state and an
action', () => {
        const action = { type: 'UNKNOWN' };
        reducer(undefined, action);
        expect(decoratedReducerSpy).toHaveBeenCalledWith(
          undefined,
          action);
      });
    });
  });
```

2. We've defined `decoratedReducerSpy` as the reducer, which we can then assert on. The reducer itself is instantiated in the `beforeEach`, as we'll need that for each test. The test itself passes an `undefined` state to the reducer, which is the required mechanism for initializing a reducer.

3. Create a new file `src/reducers/withUndoRedo.js` and make the test pass with the following code:

```
export const withUndoRedo = (reducer) => {
  return (state, action) => {
    reducer(state, action);
  };
};
```

4. Add the next test to the describe block, as shown next. This is the first time we've seen the `toMatchObject` matcher. This returns `true` if the actual value has all of the properties contained within the expected value. It doesn't need to be an exact match; if the actual value has more properties than the expected value does, the expectation will still pass:

```
it('returns a value of what the inner reducer returns', () => {
  decoratedReducerSpy.mockReturnValue({ a: 123 });
  expect(reducer(undefined)).toMatchObject({ a : 123 });
});
```

5. Make that pass by adding the `return` keyword:

```
export const withUndoRedo = (reducer) => {
  return (state, action) => {
    return reducer(state, action);
  };
}
```

6. Initially, both `canUndo` and `canRedo` should be `false`, as there are no previous or future states that we can move to. Let's add those two tests as a pair, still in the same describe block:

```
it('cannot undo', () => {
  expect(reducer(undefined)).toMatchObject({ canUndo: false });
});

it('cannot redo', () => {
  expect(reducer(undefined)).toMatchObject({ canRedo: false });
});
```

7. To make these tests pass, we need to create a new object with those properties added:

```
export const withUndoRedo = (reducer) => {
  return (state, action) => {
    return {
      canUndo: false,
      canRedo: false,
      ...reducer(state, action)
    };
  };
}
```

8. Now let's move on to the meat of the reducer. How do things change when we perform an action via our reducer? Add a new describe block with the following content. It sets up the reducer to return a new `future` state given a `present` state:

```
describe('performing an action', () => {
  const innerAction = { type: 'INNER' };
  const present = { a: 123 };
  const future = { b: 234 };

  beforeEach(() => {
    decoratedReducerSpy.mockReturnValue(future);
  });
```

```
it('can undo after a new present has been provided', () => {
  const result = reducer(
    { canUndo: false, present },
    innerAction
  );
  expect(result.canUndo).toBeTruthy();
});
});
```

9. Make that pass with the following code. Since we're no longer dealing with an undefined state, this is the moment that we need to wrap our existing code in a conditional block:

```
export const withUndoRedo = (reducer) => {
  return (state, action) => {
    if (state === undefined) return {
      canUndo: false,
      canRedo: false,
      ...reducer(state, action)
    };

    return {
      canUndo: true
    };
  };
};
```

10. Okay; now we need to actually make sure we call the reducer again since for this new block it won't happen. Write the following test:

```
it('forwards action to the inner reducer', () => {
  reducer(present, innerAction);
  expect(decoratedReducerSpy).toHaveBeenCalledWith(
    present,
    innerAction
  );
});
```

11. Let's make life difficult for ourselves and make that pass *outside* of our return statement:

```
reducer(state, action);
return {
  canUndo: true
};
```

There are various different ways we could approach this problem. This approach certainly isn't the most concise solution, since there are now *two* equivalent calls to the reducer, but it is the *simplest* solution in that it requires the least amount of code change to make the test pass.

12. As we've seen before, we need a second test to get this call in the right place, within the returned value. Add the following test:

```
it('returns the result of the inner reducer', () => {
  const result = reducer(present, innerAction);
  expect(result).toMatchObject(future);
});
```

13. Make that pass by saving off the reducer value and returning it as part of the returned object:

```
const newPresent = reducer(state, action);
return {
  ...newPresent,
  canUndo: true
};
```

This implementation is interesting because it now also passes any test we might write for canRedo in addition to canUndo. For any new state that the reducer advances to, we want canRedo to be false. We can take advantage of an undefined value being false and not bother with and then test for canRedo.

14. Finally, the reducer should not advance the state if the instruction wasn't processed due to an error. We can determine this by checking if the inner reducer advanced the nextInstructionId property. To do that, modify the present and future constants to include this parameter, and add the new test, as shown next:

```
const present = { a: 123, nextInstructionId: 0 };
const future = { b: 234, nextInstructionId: 1 };

it('returns the previous state if nextInstructionId does not
increment', () => {
  decoratedReducerSpy.mockReturnValue({
    nextInstructionId: 0
  });
  const result = reducer(present, innerAction);
  expect(result).toBe(present);
});
```

Importantly, this change means our `withUndoRedo` reducer cannot be reused outside of this one application: it is tied to the `script` reducer. Or at least, it's tied to decorating reducers that use an increment `nextInstructionId` property to determine if the inner action succeeded or not. It is left as an exercise for the reader to build a generic version of this reducer.

15. Make that pass by wrapping our new return block in a conditional, and returning the old state if the test doesn't pass:

```
const newPresent = reducer(state, action);
if (
  newPresent.nextInstructionId != state.nextInstructionId
) {
  return {
    ...newPresent,
    canUndo: true,
    canRedo: false
  };
}
return state;
```

This covers all the functionality for performing any actions *other than* undo and redo. The next two sections will cover those. It's interesting that we haven't had to save off any previous states at all yet. It does make sense, however, since there's no action to retrieve it yet.

Handling the undo action

We'll create a new action, UNDO, which causes us to push the current state into a new array called `past`:

1. For this test, we can reuse the `present` and `innerAction` properties, so push those up into the outer describe block now. Also, define a new `undoAction`. We'll use it within our first test:

```
describe('withUndoRedo', () => {
  const undoAction = { type: 'UNDO' };
  const innerAction = { type: 'INNER' };
  const present = { a: 123, nextInstructionId: 0 };
  const future = { b: 234, nextInstructionId: 1 };

  ...
});
```

2. Add a new nested describe block with the following test and setup. The
`beforeEach` block sets up a scenario where we've already performed an action
that will have "saved" a previous state. We're then ready to undo it within the
test:

```
describe('undo', () => {
  let newState;

  beforeEach(() => {
    decoratedReducerSpy.mockReturnValue(future);
    newState = reducer(present, innerAction);
  });

  it('sets present to the latest past entry', () => {
    const updated = reducer(newState, undoAction);
    expect(updated).toMatchObject(present);
  });
});
```

In this test, the *Act* phase of the test occurs in the `beforeEach` block. I've
made an educated guess that the subsequent tests will use the same setup,
since they will all be exercising the undo functionality.

3. Make that pass by modifying the function as follows. There's no need for an
array of values just yet; we can undo one level deep by using a single variable.
We also use a `switch` statement since we'll be adding a case for REDO later:

```
export const withUndoRedo = (reducer) => {
  let past;

  return (state, action) => {
    if (state === undefined) return {
      canUndo: false,
      canRedo: false,
      ...reducer(state, action)
    };

    switch(action.type) {
      case 'UNDO':
        return past;
      default:
        const newPresent = reducer(state, action);
        if (
          newPresent.nextInstructionId != state.nextInstructionId
        ) {
          past = state;
```

```
                    return {
                      ...newPresent,
                      canUndo: true
                    };
                  }
                  return state;
              }
          };
      };
```

4. Let's make sure we can undo any number of levels deep. Add the next test:

```
it('can undo multiple levels', () => {
  const futureFuture = { c: 345, nextInstructionId: 3 };
  decoratedReducerSpy.mockReturnValue(futureFuture);
  newState = reducer(newState, innerAction);

  const updated = reducer(
    reducer(newState, undoAction),
    undoAction
  );
  expect(updated).toMatchObject(present);
});
```

5. For this, we'll need to upgrade past to an array:

```
export const withUndoRedo = (reducer) => {
  let past = [];

  return (state, action) => {
    if (state === undefined) return {
      canUndo: false,
      canRedo: false,
      ...reducer(state, action)
    };

    switch(action.type) {
      case 'UNDO':
        const lastEntry = past[past.length - 1];
        past = past.slice(0, -1);
        return lastEntry;
      default:
        const newPresent = reducer(state, action);
        if (newPresent.nextInstructionId !=
state.nextInstructionId) {
          past = [ ...past, state ];

          return {
```

```
            ...newPresent,
            canUndo: true
          };
        }
        return state;
      }
    };
  };
```

6. There's one final test we need to do. Interestingly enough, it's *not* that canUndo is set to true or false. That functionality we actually get for free: the first state entry will implicitly have a false value for canUndo, since canUndo is undefined. For canUndo, we've already coded that behavior by setting it to true when we move to a new state. So the final test is in fact for canRedo:

```
it('sets canRedo to true after undoing', () => {
  const updated = reducer(newState, undoAction);
  expect(updated.canRedo).toBeTruthy();
});
```

7. Finally, make that pass by returning a new object comprised of lastEntry and the new canRedo property:

```
case 'UNDO':
  const lastEntry = past[past.length - 1];
  past = past.slice(0, -1);
  return {
    ...lastEntry,
    canRedo: true
  };
```

Handling the redo action

Redo is very similar to undo, just reversed. In our production code, however, we'll need to add a switch statement:

1. First, add a new definition for the UNDO action, in the top-level describe block:

```
describe('withUndoRedo', () => {
  const undoAction = { type: 'UNDO' };
  const redoAction = { type: 'REDO' };


  ...
});
```

2. Underneath the `undo` describe block, add the following `redo` describe block with the first test. Be careful with the setup for the spy; the call is `mockReturnValueOnce` here, not `mockReturnValue`. The test needs to ensure it takes its value from the stored redo state:

```
describe('redo', () => {
  let newState;

  beforeEach(() => {
    decoratedReducerSpy.mockReturnValueOnce(future);
    newState = reducer(present, innerAction);
    newState = reducer(newState, undoAction);
  });

  it('sets the present to the latest future entry', () => {
    const updated = reducer(newState, redoAction);
    expect(updated).toMatchObject(future);
  });
});
```

3. Let's start by declaring a `future` variable, next to the declaration for `past`:

```
let post = [], future;
```

4. Set this within the UNDO action:

```
case 'UNDO':
  const lastEntry = past[past.length - 1];
  past = past.slice(0, -1);
  future = state;
```

5. Now that it's saved, we can handle the REDO action. Add the following case clause, between the UNDO clause and the default clause:

```
case 'REDO':
  return future;
```

6. The next test is for multiple levels of redo. This is slightly more complicated than the same case in the undo block—we'll have to modify the `beforeEach` block to take us back *twice*. First, pull out the `futureFuture` value from the `undo` test and bring it into the outer scope, next to the other values, just below `future`:

```
const future = { b: 234, nextInstructionId: 1 };
const futureFuture = { c: 345, nextInstructionId: 3 };
```

7. Now update `beforeEach` to take two steps forward and then two back:

```
beforeEach(() => {
  decoratedReducerSpy.mockReturnValueOnce(future);
  decoratedReducerSpy.mockReturnValueOnce(futureFuture);
  newState = reducer(present, innerAction);
  newState = reducer(newState, innerAction);
  newState = reducer(newState, undoAction);
  newState = reducer(newState, undoAction);
});
```

8. Finally, add the test:

```
it('can redo multiple levels', () => {
  const updated = reducer(
    reducer(newState, redoAction),
    redoAction
  );
  expect(updated).toMatchObject(futureFuture);
});
```

9. To make this pass, start by initializing the `future` variable to be an empty array:

```
let past = [], future = [];
```

10. Update the UNDO clause to push the current value to it:

```
case 'UNDO':
  const lastEntry = past[past.length - 1];
  past = past.slice(0, -1);
  future = [ ...future, state ];
```

11. Update the REDO clause to pull out that value we just pushed. After this change, the test should be passing:

```
case 'REDO':
  const nextEntry = future[future.length - 1];
  future = future.slice(0, -1);
  return nextEntry;
```

 Because of the way we've set up `canUndo` and `canRedo` when handling other actions, we don't need to specifically account for setting `canRedo` and `canUndo` here, so this test essentially "completes" the basic redo action. However, we do still have an edge case which we'll get to next.

12. There's one final test we need to write for our barebones implementation, which checks that a redo followed by an undo brings us back to the original state:

```
it('returns to previous state when followed by an undo', () => {
  const updated = reducer(
    reducer(newState, redoAction), undoAction
  );
  expect(updated).toMatchObject(present);
});
```

13. Make that pass by setting the past properly in the REDO case:

```
case 'REDO':
  const nextEntry = future[future.length - 1];
  past = [ ...past, state ];
  future = future.slice(0, -1);
  return nextEntry;
```

This completes our reducer. However, our implementation has a memory leak! We never clear out the future array when we generate new states. If the user repeatedly hit undo and then performed new actions, all their old actions would remain in future but become unaccessible (due to the false canRedo value in the latest state).

If you wanted to test for this scenario, you could simulate the sequence and check that you expect to return undefined. This test isn't *great* in that we really shouldn't be sending a REDO action when canRedo returns false, but that's what our test ends up doing:

```
it('return undefined when attempting a do, undo, do, redo sequence', () =>
{
  decoratedReducerSpy.mockReturnValue(future);
  let newState = reducer(present, innerAction);
  newState = reducer(newState, undoAction);
  newState = reducer(newState, innerAction);
  newState = reducer(newState, redoAction);
  expect(newState).not.toBeDefined();
});
```

To make that pass, simply clear future when setting new state, as shown:

```
if (newPresent.nextInstructionId != state.nextInstructionId) {
  past = [ ...past, state ];
  future = [];
  return {
    ...newPresent,
    canUndo: true
  };
}
```

Attaching the new reducer

Modify `src/store.js` to hook in the new reducer. This file is not under test so you get a free pass to change your production code without a test. However, once you make this change, you'll get a whole bunch of test failures that you'll need to work through one by one:

```
import { withUndoRedo } from './reducers/withUndoRedo';

export const configureStore = (
  storeEnhancers = [],
  initialState = {}
) => {
  return createStore(
    combineReducers({
      script: withUndoRedo(scriptReducer)
    }),
    initialState,
    compose(...storeEnhancers)
  );
};
```

Your tests should be passing and the app should still run. However, the undo and redo functionality is still not accessible. For that, we need to add some buttons to the menu bar.

Building buttons

The Git tag for this section is `undo-redo-buttons`.

The final piece to this puzzle is adding buttons to trigger the new behavior by adding **Undo** and **Redo** buttons to the menu bar:

1. Open `test/MenuButtons.test.js` and add the following describe block at the bottom of the file, nested inside the `MenuButtons` describe block. It uses a couple of helper functions that have already been defined with the file, `renderWithStore` and `button`:

```
describe('undo button', () => {
  it('renders', () => {
    renderWithStore(<MenuButtons />);
```

```
      expect(button('Undo').exists()).toBeTruthy();
    });
  });
```

2. Make that pass by modifying the implementation for `MenuButtons` as shown:

```
export const MenuButtons = connect(
  ...
)((
  ...
) => {
  ...
  return (
    <React.Fragment>
      <button>Undo</button>
      <button onClick={reset} disabled={!canReset}>
        Reset
      </button>
    </React.Fragment>
  );
}};
```

3. Add the next test:

```
it('is disabled if there is no history', () => {
  renderWithStore(<MenuButtons />);
  expect(button('Undo').hasAttribute('disabled')).toBeTruthy();
});
```

4. Make that pass by adding a hard-coded disabled attribute, as shown:

```
<button disabled={true}>Undo</button>
```

5. Now we add in the code that will require us to connect with Redux:

```
it('is enabled if an action occurs', () => {
  const store = renderWithStore(<MenuButtons />);
  store.dispatch({
    type: 'SUBMIT_EDIT_LINE',
    text: 'forward 10\n'
  });
  expect(button('Undo').hasAttribute('disabled')).toBeFalsy();
});
```

6. Modify `MenuButtons` to pull out `canUndo` from the store. It already uses the `script` state for the **Reset** button behavior, so in this case, we just need to destructure it further:

```
export const MenuButtons = connect(
  ...
) (
  ({
    script: { canUndo, nextInstructionId }
  }) => {
    const canReset = nextInstructionId !== 0;
    return (
      <React.Fragment>
        <button disabled={!canUndo}>Undo</button>
        <button onClick={reset} disabled={!canReset}>
          Reset
        </button>
      </React.Fragment>
    );
  }
);
```

7. The final test for the **Undo** button is to check that it dispatches an UNDO action when it is clicked:

```
it('dispatches an action of UNDO when clicked', () => {
  const store = renderWithStore(<MenuButtons />);
  store.dispatch({
    type: 'SUBMIT_EDIT_LINE',
    text: 'forward 10\n'
  });
  click(button('Undo'));
  return expectRedux(store)
    .toDispatchAnAction()
    .matching({ type: 'UNDO' });
});
```

8. Make that pass by adding the lines highlighted next. We update `mapDispatchToProps` to include the new action and then pass that through the component props:

```
const mapDispatchToProps = dispatch => ({
  reset: () => dispatch({ type: 'RESET' }),
  undo: () => dispatch({ type: 'UNDO' })
});

export const MenuButtons = connect(
```

```
      mapStateToProps,
      mapDispatchToProps
  ) (
    ({
      script: { canUndo, nextInstructionId },
      undo
    }) => {
      const canReset = nextInstructionId !== 0;
      return (
        <React.Fragment>
          <button onClick={undo} disabled={!canUndo}>
            Undo
          </button>
          <button onClick={reset} disabled={!canReset}>
            Reset
          </button>
        </React.Fragment>
      );
    }
  );
```

9. Repeat from *Step 2* to *Step 8* for the **Redo** button. This time, you'll need to pull out the canRedo property from the script state.

That's the last change needed. Our undo and redo functionality is now complete.

Saving to LocalStorage via Redux middleware

 The Git tag for this section is local-storage.

Let's update our app to save the current state to local storage, which is a persistent data store managed by the user's web browser. Each executed statement will cause the entire set of parsed tokens to be saved. When the user opens the app, the tokens will be read and replayed through the parser.

As a reminder, the parser (in `src/parser.js`) has a function `parseTokens`. This is the function we'll call from within our middleware, and in this section, we'll build tests to assert that we've called this function.

We'll write a new piece of Redux middleware for the task. The middleware will pull out only two pieces of the `script` state: the `name` and the `parsedTokens`.

The local storage API is fairly straightforward:

- `window.localStorage.getItem(key)` returns the value of an item in local storage. The value stored is a string, so if it's a serialized object then we need to call `JSON.parse` to deserialize it. The function returns `null` if no value exists for the given key.
- `window.localStorage.setItem(key, value)` sets the value of an item. The value is serialized as a string, so we need to make sure to call `JSON.stringify` on any objects before we pass them in here.

Building middleware

The first step is to build the middleware that works with local storage:

1. Create the directories `src/middleware` and `test/middleware`, and then open the file `test/middleware/localStorage.test.js`. To make a start, let's define two spies, `getItemSpy` and `setItemSpy`, which will make up the new object. We have to use `Object.defineProperty` to set these spies because the `window.localStorage` property is write protected:

```
import { save } from '../../src/middleware/localStorage';

describe('localStorage', () => {
  const data = { a: 123 };
  let getItemSpy = jest.fn();
  let setItemSpy = jest.fn();

  beforeEach(() => {
    Object.defineProperty(window, 'localStorage', {
      value: {
        getItem: getItemSpy,
        setItem: setItemSpy
      }});
  });
});
```

2. Let's write our first test for the middleware. This test simply asserts that the middleware does what all middleware should, which is call `next(action)`. Redux middleware functions have complicated semantics, being functions that return functions that return functions, but our tests will make short work of that:

```
describe('save middleware', () => {
  const name = 'script name';
  const parsedTokens = ['forward 10'];
  const state = { script: { name, parsedTokens } };
  const action = { type: 'ANYTHING' };
  const store = { getState: () => state };
  let next;

  beforeEach(() => {
    next = jest.fn();
  });

  const callMiddleware = () => save(store)(next)(action);

  it('calls next with the action', () => {
    callMiddleware();
    expect(next).toHaveBeenCalledWith(action);
  });
});
```

3. Let's make that pass. Create the file `src/middleware/localStorage.js` and add the following definition:

```
export const save = store => next => action => {
  next(action);
};
```

4. The next test checks that we return that value:

```
it('returns the result of next action', () => {
  next.mockReturnValue({ a : 123 });
  expect(callMiddleware()).toEqual({ a: 123 });
});
```

5. Let's return that value:

```
export const save = store => next => action => {
  return next(action);
};
```

6. Now we can check that we add the stringified value to local storage:

```
it('saves the current state of the store in localStorage', () => {
  callMiddleware();
  expect(setItemSpy).toHaveBeenCalledWith('name', name);
  expect(setItemSpy).toHaveBeenCalledWith(
    'parsedTokens',
    JSON.stringify(parsedTokens)
  );
});
```

7. Now we can complete the implementation of the save middleware:

```
export const save = store => next => action => {
  const result = next(action);
  const {
    script: { name, parsedTokens }
  } = store.getState();
  localStorage.setItem('name', name);
  localStorage.setItem(
    'parsedTokens',
    JSON.stringify(parsedTokens)
  );
  return result;
};
```

8. Let's move on to the load function, which isn't middleware but we can place it in the same file, despite its location in the middleware directory. Create a new describe block with the following test. I'm doubling up the describe block here because one of the later tests will deal with a different spy setup:

```
import { load, save } from '../../src/middleware/localStorage';

...

describe('load', () => {
  describe('with saved data', () => {
    beforeEach(() => {
      getItemSpy.mockReturnValueOnce('script name');
      getItemSpy.mockReturnValueOnce(
        JSON.stringify([ { a: 123 } ])
      );
    });

    it('retrieves state from localStorage', () => {
      load();
      expect(getItemSpy).toHaveBeenCalledWith('name');
```

```
        expect(getItemSpy).toHaveBeenLastCalledWith(
          'parsedTokens'
        );
      });
    });
  });
});
```

9. Make that pass by defining a new function in the production code:

```
export const load = () => {
  localStorage.getItem('name');
  localStorage.getItem('parsedTokens');
};
```

10. Now let's send that data to the parser. For this, we'll need a `parserSpy` that we use to spy on the parser's `parseTokens` function:

```
describe('load', () => {
  let parserSpy;

  describe('with saved data', () => {
    beforeEach(() => {
      parserSpy = jest.fn();
      parser.parseTokens = parserSpy;
      ...
    });

    it('calls to parsedTokens to retrieve data', () => {
      load();
      expect(parserSpy).toHaveBeenCalledWith(
        [ { a: 123 } ],
        parser.emptyState
      );
    });
  });
});
```

 Although it isn't covered in the book, you can check out the code for the parser and `parseTokens` in the file `src/parser.js`.

11. Add the following production code to make that pass:

```
import * as parser from '../parser';

export const load = () => {
  localStorage.getItem('name');
```

```
  const parsedTokens = JSON.parse(
    localStorage.getItem('parsedTokens')
  );
  parser.parseTokens(parsedTokens, parser.emptyState);
};
```

12. Now let's make sure we return the data in the right format:

```
it('returns re-parsed draw commands', () => {
  parserSpy.mockReturnValue({ drawCommands: [] });
  expect(load().script).toHaveProperty('drawCommands', []);
});
```

13. Make that pass by returning an object with the parsed response:

```
export const load = () => {
  localStorage.getItem('name');
  const parsedTokens =
JSON.parse(localStorage.getItem('parsedTokens'));
  return {
    script: parser.parseTokens(parsedTokens, parser.initialState)
  };
};
```

14. Next, let's add the name into that data structure:

```
it('returns name', () => {
  expect(load().script.present).toHaveProperty(
    'name',
    'script name'
  );
});
```

15. To make that pass, first we need to save the name that's returned from local storage and then we need to insert it into the present object:

```
export const load = () => {
  const name = localStorage.getItem('name');
  const parsedTokens = JSON.parse(
    localStorage.getItem('parsedTokens')
  );
  return {
    script: {
      ...parser.parseTokens(parsedTokens, parser.initialState),
      name
    }
  };
};
```

16. Finally, we need to deal with the case where no state has been saved yet. The local storage API gives us `null` back in that case, but we'd like to return `undefined`, which will trigger Redux to use the default state. Add this test to the outer `describe` block, so that it won't pick up the extra `getItemSpy` mock values:

```
it('returns undefined if there is no state saved', () => {
  getItemSpy.mockReturnValue(null);
  expect(load()).not.toBeDefined();
});
```

17. Make that pass by wrapping the return statement in an `if` statement:

```
if (parsedTokens && parsedTokens !== null) {
  return {
    ...
  };
}
```

18. Open `src/store.js` and modify it to include the new middleware. I'm defining a new function, `configureStoreWithLocalStorage`, so that our tests can continue using `configureStore` without interacting with local storage:

```
import {
  createStore,
  compose,
  combineReducers,
  applyMiddleware
} from 'redux';
import { scriptReducer } from './reducers/script';
import { withUndoRedo } from './reducers/withUndoRedo';
import { save, load } from './middleware/localStorage';

export const configureStore = (
  storeEnhancers = [],
  initialState = {}
) => {
  return createStore(
    combineReducers({
      script: withUndoRedo(scriptReducer)
    }),
    initialState,
    compose(
      ...[
        applyMiddleware(save),
        ...storeEnhancers
      ]
```

```
    )
  );
};
```

```
export const configureStoreWithLocalStorage = () =>
  configureStore(undefined, load());
```

19. Finally, open `src/index.js` and replace the call to `configureStore` with a call
to `configureStoreWithLocalStorage`. You'll also need to update the import
for this new function:

```
import { configureStoreWithLocalStorage } from './store';

ReactDOM.render(
  <Provider store={configureStoreWithLocalStorage()}>
    <App />
  </Provider>,
  document.getElementById('root'));
```

That's it. If you like, this is a great time to run the app for a manual test and try it. Open the
browser window, type a few commands, and try it out!

If you're stuck for commands to run a manual test, you can use these:

```
forward 100
right 90
to drawSquare
  repeat 4 [ forward 100 right 90 ]
end
drawSquare
```

These commands exercise most of the functionality within the interpreter and display.
They'll come in handy in `Chapter 11`, *Adding Animation,* when you'll probably want to be
manually testing a lot.

Changing keyboard focus

The Git tag for this section is `focus`.

The user of our application will, most of the time, be typing in the prompt at the bottom-right of the screen. It would be a great help to them if they could see the cursor already positioned there. We should do this after launching the app for the first time, and when another element—such as the name text field or the menu buttons—steals focus.

React doesn't support setting focus, so we need to use a ref on our components and then drop into the DOM API.

We'll do this via a Redux reducer. It will have two actions: `PROMPT_FOCUS_REQUEST` and `PROMPT_HAS_FOCUSED`. Any of the React components in our application will be able to dispatch the first action. The Prompt component will "listen" for it and then dispatch the second, once it has focused.

Writing the reducer

We'll start, as ever, with the reducer:

1. Create a new file named `test/reducers/environment.test.js` and add the following `describe` block. This covers the basic case of the reducer needing to return the default state when `undefined` is passed to it:

```
import {
  environmentReducer as reducer
} from '../../src/reducers/environment';

describe('environmentReducer', () => {
  it('returns default state when existing state is undefined', ()
=> {
    expect(reducer(undefined, {})).toEqual({
      promptFocusRequest: false
    });
  });
});
```

2. Make the test pass with the following code. This isn't technically the simplest code that will make this work, but it is the simplest thing if you consider the changes that would have to be made later if we didn't go with this approach. Since we've built reducers before, we know where we're going with this one:

```
const defaultState = {
  promptFocusRequest: false
};

export const environmentReducer = (
  state = defaultState,
  action) => {
  return state;
};
```

3. Add the next test:

```
it('sets promptFocusRequest to true when receiving a
PROMPT_FOCUS_REQUEST action', () => {
  expect(
    reducer(
      { promptFocusRequest: false},
      { type: 'PROMPT_FOCUS_REQUEST' }
    )
  ).toEqual({
    promptFocusRequest: true
  });
});
```

4. Make that pass by adding in a switch statement, as shown next. Again, the `switch` statement isn't necessary here—we could have used an `if`—but since we've done this before, we're confident that we will eventually need a switch:

```
export const environmentReducer = (
  state = defaultState,
  action
) => {
  switch (action.type) {
    case 'PROMPT_FOCUS_REQUEST':
      return { promptFocusRequest: true };
  }
  return state;
};
```

5. Add the final test for this reducer:

```
it('sets promptFocusRequest to false when receiving a
PROMPT_HAS_FOCUSED action', () => {
  expect(
    reducer(
      { promptFocusRequest: true},
      { type: 'PROMPT_HAS_FOCUSED' }
    )
  ).toEqual({
    promptFocusRequest: false
  });
});
```

6. Finally, make that pass by adding another case statement:

```
case 'PROMPT_HAS_FOCUSED':
  return { promptFocusRequest: false };
```

Adding the reducer to the store

Before we can use the new reducer in our tests, we'll need to add it to the store. Open up `src/store.js` and modify it as follows. I have left out the existing imports in this code listing:

```
import { environmentReducer } from './reducers/environment';

export const configureStore = (
  storeEnhancers = [],
  initialState = {}
) => {
  return createStore(
    combineReducers({
      script: withUndoRedo(logoReducer),
      environment: environmentReducer
    }),
    initialState,
    compose(
      ...[
        applyMiddleware(save), ...storeEnhancers
      ]
    )
  );
};
```

Focusing the prompt

Let's move on to the most difficult part of this: focusing the actual prompt. For this, we'll need to introduce a ref:

1. Open `test/Prompt.test.js` and add the following `describe` block at the bottom, nested within the `Prompt` describe block. The test uses the `document.activeElement` property, which is the element that currently has focus. It's also using the `renderInTableWithStore` function, which is the same as the `renderWithStore` helper you've seen already except that the component is first wrapped in a `table`:

```
describe('prompt focus', () => {
  it('sets focus when component first renders', () => {
    renderInTableWithStore(<Prompt />);
    expect(document.activeElement).toEqual(textArea());
  });
});
```

2. Let's make that pass. We'll define a new `ref` using the `useRef` hook, and we'll use the `useEffect` hook to focus when the component mounts. Make sure to pull out the new constants from the React constant, which is at the top of the file:

```
import React, { useEffect, useRef, useState } from 'react';

export const Prompt = () => {

  ...

  const inputRef = useRef();

  useEffect(() => {
    inputRef.current.focus();
  }, [inputRef]);

  return (
    ...
      <textarea onScroll={handleScroll}
                value={editPrompt}
                style={{height: height}}
                ref={inputRef}
                onChange={handleChange}
                onKeyPress={handleKeyPress} />
    ...
  );
};
```

3. Before we add the next test, first import the `act` function, which we'll need to ensure that the `useEffect` hook runs before we proceed with our expectations:

```
import { act } from 'react-dom/test-utils';
```

4. Now let's add the next test. We'll need a new helper function that will clear focus. Because focus will be set as soon as the component mounts, we need to unset it again so we can verify the behavior of our focus request:

```
const jsdomClearFocus = () => {
  const node = document.createElement('input');
  document.body.appendChild(node);
  node.focus();
  node.remove();
}

it('calls focus on the underlying DOM element if promptFocusRequest
is true', async () => {
  const store = renderInTableWithStore(<Prompt />);
  jsdomClearFocus();
  act(() => {
    store.dispatch({ type: 'PROMPT_FOCUS_REQUEST' });
  });
  expect(document.activeElement).toEqual(textArea());
});
```

5. To make that pass, first add the new mapped state at the top of the component:

```
const mapStateToProps = ({
  script: { nextInstructionId },
  environment: { promptFocusRequest }
}) => ({ nextInstructionId, promptFocusRequest });

export const Prompt = connect(
  mapStateToProps,
  mapDispatchToProps
) (
  ({
    nextInstructionId,
    promptFocusRequest,
    submitEditLine }) => {
    ...
});
```

6. Then, add a new effect which will run when `promptFocusRequest` changes. Interestingly, the test doesn't force us to write a conditional around this, and the code will run fine without it. When `promptFocusRequest` returns to `false`, the effect will run again, but this is harmless:

```
useEffect(() => {
  inputRef.current.focus();
}, [promptFocusRequest]);
```

7. Finally, let's dispatch an action when the focus has occurred:

```
it('dispatches an action notifying that the prompt has focused', ()
=> {
  const store = renderWithStore(<Prompt />);
  store.dispatch({ type: 'PROMPT_FOCUS_REQUEST' });
  return expectRedux(store)
    .toDispatchAnAction()
    .matching({ type: 'PROMPT_HAS_FOCUSED' });
});
```

8. To make that pass, add a new dispatch function that we can call within the `Prompt` component:

```
const mapDispatchToProps = {
  submitEditLine: text => ({ type: 'SUBMIT_EDIT_LINE', text }),
  promptHasFocused: () => ({ type: 'PROMPT_HAS_FOCUSED' })
};

export const Prompt = connect(
  mapStateToProps,
  mapDispatchToProps
) (
  ({
    nextInstructionId,
    promptFocusRequest,
    submitEditLine,
    promptHasFocused
  }) => {
```

9. Finally, call `promptHasFocused` within the `useEffect` hook. Make sure to include `promptHasFocused` in the hook's dependency list:

```
useEffect(() => {
  inputRef.current.focus();
  promptHasFocused();
}, [promptFocusRequest, promptHasFocused]);
```

Requesting focus in other components

All that's left is to call the request action when required. We'll do this for `ScriptName`, but you could also do it for the buttons in the menu bar:

1. Open `test/ScriptName.test.js` and add the following test in the describe block with the name `when the user hits Enter`:

```
it('dispatches a prompt focus request', () => {
    return expectRedux(store)
        .toDispatchAnAction()
        .matching({ type: 'PROMPT_FOCUS_REQUEST' });
});
```

2. In `src/ScriptName.js`, modify the component to define a dispatch callback `promptFocusRequest`:

```
const mapDispatchToProps = {
    submitScriptName: text => ({ type: 'SUBMIT_SCRIPT_NAME', text }),
    promptFocusRequest: () => ({ type: 'PROMPT_FOCUS_REQUEST' })
};

export const ScriptName = connect(
    mapStateToProps,
    mapDispatchToProps
) (
    ({
        name,
        submitScriptName,
        promptFocusRequest
    }) => {
    ...
    }
);
```

3. Finally, call that from within the edit completion handler:

```
const completeEditingScriptName = () => {
    if (editingScriptName) {
        toggleEditingScriptName();
        submitScriptName(updatedScriptName);
        promptFocusRequest();
    }
};
```

That's it! If you build and run now, you'll see how focus is automatically given to the prompt textbox, and if you edit the script name (by clicking on it, typing something, and then hitting *Enter*), you'll see that focus returns to the prompt.

Summary

In this chapter, we've explored how React and Redux can be used together to build applications beyond form-based input. We've covered using Redux to support undo/redo behavior, and building Redux middleware to save and load existing states via the browser's LocalStorage API. Finally, we looked at how to test-drive changing the browser's focus, rounding off our additions to the user interface.

In the next chapter, we'll look at how to test-drive something much more intricate: animation.

Further learning

- Wikipedia entry on the Logo programming language: `https://en.wikipedia.org/wiki/Logo_(programming_language)`

11
Adding Animation

Animation lends itself to test-driven development just as much as any other feature. However, it also lends itself to manual testing, since it helps to observe if our code is doing the right thing according to our eyes. This is particularly true because animation is not something that most programmers do every day. When something is new, it's often better to do lots of manual tests to verify behavior in addition to your tests.

In fact, while preparing for this chapter I did a *lot* of manual testing. The walk-through that you're about to be presented with was not a start-to-finish affair for me. I had to play with a number of different approaches, taking many wrong turns. There were many times that I opened my browser to the `forward 100` or `right 90` type to verify what was actually happening.

Once my code was working, I then had to refactor it and clean it up. With each refactor, I also manually tested, just to verify I hadn't broken anything.

Much of this process won't be visible to you as you read through the chapter, but I hope that when you come to animate your components you remember this note and be liberal with your manual testing!

This chapter covers the following topics:

- Isolating components for animation
- Animating with `requestAnimationFrame`

Isolating components for animation

There are two parts to this animation:

- First, there's a movement animation that occurs when lines are being drawn. Say, for example, that the user has entered `forward 100` as an instruction. We want the turtle to move slowly 100 units along, at a given speed. As it moves, it will draw the line behind it.
- The second animation is turtle rotation. The turtle does not turn instantly; if the user types `rotate 90` then the turtle should rotate slowly until it has made a quarter turn.

The code we'll write is relatively complicated, so we need to do some up-front design first.

Designing the component

The Git tag for this section is `animation`.

As you read through this section, you might wish to open `src/Drawing.js` and read the existing code to understand what it's doing.

The current `Drawing` component shows a static snapshot of how the drawing looks at this point. It renders a set of **Scalable Vector Graphics (SVG)** lines and a triangle to represent the turtle.

We'll need to do some work to convert this from a static snapshot to an animating representation.

As it stands, the component takes a `turtle` prop and a `drawCommands` prop. The `turtle` prop is the current position of the turtle, given all the `drawCommands` have already been drawn. However, this isn't what we need when we're animating. We need the initial position of the turtle before any `drawCommands` have been animated.

This means we'll need to keep a track of the turtle in state, and remove the use of the prop entirely. The turtle value starts at the 0, 0 coordinate with an angle of 0. As we move through `drawCommands`, we can modify the turtle location as appropriate.

Another problem we face is how to keep track of which commands have already been animated. This is an issue because the user is entering commands one by one, and `Drawing` will continue receiving new props as the `drawCommands` array grows larger and larger. We need to keep track of the commands that have already appeared on screen. To do this, we'll use the `animatingCommandIndex` index to denote the index of the array item that is currently being animated. We start animating at the `0` index. Once that command has been animated, we increment the index by `1`, moving along to the next command, and animate that. The process is repeated until we reach the end of the array.

There are two types of draw commands: `drawLine` and `rotate`. Here are a couple of examples of commands that will appear in the `drawCommands` array:

```
{ drawCommand: 'drawLine', id: 123, x1: 100, y1: 100, x2: 200, y2: 100 }
{ drawCommand: 'rotate', id: 234, previousAngle: 0, newAngle: 90 }
```

The animated `Drawing` component will need to process different animations depending on which type of command is being animated.

The existing component already has a `Turtle` component that has been split out from the main component. Let's follow the same approach for our new animated lines by building a `StaticLines` component, to represent lines already drawn, and an `AnimatedLine` component, to represent the current line being animated.

Extracting out StaticLines

 The Git tag for this section is `animation`.

The current `Drawing` component already draws a set of lines. Our first job is to extract that into its own component, named `StaticLines`.

1. The test suite for the `Drawing` component contains a set of sample lines. These will be useful in the `StaticLines` test suite too, so let's extract them now. Create a new file named `test/sampleLines.js` and add the following content:

   ```
   export const horizontalLine = {
     drawCommand: 'drawLine',
     id: 123,
     x1: 100,
     y1: 100,
   ```

```
    x2: 200,
    y2: 100
};

export const verticalLine = {
  drawCommand: 'drawLine',
  id: 234,
  x1: 200,
  y1: 100,
  x2: 200,
  y2: 200
};

export const diagonalLine = {
  drawCommand: 'drawLine',
  id: 235,
  x1: 200,
  y1: 200,
  x2: 300,
  y2: 300
};
```

2. In `test/Drawing.test.js`, delete the three definitions for `horizontalLine`, `verticalLine`, and `diagonalLine` and replace them with the following import:

```
import {
  horizontalLine,
  verticalLine,
  diagonalLine
} from './sampleLines';
```

3. Create a new `test/StaticLines.test.js` file, and prime it with the following imports and outer describe block. Much of this is copied from `test/Drawing.test.js`. The only new thing is the definition of `renderSvg`, which we need because the `line` elements we'll render are only valid within a parent `svg` element:

```
import React from 'react';
import { createContainer } from './domManipulators';
import { StaticLines } from '../src/StaticLines';
import {
  horizontalLine,
  verticalLine,
  diagonalLine
} from './sampleLines';

describe('StaticLines', () => {
```

```
let container, render;

beforeEach(() => {
  ({ container, render } = createContainer());
});

const renderSvg = component => render(<svg>{component}</svg>);
const line = () => container.querySelector('line');
const allLines = () => container.querySelectorAll('line');
});
```

4. Add the first test. This is the same test that's contained within
   `test/Drawing.test.js`, but it needs to be modified since `Drawing` uses the
   Redux store to pass in props, whereas here we can just pass them in directly:

```
it('renders a line with the line coordinates', () => {
  renderSvg(<StaticLines lineCommands={[ horizontalLine ]} />);
  expect(line()).not.toBeNull();
  expect(line().getAttribute('x1')).toEqual('100');
  expect(line().getAttribute('y1')).toEqual('100');
  expect(line().getAttribute('x2')).toEqual('200');
  expect(line().getAttribute('y2')).toEqual('100');
});
```

It's a normal occurrence to have to rewrite tests in this way, whenever
you're extracting small components out of a larger Redux-connected
component.

5. Let's cheat a little here and continue moving tests across before we run them.
   Move the following three tests from the `Drawing` test suite to the
   `StaticLines` test suite. You'll need to make the same change as shown in the
   first preceding test:

```
sets a stroke width of 2
sets a stroke color of black
draws every drawLine command
```

6. If you run the tests now, you'll get four failures. The error message indicates that the StaticLines component wasn't found. Time to extract that code! In src/Drawing.js, start by defining a new functional component at the top of the file. With this change, you should now start to see test failures rather than exceptions:

```
import React from 'react';

export const StaticLines = ({ lineCommands }) => null;
```

7. In the Drawing component, the first child of the svg element is a map over lineCommands. This is exactly the code that we need, so move those two lines into StaticLines. Note that we are able to get rid of the outer curly braces surrounding the map. You could even remove the curly braces around the function definition if you wished. Running tests at this point should give you all green tests:

```
export const StaticLines = ({ lineCommands }) =>
  lineCommands.map(({ id, x1, y1, x2, y2 }) =>
    <line
      key={id}
      x1={x1}
      y1={y1}
      x2={x2}
      y2={y2}
      strokeWidth="2"
      stroke="black"
    />
  );
```

8. In test/Drawing.test.js, delete all of the tests you just moved across to StaticLines.

9. Next, it's time to update Drawing to use StaticLines. First, we'll need to import the module so we can stub it out. Add the following import at the top of test/Drawing.test.js:

```
import * as StaticLinesModule from '../src/StaticLines';
```

10. Stub out the `StaticLines` component in the `beforeEach` block:

```
beforeEach(() => {
  ...
  jest
    .spyOn(StaticLinesModule, 'StaticLines')
    .mockReturnValue(<div id="staticLines" />);
});
```

11. Add the following test, which verifies that `StaticLines` appears in our rendered output. This is the first of two tests that verify that we're using `StaticLines` correctly:

```
it('renders StaticLines within the svg', () => {
  renderWithStore(<Drawing />);
  expect(
    container.querySelector('svg > div#staticLines')
  ).not.toBeNull();
});
```

12. To make that pass, first you'll need to import the new component into `src/Drawing.js`:

```
import { StaticLines } from './StaticLines';
```

13. Now replace the component's JSX to render the new component:

```
return (
  <div id="viewport">
    <svg
      viewBox="-300 -300 600 600"
      preserveAspectRatio="xMidYMid slice"
      xmlns="http://www.w3.org/2000/svg">
      <StaticLines />
      <Turtle {...turtle} />
    </svg>
  </div>
```

14. Next, find the test does not draw any commands for the ones that aren't `drawLine` commands. Rewrite this in terms of the `StaticLines` component, as follows. This new test combines two pieces of functionality: firstly, it assigns the `lineCommands` prop, and secondly, the value passed in is filtered out:

```
it('sends only line commands to StaticLines', () => {
  const unknown = { drawCommand: 'unknown' };
  renderWithStore(<Drawing />, {
```

```
        script: {
          drawCommands: [horizontalLine, verticalLine, unknown]
        }
      });
      expect(StaticLinesModule.StaticLines).toHaveBeenLastCalledWith(
        { lineCommands: [horizontalLine, verticalLine] },
        expect.anything()
      );
    });
```

We'll now build an AnimatedLine component before we re-implement Drawing to use both StaticLines and AnimatedLine.

Building an AnimatedLine component

 The Git tag for this section is animated-line-component.

This component is straightforward: we will pass to it the line to be drawn and the current turtle position. Rather than drawing the line from x1,y1 to x2,y2 as we do with StaticLines for an animating line, we'll draw it from x1,y1 to the current turtle position. The turtle position will move at a constant speed from the x1,y1 coordinate until it reaches the x2,y2 co-ordinate, drawing a line behind it:

1. Create a new file, test/AnimatedLine.test.js, and prime it with the following imports and describe the block setup. This is very similar to what we just did for StaticLines. The main difference is that we're passing in a new turtle prop:

    ```
    import React from 'react';
    import ReactDOM from 'react-dom';
    import { createContainer } from './domManipulators';
    import { AnimatedLine } from '../src/AnimatedLine';
    import {
      horizontalLine,
      verticalLine,
      diagonalLine
    } from './sampleLines';

    const turtle = { x: 10, y: 10, angle: 10 };

    describe('AnimatedLine', () => {
    ```

```
let container, render;

beforeEach(() => {
  ({ container, render } = createContainer());
});

const renderSvg = component => render(<svg>{component}</svg>);
const line = () => container.querySelector('line');
});
```

2. Now add the first test:

```
it('draws a line starting at the x1,y1 co-ordinate of the command
being drawn', () => {
  renderSvg(
    <AnimatedLine
      commandToAnimate={horizontalLine}
      turtle={turtle}
    />
  );
  expect(line()).not.toBeNull();
  expect(line().getAttribute('x1')).toEqual(
    horizontalLine.x1.toString()
  );
  expect(line().getAttribute('y1')).toEqual(
    horizontalLine.y1.toString()
  );
});
```

3. Create a new file, `src/AnimatedLine.js`, and make your test pass by using the following implementation:

```
import React from 'react';

export const AnimatedLine = ({
  commandToAnimate: { x1, y1 }
}) => (
  <line x1={x1} y1={y1} />
);
```

4. Onto the next test. In this one, I'm explicitly setting the turtle values so that it's clear to see where the expected values come from:

```
it('draws a line ending at the current position of the turtle', ()
=> {
  renderSvg(
    <AnimatedLine
      commandToAnimate={horizontalLine}
```

```
      turtle={{ x: 10, y: 20 }}
    />
  );
  expect(line().getAttribute('x2')).toEqual('10');
  expect(line().getAttribute('y2')).toEqual('20');
});
```

5. To make that pass, we just need to set the x2 and y2 props on the line element, pulling that in from the turtle:

```
export const AnimatedLine = ({
  commandToAnimate: { x1, y1 },
  turtle: { x, y }
}) => (
  <line x1={x1} y1={y1} x2={x} y2={y} />
);
```

6. Then we need two tests to set the strokeWidth and the stroke props:

```
it('sets a stroke width of 2', () => {
  renderSvg(
    <AnimatedLine
      commandToAnimate={horizontalLine}
      turtle={turtle}
    />
  );
  expect(line().getAttribute('stroke-width')).toEqual('2');
});

it('sets a stroke color of black', () => {
  renderSvg(
    <AnimatedLine
      commandToAnimate={horizontalLine}
      turtle={turtle}
    />
  );
  expect(line().getAttribute('stroke')).toEqual('black');
});
```

7. Finish off the component by adding in those two props:

```
export const AnimatedLine = ({
  commandToAnimate: { x1, y1 },
  turtle: { x, y }
}) => (
  <line
    x1={x1}
    y1={y1}
```

```
      x2={x}
      y2={y}
      strokeWidth="2"
      stroke="black"
    />
  );
```

Now it's time to add this new component into `Drawing`. This isn't as straightforward as `StaticLines`; for this one, we'll need to consider animation.

Animating with requestAnimationFrame

This work will split into two parts: drawing lines and rotating the turtle. Each of these requires similar but different animation logic.

Drawing lines

The Git tag for this section is `request-animation-frame`.

In order to use the `AnimatedLine` component, we'll first need to implement the animation logic that helps us divide `drawCommands` up into previously drawn commands, the current animating command, and future commands to animate.

We'll use the `useEffect` hook in combination with `requestAnimationFrame` to move the turtle.

To begin, we need to first change how we determine the position of the turtle. In the existing implementation, the final turtle position is passed into the `Drawing` component. This works perfectly fine if we aren't animating. But now we need to know where the turtle starts, and move it along each line, recording where it is at every single point, including its direction:

1. In the `Drawing` tests, find the test named `passes the turtle x, y and angle as props to Turtle`. Change it to read as follows. We want the *initial* turtle to be at the origin.

   ```
   it('passes the turtle x, y and angle as props to Turtle', () => {
     renderWithStore(<Drawing />);
   ```

```
expect(TurtleModule.Turtle).toHaveBeenCalledWith(
  { x: 0, y: 0, angle: 0 },
  expect.anything()
);
});
```

This test uses the `TurtleModule.Turtle` spy, which is already defined in the `beforeEach` block.

2. In `src/Drawing.js`, at the top of the `Drawing` component, remove the turtle prop from the function definition and from `mapStateToProps`.

3. Replace it with the following constant definition, just below the current calls to `useState`. After this change, the test should pass:

```
const turtle = { x: 0, y: 0, angle: 0 };
```

4. It's time to begin using `requestAnimationFrame`. We'll need to stub out that function. In the `Drawing` describe block, add the following setup for `beforeEach` and `afterEach`:

```
beforeEach(() => {
  ...
  jest
    .spyOn(window, 'requestAnimationFrame');
});

afterEach(() => {
  window.requestAnimationFrame.mockReset();
});
```

We need to use an `afterEach` block here to ensure that our spy object is successfully reset between tests.

5. Let's add a test to verify that we call it. Add this to the bottom of the describe block. Unusually, we're performing the first render within the `beforeEach` block. Although this first test only contains an expectation, subsequent tests will contain triggers of the `requestAnimationFrame` handlers. Therefore, we can think of the render as part of the *Arrange* phase of the test:

```
describe('movement animation', () => {
  beforeEach(() => {
```

```
      renderWithStore(<Drawing />, {
        script: {
          drawCommands: [horizontalLine],
          turtle: { x: 0, y: 0, angle: 0 }
        }
      });
    });

    it('invokes requestAnimationFrame', () => {
      expect(window.requestAnimationFrame).toHaveBeenCalled();
    });
  });
```

6. Make this pass by adding in a new `useEffect` in the `Drawing` component. Add the following three lines, just above the return JSX:

> You can actually make this test pass by simply passing calling `requestAnimationFrame` within the main function body. However, you'd be breaking the "rules" of React components by doing that.

```
useEffect(() => {
  requestAnimationFrame();
}, []);
```

7. For the next test, we need a couple of new imports. The first is for `act`. Since we're now in the realms of `useEffect`, any actions that cause updates to the component state must occur within an `act` block. That includes any triggered animation frames, and we're about to trigger some. Add that import now:

```
import { act } from 'react-dom/test-utils';
```

8. We also need an import for `AnimatedLine` because, in the next test, we'll assert that we render it. Add the following import, together with its spy setup, as shown:

```
import * as AnimatedLineModule from '../src/AnimatedLine';

beforeEach(() => {
  ...
  jest
    .spyOn(AnimatedLineModule, 'AnimatedLine')
    .mockReturnValue(<div id="animatedLine" />);
});

afterEach(() => {
```

```
. . .
AnimatedLineModule.AnimatedLine.mockReset();
});
```

9. The call to requestAnimationFrame should pass a handler function as an argument. The browser will then call this function during the next animation frame. For the next test, we'll check that the turtle is at the start of the first line when the timer first fires. We need to define a new helper to do this, which is triggerRequestAnimationFrame. In a browser environment, this call would happen automatically, but in our test, we play the role of the browser and trigger it in code. It's this call that must be wrapped in an act since our handler will cause the component state to change:

```
const triggerRequestAnimationFrame = time => {
  act(() => {
    const lastCall =
      window.requestAnimationFrame.mock.calls.length - 1;
    const frameFn =
      window.requestAnimationFrame.mock.calls[lastCall][0];
    frameFn(time);
  });
};

it('renders an AnimatedLine with turtle at the start position when
the animation has run for 0s', () => {
  triggerRequestAnimationFrame(0);
  expect(AnimatedLineModule.AnimatedLine).toHaveBeenCalledWith(
    {
      commandToAnimate: horizontalLine,
      turtle: { x: 100, y: 100, angle: 0 }
    },
    expect.anything()
  );
});
```

10. Making this test pass will be a bit of a "big bang," unfortunately. That's partly because, as we make changes other tests will break, so we'll do this piece by piece. To begin with, running this test will give a cryptic error about "frameFn is not a function." That gives us a clue about where to start: we need to pass a function to requestAnimationFrame. Let's do that now, and make it update the turtle to point at the first co-ordinate. For that to happen, the turtle variable will need to become component state. Change the constant declaration for turtle to the following:

```
const [turtle, setTurtle] = useState({ x: 0, y: 0, angle: 0 });
```

11. Extend `useEffect` as shown. We need to define two variables, `commandToAnimate` and `isDrawingLine`, which we'll use to determine if we should animate at all. The `isDrawingLine` test is necessary because some of our tests send no `drawCommands` at all to the component, in which case `commandToAnimate` will be null. Yet another test passes a command of an unknown type into the component, which would also blow up if we tried to pull out `x1` and `y1` from it.

```
const commandToAnimate = drawCommands[0];
const isDrawingLine =
  commandToAnimate && isDrawLineCommand(commandToAnimate);

useEffect(() => {
  const handleDrawLineFrame = time => {
    setTurtle(turtle => ({
      ...turtle,
      x: commandToAnimate.x1,
      y: commandToAnimate.y1,
    }));
  };
  if (isDrawingLine) {
    requestAnimationFrame(handleDrawLineFrame);
  }
}, [commandToAnimate, isDrawingLine]);
```

This code uses the *functional update* variant of `setTurtle` that takes a function rather than a value, which can be used when the new state value depends on the old value. Using this form of setter means that turtle doesn't need to be in the dependency list of `useEffect` and won't cause the `useEffect` hook to reset itself.

12. At this point, we still aren't rendering an `AnimatedLine`, which is what our test expects. Let's fix that now. Start by adding the import:

```
import { AnimatedLine } from './AnimatedLine';
```

13. Insert this just below the JSX for `StaticLines`. At this point, your test should be passing:

```
<AnimatedLine
  commandToAnimate={commandToAnimate}
  turtle={turtle}
/>
```

14. We need a further test to check that we don't render an `AnimatedLine` if there are no lines being animated. Add the next test as shown, but don't add it in the movement animation block; instead, move back up above it into the parent context:

```
it('does not render AnimatedLine when not moving', () => {
  renderWithStore(<Drawing />, { script: { drawCommands: [] } });
  expect(AnimatedLineModule.AnimatedLine).not.toHaveBeenCalled();
});
```

15. Make that pass by wrapping the `AnimatedLine` component with a ternary. We simply return null if `isDrawingLine` is false:

```
{isDrawingLine ? (
  <AnimatedLine
    commandToAnimate={commandToAnimate}
    turtle={turtle}
  /> : null}
```

16. We've handled what the *first* animation frame should do; now let's code up subsequent calls. The `handleDrawLineFrame` handler, when called by the browser, will be passed a time parameter. The `handleDrawLineFrame` function should run for a particular duration. The turtle travels at a constant velocity, so the duration is based on the length of the line being drawn. We'll use the next test to get us to that implementation. In the following code, there are *two* calls to `triggerRequestAnimationFrame`. The first one is used to signify that animation is started; the second one allows us to move. We need the first call (with a time index of 0) to be able to mark the time at which animation started:

```
it('renders an AnimatedLine with turtle at a position based on a
speed of 5px per ms', () => {
  triggerRequestAnimationFrame(0);
  triggerRequestAnimationFrame(250);
  expect(
    AnimatedLineModule.AnimatedLine
  ).toHaveBeenLastCalledWith(
    {
      commandToAnimate: horizontalLine,
      turtle: { x: 150, y: 100, angle: 0 }
    },
    expect.anything()
  );
});
```

17. To make this pass, first, we need to define a couple of functions. Scroll up `src/Drawing.js` until you see the definition for `isDrawLineCommand`, and add these two new definitions there. The `distance` and `movementSpeed` functions are used to calculate the duration of the animation:

```
const isDrawLineCommand = command =>
  command.drawCommand === 'drawLine';
const distance = ({ x1, y1, x2, y2 }) =>
  Math.sqrt((x2 - x1) * (x2 - x1) + (y2 - y1) * (y2 - y1));
const movementSpeed = 5;
```

18. Now we can calculate the duration of the animation; modify `useEffect` as shown:

```
useEffect(() => {
  let duration;
  const handleDrawLineFrame = time => {
   setTurtle(turtle => ({
      ...turtle,
      x: commandToAnimate.x1,
      y: commandToAnimate.y1,
     }));
  };
  if (isDrawingLine) {
    duration = movementSpeed * distance(commandToAnimate);
    requestAnimationFrame(handleDrawLineFrame);
  }
}, [commandToAnimate, isDrawingLine]);
```

19. By declaring `duration` as the very first line in the `useEffect` block, the variable is in scope for the `requestAnimationFrame` handler to read it to calculate distance. To do that, we take the elapsed time and divide it by the total duration:

 At this point, our animations have always begun at a time of 0. That simplifies our implementation for this test, but it isn't true of the real world, for which animation will start at the current time. The next test we write will improve on this implementation.

```
useEffect(() => {
  let duration;
  const handleDrawLineFrame = time => {
    const { x1, x2, y1, y2 } = commandToAnimate;
    setTurtle(turtle => ({
      ...turtle,
      x: x1 + ((x2 - x1) * (time / duration)),
      y: y1 + ((y2 - y1) * (time / duration)),
```

```
    }));
  };
  if (isDrawingLine) {
    duration = movementSpeed * distance(commandToAnimate);
    requestAnimationFrame(handleDrawLineFrame);
  }
}, [commandToAnimate, isDrawingLine]);
```

20. Okay! Let's make sure this can work for a start time of something other than 0. Add the following test:

```
it('calculates move distance with a non-zero animation start time',
() => {
  const startTime = 12345;
  triggerRequestAnimationFrame(startTime);
  triggerRequestAnimationFrame(startTime + 250);
  expect(
    AnimatedLineModule.AnimatedLine
  ).toHaveBeenLastCalledWith(
    {
      commandToAnimate: horizontalLine,
      turtle: { x: 150, y: 100, angle: 0 }
    },
    expect.anything()
  );
});
```

21. Make that pass by introducing the `start` and `elapsed` times, as shown:

```
useEffect(() => {
  let start, duration;
  const handleDrawLineFrame = time => {
    if (start === undefined) start = time;
    const elapsed = time - start;
    const { x1, x2, y1, y2 } = commandToAnimate;
    setTurtle(turtle => ({
      ...turtle,
      x: x1 + ((x2 - x1) * (elapsed / duration)),
      y: y1 + ((y2 - y1) * (elapsed / duration)),
    }));
  };
  if (isDrawingLine) {
    duration = movementSpeed * distance(commandToAnimate);
    requestAnimationFrame(handleDrawLineFrame);
  }
}, [commandToAnimate, isDrawingLine]);
```

22. Our components need to call `requestAnimationFrame` repeatedly until the duration is reached. At that point, the line should have been fully drawn. In this test, we trigger three animation frames, and we expect `requstAnimationFrame` to have been called three times:

```
it('invokes requestAnimationFrame repeatedly until the duration is
reached', () => {
  triggerRequestAnimationFrame(0);
  triggerRequestAnimationFrame(250);
  triggerRequestAnimationFrame(500);
  expect(
    window.requestAnimationFrame.mock.calls.length
  ).toEqual(3);
});
```

23. To make that pass, we need to ensure that `handleDrawLineFrame` triggers another `requestAnimationFrame` when it's run. However, we should only do that until the time that the duration has been reached. Make that pass happen by writing the following conditional:

```
const handleDrawLineFrame = (time) => {
  if (start === undefined) start = time;
  if (time < start + duration) {
    const elapsed = time - start;
    const { x1, x2, y1, y2 } = commandToAnimate;
    setTurtle(turtle => ({
      ...turtle,
      x: x1 + ((x2 - x1) * (elapsed / duration)),
      y: y1 + ((y2 - y1) * (elapsed / duration)),
    }));
    requestAnimationFrame(handleDrawLineFrame);
  }
};
```

We use a less-than comparison here since the timestamp argument could be any time equal to or greater than the expected duration.

24. Next, we need to move to the next command when the line has been fully drawn. This new describe block needs to be placed below the describe block we've just implemented, since it uses a different render call, and different test setup.

Notice how `triggerRequestAnimationFrame` is used here—the second animation resets the clock to 0. This is clearly not how time runs in the real-world, but it helps with test readability. Our existing tests mean we've already correctly handled an ever-increasing timestamp, so we can afford to prioritize test readability in future tests.

```
describe('after animation', () => {
  it('animates the next command', () => {
    renderWithStore(<Drawing />, {
      script: { drawCommands: [horizontalLine, verticalLine] }
    });
    triggerRequestAnimationFrame(0);
    triggerRequestAnimationFrame(500);
    triggerRequestAnimationFrame(0);
    triggerRequestAnimationFrame(250);
    expect(
      AnimatedLineModule.AnimatedLine
    ).toHaveBeenLastCalledWith(
      expect.objectContaining({
        commandToAnimate: verticalLine,
        turtle: {
          x: 200,
          y: 150,
          angle: 0
        }
      }),
      expect.anything()
    );
  });
});
```

25. To make that pass, we need to introduce a pointer to the command that is currently being animated. This will start at the 0 index, and we'll increment it each time animation finishes. Add the following new state variable at the top of the component:

```
const [
  animatingCommandIndex,
  setAnimatingCommandIndex
] = useState(0);
```

26. Update the `commandToAnimate` constant to use this new variable:

```
const commandToAnimate = drawCommands[animatingCommandIndex];
```

27. Add an `else` clause to the conditional in `handleDrawLineFrame` that increments the value:

```
if (time < start + duration) {
  ...
} else {
  setAnimatingCommandIndex(
    animatingCommandIndex => animatingCommandIndex + 1
  );
}
```

28. For the final test, we want to make sure that only previously animated commands are sent to `StaticLines`. The currently animating line will be rendered by `AnimatedLine`, and lines which haven't been animated yet shouldn't be rendered at all:

```
it('places line in StaticLines', () => {
  renderWithStore(<Drawing />, {
    script: { drawCommands: [horizontalLine, verticalLine] }
  });
  triggerRequestAnimationFrame(0);
  triggerRequestAnimationFrame(500);
  expect(
    StaticLinesModule.StaticLines
  ).toHaveBeenLastCalledWith(
    { lineCommands: [horizontalLine] },
    expect.anything()
  );
});
```

29. To make that pass, update `lineCommands` to take only the portion of `drawCommands` up until the current `animatingCommandIndex`:

```
const lineCommands = drawCommands
  .slice(0, animatingCommandIndex)
  .filter(isDrawLineCommand);
```

30. Although the latest test will now pass, the existing test sends only line commands to `StaticLines`, and will now break. Since our latest test covers essentially the same functionality, you can safely delete that test now.

That's it! If you run the app you'll now be able to see lines being animated as they are placed on screen.

Cleaning up after useEffect

The `useEffect` hook we've written has `commandToAnimate` and `isDrawingLine` in its dependency list. That means that when either of these values update, the `useEffect` hook tears down and will be restarted. For the most part, this doesn't affect our application, and since the `Drawing` component never unmounts, we don't need to worry too much about that. However, one case that we will need to worry about is if the user resets their screen.

If a command is currently animating when the user clicks the **Reset** button, we don't want the current animation frame to continue. We want to clean that up. Let's add a test for that now:

1. Add the following test at the bottom of `test/Drawing.test.js`:

```
it('calls cancelAnimationFrame on reset', () => {
  renderWithStore(<Drawing />, {
    script: { drawCommands: [horizontalLine] }
  });
  renderWithStore(<Drawing />, { script: { drawCommands: [] } });
  expect(window.cancelAnimationFrame).toHaveBeenCalledWith(
    cancelToken
  );
});
```

2. You'll also need to change the `beforeEach` block, making the `requestAnimationFrame` stub return a dummy cancel token, and adding in a new stub for the `cancelAnimationFrame` function:

```
describe('Drawing', () => {
  const cancelToken = 'cancelToken';
  let container, renderWithStore;

  beforeEach(() => {
    ...
    jest
      .spyOn(window, 'requestAnimationFrame')
      .mockReturnValue(cancelToken);
    jest.spyOn(window, 'cancelAnimationFrame');
  });
});
```

3. To make the test pass, update the `useEffect` hook to save off a new `cancelToken` when `requestAnimationFrame`, and then return the cleanup function from the `useEffect` hook. This function will be called by React when it tears down the hook:

```
useEffect(() => {
  let start, duration, cancelToken;
  const handleDrawLineFrame = time => {
    if (start === undefined) start = time;
    if (time < start + duration) {
      ...
      cancelToken = requestAnimationFrame(handleDrawLineFrame);
    } else {
      setAnimatingCommandIndex(
        animatingCommandIndex => animatingCommandIndex + 1
      );
    }
  };
  if (isDrawingLine) {
    duration = movementSpeed * distance(commandToAnimate);
    cancelToken = requestAnimationFrame(handleDrawLineFrame);
  }

  return () => {
    cancelAnimationFrame(cancelToken);
  }
});
```

4. Finally, we don't want to run this cleanup if `cancelToken` hasn't been set. The token won't have been set if we aren't currently rendering a line. We can prove that with the following test, which you should add now:

```
it('does not call cancelAnimationFrame if no line animating', () =>
{
  jest.spyOn(window, 'cancelAnimationFrame');
  renderWithStore(<Drawing />, {
    script: { drawCommands: [] }
  });
  renderWithStore(<React.Fragment />);
  expect(window.cancelAnimationFrame).not.toHaveBeenCalled();
});
```

This test shows how you can mimic an *unmount* of a component in React, which is simply by rendering `<React.Fragment />` in place of the component under test. React will unmount your component when this occurs.

5. To make that pass, simply wrap the returned cleanup function in a conditional:

```
return () => {
  if (cancelToken) {
    cancelAnimationFrame(cancelToken);
  }
};
```

That's all we need to do for animating the `drawLine` commands. Next up is rotating the turtle.

Rotating the turtle

 The Git tag for this section is `rotation`.

Our lines and turtle are now animating nicely. However, we still need to handle the second type of draw commands: rotations. Just like with movement, our turtle moves with a constant speed when rotating to a new angle. A 360° rotation should take one second to complete, and we can use this to calculate the duration of rotation. For example, a 90° rotation will be 0.25 seconds to complete.

In the last section, we started with a test to check that we were calling `requestAnimationFrame`. I'm going to skip that for brevity; it's also not essential, since we've already proved the same design with drawing lines. We can jump right into the more complex tests, using the same `triggerRequestAnimationFrame` helper as before.

Let's update `Drawing` to animate the turtle's coordinates.

1. At the top of `test/Drawing.test.js`, add a new definition for `rotate90`, which we'll use in our tests. You can put it just beneath the example `drawLine` commands.

```
const rotate90 = {
  drawCommand: 'rotate',
  id: 456,
  previousAngle: 0,
  newAngle: 90
};
```

2. Add the following test to the bottom of the `Drawing` describe block. Create it in another nested describe block, just below the last test you wrote. The test follows exactly the same principle as our tests for drawing lines: we trigger two animation frames, one at time 0 ms and one at time 500 ms, and then expect the rotation to have occurred. You'll notice that I'm also testing the *x* and *y* co-ordinates; that's to make sure we continue to pass those through:

```
describe('rotation animation', () => {
  beforeEach(() => {
    renderWithStore(<Drawing />, {
      script: { drawCommands: [rotate90] }
    });
  });

  it('rotates the turtle', () => {
    triggerRequestAnimationFrame(0);
    triggerRequestAnimationFrame(500);
    expect(TurtleModule.Turtle).toHaveBeenLastCalledWith(
      { x: 0, y: 0, angle: 90 },
      expect.anything()
    );
  });
});
```

 These tests use the `TurtleModule.Turtle` stub which is defined in the `Drawing` test suite already, within the `beforeEach` block.

3. Moving to `src/Drawing.js`, start by adding a definition of `isRotateCommand`, just below the definition of `isDrawLineCommand`:

```
const isDrawLineCommand = command =>
  command.drawCommand === 'drawLine';
const isRotateCommand = command =>
  command.drawCommand === 'rotate';
```

4. In the `Drawing` component, add a new constant, `isRotating`, just below the definition of `isDrawingLine`:

```
const isDrawingLine =
  commandToAnimate && isDrawLineCommand(commandToAnimate);
const isRotating =
  commandToAnimate && isRotateCommand(commandToAnimate);
```

5. In the `useEffect` hook, define a new handler for rotations, `handleRotationFrame`, just below the definition of `handleDrawLineFrame`. For the purposes of this test, it doesn't need to do much other than set the angle to the new value:

```
const handleRotationFrame = time => {
  setTurtle(turtle => ({
    ...turtle,
    angle: commandToAnimate.newAngle
  }));
};
```

6. We can make use of that to call a `requestAnimationFrame` when a rotation command is being animated. Modify the last section of the `useEffect` hook to look as follows, ensuring that you add `isRotating` to the dependency list. The test should pass after this change:

```
useEffect(() => {
  ...

  if (isDrawingLine) {
    duration = movementSpeed * distance(commandToAnimate);
    requestAnimationFrame(handleDrawLineFrame);
  } else if (isRotating) {
    requestAnimationFrame(handleRotationFrame);
  }
}, [commandToAnimate, isDrawingLine, isRotating]);
```

7. Let's add a test to get the duration in and use it within our calculation. This is essentially the same as the last test, but with a different duration and, therefore, a different expected rotation:

```
it('rotates part-way at a speed of 1s per 180 degrees', () => {
  triggerRequestAnimationFrame(0);
  triggerRequestAnimationFrame(250);
  expect(TurtleModule.Turtle).toHaveBeenLastCalledWith(
    { x: 0, y: 0, angle: 45 },
    expect.anything()
  );
});
```

8. To make this pass, first we need to define `rotateSpeed`. You can add this definition just below the definition for `movementSpeed`:

```
const rotateSpeed = 1000 / 180;
```

9. Next, update the conditional at the bottom of the `useEffect` handler to calculate duration for the rotate command:

```
} else if (isRotating) {
  duration =
    rotateSpeed *
    Math.abs(
      commandToAnimate.newAngle -
        commandToAnimate.previousAngle
    );
  requestAnimationFrame(handleRotationFrame);
}
```

10. Update `handleRotationFrame` to use the duration to calculate a proportionate angle to move by:

```
const handleRotationFrame = (time) => {
  const { previousAngle, newAngle } = commandToAnimate;
  setTurtle(turtle => ({
    ...turtle,
    angle:
      previousAngle +
      (newAngle - previousAngle) * (time / duration)
  }));
};
```

11. Just as with `handleDrawLineFrame`, we need to ensure that we can handle start times of other than 0. Add the following test:

```
it('calculates rotation with a non-zero animation start time', ()
=> {
  const startTime = 12345;
  triggerRequestAnimationFrame(startTime);
  triggerRequestAnimationFrame(startTime + 250);
  expect(TurtleModule.Turtle).toHaveBeenLastCalledWith(
    { x: 0, y: 0, angle: 45 },
    expect.anything()
  );
});
```

12. Make that pass by adding the `start` and `elapsed` variables. After this, the test should be passing. You'll be able to notice the similarity between `handleDrawLineFrame` and `handleRotationFrame`:

```
const handleRotationFrame = (time) => {
  if (start === undefined) start = time;
  const elapsed = time - start;
```

```
      const { previousAngle, newAngle } = commandToAnimate;
      setTurtle(turtle => ({
        ...turtle,
        angle:
          previousAngle +
          (newAngle - previousAngle) * (elapsed / duration)
      }));
    };
```

13. Let's add a test to make sure we're calling `requestAnimationFrame` repeatedly. This is exactly the same test that we used for the `drawLine` handler, except now we're passing in the `rotate90` command. Remember to make sure the test belongs in the nested context, so you can be sure that there's no name clash:

```
it('invokes requestAnimationFrame repeatedly until the duration is
reached', () => {
  triggerRequestAnimationFrame(0);
  triggerRequestAnimationFrame(250);
  triggerRequestAnimationFrame(500);
  expect(
    window.requestAnimationFrame.mock.calls.length
  ).toEqual(3);
});
```

14. To make this pass, we need to do a couple of things. First, we need to modify `handleRotationFrame` in the same way we did with `handleDrawLineFrame`, by adding a conditional that stops animating after the duration has been reached. Second, we also need to fill in the second part of the conditional to set the turtle location when the animation is finished:

```
const handleRotationFrame = (time) => {
  if (start === undefined) start = time;
  if (time < start + duration) {
    ...
  } else {
    setTurtle(turtle => ({
      ...turtle,
      angle: commandToAnimate.newAngle
    }));
  }
};
```

This `else` clause wasn't necessary with the `drawLine` handler because, as soon as a line finishes animating, it will be passed to `StaticLines` which renders all lines with their full length. This isn't the case with the rotation angle: it remains fixed until the next rotation. Therefore, we need to ensure it's at its correct final value.

15. We've got one final test. We need to increment the current animation command once the animation is done. As with the same test in the previous section, this test should live *outside* the describe block we've just used, since it has a different test setup:

```
it('animates the next command once rotation is complete', async ()
=> {
  renderWithStore(<Drawing />, {
    script: { drawCommands: [rotate90, horizontalLine] }
  });
  triggerRequestAnimationFrame(0);
  triggerRequestAnimationFrame(500);
  triggerRequestAnimationFrame(0);
  triggerRequestAnimationFrame(250);
  expect(TurtleModule.Turtle).toHaveBeenLastCalledWith(
    { x: 150, y: 100, angle: 90 },
    expect.anything()
  );
});
```

16. Add the call to `setNextCommandToAnimate` into the `else` condition:

```
} else {
  setTurtle(turtle => ({
    ...turtle,
    angle: commandToAnimate.newAngle
  }));
  setAnimatingCommandIndex(animatingCommandToIndex =>
    animatingCommandToIndex + 1
  );
}
```

That's it! If you haven't done so already, it's worth running the app to try it out.

Summary

In this chapter, we've explored how to test the `requestAnimationFrame` browser API. As you've no doubt found, it's not a straightforward process, and there are multiple tests that need to be written if you wish to be fully covered. What's more, we omitted testing the `cancelAnimationFrame` call, which is fine for demonstration purposes but probably not fine for a production app.

Despite the complication involved, it is possible to test animation, and the benefit of doing so is that the complex production code is fully documented via the tests.

In the next chapter, we'll look at how acceptance testing can help add an even greater level of verification and documentation to your system.

Exercises

- Update `Drawing` so that it resets the turtle position when the user clears the screen with the Reset button.
- Our tests have a lot of duplication due to the repeated calls to `triggerRequestAnimationFrame`. Simplify how this is called by creating a wrapper function called `triggerAnimationSequence` that takes an array of frame times and calls `triggerRequestAnimationFrame` for each of those times.
- Loading an existing script (for example, on startup) will take a long time to animate all instructions, and so will pasting in code snippets. How would you modify the system to fast-forward animation in these circumstances?
- How does the undo and redo feature affect animation?

12
Working with WebSockets

In this chapter, we'll look at how to test-drive the WebSocket API within our React app. We'll use it to build a "teaching mode" where one person can share their screen and others can watch as they type out commands.

The WebSocket API isn't straightforward. It uses a number of different callbacks and requires functions to be called in a certain order. To make things harder, we'll do this all within a Redux saga: that means we'll need to do some work to convert the callback API to one that can work with generator functions.

This chapter covers the following topics:

- Designing a WebSocket interaction
- Test-driving a WebSocket connection
- Streaming events with redux-saga
- Updating the app

Designing a WebSocket interaction

Before we begin test-driving, let's think about the up-front design.

There are two modes of operation: presenting and watching. If you're presenting, then everyone watching will get a copy of your commands. A session is made up of one presenter and zero or more watchers. WebSockets are used to communicate with the server. Messages are sent in JSON format.

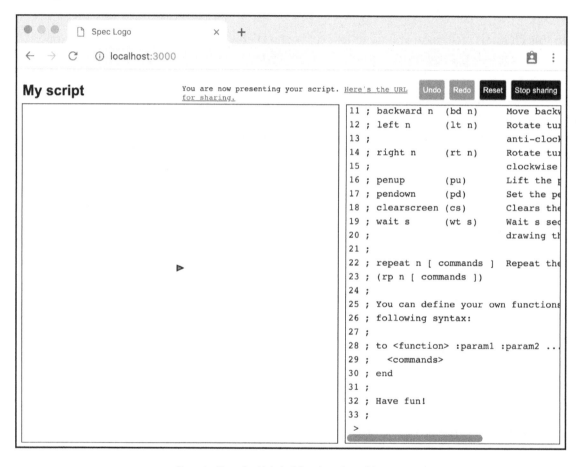

The new teaching mode, with sharing information at the top of the screen

So, how does it work?

- The presenter clicks the **Start sharing** button. The server is sent the following message.

  ```
  { type: 'START_SHARING' }
  ```

- The server then responds with the id of the session, as shown:

  ```
  { status: 'STARTED', id: 123 }
  ```

- This ID can be used to create a URL that opens the application in watching mode, linked to this ID:

  ```
  http://localhost:3000/index.html?watching=123
  ```

- The URL can be shared and opened anywhere. When the application is opened in this mode, the application immediately opens a WebSocket to the server and sends this message:

  ```
  { type: 'START_WATCHING', id: 123 }
  ```

- There can be any number of watchers that connect. On an initial connect, any commands that the presenter has already sent to the server will be replayed. Those commands are sent from the presenter for any Redux action of type SUBMIT_EDIT_LINE, and they are sent via the WebSocket to the server like this:

  ```
  {
    type: 'NEW_ACTION',
    innerAction: { type: 'SUBMIT_EDIT_LINE', text: 'forward 10\n' }
  }
  ```

- Once the server receives an action like that, it stores it in its history but also immediately sends the innerAction to all subscribers:

  ```
  { type: 'SUBMIT_EDIT_LINE', text: 'forward 10\n' } }
  ```

- When the watcher is done, they simply need to close the tab and their connection will close.
- If the presenter is done, they can either close the tab or hit the **Stop sharing** button. This closes the connection and the server clears out its internal state.

The new UI elements

Much of the UI has already been built for you, and we won't bother going over the code as the concepts have been explored in the previous chapter. Here's what you'll find:

- A new button to toggle sharing on and off. It appears in the menu buttons bar, initially named **Start sharing**, and, once sharing has started, it becomes **Stop sharing**.
- The location bar can now take a `?watching=<id>` search parameter. Having this present triggers the application to run in watching mode.
- There is a new message that appears as part of the menu buttons bar. It is either not present, or contains a message telling the user if they are presenting or if they are watching. If they are presenting, it also contains a URL that they can copy and share with others.

Splitting apart the saga

This chapter is a little different in that I've already started off the root saga. There are no tests for this yet—shock!—but it should help you understand the structure we're aiming for. We'll fill in each of the methods as we go along. Naturally, if this wasn't a teaching exercise I wouldn't have written this method first—I would have filled it out as I wrote the tests.

The file we'll be working on is named `src/middleware/sharingSagas.js`. If you open that now, you'll notice two parts to it. First, there's a middleware function named `duplicateForSharing`:

```
export const duplicateForSharing = store => next => action => {
  if (action.type === 'SUBMIT_EDIT_LINE') {
    store.dispatch({
      type: 'SHARE_NEW_ACTION',
      innerAction: action
    });
  }
  return next(action);
};
```

This is essentially a filter that provides us with all the actions that we wish to broadcast. It doesn't know anything about *if* we are currently broadcasting as a presenter. That will be including in some of the code we are about to test-drive.

The next part is the root saga, and this is what we're going to test-drive. It's split into four smaller functions, which are the functions we'll need to fill out:

```
export function* sharingSaga() {
  yield takeLatest('TRY_START_WATCHING', startWatching);
  yield takeLatest('START_SHARING', startSharing);
  yield takeLatest('STOP_SHARING', stopSharing);
  yield takeLatest('SHARE_NEW_ACTION', shareNewAction);
}
```

These four functions make up the entire workflow. Note that there's no facility to "stop watching"—if you want to do that, you'll need to manually change the browser URL to remove the watching search param.

Remember that, if you're strict with your TDD, you wouldn't write this function out until you had tests to cover it.

Test-driving a WebSocket connection

The Git tag for this section is `websockets`. It contains solutions to the exercises from the previous chapter, so if you haven't completed the *Exercises* section yourself, then you should move to this tag now so that you're up to date.

For more detailed instructions, see the *To get the most out of this book* section in the `Preface`.

Let's start by filling out that first function, `startSharing`. This function will be called as a result of receiving the `START_SHARING` action, which is triggered when the user clicks the **Start sharing** button.

1. In `test/middleware/sharingSagas.test.js` add the following imports at the top:

   ```
   import { storeSpy, expectRedux } from 'expect-redux';
   import { act } from 'react-dom/test-utils';
   import { configureStore } from '../../src/store';
   ```

2. At the bottom of the file, add a new describe block and its setup. The challenging part here is the WebSocket spy. We're stubbing out the `WebSocket` constructor function. We'll be revisiting this setup a number of times as we flesh out the spy's functions. There's also code here to set the window location—this is a little clunky, so you may prefer to extract that into its own function with a good name.

```
describe('sharingSaga', () => {
  let store;
  let socketSpyFactory;

  beforeEach(() => {
    socketSpyFactory = spyOn(window, 'WebSocket');
    socketSpyFactory.mockImplementation(() => {
      return {};
    });
    store = configureStore([storeSpy]);
    Object.defineProperty(window, 'location', {
      writable: true,
      value: {
        protocol: 'http:',
        host: 'test:1234',
        pathname: '/index.html'
      }
    });
  });

  afterEach(() => {
    socketSpyFactory.mockReset();
  });
});
```

You'll get more from this chapter if you have at least a basic understanding of the WebSocket API. It's not as straightforward as the fetch API, for example. At its core, calling the WebSocket constructor returns an object with `send` and `close` methods, and `onopen`, `onmessage`, `onclose`, and `onerror` event handlers. We'll implement most of these on our test double as we build out our test suite. If you'd like to learn more about the WebSocket API, check out the *Further learning* section at the end of this chapter.

3. Add the first test in a nested describe block. This checks that we make the WebSocket connection with the right URL:

```
describe('START_SHARING', () => {
  it('opens a websocket when starting to share', () => {
    store.dispatch({ type: 'START_SHARING' });
```

```
        expect(socketSpyFactory).toHaveBeenCalledWith(
          'ws://test:1234/share'
        );
      });
    });
```

4. Make that pass by filling in the generator function. You'll find the empty function already present in the file—you just need to fill in the content:

```
function* startSharing() {
  const { host } = window.location;
  new WebSocket(`ws://${host}/share`);
}
```

5. Modify the WebSocket spy to add an "inner" spy, sendSpy, which will be called when the user calls the send function on the WebSocket. We also need to store a reference to the socketSpy that's created, so we can call the callbacks that the user attaches to its event handlers (such as onopen and onmessage):

```
let sendSpy;
let socketSpy;

beforeEach(() => {
  sendSpy = jest.fn();
  socketSpyFactory = spyOn(window, 'WebSocket');
  socketSpyFactory.mockImplementation(() => {
    socketSpy = {
      send: sendSpy
    };
    return socketSpy;
  });
  ...
}
```

6. Let's add the next test. It's important that we mimic the exact behavior of the WebSocket API, and one important part of that is when the client receives an onopen callback. Our tests must cause that action to occur. It gets slightly tricky here because we know that in our production code this will cause a Promise to resolve, causing the saga to kick back into action. The remainder of the generator function will be run as a new task. That means once we've opened the socket, we should wait for that task to run before we carry on with our expectations. We do that with async act:

```
const notifySocketOpened = async () => {
  await act(async () => {
    socketSpy.onopen();
```

```
    });
  };

  it('dispatches a START_SHARING action to the socket', async () => {
    store.dispatch({ type: 'START_SHARING' });
    await notifySocketOpened();
    expect(sendSpy).toHaveBeenCalledWith(
      JSON.stringify({ type: 'START_SHARING' })
    );
  });
});
```

The async `act` function helps us even when we're not dealing with React components.

7. Make that pass. This code is a little tricky. We're building a `Promise` object to adapt the WebSocket callback-based API into something that we can use with the generator `yield` keyword.

```
const openWebSocket = () => {
  const { host } = window.location;
  const socket = new WebSocket(`ws://${host}/share`);
  return new Promise(resolve => {
    socket.onopen = () => { resolve(socket) };
  });
};

function* startSharing() {
  const presenterSocket = yield openWebSocket();
  presenterSocket.send(JSON.stringify({ type: 'START_SHARING' }));
}
```

In this chapter, we're only building a barebones socket implementation. For a real-world application, you would want to add support for the `onerror` callback as well as `onopen`.

8. The next test will send a message over the socket. The generator function will yield while it waits of a message to be received, in exactly the same way it waited for a connection to be opened. Therefore before we begin writing any tests we'll add a helper function to send a message and wait for the current task queue to flush. Add this helper to test/middleware/sharingSagas.test.js, just below notifySocketOpened:

```
const sendSocketMessage = async message => {
  await act(async () => {
    socketSpy.onmessage({ data: JSON.stringify(message) });
  });
};
```

9. Add the next test, using the function you've just defined:

```
it('dispatches an action of STARTED_SHARING with a URL containing
the id that is returned from the server', async () => {
  store.dispatch({ type: 'START_SHARING' });
  await notifySocketOpened();
  await sendSocketMessage({ type: 'UNKNOWN', id: 123 });
  return expectRedux(store)
    .toDispatchAnAction()
    .matching({
      type: 'STARTED_SHARING',
      url: 'http://test:1234/index.html?watching=123'
    });
});
```

10. To make this pass we'll read the message off the socket. Once that's done, we can pass the retrieved information back to the Redux store:

```
const receiveMessage = (socket) =>
  new Promise(resolve => {
    socket.onmessage = evt => { resolve(evt.data) };
  });

const buildUrl = (id) => {
  const { protocol, host, pathname } = window.location;
  return `${protocol}//${host}${pathname}?watching=${id}`;
};

function* startSharing() {
  const presenterSocket = yield openWebSocket();
  presenterSocket.send(JSON.stringify({ type: 'START_SHARING' }));
  const message = yield receiveMessage(presenterSocket);
  const presenterSessionId = JSON.parse(message).id;
  yield put({
```

```
      type: 'STARTED_SHARING',
      url: buildUrl(presenterSessionId)
    });
  }
```

That's it for the process of starting to share. Now let's deal with what happens when the user clicks the **Stop sharing** button:

1. Create a helper function inside the `sharingSaga` describe block, which will change the system to a "started sharing" state:

```
const startSharing = async sessionId => {
  store.dispatch({ type: 'START_SHARING' });
  await notifySocketOpened();
  await sendSocketMessage({ type: 'UNKNOWN', id: 123 });
};
```

2. Update the spy to include a `closeSpy` variable, which we set up in the same way as `sendSpy`:

```
let closeSpy;

beforeEach(() => {
  sendSpy = jest.fn();
  closeSpy = jest.fn();
  socketSpyFactory = spyOn(window, 'WebSocket');
  socketSpyFactory.mockImplementation(() => {
    socketSpy = {
      send: sendSpy,
      close: closeSpy
    };
    return socketSpy;
  });
  ...
});
```

3. Add the first test in a new nested context. We, first of all, start sharing, and then dispatch the `STOP_SHARING` action:

```
describe('STOP_SHARING', () => {
  it('calls close on the open socket', async () => {
    await startSharing();
    store.dispatch({ type: 'STOP_SHARING' });
    expect(closeSpy).toHaveBeenCalled();
  });
});
```

4. To make this pass, we'll fill out the `stopSharing` generator function. First, however, we need to get access to the socket that we created within the `startSharing` function. Let's extract that variable into the top-level namespace:

```
let presenterSocket;

function* startSharing() {
  presenterSocket = yield openWebSocket();
  ...
}
```

5. Then, add the following definition to the `stopSharing` function. You can then test, and everything should be passing; however, if you're running your entire test suite you'll see a large number of warnings coming from the `MenuButtons` test suite. We'll clear those up at the end of the chapter; for now, you should start running tests on this test suite only.

```
function* stopSharing() {
  presenterSocket.close();
}
```

 As a reminder, to run tests for this test suite only, use the command npm test test/middleware/sharingSagas.test.js.

6. Moving on to the next test, we want to update the Redux store with the new stopped status. This will allow us to remove the message that appeared to the user when they began sharing:

```
it('dispatches an action of STOPPED_SHARING', async () => {
  await startSharing();
  store.dispatch({ type: 'STOP_SHARING' });
  return expectRedux(store)
    .toDispatchAnAction()
    .matching({ type: 'STOPPED_SHARING' });
});
```

7. That's a simple one-liner. With this change, this function is complete:

```
function* stopSharing() {
  presenterSocket.close();
  yield put({ type: 'STOPPED_SHARING' });
}
```

Next up is broadcasting actions from the presenter to the server:

1. Create a new nested describe block with the following test:

```
describe('SHARE_NEW_ACTION', () => {
  it('forwards the same action on to the socket', async () => {
    const innerAction = { a: 123 };
    await startSharing(123);
    store.dispatch({ type: 'SHARE_NEW_ACTION', innerAction });
    expect(sendSpy).toHaveBeenLastCalledWith(
      JSON.stringify({ type: 'NEW_ACTION', innerAction })
    );
  });
});
```

2. Make it pass by filling in the following content for the `shareNewAction` function:

```
const shareNewAction = ({ innerAction }) => {
  presenterSocket.send(
    JSON.stringify({ type: 'NEW_ACTION', innerAction })
  );
}
```

3. Add the next test.

```
it('does not forward if the socket is not set yet', () => {
  store.dispatch({ type: 'SHARE_NEW_ACTION' });
  expect(sendSpy).not.toHaveBeenCalled();
});
```

This test has a subtle issue. Although it will help you add to the design of your software, it's slightly less useful as a regression test because it *could* potentially result in false positives. This test guarantees that something doesn't happen between the start and the end of the test, but it makes no guarantees about what happens *after*. Such is the nature of the async environment.

For me, this test fails before I complete the next step, and passes afterwards. But you could imagine that further down the line we might modify our production code to defer the execution of the `send` call, perhaps by using a Promise. This test would then pass, even if the conditional were removed.

4. That's simply a matter of adding a conditional around the code we have:

```
function* shareNewAction({ innerAction } ) {
  if (presenterSocket) {
    presenterSocket.send(
      JSON.stringify({ type: 'NEW_ACTION', innerAction })
    );
  }
}
```

5. We don't want to share the action if the user has stopped sharing—so let's add that in.

```
it('does not forward if the socket has been closed', async () => {
  await startSharing(123);
  socketSpy.readyState = WebSocket.CLOSED;
  store.dispatch({ type: 'SHARE_NEW_ACTION' });
  expect(sendSpy.mock.calls.length).toEqual(1);
});
```

The constant in the test above, `WebSocket.CLOSED`, and the constant in the code below, `WebSocket.OPEN`, are defined in the WebSocket specification.

6. In the next step, I'm using the condition `=== WebSocket.OPEN`, which is not exactly what the test specified. Yes, I am cutting a corner here—you could, if you wanted to be pedantic, write out tests for the other possible readyState values:

```
const shareNewAction = ({ innerAction }) => {
  if (
    presenterSocket &&
    presenterSocket.readyState === WebSocket.OPEN
  ) {
    presenterSocket.send(
      JSON.stringify({ type: 'NEW_ACTION', innerAction })
    );
  }
}
```

7. If you run your tests now, you'll find they still don't work. That's because we clobbered these constant values when we replaced `WebSocket` with our spy. So, we need to add them back in. Start by saving the real values. These constants should go right at the top of the file, underneath your imports:

```
const WEB_SOCKET_OPEN = WebSocket.OPEN;
const WEB_SOCKET_CLOSED = WebSocket.CLOSED;
```

8. Update your spy to set these constants once WebSocket has been replaced. While we're here, let's also set the default `readyState` for a socket to be `WebSocket.OPEN`, which means our other tests won't break:

```
socketSpyFactory = jest.spyOn(window, 'WebSocket');
Object.defineProperty(socketSpyFactory, 'OPEN', {
  value: WEB_SOCKET_OPEN
});
Object.defineProperty(socketSpyFactory, 'CLOSED', {
  value: WEB_SOCKET_CLOSED
});
socketSpyFactory.mockImplementation(() => {
  socketSpy = {
    send: sendSpy,
    close: closeSpy,
    readyState: WebSocket.OPEN
  };
  return socketSpy;
});
```

Your tests should now be passing. That's it for the presenter behavior. Now all that's left is the watcher behavior.

Streaming events with redux-saga

We'll repeat a lot of the same techniques in this section. There are two new concepts: first, pulling out the search param for the watcher ID, and second, using `eventChannel` to subscribe to the WebSocket `onmessage` callback:

1. Write a new describe block at the bottom of `test/middleware/sharingSagas.test.js`, but still nested inside the main describe block:

```
describe('watching', () => {
  beforeEach(() => {
    Object.defineProperty(window, 'location', {
```

```
      writable: true,
      value: {
        host: 'test:1234',
        pathname: '/index.html',
        search: '?watching=234'
      }
    });
  });

  it('opens a socket when the page loads', () => {
    store.dispatch({ type: 'TRY_START_WATCHING' });
    expect(socketSpyFactory).toHaveBeenCalledWith(
      'ws://test:1234/share'
    );
  });
});
```

2. Make it pass by filling out the `startWatching` function:

```
function* startWatching() {
  yield openWebSocket();
}
```

3. In the next test, we'll begin to make use of the search param:

```
it('does not open socket if the watching field is not set', () => {
  window.location.search = '?';
  store.dispatch({ type: 'TRY_START_WATCHING' });
  expect(socketSpyFactory).not.toHaveBeenCalled();
});
```

4. Make it pass:

```
function* startWatching() {
  const sessionId = new URLSearchParams(
    window.location.search.substring(1)
  ).get('watching');

  if (sessionId) {
    yield openWebSocket();
  }
}
```

5. Before we write the next test, add the following helper function which mimics the action that will occur on the real WebSocket, ensuring that onopen is called:

```
const startWatching = async () => {
  await act(async () => {
    store.dispatch({ type: 'TRY_START_WATCHING' });
    socketSpy.onopen();
  });
};
```

6. Use that function in the following tests:

```
it('dispatches a RESET action', async () => {
  await startWatching();
  return expectRedux(store)
    .toDispatchAnAction()
    .matching({ type: 'RESET' });
});
```

7. Make it pass by adding in a put:

```
function* startWatching() {
  const sessionId = new
URLSearchParams(location.search.substring(1)).get('watching');

  if (sessionId) {
    yield openWebSocket();
    yield put({ type: 'RESET' });
  }
}
```

8. Now we need to send a message to the server, including the ID of the session we wish to watch:

```
it('sends the session id to the socket with an action type of
START_WATCHING', async () => {
  await startWatching();
  expect(sendSpy).toHaveBeenCalledWith(
    JSON.stringify({ type: 'START_WATCHING', id: '234' })
  );
});
```

9. Thankfully, we already have our spy set up from the previous section, so this is a quick one to fix:

```
function* startWatching() {
  const sessionId = new URLSearchParams(
    window.location.search.substring(1)
```

```
).get('watching');

if (sessionId) {
  const watcherSocket = yield openWebSocket();
  yield put({ type: 'RESET' });
  watcherSocket.send(
    JSON.stringify({ type: 'START_WATCHING', id: sessionId })
  );
}
}
```

10. The next test tells the Redux store that we have started watching. This will then allow the React UI to display a message to the user telling them that they are connected:

```
it('dispatches a STARTED_WATCHING action', async () => {
  await startWatching();
  return expectRedux(store)
    .toDispatchAnAction()
    .matching({ type: 'STARTED_WATCHING' });
});
```

11. Make that pass by adding a new call to put, as shown:

```
function* startWatching() {
  const sessionId = new URLSearchParams(
    window.location.search.substring(1)
  ).get('watching');

  if (sessionId) {
    const watcherSocket = yield openWebSocket();
    yield put({ type: 'RESET' });
    watcherSocket.send(
      JSON.stringify({ type: 'START_WATCHING', id: sessionId })
    );
    yield put({ type: 'STARTED_WATCHING' });
  }
}
```

12. Now the big one. We need to add in the behavior that allows us to receive multiple messages from the server and read them in.

```
it('relays multiple actions from the websocket', async () => {
  const message1 = { type: 'ABC' };
  const message2 = { type: 'BCD' };
  const message3 = { type: 'CDE' };
  await startWatching();
  await sendSocketMessage(message1);
```

```
await sendSocketMessage(message2);
await sendSocketMessage(message3);

await expectRedux(store)
  .toDispatchAnAction()
  .matching(message1);
await expectRedux(store)
  .toDispatchAnAction()
  .matching(message2);
await expectRedux(store)
  .toDispatchAnAction()
  .matching(message3);
socketSpy.onclose();
});
```

You may think it would help to have a smaller test which handles just one message. However, that won't help us for multiple messages, as we need to use an entirely different implementation for multiple messages, as you'll see in the next step.

13. We'll use the redux-saga `eventChannel` function to do this. This is similar to the `Promise` trick we did earlier when receiving a single message, because we've provided a function that we have to call when the callback fires. With a `Promise`, it was the `resolve` function. With the `eventChannel`, we call `emitter` as many times as we want. When the socket closes, we call `emitter(END)`:

```
import { eventChannel, END } from 'redux-saga';

const webSocketListener = socket =>
  eventChannel(emitter => {
    socket.onmessage = emitter;
    socket.onclose = () => emitter(END);
    return () => {
      socket.onmessage = undefined;
      socket.onclose = undefined;
    };
  });
```

14. Now you can use the `websocketListener` to create a channel that we can repeatedly `take` events from using a loop. This loop needs to be wrapped in a `try` or `finally` block. `finally` will be called when the `emitter(END)` instruction is reached. Create a new generator function that does that, as shown:

```
function* watchUntilStopRequest(chan) {
  try {
    while (true) {
```

```
        let evt = yield take(chan);
        yield put(JSON.parse(evt.data));
      }
  } finally {
  }
};
```

15. Link the `webSocketListener` function and the `watchUntilStopRequest` generator function by calling them both from within `startWatching`. After this step, your test should be passing.

```
function* startWatching() {
  ...
  if (sessionId) {
    ...
    yield put({ type: 'STARTED_WATCHING' });
    const channel = yield call(webSocketListener, watcherSocket);
    yield call(watchUntilStopRequest(channel);
  }
}
```

Of course, we could have put the preceding code inside of `startWatching` itself, but then we would have had a very long function (10+ lines!) that would have been pretty cryptic to anyone coming to this codebase. By pulling out another generator and giving it a descriptive name, we're aiding any future readers of your code. That includes you!

16. The final test is to alert the Redux store that we've stopped watching, so that it can then remove the message that appears in the React UI:

```
it('sends a STOPPED_WATCHING action when the connection is closed',
async () => {
  await startWatching();
  socketSpy.onclose();

  return expectRedux(store)
    .toDispatchAnAction()
    .matching({ type: 'STOPPED_WATCHING' });
});
```

17. Make that pass by adding this one-liner to the finally block in
`watchUntilStopRequest`:

```
try {
    ...
} finally {
    yield put({ type: 'STOPPED_WATCHING' });
}
```

Updating the app

We've completed the work on building the sagas, but we have just a couple of adjustments to make in the rest of the app in order to integrate the new feature. First, our `MenuButtons` are functionally complete, but we need to update the tests to properly exercise the middleware, ensuring we stub out the web socket library. Second, we need to fire off a `TRY_START_WATCHING` action as soon as the app starts:

1. In `test/MenuButtons.test.js`, add in a server socket stub at the top of the describe block named `sharing button`:

```
let socketSpyFactory;
let socketSpy;

beforeEach(() => {
  socketSpyFactory = jest.spyOn(window, 'WebSocket');
  socketSpyFactory.mockImplementation(() => {
    socketSpy = {
      close: () => {},
      send: () => {}
    };
    return socketSpy;
  });
});

afterEach(() => {
  socketSpyFactory.mockReset();
});
```

2. Import `act` in the same way you did for the sagas test file:

```
import { act } from 'react-dom/test-utils';
```

3. Update the last test in the `dispatches an action of STOP_SHARING when stop sharing is clicked` file:

```
const notifySocketOpened = async () => {
  await act(async () => {
    socketSpy.onopen();
  });
};

it('dispatches an action of STOP_SHARING when stop sharing is
clicked', async () => {
  const store = renderWithStore(<MenuButtons />);
  store.dispatch({ type: 'STARTED_SHARING' });
  await notifySocketOpened();
  click(button('Stop sharing'));
  return expectRedux(store)
    .toDispatchAnAction()
    .matching({ type: 'STOP_SHARING' });
});
```

4. Finally, update `src/index.js` to call the `TRY_START_WATCHING` action when the app first loads:

```
const store = configureStoreWithLocalStorage();
store.dispatch({ type: 'TRY_START_WATCHING' });

ReactDOM.render(
  <Provider store={store}>
    <App />
  </Provider>,
  document.getElementById('root')
);
```

You can now run the app and try it out. The manual test you can try is as follows:

1. Open a session in one tab, and click **Start sharing**.
2. Right-click on the link that appears and choose to open it in a new window.
3. Move your two windows so that they are side by side.
4. In the original window, type some commands, such as `forward 100` and `right 90`. You should see the commands update.
5. Now, hit **Stop sharing** on the original window. You should see the sharing messages disappear from both screens.

Summary

In this chapter, we've covered how to test against the WebSocket API. That's not a simple feat, particularly when combined with sagas and generator functions. As ever, our tests have helped guide us to an elegant solution.

This feature isn't finished yet: our new interactive mode doesn't work too well with the existing local storage support. There's some odd behavior present.

In the next chapter, we'll take a look at fixing that using acceptance tests to help drive the change.

Exercises

- What tests could you add to ensure that socket errors are handled gracefully?

Further learning

- The WebSocket specification: https://www.w3.org/TR/websockets/

Section 4: Acceptance Testing with BDD

In this section, we advance our test-driven knowledge by introducing acceptance testing via the Cucumber framework. It extends your toolkit to include practices that can involve your whole team, not just the developers.

Finally, we end the book with a discussion of how TDD fits within the wider testing landscape, and suggestions for how you can continue your TDD journey.

This section includes the following chapters:

- Chapter 13, *Writing Your First Acceptance Test*
- Chapter 14, *Adding Features Guided by Acceptance Tests*
- Chapter 15, *Understanding TDD in the Wider Testing Landscape*

Writing Your First Acceptance Test

13

Test-driven development is a process for developers, not for the outside world. Sometimes our customers and product owners want to see automated tests too, but the kinds of tests we write are too low-level to be helpful to all members of our teams.

This chapter introduces two new software packages: Cucumber and Puppeteer.

We'll use Cucumber to build acceptance tests. There's a Cucumber package for JavaScript which incorporates a special test runner that runs **feature files**, written in a plain-English language known as Gherkin. These feature files are backed by support scripts that are written in JavaScript. Since Cucumber has its own test runner, it doesn't use Jest, although we will make use of Jest's `expect` package.

The Gherkin language is a popular syntax for writing plain-language tests that help us collaborate with our whole team. It translates into JavaScript code.

Within our support files, we'll use Puppeteer to drive a "real" web browser that can be observed and comes with all sorts of bolt-ons, like screenshot and performance testing.

 Puppeteer drives only one web browser, Google Chrome, which is enough if you're wanting to test features, such as local storage, but may not be enough for you if you're looking for cross-platform support. In that case, you may be better off looking at alternatives such as Selenium, which isn't covered in this book. However, the same testing principles apply when writing tests for Selenium. You can run through this chapter and then apply what you've learnt to Selenium or whichever driver you choose.

This chapter covers the following topics:

- Integrating Cucumber and Puppeteer into your code base
- Writing your first Cucumber test
- Using data tables to perform setup

Integrating Cucumber and Puppeteer into your code base

The Git tag for this section is `cucumber`. This tag has extra commits added on top of what was covered in the last chapter, so, if you've been following along in your own code base, then please make sure to merge the additional changes.

For more detailed instructions, see the *To get the most out of this book* section in the `Preface`.

1. Let's start by installing the packages we're after. Since Puppeteer requires Chrome, the install will download Chrome if you don't already have it on your system. Since Cucumber doesn't rely on the Jest test runner, we also need to install the `expect` package, which allows us to use Jest's `expect` functionality in a non-Jest context. Finally, `@babel/register` allows you to use ES6 syntax from within the Cucumber support files:

```
npm install --save-dev cucumber puppeteer expect @babel/register
```

2. You can run Cucumber now to see what happens:

```
$ npx cucumber-js

0 scenarios
0 steps
0m00.000s
```

3. Since we want to write out scripts with modern syntax, we'll need to wire up `@babel/register` to do that for us. Open `package.json` and add the following script:

```
"cucumber": "cucumber-js --require-module @babel/register"
```

4. Create a new folder called `features`. This should live at the same level as `src` and `test`.
5. Create another folder within that called `features/support`.

You'll now be able to run your features using the command `npm run cucumber`.

Throughout this chapter and the following one, it may be helpful to narrow down the tests you're running. You can run a single scenario by providing `npx cucumber-js` with the file name and starting line number of the scenario. You'll still need to include the `—require-module` switch. Here's an example:

```
npx cucumber-js --require-module @babel/register features/drawing.feature:5
```

If, during this chapter, you run into issues with Puppeteer on your machine, there's a Troubleshooting page on the Puppeteer GitHub that may help you: `https://github.com/GoogleChrome/puppeteer/blob/master/docs/troubleshooting.md`.

Writing your first Cucumber test

If you're reading an electronic version of this book, be careful copying and pasting sections, as you may lose formatting. Cucumber feature files are sensitive to indenting. The default indent is two spaces at each level.

We'll learn about Cucumber as we walk through an example:

1. Before we begin, it's important to ensure that your build output is up to date. Your Cucumber specs are going to run against the code built in the `dist` directory, not your source in the `src` directory. Invoke `npm run build` to make sure that happens. You'll need to remember to do this each time you modify your source files.

You could also modify your `package.json` to invoke a build before Cucumber specs are run, or to run Webpack in watch mode. See the *Further learning* section for a link.

2. Open the file `features/sharing.feature` and enter the following text. Each feature file has just one feature within it. The feature has a name and a short description, and a bunch of scenarios listed one after another.

```
Feature: Sharing

  A user can choose to present their session to any number of other
  users, who observe what the presenter is doing via their own
  browser.

  Scenario: Observer joins a session
    Given the presenter navigated to the application page
    And the presenter clicked the button 'startSharing'
    When the observer navigates to the presenter's sharing link
    Then the observer should see a message saying 'You are now
watching the session'
```

`Given`, `When`, and `Then` are analogous to the *Arrange, Act,* and *Assert* phases of your Jest tests: *given* all these things are true, *when* I perform this action, *then* I expect all these things to happen. There should really only be one `When` clause in each of your scenarios.

You'll notice that I've written the `Given` clauses in a past tense, the `When` clause in the present tense, and the `Then` clause has a "should" in there.

I've also assigned clear roles for the presenter and observer. This gives us a very simple and straightforward way of structuring each phrase: a role performed and some action with some data.

3. Go ahead and run the feature by typing `npm run cucumber` at the command line. You'll see warnings like the one in the following. Each of the Given, When, and Then phrases is backed by a step definition, which is a short function that Cucumber matches up with the phrase, passing any numbers or quotes values in as arguments to your function. In the warning, Cucumber has helpfully given you a starting point for each definition:

```
? Given the presenter navigated to the application page
    Undefined. Implement with the following snippet:
```

```
Given('the presenter navigated to the application page',
    function () {
        // Write code here that turns the phrase above
        // into concrete actions
        return 'pending';
    }
);
```

4. Let's add a step definition for the first `Given` clause. Create the file `features/support/sharing.steps.js` and add the following code. It defines a step definition that calls Puppeteer's API to launch a new browser, then open a new page, and then navigate to the URL provided. The step definition description matches up with the `Given` clause in our test scenario.

   The second parameter to Given is marked with the `async` keyword. This is an addition to what Cucumber tells us in its suggested function definition. We need async because Puppeteer's API calls all return promises that we'll need to `await`.

```
import { Given, When, Then } from 'cucumber';
import puppeteer from 'puppeteer';

const port = process.env.PORT || 3000;
const appPage = `http://localhost:${port}/index.html`;

Given('the presenter navigated to the application page',
    async function () {
        const browser = await puppeteer.launch();
        const page = await browser.newPage();
        await page.goto(appPage);
    }
);
```

> This step definition does not have anything to do with the act of screen sharing. It's to do with browsing to a web page. This step definition could undoubtedly be used across many different features, so, although we're placing it in a file named `sharing.steps.js`, it may be better to move it elsewhere when the domain becomes clearer.

5. Run your tests again. Cucumber should now point you helpfully to the next clause. For this clause, `And the presenter clicked the button 'startSharing'`, we need to get access to the `page` object we just created in the previous step. The way to do this is by accessing what's known as the `World` object in `cucumber-js`, which is really just the context for all the clauses in the current scenario. We access this through the `this` object. Before we add it to the clause, we'll need to create a `World` class. Create the file `features/support/world.js` and add the following content. It defines two methods, `setPage` and `getPage`, which allow us to save multiple pages within the world. The ability to save multiple pages is important for this test, where we have at least two pages—the presenter page and the observer page:

```
import { setWorldConstructor } from 'cucumber';

class World {
  constructor() {
    this.pages = {};
  }

  setPage(name, page) {
    this.pages[name] = page;
  }

  getPage(name) {
    return this.pages[name];
  }
};

setWorldConstructor(World);
```

6. We can now use the `setPage` and `getPage` functions from within our step definitions. Our approach will be to call `setPage` from the first step definition—the one we wrote in step 3—and then use `getPage` to retrieve it in subsequent steps. Modify the first step definition now to include the call to `setPage`, as shown in the following:

```
Given('the presenter navigated to the application page',
  async function () {
    const browser = await puppeteer.launch();
    const page = await browser.newPage();
    await page.goto(appPage);
    this.setPage('presenter', page);
  }
);
```

You may be wondering why we are defining anonymous functions (`async function (...) { ... }`) rather than lambda expressions (`async (...) => { ... }`). It allows us to take advantage of the implicit context binding that occurs with anonymous functions. If we used lambdas, we'd need to call `.bind(this)` on them.

7. Moving on to the next step definition, `the presenter clicked the button 'startSharing'`, we'll write a function that uses the Puppeteer function `Page.click` to find a button with an ID of `startSharing`. As in the last test, we'll use a variable so that this step definition can be used with other button IDs in future scenarios:

```
Given('the presenter clicked the button {string}',
  async function (buttonId) {
    await this.getPage('presenter').click(`button#${buttonId}`);
  }
);
```

8. The next step definition, `the observer navigates to the presenter's sharing link`, is similar to the first definition in that we want to open a new browser. The difference is that, this time, it's for the observer, and we first need to look up the path to follow. The path is given to us through the URL that the presenter is shown once they start searching, so we can look that up using the `Page.$eval` function.

There's some duplication building up between our step definitions. Later on, we'll extract this commonality into its own function.

```
When('the observer navigates to the presenter\'s sharing link',
  async function () {
    await this.getPage('presenter').waitForSelector('a');
    const link = await this.getPage('presenter').$eval('a', a =>
      a.getAttribute('href')
    );
    const url = new URL(link);
    const browser = await puppeteer.launch();
    const page = await browser.newPage();
    await page.goto(url);
    this.setPage('observer', page);
  }
);
```

9. The final step definition uses the Puppeteer function `Page.$eval` again, this time to retrieve the value of the body. This function calls `document.querySelector` to find an HTML node and then runs a function to transform that node into a "plain" JavaScript object. We then test that using the `expect` function in the normal way. Make sure to place the listed import at the top of your file:

```
import expect from 'expect';

Then('the observer should see a message saying {string}',
  async function (message) {
    const pageText = await this.getPage('observer').$eval(
      'body',
      e => e.outerHTML
    );
    expect(pageText).toContain(message);
  }
);
```

10. Run your tests with `npm run cucumber`. The output from your test run will look as follows. While our step definitions are complete, something is amiss. We still need to spin up a server:

```
1) Scenario: Observer joins a session
   ✖ Given the presenter browsed to 'index.html'
       Error: net::ERR_CONNECTION_REFUSED
           at http://localhost:3000/index.html
```

11. Add the following two functions to the `World` class in `features/support/world.js`, including the import for app at the top of the file. The `startServer` function is equivalent to how we start the server in `server/src/server.js`. The `closeServer` function stops the server, but, before it does this, it closes all Puppeteer browser instances. It's important to do this before closing the server. That's because the server does not kill any "live" connections—such as our WebSockets—when the close method is called. We need to ensure they are closed first, otherwise the server won't close.

We are lucky that all our code lives within the same project, so starting it is straightforward. If your code base is split over multiple projects, this step is likely to be more involved.

```
import { app } from '../../server/src/app';

startServer() {
```

```
const port = process.env.PORT || 3000;
this.server = app.listen(port);
}

closeServer() {
  Object.keys(this.pages).forEach(name =>
    this.pages[name].browser().close()
  );
  this.server.close();
}
```

12. Make use of these new functions with the `Before` and `After` hooks. Create a new file, `features/support/hooks.js`, and add the following code:

```
import { Before, After } from 'cucumber';

Before(function() {
  this.startServer();
});

After(function() {
  this.closeServer();
});
```

13. Run the command `npm run cucumber` and observe the output. Your scenario—and feature—should now be passing.

 Remember to run `npm run build` before running Cucumber.

```
> spec-logo@1.0.0 cucumber /Users/daniel/work/react-tdd/spec-logo
> npx cucumber-js --require-module babel-register

......

1 scenario (1 passed)
4 steps (4 passed)
0m00.848s
```

14. Let's go back and tidy up that repeated code. We'll extract a function called `browseToPageFor` and we'll place it within our `World` class. Open `features/support/world.js` and add the following method at the bottom of the class:

```
async browseToPageFor(role, url) {
  const browser = await puppeteer.launch();
  const page = await browser.newPage();
  await page.goto(url);
  this.setPage(role, page);
}
```

15. You'll also need to move the Puppeteer import across from `features/support/sharing.steps.js` into `features/support/world.js`:

```
import puppeteer from 'puppeteer';
```

16. Finally, rewrite the two steps that open the browser in terms of `browseToPageFor`:

```
Given('the presenter navigated to the application page',
  async function () {
    await this.browseToPageFor('presenter', appPage);
  }
);

When('the observer navigates to the presenter\'s sharing link',
  async function () {
    await this.getPage('presenter').waitForSelector('a');
    const link = await this.getPage('presenter').$eval('a', a =>
      a.getAttribute('href')
    );
    const url = new URL(link);
    await this.browseToPageFor('observer', url);
  }
);
```

That's really all there is to writing an acceptance test with Cucumber and Puppeteer.

The tests we've written run Puppeteer in headless mode, meaning that an actual Chrome browser window doesn't launch. If you'd like to see that happen, you can turn headless mode off by modifying the launch commands (remember there are two in the previous step definitions) to read as follows:

```
const browser = await puppeteer.launch({ headless: false });
```

If you're using console logging to assist in your debugging, you'll need to provide another parameter to dump console output to stdout:

```
const browser = await puppeteer.launch({ dumpio: true });
```

Using data tables to perform setup

 The Git tag for this section is `cucumber-data-tables`.

Let's quickly look at one more feature of Cucumber that you can use within your tests: data tables. We'll write another test that will pass in our system, before we move on to new functionalities in the next chapter:

1. Create a new feature file called `features/drawing.feature`. Write out the following content. It contains a set of instructions to draw a square using a Logo function. You'll note I'm using a small side length of 10; that's to make sure the animation occurs quickly:

```
Feature: Drawing

  A user can draw shapes by entering commands at the prompt.

  Scenario: Drawing functions
    Given the user navigated to the application page
    When the user enters the following instructions at the prompt:
      | to drawsquare |
      | repeat 4 [ forward 10 right 90 ] |
      | end |
      | drawsquare |
    Then these lines should have been drawn:
      | x1 | y1 | x2 | y2 |
      | 0  | 0  | 10 | 0  |
      | 10 | 0  | 10 | 10 |
      | 10 | 10 | 0  | 10 |
      | 0  | 10 | 0  | 0  |
```

2. The first phrase does the same thing as our previous step definition, except we've renamed "presenter" to "user." Being more generic makes sense in this case as the role of presenter is no longer relevant to this test. We can use the `World` function `browseToPageFor` for this first step. However, if you look back at how we wrote this step definition for the Sharing feature, you'll see we used this function and also an `appPage` constant, which contained the URL to navigate to. We don't yet have access to `appPage`, so let's pull that into `World` now. In `features/support/world.js`, add the following constant at the top of the file, above the `World` class:

```
const port = process.env.PORT || 3000;
```

3. Add the following method to `World`:

```
appPage() {
  return `http://localhost:${port}/index.html`;
}
```

4. In `features/support/sharing.steps.js`, remove the definitions for `port` and `appPage`, and update the first step definition as shown:

```
Given('the presenter navigated to the application page',
  async function () {
    await this.browseToPageFor('presenter', this.appPage());
  }
);
```

5. It's time to create a new step definition for a `'user'` page. Open the file `features/support/drawing.steps.js` and add the following code:

```
import { Given, When, Then } from 'cucumber';
import expect from 'expect';

Given('the user navigated to the application page',
  async function () {
    await this.browseToPageFor('user', this.appPage());
  }
);
```

6. Now what about the second line, with the data table? What should our step definition look like? Well, let's ask Cucumber. Run the command `npm run cucumber` and have a look at the output. It gives us the starting point of our definition:

```
1) Scenario: Drawing functions # features/drawing.feature:5
   ✔ Before # features/support/sharing.steps.js:5
   ✔ Given the user navigated to 'index.html'
   ? When the user enters the following instructions at the prompt:
       | to drawsquare |
       | repeat 4 [ forward 10 right 90 ] |
       | end |
       | drawsquare |
       Undefined. Implement with the following snippet:

          When('the user enters the following instructions at the
   prompt:',
                  function (dataTable) {
                    // Write code here that turns the phrase above
                    // into concrete actions
                    return 'pending';
                  }
          );
```

7. Go ahead and add the suggested code to `features/supports/drawing.steps.js`. If you run `npm run cucumber` at this point, you'll notice that Cucumber successfully notices that the step definition is pending:

```
When('the user enters the following instructions at the prompt:',
    function (dataTable) {
      // Write code here that turns the phrase above
      //into concrete actions
      return 'pending';
    }
);
```

8. The `dataTable` variable is a `DataTable` object with a `raw()` function that is, in fact, an array of arrays. The outer array represents each row and the inner arrays represent the columns of each row. In this step definition, we want to take every single line and insert it into the edit prompt. Each line should be followed by a press of the *Enter* key, as shown here:

```
When('the user enters the following instructions at the prompt:',
  async function (dataTable) {
    for (let instruction of dataTable.raw()) {
      await this.getPage('user').type(
        'textarea',
        `${instruction}\n`
      );
    }
  }
);
```

9. The final step requires us to look for line elements with the right attribute values and compare them to the values in our second data table. The following code does exactly that. Copy it out now and run your tests to convince yourself that it works and that the test will pass. An explanation of all the detailed points will follow.

If you're seeing any failures, make sure your build is up to date by running `npm run build`.

```
Then('these lines should have been drawn:',
  async function(dataTable) {
    await this.getPage('user').waitFor(3000);
    const lines = await this.getPage('user').$$eval(
      'line',
      lines =>
        lines.map(line => {
          return {
            x1: parseFloat(line.getAttribute('x1')),
            y1: parseFloat(line.getAttribute('y1')),
            x2: parseFloat(line.getAttribute('x2')),
            y2: parseFloat(line.getAttribute('y2'))
          };
        })
    );
    for (let i = 0; i < lines.length; ++i) {
      expect(lines[i].x1).toBeCloseTo(
        parseInt(dataTable.hashes()[i].x1)
```

```
    );
    expect(lines[i].y1).toBeCloseTo(
      parseInt(dataTable.hashes()[i].y1)
    );
    expect(lines[i].x2).toBeCloseTo(
      parseInt(dataTable.hashes()[i].x2)
    );
    expect(lines[i].y2).toBeCloseTo(
      parseInt(dataTable.hashes()[i].y2)
    );
  }
});
```

That last test contained some complexity that's worth diving into:

- We used `Pages.waitFor` to wait for 3 seconds, which gives the system time to complete animations. Including a timeout like this is not great practice, but it'll work for now. We'll look at a way of making this more specific in the next chapter—we'll need to modify our production code in order to do that.

- The `Page.$$eval` function is like `Page.$eval` but returns an array under the hood, and calls `document.querySelector` rather than `document.querySelectorAll`.

- It's important that we do all of the attribute transformation logic—moving from HTML `line` elements and attributes to "plain" integer values of x1, y1, and so on—within the page function of `Page.$$eval`. This is because Puppeteer will garbage collect any DOM node objects once the eval call is done.

- Our line values need to be parsed with `parseFloat` because the `requestAnimationFrame` logic we coded doesn't perfectly line up with the integer endpoints—they are out by very slight fractional amounts.

- That also means we need to use the Jest matcher `toBeCloseTo` rather than `toBe`, which we need because of the fractional value difference described previously.

- Finally, we use the `DataTable hashes()` function here to pull out an array of objects which has a key for each of the columns in the data table, based on the header row that we provided in the feature definition. So, for example, we can call `hashes()[0].x1` to pull out the value in the x1 column for the first row.

Go ahead and run your tests again with `npm run cucumber`. Everything should be passing.

Summary

Cucumber tests (and acceptance tests in general) are similar to the tests we've been writing in the rest of the book. They are focused on specifying examples of behavior. They should be specific in nature: they should not talk in abstract terms, but make use of real data and numbers as a means to test a general concept, just as we've done in the two examples in this chapter. All this is in common with unit tests.

The essential difference from our unit tests is that acceptance tests are done at a much higher level. You don't need to test every single detail in your features, unlike in your unit tests, which will get all the details ironed out.

Just as with unit tests, it's important to find ways to simplify the code. The number one rule is to try to write generic Given, When, and Then phrases that can be reused across classes and extracted out of step definition files, either into the World class or some other module. We've seen an example of how to do that in this chapter.

In the next chapter, we'll follow the whole process for a new scenario, from a failing test passed to us by a product owner, through to building out the step definitions, and then to adding value to the production code so that our Cucumber test then passes.

14
Adding Features Guided by Acceptance Tests

In the last chapter, we studied the basic elements of writing Cucumber features and how to use Puppeteer to manipulate our UI. But we haven't yet explored how they can fit into our development process. In this chapter, we'll implement a new feature starting with our Cucumber acceptance tests.

Imagine that our product owner has seen the great work that we've done building *Spec Logo*. They have suggested that the share screen functionality is good, but it can do with an addition: it should give the presenter the option of resetting their state before sharing begins as shown below:

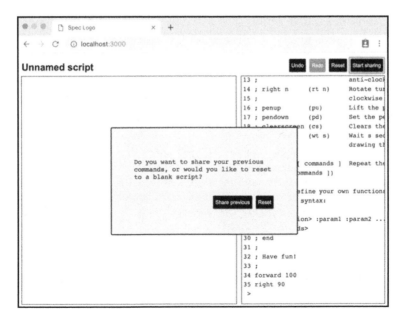

The new sharing dialog

The product owner has provided us with some Cucumber acceptance tests that are currently red and have passed them to you for implementation—both the step definitions and the production code.

This chapter covers the following topics:

- Adding acceptance tests for a dialog box
- Fixing acceptance tests by test-driving production code
- Adding better wait support

Adding acceptance tests for a dialog box

 The Git tag for this section is new-sharing-scenarios.

Let's start by taking a look at the new feature:

1. Open the features/sharing.feature file and take a look at the first feature that you've been given. Read through the steps and try to understand what our product owner is describing. The test covers quite a lot of behavior – unlike our unit tests. That is to say, it tells a complete story, or use case:

```
Scenario: Presenter chooses to reset current state when sharing
  Given the presenter navigated to the application page
  And the presenter entered the following instructions at the
prompt:
    | forward 10 |
    | right 90 |
  And the presenter clicked the button 'startSharing'
  When the presenter clicks the button 'reset'
  And the observer navigates to the presenter's sharing link
  Then the observer should see no lines
  And the presenter should see no lines
  And the observer should see the turtle at x = 0, y = 0, angle = 0
  And the presenter should see the turtle at x = 0, y = 0, angle =
0
```

We'll implement these step definitions one by one. Some of them will already work, some will be completely new, and some will require refactoring of existing step definitions.

2. The first `Given` phrase, `the presenter navigated to the application page`, already works, and you can verify this if you run `npm run cucumber`.

3. The next step, `the presenter entered the following instructions at the prompt`, is very similar to a step from Chapter 13, *Writing Your First Acceptance Test*, in `drawing.steps.js` and `the user entered the following instructions at the prompt`. We could choose to refactor here, just as we did with the `browseToPageFor` function; however, we shouldn't do that while our feature is red. We'll do that on green, just as with our unit tests. For now, we'll duplicate the code. Open `features/support/sharing.steps.js` and add the following step definition at the bottom of the code:

```
When(
    'the presenter entered the following instructions at the
prompt:',
    async function(dataTable) {
       for (let instruction of dataTable.raw()) {
         await this.getPage('presenter').type(
           'textarea',
           `${instruction}\n`
         );
         await this.getPage("presenter").waitFor(3500);
       }
    }
);
```

4. Next up is a `Given` clause that we have already: `the presenter clicked the button 'startSharing'`. But the line that appears after this is the first `When` clause, which will need to be implemented. Run `npm run cucumber` and you'll be given a template code for this function. Copy and paste the template code into your step definition file, as shown in the following code:

```
When('the presenter clicks the button {string}',
    function (string) {
       // Write code here that turns the phrase above
       // into concrete actions
       return 'pending';
    }
);
```

This scenario has *two* When phrases, which is unusual. Just as with your unit tests in the Act phase, you generally want just one When phrase. However, since there are two users working together at this point, it makes sense to have a single action for both of them, so we'll let our product owner off the hook on this occasion.

5. This is very similar to other step definitions that we've had before. We can think about removing the duplication later, but, for now, just fill out the function as shown in the following code block. Note that there is a new call to waitForSelector. This waits for the button to appear on the page before we continue, which gives the dialog time to render:

```
When('the presenter clicks the button {string}', async function (
  buttonId
) {
    await this.getPage('presenter').waitForSelector(
      `button#${buttonId}`
    );
    await this.getPage('presenter').click(`button#${buttonId}`);
});
```

6. The second When clause already has a definition from our previous test, so we move on to the Then clauses. The first is the observer should see no lines; run npm run cucumber and copy and paste the template function that Cucumber provides, as shown in the following code block:

```
Then('the observer should see no lines', function () {
  // Write code here that turns the phrase above
  // into concrete actions
  return 'pending';
});
```

7. For this step, we want to assert that there are no line elements on the page:

```
Then('the observer should see no lines', async function () {
  const numLines = await this.getPage('observer').$$eval(
    'line',
    lines => lines.length
  );
  expect(numLines).toEqual(0);
});
```

8. Running `npm run cucumber`, you should see that this step passes, and the next one is very similar. Copy the step definition you just wrote and modify it to work for the presenter, as shown in the following code block. Again, we can clean up the duplication later:

```
Then('the presenter should see no lines', async function () {
    const numLines = await this.getPage('presenter').$$eval(
        'line',
        lines => lines.length
    );
    expect(numLines).toEqual(0);
});
```

9. Run Cucumber now, and you'll see that this step fails; this is the first failure that we've got. It points to the specific change that we'll need to make in the code base:

```
✖ And the presenter should see no lines
    Error: expect(received).toEqual(expected)

    Expected value to equal:
      0
    Received:
      1
```

10. Since we have hit a red step, we could now go back and start working on our code to make this green. However, because we just have two almost identical clauses to complete, I'm going to choose to complete these definitions before continuing. Cucumber tells us the template function that we should use, so add that in now, as follows:

```
Then(
    'the observer should see the turtle at x = {int}, y = {int},
angle = {int}',
    function (int, int2, int3) {
    // Write code here that turns the phrase above
    // into concrete actions
    return 'pending';
});
```

11. We need to define a number of helpers that can tell us the current *x*, *y*, and angle of the turtle. We need this because all we have is the **Scalable Vector Graphics (SVG)** polygon element, which uses a `points` string and a `transform` string to position the turtle. Our helpers will take these strings and convert them back to numbers for us. As a reminder, here's how the turtle is initially positioned:

```
<polygon
  points="-5,5, 0,-7, 5,5"
  fill="green"
  stroke-width="2"
  stroke="black"
  transform="rotate(90, 0, 0)" />
```

12. We can use the first `points` coordinate to calculate *x* and *y*, by adding 5 to the first number and subtracting 5 from the second. The angle can be calculated by taking the first parameter to rotate and subtracting 90. Create a new file named `features/support/turtle.js`, and then add the following two definitions:

```
export const calculateTurtleXYFromPoints = points => {
  const firstComma = points.indexOf(',');
  const secondComma = points.indexOf(',', firstComma + 1);
  return {
    x: parseFloat(points.substring(0, firstComma)) + 5,
    y:
      parseFloat(points.substring(firstComma + 1, secondComma)) - 5
  };
};

export const calculateTurtleAngleFromTransform = transform => {
  const firstParen = transform.indexOf('(');
  const firstComma = transform.indexOf(',');
  return (
    parseFloat(transform.substring(firstParen + 1, firstComma)) -
    90
  );
}
```

13. In `feature/sharing.steps.js`, update the step definition, as shown in the following code block:

```
Then(
  'the observer should see the turtle at x = {int}, y = {int},
angle = {int}',
  async function (expectedX, expectedY, expectedAngle) {
  await this.getPage('observer').waitFor(4000);
```

```
const turtle = await this.getPage('observer').$eval(
  'polygon',
  polygon => ({
    points: polygon.getAttribute('points'),
    transform: polygon.getAttribute('transform')
  })
);
const position = calculateTurtleXYFromPoints(turtle.points);
const angle = calculateTurtleAngleFromTransform(
  turtle.transform
);
expect(position.x).toBeCloseTo(expectedX);
expect(position.y).toBeCloseTo(expectedY);
expect(angle).toBeCloseTo(expectedAngle);
});
```

14. Finally, repeat this step definition for the presenter, as follows:

```
Then(
  'the presenter should see the turtle at x = {int}, y = {int},
angle = {int}',
  async function (expectedX, expectedY, expectedAngle) {
  await this.getPage('presenter').waitFor(4000);
  const turtle = await this.getPage('presenter').$eval(
    'polygon',
    polygon => ({
      points: polygon.getAttribute('points'),
      transform: polygon.getAttribute('transform')
    })
  );
  const position = calculateTurtleXYFromPoints(turtle.points);
  const angle = calculateTurtleAngleFromTransform(
    turtle.transform
  );
  expect(position.x).toBeCloseTo(expectedX);
  expect(position.y).toBeCloseTo(expectedY);
  expect(angle).toBeCloseTo(expectedAngle);
});
```

That's the first test; now let's move on to the second scenario:

1. Take a look at the second scenario in features/sharing.feature. Nearly all of these are already implemented; the only ones that we'll need to implement are these lines should have been drawn for the observer and these lines should have been drawn for the presenter:

```
Scenario: Presenter chooses to keep and replay state when sharing
  Given the presenter navigated to the application page
```

And the presenter entered the following instructions at the prompt:
```
| forward 10 |
| right 90 |
```
And the presenter clicked the button 'startSharing'
When the presenter clicks the button 'keep'
And the observer navigates to the presenter's sharing link
Then these lines should have been drawn for the observer:
```
| x1 | y1 | x2 | y2 |
| 0  | 0  | 10 | 0  |
```
And these lines should have been drawn for the presenter:
```
| x1 | y1 | x2 | y2 |
| 0  | 0  | 10 | 0  |
```
And the observer should see the turtle at x = 10, y = 0, angle = 90
And the presenter should see the turtle at x = 10, y = 0, angle = 90

2. We already have a step definition that is very similar to these two in
   features/support/drawing.steps.js. Let's extract that logic into its own
   module so that we can reuse it. Create a new file named
   features/support/svg.js and then add the following code. Note that this is
   exactly the same code that was originally in drawing.steps.js:

```javascript
import expect from 'expect';

export const checkLinesFromDataTable = page =>
  return async function (dataTable) {
    await this.getPage(page).waitFor(2000);
    const lines = await this.getPage(page).$$eval('line', lines =>
      lines.map(line => ({
        x1: parseFloat(line.getAttribute('x1')),
        y1: parseFloat(line.getAttribute('y1')),
        x2: parseFloat(line.getAttribute('x2')),
        y2: parseFloat(line.getAttribute('y2'))
    })));
    for (let i = 0; i < lines.length; ++i) {
      expect(lines[i].x1).toBeCloseTo(
        parseInt(dataTable.hashes()[i].x1)
      );
      expect(lines[i].y1).toBeCloseTo(
        parseInt(dataTable.hashes()[i].y1)
      );
      expect(lines[i].x2).toBeCloseTo(
        parseInt(dataTable.hashes()[i].x2)
      );
      expect(lines[i].y2).toBeCloseTo(
```

```
        parseInt(dataTable.hashes()[i].y2)
      );
    }
  };
```

3. In `features/support/drawing.steps.js`, modify the `these lines should have been drawn in order` step definition so that it now uses this function:

   ```
   import { checkLinesFromDataTable } from './svg';

   Then(
     'these lines should have been drawn:',
     checkLinesFromDataTable('user')
   );
   ```

4. The two new step definitions for our latest sharing scenario are now straightforward. In `features/support/sharing.steps.js`, add the following import and step definitions.

   ```
   import { checkLinesFromDataTable } from './svg';

   Then(
     'these lines should have been drawn for the presenter:',
     checkLinesFromDataTable('presenter')
   );
   Then(
     'these lines should have been drawn for the observer:',
     checkLinesFromDataTable('observer')
   );
   ```

With the step definitions complete, it's time to make both of these scenarios pass.

Fixing acceptance tests by test-driving production code

 The Git tag for this section is `implementing-new-scenarios`.

- When the user clicks on **Start sharing**, a dialog should appear with a **Reset** button.
- If the user chooses to reset, the Redux is sent a `START_SHARING` action with a new `reset` property that is set to `true`:

  ```
  { type: 'START_SHARING', reset: true }
  ```

- If the user chooses to share their existing commands, then the `START_SHARING` action is sent with `reset` set to `false`:

  ```
  { type: 'START_SHARING', reset: false }
  ```

- When the user clicks on **Reset**, a `RESET` action should be sent to the Redux store.
- Sharing should not be initiated until *after* the `RESET` has occurred.

Adding a dialog box

Now that we know what we're building, let's go for it! To do so, perform these steps:

1. Open `test/MenuButtons.test.js` and skip the test that is titled `dispatches an action of START_SHARING when start sharing is clicked` – we'll come back to fix this later:

   ```
   it.skip('dispatches an action of START_SHARING when start sharing
   is clicked', () => {
     ...
   });
   ```

2. Add in a new import for the `Dialog` component, and stub it out in the `beforeEach` function. The `Dialog` component already exists in the code base but has remained unused until now:

```
import * as DialogModule from '../src/Dialog';

describe('MenuButtons', () => {
  beforeEach(() => {
    ...
    DialogModule.Dialog = jest.fn(() => null);
  });
});
```

3. Add this new test just below the one you've skipped. It displays a dialog with a customizable message and buttons. We'll need to add in four props: `message`, `buttons`, `onClose`, and `onChoose`, as follows:

```
it('opens a dialog when start sharing is clicked', () => {
  renderWithStore(<MenuButtons />);
  click(button('Start sharing'));
  expect(DialogModule.Dialog).toHaveBeenCalled();
  const dialogProps = DialogModule.Dialog.mock.calls[0][0];
  expect(dialogProps.message).toEqual(
    'Do you want to share your previous commands, or would you like
to reset to a blank script?'
  );
});
```

4. In `src/MenuButtons.js`, make that pass by adding it to the JSX, including the import at the top of the file. The new component should be placed at the very bottom of the returned components:

```
import { Dialog } from './Dialog';

return (
  <React.Fragment>
    ...
      <Dialog
        message="Do you want to share your previous commands, or
would you like to reset to a blank script?"
      />
  </React.Fragment>
);
```

5. Now we need to make sure the dialog isn't shown until the start sharing button is clicked on; add the following test:

```
it('does not initially show the dialog', () => {
  renderWithStore(<MenuButtons />);
  expect(DialogModule.Dialog).not.toHaveBeenCalled();
});
```

6. Make this pass by adding in a new state variable, isSharingDialogOpen. The sharing button will set this to true when it's clicked on. You'll need to add the import for useState at the top of the file:

```
const { useState } = React;

export const MenuButtons = connect(
  ...
)(
  (...) => {
    const [ isSharingDialogOpen, setIsSharingDialogOpen ] = useState(
      false
    );
    const openSharingDialog = () => setIsSharingDialogOpen(true);

    ...

    return (
      <React.Fragment>
        ...
        {environment.isSharing ? (
          <button id="stopSharing" onClick={stopSharing}>
            Stop sharing
          </button>
        ) : (
          <button id="startSharing" onClick={openSharingDialog}>
            Start sharing
          </button>
        )}
        {isSharingDialogOpen ? (
          <Dialog
            message="Do you want to share your previous commands, or
would you like to reset to a blank script?"
          />
        ) : null}
      </React.Fragment>
    );
  });
```

7. Now let's add a test for adding buttons into the dialog:

```
it('passes Share and Reset buttons to the dialog', () => {
  renderWithStore(<MenuButtons />);
  click(button('Start sharing'));
  const dialogProps = DialogModule.Dialog.mock.calls[0][0];
  expect(dialogProps.buttons).toEqual([
    { id: 'keep', text: 'Share previous' },
    { id: 'reset', text: 'Reset' }
  ]);
});
```

8. Make this pass by adding in a `buttons` prop to the `Dialog` component, as follows:

```
{isSharingDialogOpen ?
  <Dialog
    message="Do you want to share your previous commands, or would
you like to reset to a blank script?"
    buttons={[
      { id: 'keep', text: 'Share previous' },
      { id: 'reset', text: 'Reset' }
    ]} />
  ) : null}
```

9. For the next test, we'll test that the dialog closes. Start by defining a new `closeDialog` helper:

```
const closeDialog = () =>
  act(() => {
    const lastCall =
      DialogModule.Dialog.mock.calls[
        DialogModule.Dialog.mock.calls.length - 1
      ];
    lastCall[0].onClose();
  });
```

10. Add the next test, which checks that the `Dialog` component disappears once the dialog has had its `onClose` prop invoked:

```
it('closes the dialog when the onClose prop is called', () => {
  renderWithStore(<MenuButtons />);
  click(button('Start sharing'));
  closeDialog();
  expect(container.querySelector('#dialog')).toBeNull();
});
```

11. Make this pass by adding the following line into the `Dialog` JSX:

```
<Dialog
  onClose={() => setIsSharingDialogOpen(false)}
  ...
/>
```

12. Now go back to the test that you skipped, and modify it so that it reads the same as the following code block. We're going to modify the START_SHARING Redux action to take a new `reset` Boolean variable:

```
const makeDialogChoice = button => {
  const lastCall =
    DialogModule.Dialog.mock.calls[
      DialogModule.Dialog.mock.calls.length - 1
    ];
  lastCall[0].onChoose(button);
};

it('dispatches an action of START_SHARING when dialog onChoose prop
is invoked with reset', () => {
  renderWithStore(<MenuButtons />);
  click(button('Start sharing'));

  makeDialogChoice('reset');

  return expectRedux(store)
    .toDispatchAnAction()
    .matching({ type: 'START_SHARING', reset: true });
});
```

13. To make this pass, move to `src/MenuButtons.js` and modify `mapDispatchToProps` so that the `startSharing` property is passed the new `reset` Boolean:

```
startSharing: () => ({ type: 'START_SHARING', reset: true })
```

14. In the `MenuButtons` component, set the `onChoose` prop on the `Dialog` component:

```
return (
  <React.Fragment>
    ...
    {isSharingDialogOpen ? (
      <Dialog
        onClose={() => setIsSharingDialogOpen(false)}
        onChoose={startSharing}
```

```
        . . .
      />
    ) : null}
  </React.Fragment>
);
```

15. Finally, we need to add a new test for sending a value of `false` through for the `reset` action property:

```
it('dispatches an action of START_SHARING when dialog onChoose prop
is invoked with share', () => {
  renderWithStore(<MenuButtons />);
  click(button('Start sharing'));

  makeDialogChoice('share');

  return expectRedux(store)
    .toDispatchAnAction()
    .matching({ type: 'START_SHARING', reset: false });
});
```

16. This is simple to make pass; modify `startSharing` to take a `button` parameter, and then use that to set the `reset` property:

```
startSharing: button => ({
  type: 'START_SHARING',
  reset: button === 'reset'
})
```

Updating sagas to reset or replay state

We've now updated the `START_SHARING` action object that is sent to Redux. Now, we need to update the sharing sagas to handle this change:

1. Open `test/middleware/sharingSagas.test.js` and add the following test to the end of the `START_SHARING` nested describe block:

```
it('puts an action of RESET if reset is true', async () => {
  store.dispatch({ type: 'START_SHARING', reset: true });
  await notifySocketOpened();
  await sendSocketMessage({ type: 'UNKNOWN', id: 123 });
  return expectRedux(store)
    .toDispatchAnAction()
    .matching({ type: 'RESET' });
});
```

2. In `src/middleware/sharingSagas.js`, modify `startSharing` so that it reads the same as the following code block. Don't forget to add the new `action` parameter in the top line:

```
function* startSharing(action) {
  ...
  if (action.reset) {
    yield put({ type: 'RESET' });
  }
}
```

3. Now for the tricky second test. If the `reset` is `false`, we want to replay all the current actions:

```
it('shares all existing actions if reset is false', async () => {
  const forward10 = {
    type: 'SUBMIT_EDIT_LINE',
    text: 'forward 10'
  };
  const right90 = {
    type: 'SUBMIT_EDIT_LINE',
    text: 'right 90'
  };
  store.dispatch(forward10);
  store.dispatch(right90);
  store.dispatch({ type: 'START_SHARING', reset: false });
  await notifySocketOpened();
  await sendSocketMessage({ type: 'UNKNOWN', id: 123 });
  expect(sendSpy).toHaveBeenCalledWith(
    JSON.stringify({
      type: 'NEW_ACTION',
      innerAction: forward10
    })
  );
  expect(sendSpy).toHaveBeenCalledWith(
    JSON.stringify({
      type: 'NEW_ACTION',
      innerAction: right90
    })
  );
});
```

4. To make this pass, we can use the `toInstructions` function from the export namespace. We also need to make use of two new redux-saga functions: `select` and `all`. `select` is used to retrieve state, and `all` is used with `yield` to ensure that we wait for all the passed calls to complete before continuing. Add those imports in now, in `src/middleware/sharingSagas.js`:

```
import {
  call,
  put,
  takeLatest,
  take,
  all,
  select
} from 'redux-saga/effects';

import { eventChannel, END } from 'redux-saga';
import { toInstructions } from '../language/export';
```

5. Now modify the `startSharing` function by tacking on an `else` block to the conditional:

```
if (action.reset) {
  yield put({ type: 'RESET' });
} else {
  const state = yield select(state => state.script);
  const instructions = toInstructions(state);
  yield all(
    instructions.map(instruction =>
      call(shareNewAction, {
        innerAction: {
          type: 'SUBMIT_EDIT_LINE',
          text: instruction
        }
      })
    )
  );
}
```

6. If you run the tests now, you'll notice that there are a couple of unrelated failures. We can fix these by adding in a default value for the `reset` property in the `startSharing` helper method in our tests:

```
const startSharing = async sessionId => {
  store.dispatch({ type: 'START_SHARING', reset: true });
  await notifySocketOpened();
  await sendSocketMessage({ type: 'UNKNOWN', id: 123 });
};
```

Adding better wait support

Many of our step definitions contain waits that pause our test script interaction with the browser while we wait for the animations to finish. Here's an example from our tests, which waits for a period of three seconds:

```
await this.getPage('user').waitFor(3000);
```

Unfortunately, this kind of wait is brittle as there are likely to be occasions when the timeout is slightly too short and the animation hasn't finished. In this case, the test will intermittently fail. Conversely, the wait period is actually quite long. As more tests are added, the timeouts add up and the test runs suddenly take forever to run.

What we can do instead is modify our production code to alert us when it is animating. We do this by adding an `isAnimating` class to the `viewport div` when an animation is running. We then use the Puppeteer `waitForSelector` function to check for a change in the value of this class.

Alerting when the animation is complete

 The Git tag for this section is `is-animating`.

We'll do this by introducing a new state variable in the `Drawing` component, named `isAnimating`, and toggle it to true if we're currently animating, and false otherwise:

1. In `test/Drawing.test.js`, add a new nested `describe` block within the main `Display` context, just below the context for `resetting`. Then, add the following test:

```
describe('isAnimating', () => {
  describe('draw line animation', () => {
    it('adds isAnimating class to viewport when animation begins',
() => {
      renderWithStore(<Drawing />, {
        script: { drawCommands: [horizontalLine] }
      });
      triggerRequestAnimationFrame(0);
      expect(
        container.querySelector('#viewport').className
      ).toContain('isAnimating');
```

```
      });
    });
  });
```

2. In `src/Drawing.js`, update the JSX to include this class name on the `viewport` element:

```
return (
  <div id="viewport" className="isAnimating">
    ...
  </div>
);
```

3. Let's triangulate in order to get this state variable in place. To do this, add the following test – I've placed it *above* the draw line animation context, at the top of the `isAnimating` block:

```
it('initially does not have the isAnimating class set', () => {
  renderWithStore(<Drawing />, {
    script: { drawCommands: [] }
  });
  expect(
    container.querySelector('#viewport').className
  ).not.toContain('isAnimating');
});
```

4. To make this pass, update `className` to only set `isAnimating` if `commandToAnimate` is not null:

```
className={commandToAnimate ? 'isAnimating' : ''}>
```

We also need to be careful about removing the `isAnimating` class once the animation is finished. However, this is taken care of for us automatically, as `commandToAnimate` will be set to undefined again when that happens. In other words, we don't need an explicit test for this, and we're done with this addition.

Updating step definitions to use waitForSelector

 The Git tag for this section is `wait-for-selector`.

We're ready to use this new behavior in our step definitions:

1. In `features/support/world.js`, add the following two methods to the `World` class. The first waits for the `isAnimating` selector to appear within the DOM, and the second waits for it to disappear:

```
waitForAnimationToBegin(page) {
  return this.getPage(page).waitForSelector('.isAnimating');
}

waitForAnimationToEnd(page) {
  return this.getPage(page).waitForSelector('.isAnimating', {
    hidden: true
  });
}
```

2. In `features/support/drawing.steps.js`, search for the single `waitFor` invocation in this file and replace it with the code in the following block:

```
When(
  'the user enters the following instructions at the prompt:',
  async function (dataTable) {
    for (let instruction of dataTable.raw()) {
      await this.getPage('user').type(
        'textarea',
        `${instruction}\n`
      k);
      await this.waitForAnimationToEnd('user');
    }
  }
);
```

We're waiting for animation after *each* instruction is entered. This is important as it mirrors how the isAnimating class will be added and removed from the application. If we only had one waitForAnimationToEnd function as the last instruction on the page, we may end up exiting the step definition early if the wait catches the removal of an isAnimating class in the *middle* of a sequence of instructions, rather than catching the *last* one.

3. Now open features/support/sharing.steps.js; this file has a similar step in it as the previous one, so update that one now, in the same way:

```
When(
    'the presenter entered the following instructions at the
prompt:',
    async function(dataTable) {
      for (let instruction of dataTable.raw()) {
        await this.getPage('presenter').type(
          'textarea',
          `${instruction}\n`
        );
        await this.waitForAnimationToEnd('presenter');
      }
    }
);
```

4. Toward the bottom of the file, update the two-step definitions that check the turtle position:

```
Then(
    'the observer should see the turtle at x = {int}, y = {int},
angle = {int}',
    async function (expectedX, expectedY, expectedAngle) {
    await this.waitForAnimationToEnd('observer');
    ...
});

Then(
    'the presenter should see the turtle at x = {int}, y = {int},
angle = {int}',
    async function (expectedX, expectedY, expectedAngle) {
    await this.waitForAnimationToEnd('presenter');
    ...
});
```

5. Open `features/support/svg.js` and update the function within it as follows:

```
export const checkLinesFromDataTable = page => {
  return async function (dataTable) {
    await this.waitForAnimationToEnd(page);
    ...
  }
};
```

6. If you run `npm run cucumber` now, you'll see that we have one test failure, which is related to the output on the observer's screen. It indicates that we need to wait for the animations when we load the observer's page. In this case, we need to wait for the animation to start before we can wait for it to finish. We can fix this by adding a new step in the feature. Open `features/sharing.feature` and modify the last test to include a *third* entry in the When section:

```
When the presenter clicks the button 'keep'
And the observer navigates to the presenter's sharing link
And the observer waits for animations to finish
```

If you aren't happy with having three When steps, then you can always compose these three steps into a single step.

Back in `features/support/sharing.steps.js`, add this new step definition just underneath the other When step definitions:

```
When('the observer waits for animations to finish', async function
() {
  await this.waitForAnimationToBegin('observer');
  await this.waitForAnimationToEnd('observer');
});
```

Your tests should now be passing, and they should be much faster. On my machine, they now only take a quarter of the time that they did before.

Exercises

- Remove as much duplication as possible from your step definitions.

Summary

In this chapter, we looked at how you can integrate acceptance tests into your programming workflow. In particular, we looked at some of the ways that acceptance tests differ from unit tests. We also learned how extra thinking and care must be taken to ensure our tests aren't brittle, especially around timeouts.

We're now finished with our journey into Logo. I hope you enjoyed it!

In the final chapter of the book, we'll look at how TDD compares to other developer processes.

15
Understanding TDD in the Wider Testing Landscape

At the beginning of this book, I spoke about dogma and how this book is a written form of *my* dogma. It details how I prefer to write applications and summarizes everything I've learnt about test-driven development up until this point in time.

There have been a number of recurring themes that many chapters have touched on across the book: the notion of 'strict' test-driven development, how and when to 'cheat', systematic refactoring, and so on.

Some dev teams like to adopt the mantra of move fast and break things. TDD is the opposite—we must go slow and think about things. To understand what this means in practice, we can compare TDD with various other popular testing techniques.

The following topics will be covered in this chapter:

- Test-driven development as a testing technique
- Manual testing
- Automated testing
- Not testing at all

Test-driven development as a testing technique

Is test-driven development a testing technique at all? It's not uncommon to hear the belief that TDD is not about testing; rather, it's about design, behavior, or specification, and the automated tests we have at the end are simply an added bonus.

Yes, TDD is about design, but TDD is certainly about testing, too. TDD practitioners care that their software has a high level of quality, and this is the same thing that all testers care about. That's why we use the term Quality Assurance to describe the role of tester within our teams.

People question the naming of test-driven development because they feel that the notion of 'testing' confuses the actual process. This is often true, and many people struggle with TDD. It's easier to do it badly than it is to do it well. Some often end up missing out tests, building brittle tests, writing loose expectations, over-complicating solutions, forgetting to refactor, and so on.

It's not just novices who struggle with this – everyone does it, experts included. People make a mess all the time. That's also part of the fun. Discovering the joy of TDD requires a certain degree of humility.

If you are lucky enough to have a tester on your team, you may think that TDD encroaches on their work, or may even put them out of a job. If you ask them their opinion, however, you'll undoubtedly find they are only too keen for you, the prized developer, to start taking an interest in the quality of your work. With TDD, you'll catch all those trivial logic errors yourself. The testers can then better use their time by focusing on testing complex use cases and hunting down missed requirements.

Best practices for your unit tests

Great unit tests are:

- Independent: Each test should test just one thing, and invoke only one unit. There are many techniques that we can employ to achieve this goal. To take just two examples: collaborators are often (but not always) mocked, and example data should be the minimum set of data required to correctly describe the test.

You may have heard of the 'great TDD debate' of *classicist* vs *mockist* TDD, sometimes called Detroit school and London school. The idea is that the classicist will not use mocks and stubs, and the mockist will mock *all* collaborators. I think this is a false dichotomy. Both techniques are important, and you have seen both in use in this book. I would encourage you to not limit yourself to a single approach, but instead experiment and learn to be comfortable with both.

- Short, with a high level of abstraction: The test description should be concise. The test code should highlight all the pieces of code that are important to the test, and hide any apparatus that's required but not relevant.

- Quick to run: Use test doubles instead of interacting with system resources (files, network connections, and so on) or other processes. Do not use sleep in your code, or rely on the passing of time.

- Focused on observable behavior: The system is interesting for what it does to the outside world, not for how it does it. In the case of React, we care about DOM interaction.

- In three parts: These parts are `arrange`, `act`, and `assert`. Each test should follow this structure.

- DRY: Always take the time to refactor and clean up your tests, aiming for readability. DRY, of course, stands for Don't Repeat Yourself.

- A design tool: Great tests help you figure out how to design your system. That's not to say that up-front design isn't important. In the first three chapters, we always did a little design before we embarked on our tests. It's important to do some thinking so that you have an idea of the general direction you're headed. Just don't try to plan too far ahead, and be prepared to throw out your design entirely as you proceed.

TDD is not a replacement for great design. To be a great TDD practitioner, you should also learn about and practice software design. There are many books about software design. Do not limit yourself to books about JavaScript; good design transcends language.

I would suggest looking for authors who continually write books about design. A few of my favorite authors in this area include Kent Beck, Sandi Metz, Corey Haines, and Martin Fowler.

Improving your technique

The following are some general tips for improving:

- Work with others: Beyond reading this book, the best way to 'level up' in TDD is to work with experts. Since TDD lends itself so well to pair and mob programming, it can give structure to teams of mixed experience. More experienced developers can use the granularity of small tests to help improve the work of less experienced developers.

- Experiment with design: TDD gives you a safety net that allows you to experiment with the style and shape of your programs. Make use of that safety net to learn more about design. Your tests will keep you safe.

- Learn to slow down: TDD requires a great deal of personal discipline. Unfortunately, there is no room for sloppiness. You must not cut corners; instead, take every opportunity to refactor. Once your test passes, sit with your code. Before moving on to the next test, stare at your current solution and think carefully about whether it is the best it can possibly be.

- Don't be afraid to defer design decisions: Sometimes we're faced with a number of design options, and it can be tricky to know which option to choose. Even the simple act of naming variables can be difficult. Part of having a sense of design is knowing when to defer your thinking. If you're in the refactor stage and feel yourself weighing up two or more options, move on and add another test, and then revisit your design. You'll often find you have more design knowledge and will be closer to the right answer.

- Solve a kata each day: A kata is a short exercise designed to be practiced repeatedly with the aim of teaching you a certain technique. Two basic katas are coin changer and Roman numerals. More complex katas include the bowling game kata, the bank kata, and Conway's Game of Life. The diamond kata is a favorite of mine, as are sorting algorithms.

- Attend a Coderetreat: Coderetreat is a day of pairing and TDD that revolves around the Game of Life kata. The Global Day of Coderetreat is held in November. Groups from all around the world get together to solve this problem. It's not only fun, but a great way to expand your TDD horizons.

Manual testing

Manual testing means starting your application and using it. It takes up a lot of time, not just because you'll be actually using the application, but also because it takes time to get test environments set up and primed with the relevant test data.

For this reason, it's important to avoid manual testing where possible. There are, however, times when it's necessary, as we'll discover in this section.

Since you're engaging with your own creative work, you are undoubtedly interested to find out how it performs. You should certainly take the time to do this, but think of it as downtime and a chance to relax, rather than a formal part of your development process.

There is always a temptation to manually test software after each feature is complete, just to verify that it actually works. If you have to do this a lot, consider how much confidence you have in your unit tests. If you said, "I have 100% confidence in my unit tests", why would you ever need to use software to prove it?

Demonstrating software

There are at least two important occasions on which you should *always* manually test: when you are demonstrating your software to your customers and users, and when you are preparing to demonstrate your software.

Preparing means writing down a demo script that lists every action you want to perform. Rehearse your script at least a couple of times before you perform it live. Very often, rehearsals will bring about changes to the script, which is why rehearsals are so important. Always make sure you've done at least one full run-through that didn't require changes before you perform a live demo.

Testing the whole product

Front-end development includes a lot of moving parts, including:

- Multiple browser environments requiring support
- CSS
- Distributed components, such as proxies and caches
- Authentication mechanisms

Manually testing is necessary not because of test-driven code, but because of all the other complexities that go along with it. We need to check that everything sits together nicely.

Alternatively, you can use end-to-end tests for the same coverage; however, these are costly to develop and maintain.

Exploratory testing

Exploratory testing is what you want your QA team to do. If you don't have a QA team, you should allocate time to do this yourself. Exploratory testing involves exploring software and hunting for missing requirements or complex use cases that your team has not yet thought about.

Because TDD works at a very low level, it can be easy to miss or even misunderstand requirements. Your unit tests might cover 95% of cases, but you can accidentally forget about the remaining 5%. This happens a lot when a team is new to TDD, or is made up of novice programmers. It happens all the time with experienced TDDers, too – even those of us who write books on TDD! We all make errors from time to time.

What's more, when mocking is involved, it can be easy to generate false positives. We saw this in an earlier chapter, when we reworked the public interface of our component, but the component that used it still passed.

 TDD can give you more confidence, but there is absolutely no way that TDD guarantees bug-free software.

With time and experience, you'll get better at spotting all those pesky edge cases before they make it to the QA team.

An alternative to exploratory testing is automated acceptance tests, but as with end-to-end tests, these are costly to develop and maintain, and they also require a high level of expertise and team discipline.

Debugging in the browser

For the TDD practitioner, debugging should – in theory – be a very rare experience, or at least something that is actively avoided. In practice, however, you will need these skills from time to time.

A downside of TDD is that your debugging skills suffer. Debuggers are complex and highly sophisticated pieces of software.

Print-line debugging is the name given to the debugging technique where a codebase is littered with `console.log` statements in the hope that they can provide runtime clues about what's going wrong. I've worked with many programmers who began their careers with TDD; for many of them, print-line debugging is the only form of debugging they know. Although it's a simple technique, it's also time-consuming, involves a lot of trial and error, and you have to remember to clean up after yourself when you're done. There's a risk of accidentally forgetting about a stray `console.log` and it then going live in production.

Modern browsers have very sophisticated debugging tools that, until just recently, would have been imaginable only in a 'full-fat' IDE. You should make time to learn about all of the standard debugging techniques, including setting breakpoints (including conditional breakpoints), stepping in, out and over, watching variables, and so on.

Whatever form of debugging you use, it's always an epic time sink. It can be an incredibly frustrating experience, with a lot of hair-pulling. That's a big reason we test-drive: so we never have to debug. Our tests do the debugging for us.

A common anti-pattern is to use debugging techniques that track down a bug, and once it's discovered, fix it and move on to the next task. What you should be doing instead is writing a failing test to prove the existence of a bug. As if by magic, the test has done the debugging for you. You can then fix the bug *and* immediately the test will tell you if the issue is fixed, without the need to manually re-test. Think of all the time you'll save!

 Check out the *Further learning* section for resources on the Chrome debugger.

Automated testing

TDD is a form of automated testing. This section lists some other popular types of automated testing and how they compare to TDD.

Integration tests

These tests check how two or more independent processes interact. Those processes could either be on the same machine or distributed across a network. However, your system should exercise the same communication mechanisms as it would in production, so if it makes HTTP calls out to a web service then it should do so in your integration tests, regardless of where the web service is running.

Integration tests should be written in the same unit test framework that you use for unit tests, and all of the same rules about writing good unit tests apply to integration tests.

The trickiest part of integration testing is the orchestration code, which involves starting and stopping processes, and waiting for processes to complete their work. Doing that in a reliable way can be difficult.

Acceptance tests

Acceptance tests are written by the customer, or a proxy to the customer such as a product owner, where 'acceptance' refers to a quality gate that must be passed for the released software to be accepted as complete. Of course, your unit tests should be accepted too, but since they are at a very low level, it's unlikely you'll discuss them with your customer.

Now, the problem involves customers writing tests; the Gherkin syntax that we saw in Chapters 13 & 14 is one way of doing this.

Acceptance tests will often cover multiple processes, just like integration tests, and may run in a distributed environment to mimic production.

Acceptance tests are costly to build and maintain. Fortunately, they can be introduced gradually, so you can start small and prove their value before increasing their scope.

I find acceptance tests most useful when manual exploratory testing starts taking an inordinate amount of time. This can happen when TDD isn't performed strictly and there is a lower level of confidence in the finished product, but it also happens on codebases with great test coverage as they grow in size and in age.

I'll come back again to the point about mocking collaborators – if you're choosing to mock collaborators, you will need at least *some* coverage of those interactions when they *aren't* mocked, and acceptance tests often fit that role nicely.

As you can see, acceptance tests often become a necessity as software products grow beyond the realms of a simple application.

Acceptance tests can also be used to build trust between developers and product stakeholders. If the customer is endlessly testing your software looking for bugs, that points to a low level of trust between the development team and the outside world. Acceptance tests could help improve that trust if they start catching bugs that would otherwise be found by your customer. At the same time, however, you should be asking yourself why TDD isn't catching all those bugs in the first place and consider how you can improve your overall testing process.

Property-based and generative testing

In traditional TDD, we find a small set of specifications or examples to test our functions against. Property-based testing is different: it generates a large set of tests based on a definition of what the inputs to those functions should be. The test framework is responsible for generating the input data and the tests.

For example, if I had a function that converted Fahrenheit to Celsius, I could use a generative test framework to generate tests for a large, random sample of integer-valued Fahrenheit measurements and ensure that each of them converts to the correct Celsius value.

This kind of testing does not replace TDD, but is another tool in the TDD practitioner's toolbox.

Property-based testing is just as hard as TDD. It is no magic bullet. Finding the right properties to assert on is challenging, particularly if you aim to build them up in a test-driven style.

Snapshot testing

This is a React-specific type of testing that has a long history of recording the appearance of user interfaces. React component trees are serialized to disk as a JSON string and then compared between tests runs.

React component trees are useful in a couple of important scenarios, including the following:

- When your team has a low level of experience with TDD and general program design, and can become more confident with a safety net of snapshot testing

- When you have zero test coverage of software that is already being used in production, and you would like to quickly gain some level of confidence before making any changes

QA teams are sometimes interested in how software changes visually between releases, but they will probably not want to write tests in your unit tests' codebase; they'll have their own specialized tool for that.

Snapshot testing is certainly a useful tool to know about, but be careful about the following issues that can present themselves:

- Snapshots are not descriptive. They do not go beyond saying, "this component tree looks the same as it did before." This means that if they break, it will not be immediately clear why they broke.

- If snapshots are rendered at a high level in your component tree, they are brittle. Brittle tests break frequently and therefore take a lot of time to correct. Since the tests are at a high-level, they do not pinpoint where the error is, so you'll spend a lot of time hunting down failures.

- Snapshot tests can pass in two scenarios: first, when the component tree is the same as the previous version that was tested, and second, when no snapshot artefacts from the previous test run are found. This means that a green test does not give you full confidence – it could simply be green because previous artefacts are missing.

When writing good tests (of any kind), you want the following to be true of any test failure that occurs:

1. It is very quick to ascertain if the failure is due to an error or due to a change in specification.

2. In the case of errors, it is very quick to pinpoint the problem and the location of the error.

With TDD, it's well known how to write good tests. We aren't quite there with snapshot testing, however, so if you do employ it in your codebase, make sure to measure how much value it is providing you and your team.

Canary testing

Canary testing is when you release your software to a small proportion of your users and see what happens. It can be useful for web applications with a large user-base. One version of canary testing involves sending each request to two systems: the live system and the system under test. Users only sense the live system but the test system results are recorded and analyzed by you. Differences in functionality and performance can then be observed, while your users are never subjected to test software.

Canary testing is attractive because, on the surface, it seems very cost effective, and also requires next to no 'thinking' from the programmer.

Unlike TDD, canary testing cannot help you with the design of your software, and it may take a while for you to get any feedback.

Not testing at all

There is a belief that TDD doesn't apply to some scenarios in which it clearly does – for example, if your code is 'throwaway' (whatever that means), or if it's presumed to never need modification once it's deployed. Believing this, is almost ensuring the opposite to be true. Code, particularly code without tests, has a habit of living on beyond its intended lifespan.

In addition to reducing the fear of changing code, tests also reduce the fear of *removing* code. Without tests, you'll read some code and think "maybe something uses this code for some purpose I don't quite remember...". With tests in place, this won't be a concern. You'll read the test, see that the test no longer applies due to a changed requirement, and then delete the test and its corresponding production code.

However, there are in fact a number of scenarios in which not writing tests is acceptable. The two most important ones are as follows.

When quality doesn't matter

Unfortunately, in many environments, quality doesn't matter. Many of us can relate to this. We've worked for employers who actively disregard quality. These people make enough profit that they don't *need* or *want* to care. Caring about quality is, unfortunately, a personal choice. If you are in a team that does not value quality, it will be hard to convince them that test-driven development is worthwhile.

If you're in this situation and you have a burning desire to use TDD, then you have a few options. You can spend time convincing your colleagues that it is a good idea. This is never an easy task. You could also play the TDD-by-stealth game, in which you don't ask permission before you start. Failing these options, those of us who are fortunate enough to be able to take such a risk can seek out an alternative employer that *does* value quality.

Spiking and deleting code

Spiking, in the test-driven sense of the word, simply means coding without tests. We spike when we're in uncharted territory. We need to find a workable approach to a problem we've never solved before, and there is likely to be a great deal of trial and error, along with a lot of backtracking. There is a high chance of finding *un*workable approaches before a workable one. Writing tests doesn't make much sense in this situation because many of the tests written along the way will ultimately end up being scrapped.

Let's say, for example, that I'm building a Websocket server and client, but it's the first time I've used Websockets. This would be a good candidate for spiking – I can explore the Websocket API in a safe way until I'm comfortable baking it into my application.

It's important to stop spiking when you feel that you've hit on a workable approach. You don't need a complete solution, just one that teaches you enough to set you off on the right path.

In the purist vision of TDD, spiking must be followed by deleting. If you're going to spike, you must be comfortable with deleting your work. Unfortunately, that's easier said than done; it's hard to scrub out creative output. You must shake off the belief that your code is sacred. Be happy to chuck it away.

In the pragmatic vision of TDD, spiking can often be followed by writing tests around the spiked code. I use this technique all the time.

Spiking is related to the practice of *test last*, but for me, there's a subtle difference. Writing code around a spike is a TDD cheat in that you want your finished tests to look as if you used TDD in the first place. Anyone else coming along after you should never know that you cheated.

Test last, however, is a more loosely-defined way of testing where you write all the production code and then write some unit tests that prove *some* of the more important use cases. Writing tests like this gives you some level of regression coverage but none of the other benefits of TDD.

Speaking from a personal perspective, I think spiking often only works when a developer has enough experience to effectively predict the order of tests. If you're new to TDD, it may be wise to avoid this particular cheat until you're confident that you can think out a test sequence of required tests that will cover all the required functionality within a spike code.

At this point, a purist will say that your spike code can include redundant code, although it may not be the simplest solution because any tests will not have driven the implementation. There is some merit to this argument, but, as previously mentioned, it's always worth experimenting and figuring out what works best for you.

Summary

Becoming a great practitioner of test-driven development takes a great deal of effort. It requires practice, experience, determination, and discipline.

Many people have tried TDD and failed. Some of them will conclude, erroneously, that TDD is broken. But it's not broken, and it's not even difficult – it just takes effort and patience to 'get right'.

But what is getting it right, anyway?

At the very beginning of this book I stated that this is a book about *my* dogma. There is a great deal of dogma around software development. Plenty of people believe that they know the *right* way to write code, and everyone else is *wrong*. This goes for testing, too: some people will have read this book and disagreed with much of what I've said, believing that these ideas just don't work.

Of course, all software development techniques are subjective. Everything in this book is subjective; it is not the "right" way. It is a collection of techniques that *I* like to use, and that I have found success with. I am aware that other people find success with other other techniques. And that's okay.

For me, the exciting part of TDD is not the black-and-white, strict form of the process; it is the greys in which we can define (and refine) our own development process that works for us and for our colleagues. The TDD cycle gives us just enough structure that we can find joy in fleshing it out with our rules, and our own dogma.

I hope you have found this book valuable and, more than that, I hope you've found it enjoyable. There are many, many ways to test-drive React applications and my wish is that you will now begin to evolve your own testing practice, just as I have done and continue to do.

Further learning

- Two catalogs of code katas:
    - http://codingdojo.org/kata/
    - http://codekata.com
- Global Day of Coderetreat: https://www.coderetreat.org
- Kata Log: http://kata-log.rocks
- The bank kata: https://github.com/sandromancuso/Bank-kata
- Getting Started with Debugging JavaScript in Chrome DevTools: https://developers.google.com/web/tools/chrome-devtools/javascript/
- Property-based testing for JavaScript: https://github.com/leebyron/testcheck-js
- The diamond kata with property-based tests: http://www.natpryce.com/articles/000807.html

Other Books You May Enjoy

If you enjoyed this book, you may be interested in these other books by Packt:

React Design Patterns and Best Practices - Second Edition
Carlos Santana Roldán

ISBN: 9781789530179

- Get familiar with the new React features,like context API and React Hooks
- Learn the techniques of styling and optimizing React components
- Make components communicate with each other by applying consolidate patterns
- Use server-side rendering to make applications load faster
- Write a comprehensive set of tests to create robust and maintainable code
- Build high-performing applications by optimizing components

React Material-UI Cookbook

Adam Boduch

ISBN: 9781789615227

- Learning to build the overall structure, layout, and navigation for your Material UI app.
- Learning to present simple and complex information in a variety of ways.
- Build interactive and intuitive controls.
- Designing portable themes and styles for all of your Material UI apps.

Leave a review - let other readers know what you think

Please share your thoughts on this book with others by leaving a review on the site that you bought it from. If you purchased the book from Amazon, please leave us an honest review on this book's Amazon page. This is vital so that other potential readers can see and use your unbiased opinion to make purchasing decisions, we can understand what our customers think about our products, and our authors can see your feedback on the title that they have worked with Packt to create. It will only take a few minutes of your time, but is valuable to other potential customers, our authors, and Packt. Thank you!

Index

Made in United States
North Haven, CT
27 March 2022